ADVANCES IN
LIBRARY ADMINISTRATION
AND ORGANIZATION

Volume 8 • 1989

ADVANCES IN LIBRARY ADMINISTRATION AND ORGANIZATION

A Research Annual

Editors: **GERARD B. McCABE**
Director of Libraries
Clarion University of Pennsylvania

BERNARD KREISSMAN
University Librarian, Emeritus
University of California, Davis

VOLUME 8 • 1989

 JAI PRESS, INC.

Greenwich, Connecticut   *London, England*

CONTENTS

INTRODUCTION
  Bernard Kreissman   vii

QUALITY IN BIBLIOGRAPHIC DATABASES:
AN ANALYSIS OF MEMBER-CONTRIBUTED
CATALOGING IN OCLC AND RLIN
  Sheila S. Intner   1

THE LIBRARY LEADERSHIP PROJECT:
A TEST OF LEADERSHIP EFFECTIVENESS
IN ACADEMIC LIBRARIES
  Eugene S. Mitchell   25

APPLYING STRATEGIC PLANNING
TO THE LIBRARY: A MODEL FOR PUBLIC
SERVICES
  Larry J. Ostler   39

MANAGEMENT ISSUES IN SELECTION,
DEVELOPMENT, AND IMPLEMENTATION
OF INTEGRATED OR LINKED SYSTEMS
FOR ACADEMIC LIBRARIES
  Elaine Lois Day   69

ACQUISITIONS MANAGEMENT: THE
INFRINGING ROLES OF ACQUISITIONS
LIBRARIANS AND SUBJECT SPECIALISTS–
AN HISTORICAL PERSPECTIVE
  Barbara J. Henn   113

DEVELOPMENT AND USE OF THEATRE
DATABASES
  Helen K. Bolton   131

THE ACADEMIC LIBRARY AND THE
LIBERAL ARTS EDUCATION OF YOUNG
ADULTS: REVIEWING THE RELEVANCE
OF THE LIBRARY-COLLEGE IN THE 1980S
Peter V. Deekle   145

COLLEGE LIBRARIES: THE COLONIAL
PERIOD TO THE TWENTIETH CENTURY
Eugene R. Hanson   171

LIBRARY ADMINISTRATORS' ATTITUDES
TOWARD CONTINUING PROFESSIONAL
EDUCATION ACTIVITIES
John A. McCrossan   201

A CORE REFERENCE THEATRE ARTS
COLLECTION FOR RESEARCH
Sharon Lynn Schofield, Helen K. Bolton,
Rashelle S. Karp, and Bernard S. Schlessinger   215

THE LIBRARY BUILDINGS AWARD
PROGRAM OF THE AMERICAN INSTITUTE
OF ARCHITECTS AND THE AMERICAN
LIBRARY ASSOCIATION
Roscoe Rouse, Jr.   241

BIBLIOGRAPHY OF SUB-SAHARA AFRICAN
LIBRARIANSHIP, 1986-1987
Glenn L. Sitzman   253

BIOGRAPHICAL SKETCHES
OF THE CONTRIBUTORS   293

INDEX   297

INTRODUCTION

In a professional world replete with networks, CD-ROM, and computerized everything, is it refreshing or just old fashioned to find a half score of lengthy studies devoted to budget, acquisition management, professional education, personnel, and bibliography. The editors of Advances in Library Administration and Organization found it extremely interesting to note that the concerns voiced in Carl Jackson's introduction to volume 1 (1982) continue to be some of the same concerns we are presenting in 1989, despite the fact that all of us are aware that the face and guts of librarianship have changed remarkably in the last eight years.

The newer issues are here also as Day's paper on on-line public access catalogs and Intner's study of our major databases confirms. Nevertheless, as you are about to discover the traditional problems of library management and organization are still very much with us.

Welcome to volume 8.

Bernard Kreissman
Series Editor

QUALITY IN BIBLIOGRAPHIC DATABASES:

AN ANALYSIS OF MEMBER-CONTRIBUTED CATALOGING IN OCLC AND RLIN

Shelia S. Intner

SUMMARY OF FINDINGS

This study examined 215 matched pairs of catalog entries of OCLC and RLIN for errors and differences in fullness. The variation in quality of this original cataloging, as measured by comparing the accuracy and fullness of the 430 records, appears negligible. Differences were not statistically significant.

A total of 1,067 errors of all types were found, an average of 2.48 errors per record. The 215 OCLC records contained a total of 537 errors of all kinds, while the 215 RLIN records contained a total of 530. More than one-third of all errors occurred in the interpretation and application of descriptive cataloging rules: of

Advances in Library Administration and Organization,
Volume 8, pages 1-24.
Copyright © 1989 by JAI Press Inc.
All rights of reproduction in any form reserved.
ISBN: 0-89232-967-X

OCLC, 38.2 percent; RLIN 36.0 percent. The distribution of these errors showed that most were made in recording publication, distribution information.

While a total of 84 errors of all kinds occurred in OCLC's descriptive headings (main entries, series headings, and descriptive added entries), only 26 affected retrieval; and, while a total of 94 errors of all kinds occurred in RLIN's descriptive headings, only 29 affected retrieval.

Fifty-nine subject-related errors occurred in all records: 36 in OCLC and 23 in RLIN. More latitude was allowed in analyzing subject headings and classification numbers. Subject headings diverging widely from a book's content, employing unacceptable terms, or representing clear instances of misuse of terms counted as substantive errors. Absence of subject headings counted as an error although they are not required. Six errors occurred in OCLC's subject headings and five in RLIN's.

Similar criteria were applied to classification numbers. Two RLIN records had classification numbers diverging widely from the subject headings for the works. Ten OCLC records and three RLIN records lacked classification numbers.

Errors in the punctuation, capitalization, spelling, and tagging of subject fields totalled 33 in all records, 20 in OCLC, and 13 in RLIN.

The hypothesis that RLIN records were more complete was not upheld: Of 269 instances in which data was missing from one record in the pair that appeared in the other, 112 were attributable to OCLC records and 157 to RLIN records. Most fullness differences were for optional data in non-heading fields, but OCLC catalogers assigned more subject headings with subheadings as well as more descriptive headings than did RLIN catalogers.

A total of 1,137 subject headings were assigned to the 430 records. RLIN records averaged 2.76 subject headings per record, while OCLC averaged 2.50 per record. In 70 record pairs, RLIN entries had more subject headings; in 46 record pairs, OCLC entries had more; and 99 record pairs had equal numbers of subject headings.

The small sample size mandates additional testing to uphold the investigators' assumption as a result of this study that quality does not differ markedly between original cataloging records in the two databases.

BACKGROUND

In the early years of the two major national bibliographic networks of the United States, Online Computer Library Center (OCLC) and the Research Libraries Information Network (RLIN), Library of Congress machine-readable cataloging (LC MARC records) formed the nucleus and large majority of records in both databases. Although LC cataloging was not without error, it was and still is the highest standard of quality in the United States. Since that time, the proportion of bibliographic records in OCLC and RLIN contributed by member libraries, i.e., their original cataloging of works for which there were no LC records, has been growing. Over the last several years, the balance tipped the other way, with member-contributed cataloging constituting a greater proportion of records in both databases than LC's contributions.[1] Quality control for cataloging contributed by libraries other than LC, although always an issue of concern, became more important as the databases expanded and as the proportion of LC's standard quality cataloging diminished relative to member-contributed cataloging.

One of the differences between the two networks was their approach to maintaining quality control, i.e., ensuring the entry of high quality original cataloging into the databases, and the methods employed to ensure that standards for accuracy and fullness of records were met by members. Four factors affected quality control: network objectives; pricing structures and other influences on quality; members' own cataloging capabilities and needs; and their historic development.

OCLC began a full decade before publication of the *Anglo-American Cataloguing Rules*, second edition (AACR 2)—descriptive cataloging rules in current use.[2] The RLIN database, although an extension of an earlier system originating at Stanford University in the 1960s, began its existence as a shared cataloging database simultaneously with AACR 2's publication in 1978. While these new rules were not implemented by the research library community, including LC, until 1981, many fewer records pre-existed their adoption in RLIN than in OCLC, making for greater uniformity among the records in that database.

In its early years, OCLC, whose primary objective was building the database, was thought by some to be less demanding about quality control, offering the institution that entered a new record for the first time a small financial reward, without regard for record quality as measured by accuracy and fullness. A record containing only the minimum number of required fields (K-level), if entered for the first time, was not charged, just as one containing all the fields required by AACR 2 and the network (I-level) was not. OCLC set bibliographic input standards, but quality control was largely a voluntary effort of individual librarians, whose adherence to the standards was not carefully controlled. Accuracy could only be monitored by calculating the number of errors noted by members and brought to the attention of the network or found by periodic network checks. If a member library chose merely to edit away the errors for its local entries, failing to submit a report to headquarters, the problems could remain uncorrected. (OCLC, unlike RLIN, has only one master record for each entry in its database. Except for LC cataloging, which replaces a member-contributed record, and the activities of ''Enhance libraries,'' explained below, only the entering library can change an I-level record and only so long as no additional holding symbol has been added. The headquarters quality control unit may alter master records and K-level records may be augmented by any library.)

Later, OCLC instituted a number of programs to help members improve the quality of their cataloging, including the formation of a quality control unit at its headquarters, development of local peer councils (groups that monitored performance and exerted peer pressure to comply with the standards) and buddy groups (pairing of a veteran, high quality cataloger with a new member), presentation of workshops teaching coding, tagging, and even cataloging, and appointment of "Enhance" libraries, libraries whose cataloging was consistently superior, whose catalogers were permitted to correct and improve other members' records in OCLC's database. Generally, these efforts were based in the regional networks rather than being developed and executed directly by the national network.

RLIN, whose primary stated objective was to maintain the research value of its database, emphasized and rewarded higher quality cataloging. From the first, quality control was an issue of importance. RLIN, too, relied on voluntary adherence to standards, but its pricing varied with a record's fullness and accuracy. Most of the small group libraries comprising the Research Libraries Group represented institutions dedicated to providing scholarly research materials for graduate and post-graduate study. In order to serve those needs, full and accurate catalog records were important. Also, these institutions collected large numbers of relatively esoteric materials requiring original cataloging, e.g., primary research materials, foreign language materials, technical reports, etc.; therefore, they maintained cataloging departments with large numbers of expert catalogers. Since each library's own records entered in RLIN's database are retrievable individually, not just a single master record with the library's holding symbol attached as with OCLC's, inputting the best record possible was more beneficial and cost effective in the long run.

In contrast with RLIN, OCLC's membership included large numbers of colleges, smaller universities, and an important minority of public libraries, whose clients were not primarily researchers and who placed less emphasis on accurate and extensive catalog records. Their acquisitions tended to be more homogeneous and duplicative, often coinciding with materials acquired and cataloged by LC. (There were always research institutions in OCLC and colleges and small public libraries in RLIN, but the relative proportions differed.) A good many of these institutions joined the network expecting to shrink their professional cataloging staff, if not eliminate it altogether, relying instead on the data supplied by LC and the largest members. Thus, network participation tended to deprofessionalize cataloging in these libraries, making it difficult for them to produce the kind of high quality original cataloging that is done by expert professional staff.[3]

PURPOSE OF THIS STUDY

It is a commonly-held belief among catalogers that the quality of original cataloging in OCLC and RLIN differs markedly. One might be led to believe that this was inevitable, given the differing objectives, attitudes, quality control activities, and histories of the two networks described above. This study had two purposes and the researchers conducted two analyses: first, to see if there were recognizable differences between original cataloging from the two databases with regard to fullness and acuracy; and, second, to discover whether there were particular areas in the record in which the errors that occurred were found most frequently.

The first analysis, which tested the hypothesis that quality differed markedly between OCLC and RLIN, was intended to do more than satisfy mere curiosity. A finding that such differences existed could lead to an investigation of policies and practices to improve quality control. A finding that such differences did not exist might indicate that quality control was not a matter of goals, pricing, peer pressure, or even the availability of expert catalogers, but a function of other factors.

The second analysis, to identify particular areas in the catalog record containing the greatest number of errors, i.e., misinterpretations of cataloging rules, misapplications of cataloging or encoding principles, and/or simple errors in spelling and punctuation, if, indeed, these were identifiable, was intended to point toward specific solutions to these specific quality control problems. If such problem areas were found, solutions could be devised, including special emphasis on these areas in library school cataloging curricula, network- or professional association-sponsored workshops, institutes, and/or inservice training programs, and in books and articles directed toward staff responsible for original cataloging.

AREAS OF STUDY

Areas of study included elements of description, subject headings, and classification as well as MARC coding, i.e., correct assignment of tags, indicators and subfield codes.

The researchers reasoned that, of the four parts of the records under scrutiny (description, subjects; classification; and encoding) the descriptive cataloging was likely to contain the most errors, since it depended on complicated rules and rule interpretations requiring expert knowledge. (This assumption was based on the investigators' experiences training new staff and teaching formal cataloging courses as well as conducting network- and professional association-sponsored institutes and workshops.)

Aside from errors in punctuation, capitalization, spelling, and MARC coding, "accuracy" in the assignment of subject headings was a matter of judgment regarding the content of works and might well elicit different responses from different catalogers, regardless of their training. The same was true of classification numbers. Substantive errors in subject headings and classification numbers were confined to obvious discrepancies between the content of books and assignments of subject headings and class numbers, illogical judgments (e.g., classification numbers that failed to match the subject headings), the use of clearly unacceptable headings or numbers (i.e., long outdated or never established in the current standard tools), and the absence of any subject headings or classification numbers. (While the absence of subject headings and class numbers is not a contravention of bibliographic input standards, the investigators limited the study to materials that would normally be given both, therefore, their absence was considered an error.)

Finally, accuracy of the MARC encoding for entry into the networks was tested. These errors might render a record less than useful depending on the number and types of errors involved.

METHODOLOGY

The study had four phases: (1) data gathering; (2) construction of an error schedule; (3) identification of record errors; and (4) statistical analysis of the results.

Data Gathering. First, a sample of bibliographic records from each database was drawn that satisfied three parameters:

1. there was no cataloging for the item from the Library of Congress or from any national library or national agency;
2. the item was represented in both databases; and
3. the record represented full cataloging, i.e., I-level records in OCLC and 9114, 9116 or 9118 in RLIN.

The universe of data was limited to original cataloging records for books published in 1983 or later in the two databases. Selecting this date, two years from the data on which LC began implementing AACR 2 cataloging, allowed for a period of time to elapse during which errors attributable to the changeover from earlier descriptive cataloging rules might occur. The researchers expected that training for experienced catalogers might take time and that newly graduated catalogers might have been taught the earlier rules up to the end of the 1981 academic year, when the official policies of LC and members of the Association of Research Libraries (ARL) mandating use of AACR 2 began.

The study was limited to books and, in order that various kinds of books might be included, 12 subject areas—four each in the sciences, social sciences, and humanities—were searched to gather entries that satisfied the three parameters listed above. The group of subjects searched excluded unclassified popular fiction, which is rarely assigned any subject headings, but literary works or critical editions classified as literature were included (8xx in the Dewey Decimal Classification or Px in the Library of Congress Classification). Also excluded were children's books, dissertations, and microform representations of books. In addition, editions subsequent to the first were excluded from the study because catalog entries for such works might legitimately be based on earlier cataloging.

To draw a sample of records to be analyzed, the RLIN database was searched first by subject in designated disciplines and entries were printed for all books published in 1983 or later for which there was no LC cataloging. RLIN was chosen to be searched first because its software permitted subject retrieval. At the time of the study, OCLC was not searchable by subject directly, although one could retrieve records by subject from the OCLC file on DIALOG.

An RLIN hit was determined by examining the main cluster record. All of the RLIN hits were searched in OCLC and any entries appearing there as cataloging from LC or any other national agency or national library were eliminated. If the entries found in OCLC appeared as microforms, dissertations, or editions subsequent to the first, they also were eliminated. Based on results of a pilot search of records in both databases bearing the subject heading GEOLOGY, which yielded approximately 20 valid record pairs, it was estimated that a body of 200 to 250 matched pairs of bibliographic records in ten or more disciplines would constitute the data to be analyzed. In fact, the final data totalled 215 matched pairs of records from the 12 disciplines, culled from an initial group of 520 record pairs after excluding all records deemed unsuitable for the study.

Construction of an Error Schedule.   At first, the following error categories were proposed: (1) typographical or transcription errors, e.g., misspelling or misspacing; (2) contravention of AACR 2; (3) contravention of LC rule interpretations (LCRIs);[4] (4) omission of data called for in second level bibliographic description;[5] (6) omission/incorrect application of standard descriptors;[6] (7) omission/incorrect application of standard classification numbers;[7] and (8) incorrect application of fixed or variable field tagging conventions.[8] However, it quickly became clear that some of these categories were not mutually exclusive and others were ambiguous. For example, if a required mark of punctuation was missing, should it be called a punctuation error or a rule error? To be certain one would have to decide what was in the mind of the inputter. Thus, the proposed error table was revised to avoid subjectivity in interpreting the reason for any particular error. An error in punctuation was called simply a punctuation error, with one exception: the use or omission of square brackets to show that cataloging information was or was not taken from prescribed sources was defined as a rule error, since AACR 2 specifies this rule apart from its general punctuation rules. Errors in the punctuation used to identify descriptive elements according to the rules of International Standard Bibliographic Description (ISBD punctuation), while specified in AACR 2, were not considered rule errors—only punctuation errors.

Both errors and differences in fullness were regarded and counted in the analysis and the error table distinguished between them. The absence of any data element was counted only as a difference in fullness if it was an optional or judgmental element; but, if it was mandatory to include that element, it was counted as a rule error. The final error table included nine types of errors and eight types of differences in fullness (see Table 1).

Different classes of errors were recognized, based on priorities that determined as most serious those errors occurring in access points, in matters of mandatory rules, and in matters of fact, not interpretation. The majority of errors, while representing mistakes, did not affect access.

Books were examined to resolve discrepancies that could not be judged from catalog entries alone, and several record pairs were eliminated from the study because the books themselves were unavailable for examination.

Identification of Errors. Each investigator examined the record pairs separately, marking any errors she detected and noting any differences in the fullness of data. Each record pair was scrutinized twice before final determinations were made about what should be counted as true errors and what were matters in which a cataloger might legitimately exercise various options. Since the bibliographic input standards of both networks mandate following LC practice, there was less leeway in descriptive cataloging than one finds in the cataloging rules themselves. When an element of data contravened an LCRI, it was counted as an interpretation error, but not as an AACR 2 rule error (see Table 1).

Special care was exercised with regard to differences of fullness. Some differences of fullness affected consistency with the rules of AACR 2. When a rule was contravened by missing data, it was counted as a rule error. This was also true of a difference in fullness that affected consistency with the LCRIs. In that instance, the difference in fullness was counted as an interpretation error. If, however, a difference in fullness represented optional data, it was counted only as missing data.

Table 1. Errors and Differences of Fullness

Errors	Differences of Fullness
1. *AACR 2* rule error	1. Control field absent
2. *LCRI* error, including differences from LC's name authority file (NAF)	2. Call number absent
	3. Descriptive field absent
3. Mandatory fixed field error	4. Descriptive subfield absent
4. Call number error	5. Less data in field/subfield
5. Punctuation error	6. Added entry absent
6. Capitalization error	7. Subject headings absent
7. Spelling error	8. Less data in subject heading
8. Tagging error	
9. Subject heading error	

The assignment of at least one subject heading and a classification number was considered mandatory for the purposes of this study. If there were no subject headings or no call numbers, they were counted as errors. Beyond this, added subject headings were considered entirely optional and the number of headings was counted as data that was present or absent in the record (a difference in fullness), but not as an error, unless other errors occurred in these headings.

When the classification number assigned differed widely from the subject headings, for instance, in the choice of a main class, it was counted as an error unless the record was for a part of a series classified as a whole. Otherwise, catalogers were assumed to be correct in exercising any one of a variety of options available in the assignment of classification numbers to works. The assignment of widely different classification numbers to the same work by the OCLC and RLIN catalogers was counted as a difference (call number difference), but not as an error.

Error in the spelling or capitalization of a legitimate subject heading was counted only as a spelling or capitalization error, not as a subject heading error. Use of unused or long-dropped subject terms or subdivisions, on the other hand, were counted as subject heading errors.

Last of all, any error in the assignment of field tags, indicators, or subfield codes was considered a tagged error. Failure to encode a fixed field required to meet bibliographic input standards was also counted, but separately, as a mandatory fixed field error. Absent control fields (tagged 01x–049 in the MARC formats) that were optional according to bibliographic input standards were counted separately from those that were required, the former counted only as a missing control field and the latter counted as a mandatory fixed field error. This difference in terminology was necessary because both OCLC and RLIN reconfigure the 008 control field from the LC MARC (USMARC) format into a series of alphabetically-coded *fixed field data* appearing at the top of the record. Some fixed field data are mandatory, while some are optional. The investigators wished to emphasize the omission of mandatory data.

Statistical Analysis of Results. A database recording all of the differences— both errors and differences in fullness—between the pairs of OCLC and RLIN records was created using *StatPac*.[9] Each pair of records was assigned a control number for the study, used to identify it in the database as one unit. A profile for each of the two records making up a unit was defined, listing the errors and/or data differences between them and, for each individual bibliographic record, giving the specific occurrences of each error or fullness difference by the MARC tag number assigned to the field. For example, if an OCLC record contained an error in the date of publication (such as failure to record the ''c'' for a copyright date), it was recorded as ORE/260—an OCLC Rule Error in the 260 field. If an RLIN record had this error, it was recorded as RRE/260—an RLIN Rule Error in the 260 field. Occasionally, both entries contained the same error.[10] In this instance, the error was marked against both in order to obtain a true picture of the total number of errors among the 430 records.

Once the database was completed, statistics were computed for the number and distribution of errors and fullness differences. Comparisons could be made between units (i.e., record pairs), between records from OCLC and records from RLIN, between types of errors, and between individual fields in the entries. (See Tables 2 and 3 for these summary statistics.) In addition to the frequency distributions, correlations and tests of significance were performed.

Individual libraries that contributed the catalog records being analyzed were not identified during any part of the analysis, nor was any effort made to identify institutions making any particular error or group of errors.

FINDINGS

Analysis of the data showed that a great many errors occurred in the original cataloging studied from both databases: a total of 1,067 errors of all types occurred in the 430 records in the study—an average of almost two and one-half errors per record (2.48 errors per record). The data showed more similarity in the overall quality of original cataloging between OCLC and RLIN, as determined by comparing error totals, than the investigators had hypothesized: The 215 OCLC records contained a total of 537 errors of all kinds, while the 215 RLIN records contained a total of 530—virtually no difference (and statistically insignificant).

Descriptive Cataloging. Examining the types of errors more closely revealed that OCLC's 215 records contained 152 AACR 2 rule errors and 53 LC rule interpretation errors, while the 215 RLIN records had 136 AACR 2 rule errors

Table 2. Occurrence of Errors

Error Type	OCLC # (%)	RLIN # (%)	Total # (%)
AACR 2	152 (14.2)	136 (12.7)	288 (26.9)
LCRI	53 (5.0)	55 (5.2)	108 (10.2)
Punctuation	145 (13.6)	144 (13.5)	289 (27.1)
Capitalizing	36 (3.4)	53 (5.0)	89 (8.4)
Spelling	36 (3.4)	50 (4.7)	86 (8.1)
Tagging	36 (3.4)	30 (2.8)	66 (6.2)
Fixed fields	61 (5.7)	51 (4.8)	112 (10.5)
Subjects	8 (0.7)	6 (0.5)	14 (1.2)
Call numbers	10 (0.9)	5 (0.5)	11 (1.4)
Total errors	537 (50.3)	530 (49.7)	1,067 (100.0)

Table 3.   Cataloging Errors: Errors in *AACR 2* Rules
and *LCRI* Interpretations

Descriptive Area	OCLC # (%)	RLIN # (%)	Total # (%)
Title	24 (6.1)	21 (5.3)	45 (11.4)
Edition	1 (0.3)	2 (0.5)	3 (0.8)
Publication data	64 (16.2)	52 (13.1)	116 (29.3)
Physical data	12 (3.0)	13 (3.3)	25 (6.3)
Series	18 (4.5)	22 (5.5)	40 (10.0)
Notes	35 (8.8)	41 (10.4)	76 (19.2)
ISBN	0 (0.0)	0 (0.0)	0 (0.0)
Main entry	10 (2.5)	11 (2.8)	21 (5.3)
Added entries*	41 (10.4)	29 (7.3)	70 (17.7)
Total errors	205 (51.8)	191 (48.2)	396 (100.0)

* Includes *LCRI* errors in name headings used as subject headings.

and 55 LC rule interpretation errors. The number of errors in the application of descriptive cataloging rules between the two databases (i.e., AACR 2 rule errors plus LCRI errors in the 215 records from each database) differed by seven. The average occurrences of descriptive cataloging errors in OCLC records was almost one per record (205/215 = 95.3 percent) and in RLIN, slightly less (191/215 = 88.8 percent). The difference was not statistically significant and could be attributed to chance.

All errors in descriptive cataloging were not considered equally serious. A profile of their distribution among the areas of description (see Table 3) showed that most of them—116 errors in AACR 2 and LCRIs—occurred in the publication, distribution area (AACR 2—Area 4, see Figure 1), followed by the note area (i.e., 76 errors in AACR 2—Area 7, see Figure 2).

Descriptive cataloging errors in the title area (AACR 2—Area 1) totalled 45, primarily in AACR 2 rules, with 24 occurring in OCLC records and 21 in RLIN records. In the remaining areas of descriptive cataloging, 40 occurred in the series statement area (AACR 2—Area 6), 25 in the physical description area (AACR 2—Area 5), three in the edition area[11] (AACR 2—Area 2), and none in the standard number area (AACR 2—Area 8).

Errors in main and added entries (descriptive headings, excluding subject headings) were more important then errors in other descriptive fields, because they affect access most seriously, causing searchers to fail to locate desired entries in the database even though they may be there. A total of 74 errors in the application of cataloging rules and rule interpretations occurred in the main and added entry fields of both databases (i.e., in fields 1xx, 4xx, 7xx, and 8xx and 6xx name headings), with 36 appearing in OCLC records and 38 in RLIN's (see Table 4). The differences were not statistically significant.

Figure 1. Examples of Errors in Publication, Distribution Data

1. *Found in OCLC database:*
   Washington, D.C. : $b The Foundation of the American Society of Association Executives, $c c1984.
   Correction: Information from outside prescribed sources should be bracketed:
   [Washington, D.C.] : $b Foundation of the American Society of Association Executives, $c [c1984]

2. *Found in RLIN database:*
   [Paris] : $b OECD, $c 1986.
   Correction: There is no publication date in book; this is a copyright date and should be identified as such:
   [Paris] : $b OECD, $c c1986.

3. *Found in OCLC database:*
   Washington, D.C. : $b Federal Reserve System, $c 1986.
   Corrections: Date came from outside prescribed sources; wrong name was selected for publisher:
   Washington, D.C. : $b Board of Governors of the Federal Reserve System, $c [1986]

4. *Found in RLIN database:*
   Lanham, MD : $b Center for International Affairs, Harvard University : $b University Press of America, $c c1985.
   Correction: Wrong place of publication for first publisher: [Cambridge, Mass.] : $b Center for International Affairs, Harvard University : $a Lanham, MD: $b University Press of America, $c c1985.

Twenty-five AACR 2 rule errors occurred in descriptive headings in OCLC's records; 29 occurred in RLIN's. These errors related mainly to the choice of main entry vs. added entry and the choice of added entries. Though this relatively large number of rule errors relating to headings exhibits a startling lack of understanding of AACR 2's Chapters 21–25 among cataloging experts, they did not affect retrieval when all names and titles were retrievable in their proper forms although certain types of collocation might be lost. Thus, AACR 2 rule errors in headings were only considered as serious as errors in LCRIs, spelling, and tagging—discussed below—if they resulted in the omission of a heading.

The number of LCRI errors occurring in descriptive headings was small relative to the AACR 2 errors, only 20 in all, 11 in OCLC records and nine in RLIN. LCRI errors, which consisted mainly of failure to use the correct form of name established in the LC Name Authority File, available to catalogers as an unlinked file on both networks, were most serious because they affected retrieval negatively;[12] however, other types of errors occurring in descriptive headings affected retrieval just as much as errors in cataloging and interpretation. Simple spelling and tagging errors, troublesome wherever they occurred, affected retrieval negatively in headings, while errors in capitalization and punctuation

Figure 2. Examples of Errors in Notes

---

1. *Found in OCLC database:*
504   Bibliography: p. [243–249]
       Correction: Two sets of brackets are required here:
504   Bibliography: p. [243–249]

2. *Found in RLIN database:*
500   Summary in English and French.
       Correction: This is a German-language text and the summary appears in three languages. Note should reflect this:
500   Summary also in English and French.

3. *Found in OCLC database:*
504   Bibliography: p. 195–227.
500   A revision of the author's doctoral thesis.
       Correction: Order of notes is wrong, since the second note is not a dissertation note, but a bibliographic history note:
500   A revision of the author's doctoral thesis.
504   Bibliography: p. 195–227.

4. *Found in RLIN database:*
500   Includes index.
504   Bibliography: p. 329–356.
       Correction: Order should be reversed here, too; while not mandated, bibliographies precede indexes in most items:
504   Bibliography: p. 329–356.
500   Includes index.

5. *Found in OCLC database:*
504   Includes index and bibliographical references.
       Correction: Bibliographical references should come first:
504   Includes bibliographical references and index.

6. *Found in RLIN database:*
504   Bibliography: p. [211]–267.
       Corrections: There are two errors here, the spelling error and an error in recording the first page of the bibliography:
       504 Bibliography: p. [255]–267.

(Most errors in the note area are of small import. These examples merely establish that, given the instructions in AACR 2 regarding notes, they do occur. The only error with important implications is the last one, in which the bibliography is purported to have 44 more pages than it actually does.)

usually did not, although they look peculiar. Thus, spelling, tagging, and LCRI errors were considered the most serious of all error types. All records had a total of 55 serious errors in their descriptive headings (18 spelling, 17 tagging, and 20 LCRIs). The OCLC records contained a total of 28 serious errors (seven spelling, eight tagging, and eleven LCRI errors in headings); and the RLIN records had 29 serious errors. The variations were not statistically significant.

Figure 3.   Examples of Errors in Series Data

1. *Found in OCLC database:*
   490 0 Volume no. 38
   Correction: This is not a series statement.

2. *Found in RLIN database:*
   440 0 Biblioteca dell' "Archivum Romanicum." $n Ser 1, $p Storia, letteratura, paleografia ; $v v. 172
   Correction: This should be a direct transcription from the item and should not be abbreviated or manipulated:
   440 0 Biblioteca dell' "Archivum Romanicum." $n Serie I, $p Storia, letteratura, paleografia ; $v v. 172

3. *Found in OCLC database:*
   830 4 The family (United Nations. Dept. of International Economic and Social Affairs) ; $v no. 2
   Correction: When series uniform titles are established, they should omit articles and add a full stop at the end:
   830 0 Family (United Nations. Dept. of International Economic and Social Affairs) ; $v no. 2.

4. *Found in RLIN database:*
   490 0 Public Affairs Committee. Public Affairs Pamphlet ; $v no. 635
   Corrections: AACR 2 does not permit statement of responsibility to preceded series title proper; also, capitalization of title is incorrect:
   490 0 Public affairs pamphlet ; $v no. 635

In addition to cataloging and interpretation errors, punctuation, capitalization, spelling, and tagging errors were counted in all descriptive areas of the records, not just in the headings. Punctuation errors far outpaced all others (see Figure 4), totalling 264 errors in all parts of all the descriptions, compared with 87 capitalization, 77 spelling, and 51 tagging errors (see Table 5).

In AACR 2 Areas 1 through 8, the 215 OCLC records had 182 errors, 107 in

Table 4.   Errors in Descriptive Headings[1]

Error Type	OCLC # (%)	RLIN # (%)	Total # (%)
AACR 2	25 (14.0)	29 (16.3)	54 (30.3)
*LCRI**	11* (6.2)	9* (5.1)	20* (11.3)
Punctuation	25 (14.0)	30 (16.8)	55 (30.9)
Capitalizing	8 (4.5)	6 (3.4)	14 (7.9)
Spelling*	7* (3.9)	11* (6.2)	18* (10.1)
Tagging*	8* (4.5)	9* (5.1)	17* (9.6)
Total errors	84 (47.1)	94 (52.9)	178 (100.0)
Total errors affecting retrieval	26 (14.6)	29 (16.3)	55 (30.9)

[1] Descriptive headings include main entries, series headings, and added entry headings, excluding subject headings.
* Errors likely to affect retrieval most seriously.

Figure 4. Examples of Errors in Punctuation

---

1. *Found in OCLC database:*
   710 20 Royal Society (Great Britain).
   Correction: No full stop at end:
   710 20 Royal Society (Great Britain)

2. *Found in RLIN database:*
   260 0 Croton-on-Hudson, N.Y. : $b Policy Studies Associates, $c 1983.
   Corrections: The state abbreviation should omit periods since it is given in the book
   that way; also, there is no publication date in book; this is a copyright date and
   should be identified as such:
   260 0 Croton-on-Hudson, NY : $b Policy Studies Associates, $c c1983.

3. *Found in OCLC database:*
   300 241 p. : $b ill. maps ; $c 23 cm.
   Correction: Ill. and maps should be separated by a comma.
   300 241 p. : $b ill., maps ; $c 23 cm.

4. *Found in RLIN database:*
   260 0 Brighton, Sussex : $b Harvester Press; $a New York: $b St. Martin's Press,
   $c 1982.
   Correction: ISBD requires a space before and after the semicolon separating the
   first name from the second:
   260 0 Brighton, Sussex : $b Harvester Press ; $a New York : $b St. Martin's Press,
   $c 1982.

5. *Found in OCLC database:*
   300 vi, 330 p. : $c 24 cm.
   Correction: ISBD requires a space-semicolon-space preceding the dimensions of the
   book (i.e., height of spine):
   300 vi, 330 p. ; $c 24 cm.

6. *Found in RLIN database:*
   700 10 Dissanayake Winal.
   Corrections: Surname and forename should be separated by a comma; also, the
   forename is misspelled in the heading, although it is correctly spelled in the
   statement of responsibility in this record.
   700 10 Dissanayake, Wimal.

---

punctuation, 34 in capitalization, 25 in spelling, and 19 in tagging. In the same areas, the 215 RLIN records had 221 errors, 120 in punctuation, 49 in capitalization, 34 in spelling, and 18 in tagging.

These errors tended to occur most frequently in the note and title areas, although the publication area was not error-free and every area had some errors, but not of all types.

Subject Analysis. Since the assignment of subject headings is not bound by specific rules such as those that govern descriptive cataloging, more latitude was allowed in defining substantive errors in subject headings. The investigators did not examine the content of subject headings except in the broadest possible terms, and a substantive error was counted only when there was wide divergence

Table 5. Errors in Areas of Description

Area	Punctuation OCLC/RLIN	Capitals OCLC/RLIN	Spelling OCLC/RLIN	Tagging OCLC/RLIN	AACR/LCRI OCLC/RLIN	Total
Title	26 / 23	10 / 25	9 / 9	4 / 8	24 / 21	159
Edition	1 / 2	0 / 1	0 / 0	0 / 0	1 / 2	7
Publication data	26 / 20	5 / 5	4 / 6	4 / 3	64 / 52	189
Physical data	9 / 7	0 / 0	5 / 4	2 / 0	12 / 13	52
Series	15 / 24	6 / 6	2 / 6	6 / 5	18 / 22	110
Notes	27 / 40	13 / 12	5 / 9	3 / 2	35 / 41	187
ISBN	3 / 4	0 / 0	0 / 0	0 / 0	0 / 0	7
Main entry	7 / 1	0 / 1	3 / 8	1 / 4	10 / 11	46
Added entry	13 / 16	2 / 1	4 / 3	5 / 4	41* / 29*	108
Total	127 / 137	36 / 51	32 / 45	25 / 26	205 / 191	875

* Includes variant name forms used in subject headings.

between assigned subject headings and the content of the book being cataloged, if unacceptable subject headings were used, or if subject headings clearly were misused. In addition the complete absence of subject headings was counted as an error for the purposes of this study.

Few substantive errors occurred in subject headings (i.e., unacceptable terms used, terms clearly bearing no relation to the work in question, etc.): there were only five in OCLC and four in RLIN. In addition, one OCLC record and one RLIN record lacked any subject headings. Classification numbers were absent (also counted as an error although the investigators recognize that classification is optional) from ten OCLC records and three RLIN records, and two more RLIN records contained classification numbers that diverged widely from assigned subject headings. Thus, the total number of subject-related errors in OCLC was 18 and in RLIN was 10. The differences were not statistically significant.

Although the number of subject headings for individual records seemed to be higher in the RLIN records when the investigators examined the record pairs, the intuitive conclusion that RLIN records contained more subject headings on average was not confirmed. In 99 of the record pairs, the same number of subject headings appeared, although of the 363 headings in these pairs, 93 differed in their subdivisions; in 46 of the record pairs, the OCLC records had more headings; and in 70 of the record pairs, the RLIN records had more headings (see Figure 5). However, the average number of subject headings per record varied only slightly between the two databases: 2.5 per record in OCLC's 215 records and 2.8 per record in RLIN's. The variance was not statistically significant.

Tagging Errors. Sixty-six tagging errors occurred in the 430 records, 36 in OCLC records and 30 in RLIN records. In addition there were 112 errors in the

Figure 5.   Number of Subject Headings Assigned

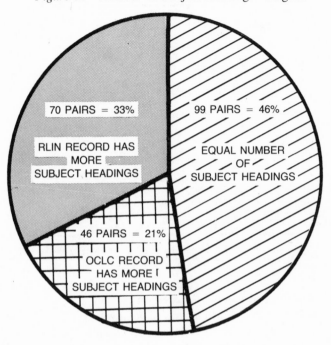

70 PAIRS = 33%

RLIN RECORD HAS
MORE
SUBJECT HEADINGS

99 PAIRS = 46%

EQUAL NUMBER
OF
SUBJECT HEADINGS

46 PAIRS = 21%

OCLC RECORD
HAS MORE
SUBJECT HEADINGS

coding of fixed field data, bringing the total number of encoding errors to 178 (see Table 6). The majority of tagging errors were found in the title field (MARC tag 245) and the control and series fields (MARC tags 0xx and 4xx, respectively): 12 tagging errors occurred in 245, and 11 each in 0xx and 4xx fields. These findings were particularly unfortunate, first, because the 245 and 440 fields contain data vital to virtually every searcher (title, subtitle, and statement of responsibility) and the first subfield is used to create title added entries; and second, because the control fields, as their name implies, have great potential for data management in online systems, both small local systems and larger ones.

Error Free Records.   Only five record pairs were completely error free. A total of only 39 individual records out of the 430 were error free, 22 in OCLC and 17 in RLIN. The higher number of error free records in OCLC was not a statistically significant difference.

Differences in Fullness.   There were 269 instances in which one record in a pair had more data than its companion, although only 112 of these involved complete absence of the data element. In the rest of the occurrences, part of the data found

Table 6. Errors in MARC Tagging

TAG	OCLC # (%)	RLIN # (%)	Total # (%)
Fixed fields	61 (34.3)	51 (28.7)	112 (63.0)
0xx	7 (3.9)	4 (2.2)	11 (6.2)*
1xx	1 (0.6)	4 (2.2)	5 (2.8)
245	4 (2.2)	8 (4.5)	12 (6.7)
250	0 (0.0)	0 (0.0)	0 (0.0)
260	4 (2.2)	3 (1.7)	7 (3.9)
300	2 (1.1)	0 (0.0)	2 (1.1)
4xx	6 (3.4)	5 (2.8)	11 (6.2)
5xx	3 (1.7)	2 (1.1)	5 (2.8)
6xx	4 (2.2)	2 (1.1)	6 (3.4)
7xx	4 (2.2)	2 (1.1)	6 (3.4)
8xx	1 (0.6)	0 (0.0)	1 (0.6)
Total	97 (54.4)	81 (45.5)*	178 (99.9)*

* Variations between individual and total percentages reflect rounding off to one place beyond the decimal point.

in an element was missing from one record of the pair. Even fewer instances—only 30 in all—occurred in which a retrieval point was present in one record, but absent in the other. These do not include instances in which the absence of the element was considered an error because the access point was mandated by an AACR 2 rule.

No clear pattern emerges here with regard to the databases, i.e., that OCLC or RLIN catalogers tended to include more data in their records. In some instances OCLC catalogers put in more data, e.g., in the larger number of subject headings assigned with added subdivisions (representing more specific headings); in other instances, RLIN catalogers included more data, e.g., the slightly larger number

Table 7. Differences of Fullness

Difference Type	OCLC # (%)	RLIN # (%)	Total # (%)
Descriptive element absent	43 (16.0)	39 (14.5)	82 (30.5)
Descriptive subelement absent	14 (5.2)	18 (6.7)	32 (11.9)
Descriptive element, less data	27 (10.0)	43 (16.0)	70 (26.0)
Added entry absent	12 (4.5)	16 (5.9)	28 (10.4)
Subject heading with less data	15 (5.6)	40 (14.9)	55 (20.5)
Subject headings absent	1 (0.4)	1 (0.4)	2 (0.7)*
Total differences	112 (41.6)*	157 (58.4)	269 (100.0)

* Variation between individual and total percentages reflect rounding off to one place beyond the decimal point.

of descriptive elements in their records. However, the mere presence of additional data does not mean a record is "better"; other judgments must be made to determine whether the additional data is useful or not that were not germane to this study.

CONCLUSIONS

Bearing in mind that the differences between the records were not statistically significant and might have occurred by chance, the following conclusions were drawn from the foregoing analysis:

1. The quality of records entered into OCLC and RLIN by member libraries appears to be quite similar and does not support the commonly-held belief that there is wide disparity in the quality of original cataloging between the databases.

2. Most records in both databases contain errors of some kind, making it difficult, if not impossible, for student or neophyte catalogers in libraries to learn accurate, high quality cataloging by emulating them.

3. The largest proportion of errors occurred, as expected, in the application of AACR 2, the descriptive cataloging rules, according to the practices established at the Library of Congress. Fewer errors were detected in subject headings, classification numbers, or in the encoding of data according to the OCLC and RLIN versions of the MARC format.

4. Of all the elements of descriptive cataloging, the greatest concentration of errors occurred in AACR 2 Areas 1, 4, 6 and 7—titles, publication data, series, and notes—and in added entries.

5. Punctuation errors occurred much more frequently than errors in capitalization, spelling, or tagging.

RECOMMENDATIONS

In view of these conclusions, the following recommendations are made to address the problems:

1. *Greater emphasis be placed on the application of AACR 2 according to the Library of Congress' policies and practices, especially in the title, publication, series, and note areas as well as in the choice and form of added entry headings.*

More time should be spent explaining the AACR 2 rules for these areas and their associated LCRIs as well as illustrating their application with examples extracted from a wide variety of books. Because there is a detailed standard that must be followed for descriptive data, one must do more than merely record whatever data one finds on an item being cataloged. The data must be recorded in the proper manner and organized according to the proper order of elements, and it must be capitalized, abbreviated and punctuated properly.

Regarding publication information, cataloging teachers and trainers might assume their students have sufficient knowledge of the publishing world to follow AACR 2 instructions that permit latitude in interpretation, e.g., "Give the name of a publisher, distributor, etc., in the shortest form in which it can be understood and identified internationally."[13] However, the findings of this study negate such assumptions. Ascertaining the appropriate data can be difficult if many dates appear in a book. Catalogers are not always knowledgeable about the differences between *printings, issues*, and other terms used in the book trade to refer to activities that might affect the choice of a date for cataloging purposes. It may be problematic to choose an appropriate place and name for the publisher when multiple names and places appear on the book.

Direct transcription of data from title pages is not always simple, either. The large number of AACR 2 and LCRI errors occurring in the title and series areas (AACR 2—Area 1 and Area 6), in which data is to be transcribed as it appears on the book, demonstrates that. Title pages perform several functions simultaneously, not only the expression of bibliographic data. Perhaps some of the other functions—to attract attention and to sell books—interfere with that expression when they are served by graphic designers and house editors. Furthermore, the data given on title pages can be very complex when the process of writing, editing, and producing a book involves many people, not just one writer, one editor, and/or one publisher.

Other areas of description, especially those governing the choice and form of main and added entries, including series entries, are not sufficiently well-understood and stand in need of more explanation and illustration, too.

Regarding the note area, one professional cataloger with several years experience in an academic library of some size said at a recent workshop, "I'm just glad if I can get them in, regardless of their order or anything else in the rules." That kind of attitude is obviously counterproductive if uniformity is a primary objective and it needs to be addressed both by graduate school teachers and inservice trainers. Or, perhaps the cataloging community might reevaluate prescribing the order of notes and allow them to be entered without regard to their order.

    2. *Correct punctuation should be emphasized.*

The fact that ISBD punctuation does not follow ordinary punctuation rules, that spaces sometimes are and sometimes are not used before and after a mark of punctuation, and that the meanings behind these punctuations are unknown to anyone but catalogers may be reasons why there are so many errors in punctuation.

The findings of this study show, given the large differential between punctuation errors and other types of errors, that it requires much more emphasis in programs that educate and train catalogers as well as in those for inputters, who may believe they are "correcting" catalogers' mistakes in punctuation by altering what they are given in order to conform to ordinary punctuation rules.

3. *AACR 2 and the LCRIs should be examined carefully to clarify them whenever possible, eliminating large numbers of exceptions to the rules as written or numerous special cases, so that rules may be understood and applied more easily.*

One example of current activity of this nature is the appointment by the American Library Association's Committee on Cataloging: Description and Access of a task force on brackets to investigate whether any changes are needed in the rules governing the use of brackets. In past years, the committee responded similarly to proposals from librarians in the field and task forces were formed to study major changes to the rules, such as the elimination of ISBD punctuation.

4. *Greater emphasis should be placed on accurate encoding of data for the MARC formats, particularly the fixed fields.*

In view of the disproportionately large number of errors that occurred in the fixed fields, it would appear that this area of the MARC record should receive more time and clearer explanation.

5. *Education and training of catalogers should be coordinated by forging closer ties among those people who teach cataloging as well as by bringing cataloging curricula into harmony whether instruction is given in a school, workshop, or inservice training course.*

Four kinds of entities support cataloging curricula and employ people to instruct others in cataloging: (1) schools of library and information science, (2) cataloging networks, (3) professional associations and organizations, and (4) individual libraries with large cataloging departments. There are some relationships among these entities now, but they are sporadic and unsystematic. Sometimes, the same faculty who teach cataloging in library/information science schools act as faculty for cataloging network workshops or for workshops sponsored by local, state, regional or national professional associations. Sometimes, the same trainers who teach newly hired staff to catalog in local libraries act as adjunct faculty in library/information science schools and/or association-sponsored workshops. Rarely is this crossover of instructional responsibilities systematic. Lists of credentialed cataloging teachers/trainers might be compiled for use by all of the entities mentioned above. The important element in such a plan is the credentials that qualify someone for inclusion.

One can imagine credentials that include appropriate preparation in formal courses, experience in the field, and/or demonstrations of excellence on examinations. Special training at the Library of Congress might be required. Several different combinations might be determined to be sufficient. Clearly, such guidelines might be flexible or rigid, might address minimum requirements or target all desired abilities, and might involve a formal regulating body or an informal consensus.

If Hafter is correct that a cadre of master catalogers plus an army of clerical workers has emerged in academic cataloging departments as a result of the rise of cataloging networks, replacing the much larger pool of variously-qualified professional catalogers that existed in pre-network days, perhaps it will be easy to identify the masters. Yet, the need to prove one's abilities might require more than just survival in the ranks of professional catalogers.

The notion of coordination among sectors of the library community teaching cataloging need not be achieved by means of any formal list or method. Just as the "national" network is made up of many kinds of networks—some international in scope and others strictly local—so the "certified" cataloging teacher/trainer might be many kinds of persons, some having one kind of credential and some having others. Perhaps coordination is possible only within limits—geographical, financial, and logistical. If so, there is much to be gained by seeking to push back the limits as far as possible.

A FINAL WORD

Although the findings reported here focus mainly on what was wrong with the 430 records examined in the course of the study, in general, many positive elements were found in this cataloging, e.g., in most entries, the choice of entry was correct, titles were correctly transcribed, etc. Given the large number of data elements and characters in this universe of records, one cannot conclude that it represents "bad" cataloging because it contained errors. On the contrary, the proportion of errors affecting retrieval was lower than, but not inconsistent with, the findings of other researchers, e.g., Taylor and Simpson.[14]

Replication of this research with a larger pool of data that might uphold or deny its findings would be extremely helpful. The records used in this study did not seem to include large numbers of particularly complicated materials, such as conference proceedings, that might have resulted in the occurrence of more errors per record. A good many of the materials included here were foreign language items, but they, as well as their English language counterparts, appeared to involve only a limited number of the problems usually thought of as difficult to resolve, e.g. corporate body responsibility, multiple authors or dates, exceptional titles, etc. Having completed this study, the investigators hypothesize that a larger group of entries with many complicated items would contain a larger proportion of errors.

Another area for future research is determination of the number of corrections made to the errors found in this study. In RLIN, other records in the cluster derived from the one used for this study might have included such corrections and in OCLC, editing by catalogers using the records might have eliminated the errors found by the investigators. One surprising phenomenon was the large number of RLIN hits that were matched by LC or other national agency or national library cataloging in OCLC. As a result, many of the original RLIN hits had to be discarded as candidates for the study.

Recommendations involving teaching/training issues should be incorporated into formal courses in cataloging being taught in schools of library and information science as well as in continuing education programs developed by the bibliographic utilities and concerned professional associations, and inservice training conducted in individual libraries. Only when a concerted effort is made to address these issues in all components of cataloging education and training is the achievement of standard, uniform cataloging data likely to be realized. An immediate advantage to such an achievement is that all libraries that use network records could do so without as much costly and time consuming editing as they now do.

Recommendations for clarifying the cataloging rules and rule interpretations might be pursued by means of a study identifying those rules and rule interpretations that appear to be candidates for such treatment. Since the publication of AACR 2, rule changes and, by definition, rule interpretations, have been largely reactive, correcting errors or concepts that proved hard to apply in practice and added needed rules that were omitted in the original document. A different kind of investigation is needed to show where the evolution of the rules has resulted in burdensome elaboration, or the proliferation of numerous exceptions and special cases.

Finally, the implementation of other recommendations depend on the interest and commitment of organizations of catalogers, including those in the networks and professional associations. Activities intended to enhance the quality of the process of cataloging and its end product—the catalog itself—will result, ultimately, in greater recognition for and appreciation of the catalog as a primary instrument of information service.

ACKNOWLEDGMENTS

This study is based on research conducted by Shelia S. Intner and Dorothy McGarry, Principal Cataloger, UCLA Science and Technology Library, funded by a joint educator-practitioner grant from the Council on Library Resources.

Many people lent their time and expertise to help in the conduct of this study, especially John W. Haeger and James Schmidt of the Research Libraries Group and Michael McGill and Martin Dillon of OCLC, who permitted the use of catalog records from their databases. Robert M. Hayes and Robert D. Stueart, deans of the graduate library/information science schools at UCLA and Simmons, respectively, and Russell Shank and Artemis Kirk, chief executive officers of the libraries at UCLA and Simmons, respectively, encouraged use of their facilities and services.

Special thanks are due Shirley Nordhaus, UCLA Computer Center, who lent expertise during the data gathering phase; to Allyson Carlyle, Alexandra Herz and Marianne

McGowan, for searching the databases; to Sara Shatford Layne and Susan Garet of UCLA, who expedited interlibrary loans for some of the books that required examination, to Linda Willey and Christopher Willey, who assisted with data preparation, and to Claudia Jensen, who did the final input and initial analysis. It is difficult to imagine completing the study without their help.

NOTES AND REFERENCES

1. A report of OCLC distributed at the February, 1986, meeting of its Users Council, of the origin of records in the OCLC database in January 2, 1986, revealed that only 2,644,940 out of a total of 12,721,827 records were contributed by LC.

2. The standard cataloging rules are given in the *Anglo-American Cataloguing Rules*, 2nd edition, edited by Michael Gorman and Paul W. Winkler (Chicago: American Library Association, 1978), plus 1983, 1984 and 1985 revisions, and subsequent updates appearing in the Library of Congress publication, *Cataloging Service Bulletin*.

3. Ruth Hafter, *Academic Librarians and Cataloging Networks: Visibility, Quality Control, and Professional Status* (New York: Greenwood Press, 1986), 63–78.

4. Interpretations of the cataloging rules by the Library of Congress (LCRIs) are published in its periodical publication *Cataloging Service Bulletin*. LCRIs may also be found in privately prepared and published compilations, and indexes to LCRIs are available, too.

5. *Anglo-American Cataloguing Rules*, 15. No minimal-level records were included in the study, partly because definitions of "minimal-level" vary and what is considered acceptable differs from place to place and partly because these records are clearly identified as less-than-full standard.

6. Standard descriptors are defined to mean subject headings from the *Library of Congress Subject Headings*, 9th ed. Washington: the Library, 1980, and its updates; or, properly identified and coded alternatives.

7. Standard classification numbers are defined to mean *Library of Congress* or *Dewey Decimal* classification numbers, assigned according to the latest edition of either classification system.

8. Errors in field tags, indicators and subfield codes were judged according to published OCLC-MARC or RLIN-MARC formats for printed monographs, as appropriate.

9. David S. Walonick, *StatPac: Statistical Analysis Package for the IBM*, version 6.0 (Minneapolis: Walonick Associates, 1986).

10. Indeed, the presence of the same error in both records in a pair led to the discovery and subsequent exclusion of a number of tape loaded records—originally input into one database and later sent by magnetic tape to be loaded into the other—that had been overlooked during the first examination of the record pair.

11. The investigators counted the errors found in the edition area, but, since editions subsequent to the first were excluded from the study, errors in this area were few, as expected.

12. When more than one form of an author's name appears in the catalog, his/her works then are dispersed under two or more heading forms. Searching either form alone will not retrieve all the works, since links do not exist between forms to direct searchers to the variants.

13. *Anglo-American Cataloguing Rules*, rule 1.4D2., p. 33.

14. Arlene G. Taylor and Charles W. Simpson, "Accuracy of LC Copy: A Comparison between Copy That Began as CIP and Other LC Cataloging," *Library Resources and Technical Services* 30 (Oct./Dec.): 375–387. The researchers reported approximately 20 percent of the LC records studied contained significant errors; regarding shared cataloging, they said it had "smaller proportions of significant errors, even though they had higher proportions of errors overall" (p. 385).

THE LIBRARY LEADERSHIP PROJECT:
A TEST OF LEADERSHIP EFFECTIVENESS
IN ACADEMIC LIBRARIES

Eugene S. Mitchell

Almost 20 years ago, one writer commented that "we know very little about what makes a supervisor effective or why a supervisor is effective in one situation but not another" (Hill, 1969). About ten years later, James MacGregor Burns (1978), in his Nobel Prize-winning book, *Leadership*, described the same situation. "Leadership is one of the most observed and least understood phenomena on earth."

The situation does not appear to have improved much since Burns's lament. What's more, the lack of understanding extends to the field of librarianship. Dragon (1976) has commented that "Leadership, although recognized by management theorists as an element in the management process, is generally ne-

Advances in Library Administration and Organization,
Volume 8, pages 25-38.
Copyright © 1989 by JAI Press Inc.
All rights of reproduction in any form reserved.
ISBN: 0-89232-967-X

glected in the literature of library administration. Little is known about the leader behavior pattern of library administrators.''

Libraries seem to be excellent places to study leadership. Although there are formal leadership positions in libraries, many non-administrative librarians assume leadership positions in task forces, committees and the like. There are a variety of both structured and unstructured tasks to be supervised. Staff members discharge duties with relative independence; performance depends largely on their own abilities and skills. Finally, libraries are complex organizations with two related but different dimensions: a nonprofessional dimension providing support services by clerks and pages and a professional one providing information services by highly educated and experienced professionals.

Consequently, there may be a need for various leadership styles within the same organization. This suggests that there is no one *best* way to lead or manage a group. In fact, this is just what much of the research shows. "Some studies have shown that directive, autocratic, managing types of leadership promote effective work performance in some situations. Other studies have shown that permissive, nondirective, human relations-oriented leadership is comparatively more effective under other situations" (Hunt, 1967).

This inconsistency has also been shown in some of the research involving teachers and educational administrators. VanGundy and Haynes (1978) have suggested that different situational requirements for college presidents (for example, president as leader of the institution versus president as leader of an administrative cabinet) will dictate leadership effectiveness and therefore may demand different types of leadership behavior. Reavis and Derlega (1976) have identified studies of teacher effectiveness which have shown that teachers with both "task-oriented" and "person-oriented" leadership styles have positive effects on student learning.

In order to better understand the role of certain variables in the leadership process, the Library Leadership Project was undertaken to examine the relationship between situational factors and the leadership effectiveness of academic library department heads.

MAJOR TRENDS IN LEADERSHIP RESEARCH

Discussions of leadership can be found in the writings of the ancient Chinese and Egyptians, but it was not until the early 1900s that scientific research into the topic began. The research at the beginning of this century first focused on the personality characteristics presumed to set leaders apart from others. This line of research was known as the Great Man Theory. Some of the characteristics which were identified and studied included physical factors (height, weight, age, appearance), fluency of speech, intelligence, self confidence, emotional control, social and economic status, popularity, and prestige. Although some correlations were shown between these traits and effectiveness, this line of research did not prove to be very fruitful because the relationships discovered (although statistically significant) were weak and of limited predictive value. In addition, longitudinal comparisons of effective and ineffective leaders in identical or similar roles were not conducted. The methodology used instead was to compare the traits of leaders to the traits of followers. Finally, too many inconsistencies and contradictions appeared as researchers tried to develop a universal theory of leadership. Some of the same traits were found in both leaders and followers.

By the early 1950s, researchers had begun to become disenchanted with the trait approach and had begun to study leader behaviors, that is, what leaders actually *do*. A wide variety of activities in which leaders engaged were identified and researchers tried to group them together.

At Ohio State University, two major dimensions were identified: consideration and initiating structure (Fleishman, 1973). Consideration referred to "the extent to which a leader exhibited concern for the welfare of the other members of the group"; initiation of structure referred to "the extent to which a leader initiated activity in the group, organized it, and defined the way the work was to be done" (Stogdill, 1981). The greatest effectiveness was usually achieved when a combination of both factors was present, the actual mix of the two being influenced by situational variables. At the University of Michigan, Likert (1961) also identified two dimensions in effective leader behavior which he distinguished as job-centered and employee-centered. His studies suggested that both sets of behavior improve performance, but that employee-centered behaviors led to better group morale. While suggesting the best ways to lead a group, these models failed to account for the situational variables which must be considered in determining leadership effectiveness.

By the 1970s, the important role played by situational variables in predicting organizational outcomes was realized and led to a situational approach in the study of research. Four of the most prominent approaches are: *Situational Leadership Theory* (Hersey and Blanchard, 1977), which considers the maturity of the group being led; *Vertical Dyad Linkage Theory* (Graen and Cashman, 1975), which concentrates on the formation of relationships between leaders and individual subordinates; *Path Goal Theory* (House, 1971), which suggests means by which the leader can identify paths to convergent organizational and individual goals; and the *Contingency Model of Leadership Effectiveness* (Fiedler, 1967), which proposes an interaction between leader style and the favorableness of the situation for the leader.

THE MODEL

The model used in this study was Fiedler's Contingency Model of Leadership Effectiveness. Fiedler contends that a group's effectiveness is contingent upon "the appropriate match between leadership personality attributes, reflecting his or her motivational structure, and the degree to which the leader has situational control and influence." There are two basic motivational structures: task motivation and relationship motivation. A task-motivated leadership style satisfies the leader's need to gain satisfaction from performing the task; a relationship-motivated leadership style is oriented toward achieving good interpersonal relations within the work group and satisfies the leader's need to gain a position of prominence.

According to Fiedler, neither style is appropriate in all organizational situations. The nature of the situation for the leader can run from very unfavorable to very favorable and leadership style can run from task to relationship motivation. Task-motivated leaders perform best in situations which are highly favorable or in those which are highly unfavorable. Relationship-oriented leaders tend to perform best in situations which have only moderate favorableness.

Motivational structure (or leadership style) is determined by an 18-item bipolar adjective scale called the Least Preferred Co-Worker (LPC) Scale in which individuals are asked to rate a co-worker with whom they have worked least well. The assumption is not that the rater's score will necessarily reflect an accurate perception of the least preferred co-worker, but rather that the way in which the rater perceives another will affect his relations with him or her. The LPC score is interpreted as a reflection of the relative motivation toward task versus interpersonal success. A person who describes the least preferred co-worker in a negative way is considered task-motivated. A person who sees the least preferred co-worker in a relatively more positive way is considered relationship-motivated.

Situational control is the moderating variable in the relationship between leadership style and effective performance. It refers to the degree to which the dimensions of the group situation give the leader power and influence over the group.

Fiedler's Model considers three situational dimensions confronting the leader. In order of importance, they are: (a) leader-member relations, the degree of trust and respect group members have for their leader; (b) task structure, the degree of structure in the task to be performed by the group; and (c) position power, the degree of formal authority and power within the leader's job. The particular mix of these three variables determines situational control.

In the Contingency Model, these variables are dichotomized to provide eight categories or octants of situations ranging from highly favorable to highly unfavorable for the leader. Octant 1 is the most favorable and Octant 8 is the least. See Table 1.

Since its appearance, there have been numerous test and extensions of the Model, but none in libraries. The validation studies have almost all been laboratory experiments. Extensions of the Model have been attempted for research firms, supermarket chains, manufacturing firms, hospitals, classrooms, Army training classes, and volleyball teams. Applications of the Model are prolific and attempts to validate it have presented evidence which is not uni-

Table 1. Octant Characteristics

| | Situation Classification | | | | |
Octant	Leader- Member Relations	Task Structure	Position Power	Motivation	Situation Favorableness
1	Good	High	Strong	Task	Most
2	Good	High	Weak	Task	Favorable
3	Good	Low	Strong	Task	
4	Good	Low	Weak	Relationship	
5	Poor	High	Strong	Relationship	
6	Poor	High	Weak	Relationship	
7	Poor	Low	Strong	Relationship	Least
8	Poor	Low	Weak	Task	Favorable

formly supportive and the Model is still somewhat controversial. It is still important, therefore, to investigate its descriptive and predictive ability.

PURPOSE

The primary purpose of this study was to investigate in academic libraries the validity of Fiedler's Model in predicting the relationships between leader motivation and leadership effectiveness under varying conditions of situational control. A second purpose of this study was to determine the situational favorableness in various specific library departments, namely, acquisitions, catalog maintenance, cataloging, circulation, collection development, processing, and reference. By analyzing the situational variables in these departments, the intent was to place each one along what can be called an "advantage for the leader" continuum represented by the line on the right of the table above. In other words, could library departments in an academic library be placed in specific Fiedler octants?

METHOD

Four hypotheses were developed to test Fiedler's Model:

1. There is no significant difference in the mean situational control for the library departments being examined.
2a. Task-motivated leaders are not significantly more effective than relationship-motivated leaders when the leader-member relations are

good and the leader's position power is strong regardless of the amount of task structure.

2b.   No significant interaction effect exists between leadership style and task structure when leader-member relations are good and the leader's position power is strong.

3.   There is no relationship between the four combined independent variables of leader motivation, leader-member relations, task structure, and position power and the dependent variable of effectiveness.

The field study approach was chosen for several reasons. Actual managers and their associates could be examined in real-life situations. Since constraints did not allow control over the assignment of subjects to groups or over independent variables, the situation demanded ex post facto research. Finally, the real test of any theory is its ability to withstand the test of validation under real-life field conditions.

The units of analysis in this study were academic library department heads responsible for acquisitions, catalog maintenance, cataloging, circulation, collection development, processing, and reference. A total of 278 department heads were randomly selected from 137 U.S. academic libraries. The libraries were affiliated with schools that shared the following characteristics: (1) medium to large enrollment (5–20,000); (2) four-year colleges and universities both with and without graduate work; and (3) overall entrance difficulty from moderate to most difficult, meaning more than 75 percent of freshman were in the top 50 percent of their high school class and scored over 900 on the SAT or over 18 on the ACT. Up to 85 percent of the applicants were accepted. A total of 209 usable responses were received for a response rate of 75 percent.

All of the independent variables in this study were measured using scales developed by Fiedler. The leader's motivational structure was determined by using the Least Preferred Co-Worker Scale. This scale and another designed to measure leader-member relations were administered to the department heads being studied. Other scales to measure task structure and position power were completed by the immediate supervisors of the managers being studied.

The dependent variables of leader and group effectiveness were measured using two scales. One, developed by Bare (1978), determined *group* effectiveness (the usual approach). The second scale, developed by Morse and Wagner (1978), determined *managerial* effectiveness (a better surrogate for leadership effectiveness than group performance). This second scale was used to rate a department head's effectiveness by identifying and judging observable actions and behavior leading to the accomplishment of the organization's goals. The instrument was concerned with six managerial roles: managing the organization's resources and its environment, organizing and coordinating, information handling, providing for growth and development, motivating and conflict handling, and strategic problem solving. Both effectiveness scales were administered to the immediate supervisors.

The data to test the first hypothesis consisted of the scores on the situational control scales (Leader-Member Relations, Task Structure, and Position Power). The data were analyzed using a one-way analysis of variance in order to see if the mean scores on each scale and the mean total (i.e., situational control) scores of all the scales for each department were significantly different from one another.

The data to test Hypothesis 2 consisted of the scores on the LPC, Task Structure Rating, Managerial Performance Effectiveness, and Group Effectiveness Scales. The data were analyzed using analysis of variance to determine any significant main or interaction effects.

To test Hypothesis 3, scores from all the scales were used. Step-wise multiple regression analysis was used to determine if leader motivation, leader-member relations, task structure and position power were useful predictors of leadership effectiveness.

RESULTS

The first step in operationalizing the Contingency Model was to determine the motivational structure of the department heads. On the version of the LPC scale used in this study, the minimum score obtainable was 18 and the maximum score was 144. Scores of 64 or above were considered high indicating a relationship motivation on the part of the leader while scores of 57 or below were considered low suggesting a task-motivated leader. For all department heads, the mean score was 62.0, the median was 61.0, and the standard deviation was 22.2.

The three intermediate variables of situational control were then determined in order to describe how favorable or unfavorable the situation was for the leader. The degree to which the group supported the leader was determined by using the Leader-Member Relations Rating Scale. The possible scores obtainable ranged from 8 to 40. A score of 30 or above indicated good leader-member relations and a score of below 20 indicated poor relations. The degree to which the task was clearly spelled out by objectives, procedures, and specific guidelines was determined by the Task Structure Rating Scale. The minimum score obtainable was 0 and the maximum was 20. A total of 6 or below indicated a task low in structure; a score of 14 or above indicated a highly structured task. The degree to which the leader's position gave him or her authority to reward or punish subordinates was determined by the Position Power Rating Scale. The minimum score obtainable was 0 and the maximum was 10. A score of 7 or more indicated high position power and a score of 3 or below denoted low position power.

The means, medians and standard deviations for these variables are shown on Table 2. The results suggest that the library activities selected for this study represent favorable leadership situations. Overall, the department heads had

Table 2.   Situational Control Results

Variable	Range of Scores	Mean	Median	Standard Deviation
Leader-Member Relations	8–40	33.8	34.0	4.8
Task Structure	0–20	12.7	13.0	4.6
Position Power	0–10	8.2	8.0	1.8

good relations with the members of their groups and possessed strong position power. Although some faced structured tasks and others unstructured, the combination of these results placed all the department heads in highly favorable octants.

The dependent variable of leadership effectiveness was determined in two ways. One examined a set of activities identified with good managerial performance and was designed to focus on the individual leader. The second examined the performance of the groups led by the department heads. The latter approach is the one traditionally followed by Fiedler and tests of his Model. The former was included because it was assumed to more realistically examine the behavior under study, namely, leader behavior rather than group behavior.

The minimum score obtainable on the Managerial Effectiveness Scale used to determine the effectiveness of the individual under study was -204 and the maximum was $+204$. Higher scores suggested greater effectiveness. For all department heads, the mean score was 96.2, the median was 114.0, and the standard deviation was 66.2.

The minimum score obtainable on the Group Effectiveness Scale used to determine the effectiveness of the group in the performance of its assigned task was 9 and the maximum was 45. Once again, a higher score suggested greater effectiveness. For all department heads, the mean score was 35.1, the median was 36.0, and the standard deviation was 6.1.

Hypothesis 1

The purpose of this hypothesis was to determine whether academic library departments could be arranged along Fiedler's continuum.

ANOVA testing of Hypothesis 1 showed significant differences in the amount of situational control among the seven library tasks under study. However, when each of the situational control variables were tested individually, a significant difference was found only among task structure scores. See Table 3.

The first hypothesis was supported. It was possible to place all of the departments into one of two of Fiedler's octants. Acquisitions, Catalog Maintenance, Cataloging, Circulation, and Processing were all Octant 1 situations, that is, they had good leader-member relations, high task structure, and strong position power. Collection Development and Reference were Octant 3 situations. They

Table 3.   Summary of Analysis of Variance
for Situational Control Variables

Source of Variation	df	Sum of Squares	Mean Square	F
Situational Control:				
Between departments	6	1868.75	311.46	5.58*
Within departments	202	11267.68	55.78	
Total	208	13136.43		
Leader-Member Relations:				
Between departments	6	225.22	37.54	1.65
Within departments	202	4608.82	22.82	
Total	208	4834.04		
Task Structure:				
Between departments	6	875.04	145.84	8.55*
Within departments	202	3446.84	17.06	
Total	208	4321.88		
Position Power:				
Between departments	6	19.16	3.19	0.95
Within departments	202	678.63	3.36	
Total	208	697.79		

* $p = .0001$

had good leader-member relations, a low amount of task structure, and the leader possessed strong position power. Both Octants 1 and 3 are considered favorable situations for the leader.

It was not surprising that departments clustered in two octants. This is the usual pattern found in this type of research. It would be highly unlikely, if not impossible, to find all octants in the same work situation. Furthermore, it was suspected that task structure would be the differentiating variable. Catalog maintenance, cataloging, acquisitions, and circulation are much more routinized (and therefore more structured) than tasks like collection development and reference.

The fact that leader-member relations and position power showed no significant differences was also not surprising. People tend to accept legitimate authority and appointed leaders are generally likely to be at least accepted and perhaps even liked. With respect to position power, it is probable that all department heads have some say in retention and promotion decisions. Therefore, they have strong position power.

The significant difference among task structure scores was also anticipated. The tasks performed in Octant 1 departments are all carried out to more or less detailed standard operating procedures. The tasks, therefore, are structured. In the context of the Model, they represent the most favorable leadership situation.

The tasks performed in Octant 3 departments are more creative, resulting in a situation not commonly found in real-life except in such organizations such as research or planning groups. The creative performance required in these situations cannot, generally speaking, be commanded. The significant difference among task structure scores supported the assumption that task structure would be the variable by which academic library task groups could be ordered along the favorableness continuum.

Hypothesis 2

The purpose of this hypothesis was to determine if one leadership style was more effective than another. Since Octants 1 and 3 represent favorable situations, a main effect was anticipated between leadership style and effectiveness in which task-motivated leaders would be more effective than relationship-motivated leaders. An interaction effect was also expected between style and task structure.

Because the differences among the department scores for leader-member relations and position power were not significant, these variables were not considered in the testing of hypothesis 2. Since Octants 1 and 3 represent favorable situations, a main effect was anticipated between LPC and effectiveness in which the task-motivated leaders would be more effective than the relationship-oriented leaders. An interaction effect was also expected between LPC and task structure.

To analyze the data, a 2x2 factorial design between LPC (high and low) and task structure (structured and unstructured) was used. Analysis of variance with leader LPC treated as a dichotomous factor was performed. Both the manager's effectiveness and the group's effectiveness were used as the dependent variables.

The median-split method was used to distinguish between high- and low-LPC leaders. That is, department heads with scores above 61 were considered high-LPC, relationship-motivated leaders, while those with scores below 61 were considered low-LPC, task-motivated leaders.

Task structure scores were also split at the median to distinguish between structured and unstructured tasks. Those scores above 13 were assumed to indicate structured tasks; scores below 13 were assumed to indicate unstructured tasks.

As a result of splitting scores at the median, 28 department heads were deleted and not considered in testing Hypothesis 2. The results of the analysis of variance are shown in Table 4.

No main effect was found between style and effectiveness but a main effect was found between task structure and effectiveness. No significant interaction effect was found between style and structure when managerial effectiveness was used. No interaction effect *at all* was found between style and structure when group effectiveness was used.

Table 4.   Summary Table for Two-Dimensional Analysis of Variance
for Managerial and Group Effectiveness Scores

Source of Variation	df	Sum of Squares	Mean Square	F
Managerial Effectiveness				
Main Effects		(74956.29)		
LPC	1	11551.29	11551.29	2.84
Task Structure	1	61550.42	61550.42	15.16*
LPC x Task Structure	1	1854.57	1854.57	0.46
Residual	177	718824.76	4061.16	
Total	180	793781.05		
Group Effectiveness				
Main Effects		(419.83)		
LPC	1	95.63	95.63	2.56
Task Structure	1	361.75	361.75	9.69**
LPC x Task Structure	1	0.00	0.00	1.00
Residual	177	6609.38	37.34	
Total	180	7029.20		

* $p = .0001$
** $p = .002$

These findings provide no support for the role that LPC is supposed to play in determining effectiveness. Effectiveness does not appear to be dependent upon any relationship between LPC and task structure, but rather upon task structure alone. The data obtained in testing Hypothesis 2 for this study suggest that differences in leadership effectiveness are attributable to task structure alone and that LPC and the interactions between the independent variables play a small role, if any. Nevertheless, the fact that task structure had an effect supports the idea that *some* situational variables have an impact on leadership effectiveness.

Hypothesis 3

The aim of this hypothesis was to take a closer look at the dependent variables to see what effect, if any, each one had on effectiveness. This would determine whether the situational variables actually impact on a situation in the way Fiedler suggests, namely, leader-member relations twice as much as task structure and task structure twice as much as position power.

Because there is some overlap in the contribution of each of the independent variables, stepwise multiple regression analysis was used to test Hypothesis 3. The assumption is that a knowledge of all the independent variables provides for a better job of predicting leadership effectiveness than knowledge of any of those variables taken alone. Multiple regression analysis identifies the best combination of predictor variables.

All variables were treated as continuous and all 209 department heads were included in the test of Hypothesis 3. The minimum significance level considered was .1500. The results of the analysis are shown in Table 5. This table shows that the variables of task structure, position power, and LPC (in that order) controlled almost 20 percent of the total variance in managerial effectiveness. Task structure and position power controlled 13.4 percent of the total variance in group effectiveness.

Although these are meaningful amounts of variance to account for, it should be noted that between 80 percent and 87 percent of the variance in effectiveness

Table 5. Summary Table for the Analysis of Regression for Managerial and Group Effectiveness Scores

Source of Variation	df	Sum of Squares	Mean Square	F	R Square
Managerial Effectiveness					
Task Structure	1	119909.09	119909.09	31.40*	.1317
Residual	207	790584.71	3819.25		
Total	208	910493.80			
Task Structure and Position Power	2	173784.61	86892.30	24.30*	.1909
Residual	206	736709.19	3576.26		
Total	208	910493.80			
Task Structure and Position Power and LPC	3	181734.72	60578.24	17.04*	.1996
Residual	205	728759.08	3554.92		
Total	208	910493.80			
Group Effectiveness					
Task Structure	1	761.83	761.83	22.91*	.0996
Residual	207	6883.79	33.25		
Total	208	7645.62			
Task Structure and Position Power	2	1027.61	513.80	15.99*	.1344
Residual	206	6618.01	32.13		
Total	208	7645.62			

* $p = .0001$

still remains unexplained. This obviously suggests that other variables relevant to leadership effectiveness exist.

Contrary to expectations based on Fiedler's Model, the degree of task structure was the variable most strongly related to effectiveness. Position power also played a major role since it increases the amount of controlled variance by 3.5 percent for group effectiveness and by almost 6 percent for managerial effectiveness.

LPC played a minor role in determining managerial effectiveness, since it increased the amount of controlled variance by less than 1 percent. It failed to play any significant role in accounting for the variance in group effectiveness.

DISCUSSION

Little support was found for Fiedler's Model in academic libraries. However, there do appear to be situational variables which can predict effectiveness. There is strong evidence to show that task structure does, and so (perhaps) does position power. Certainly there are others since task structure and position power account for only 13.4 percent of the variance. Furthermore, the nature of leadership situations in academic libraries was illuminated. They are favorable with good leader-member relations and strong position power, but there is enough difference among task structure to affect performance.

The Library Leadership Project was significant for several reasons. First, it investigated the external validity of the Contingency Model as it applies to academic libraries.

Secondly, it study examined the Model in coacting groups. Much of Fiedler's research has dealt with interacting groups which are highly interdependent groups requiring the close coordination of several team members in the performance of the primary task. Examples are basketball teams, assembly lines, and orchestras. Library departments more closely resemble coacting groups in which each group member works relatively independently of other team members. Each group member is usually on his or her own and performance depends on individual ability, skill, and motivation. Other examples of coacting groups are bowling teams and department stores.

Thirdly, this study was significant in that it examined the dependent variable of leadership effectiveness directly. Fiedler and most other researchers examining his Model use *group* effectiveness as a surrogate measure for leadership effectiveness. Fiedler readily admits, however, that group performance is not entirely a function of leadership skills. Other factors may also come into play such as personality clashes, bad luck, member abilities, motivation, and organizational support.

Finally, there were some aspects of this study which should have more direct and practical (or policy) effects. This study provided information on an important aspect of organizational behavior to librarians. To the extent that we can understand some of the variables in the leadership function, we can better perform when we are called upon to lead.

The results also broaden our awareness of the effects of different leadership styles in different situations. There are many different types of library tasks, both structured and not, and each may require a different type of leadership. Understanding the nature of the situation can lead to better placement decisions.

Finally, this study provides guidance to library educators who seek to improve the preparation of their students for the assumption of management positions. Better understanding of the theoretical foundations of management will improve the education given to new and potential leaders.

In conclusion, the Library Leadership Project provided information on an important aspect of organizational behavior to librarians. Guided by theory and tested under real conditions, it helped bridge the gap between theory and practice. Where the results agree with the Model, they provide some validity for Fiedler's position; where they disagree, they raise further questions and suggest directions for further research.

REFERENCES

Bare, A. C. (1978). Staffing and training: Neglected supervisory functions related to group performance. *Personnel Psychology, 31*, 107–117.

Burns, J. M. (1978). *Leadership*. New York: Harper and Row.

Dragon, A. C. (1976). Self-descriptions and subordinate descriptions of the leader behavior of library administrators. *Dissertation Abstracts International, 37*, 7380A–7381A. (University Microfilms No. 77–12, 796).

Fiedler, F. E. (1967). *A theory of leadership effectiveness*. New York: McGraw-Hill.

Fleishman, E. A. (1973). Twenty years of consideration and structure. In E. A. Fleishman and J. G. Hunt (Eds.), *Current developments in the study of leadership* (pp. 1–40). Carbondale, IL: Southern Illinois University Press.

Graen, G., and Cashman, J. F. (1975). A role-making model of leadership in formal organizations: A developmental approach. In J. G. Hunt and L. L. Larson (Eds.), *Leadership frontiers* (pp. 143–165). Kent, OH: Kent State University Press.

Hersey, P., and Blanchard, K. (1977). *Management of organizational behavior*. (3rd ed.). Englewood Cliffs, NJ: Prentice-Hall.

Hill, W. (1969). The validation and extension of Fiedler's theory of leadership effectiveness. *Academy of Management Journal, 12*, 33–47.

House, R. J. (1971). A path-goal theory of leader effectiveness. *Administrative Science Quarterly, 16*, 321–338.

Hunt, J. G. (1967). Fiedler's leadership contingency model: An empirical test in three organizations. *Organizational Behavior and Human Performance, 2*, 290–308.

Likert, R. (1961). *New patterns of management*. New York: McGraw-Hill.

Morse, J. J., and Wagner, F. R. (1978). Measuring the process of managerial effectiveness. *Academy of Management Journal, 21*, 23–35.

Reavis, C. A., and Derlega, V. J. (1976). Test of a contingency model of teacher effectiveness. *The Journal of Educational Research, 69*, 221–225.

Stogdill, R. M. (1981). *Stogdill's handbook of leadership*. New York: The Free Press.

VanGundy, A. B., and Haynes, L. L., III. (1978). A comparison of college presidents using Fiedler's contingency model. *Journal of Negro Education, 47*, 215–229.

APPLYING STRATEGIC PLANNING TO THE LIBRARY:

A MODEL FOR PUBLIC SERVICES

Larry J. Ostler

The 1980s have been a particularly turbulent time for libraries. With declining budgets, academic libraries have been losing support since 1977, and according to Leach (1984: 3) they may never recover this loss. Reduced buying power due to inflationary price increases for library materials during the past ten years has caused substantial declines in serials subscriptions. Book purchases have also declined, but not as sharply as journal purchases. For example, in *Library Issues* (1987: 4) Leach notes:

> The declining purchasing power of library budgets in recent years is taking a heavy toll on the quality of library collections. Most academic libraries—forced to confront materials price increases far in excess of either the CPI or their own budgetary increases—are able to obtain fewer book titles. Exacerbating this situation is the necessary reallocation of funds from book to periodical purchasing to cover the unusually high inflation rate in subscription prices.

Advances in Library Administration and Organization,
Volume 8, pages 39-67.
Copyright © 1989 by JAI Press Inc.
All rights of reproduction in any form reserved.
ISBN: 0-89232-967-X

Faculty and administrators should be mindful of this fiscal struggle and realize that highly inflated library materials costs and the declining purchasing power of the dollar are conspiring to harm the library's ability to maintain local collections adequate for the research and scholarship needs of their communities.

Not only have materials costs risen sharply, but numerous other problems remain: space is at a premium; library book collections are deteriorating physically; services suffer from chronic understaffing; and library collections are inadequate to satisfy the research needs of students and scholars (Dougherty 3). While admitting that his "predecessors also wrestled with space crises, paper deterioration, understaffing and inadequate acquisition budgets," Dougherty noted:

> The principal difference today is one of magnitude. Many traditional library procedures such as book purchasing, invoice payment, circulation, cataloging, and interlibrary loan are labor intensive and are becoming prohibitively expensive. Research libraries have no option but to adopt labor-saving technologies, if services are to be maintained at traditional levels of quality; it is the need to assimilate new technologies coupled with the accelerating rate of change that will test the fiber of our organizations (4).

Another clear indicator of economic decline in libraries is displayed in Figure 1, which shows the percentage dollar increases experienced by other segments of society as compared to books and periodicals. Another complicating economic factor, according to Sandler (1), is the steady erosion in foreign buying power (see Figure 2).

Economic predictions for colleges and universities continue to point toward decline. This changing environment is characterized by declining enrollment trends, financial exigencies, and other unexpected disasters. Institutions of

Figure 1.   How Prices Rose 1977–1986[1]

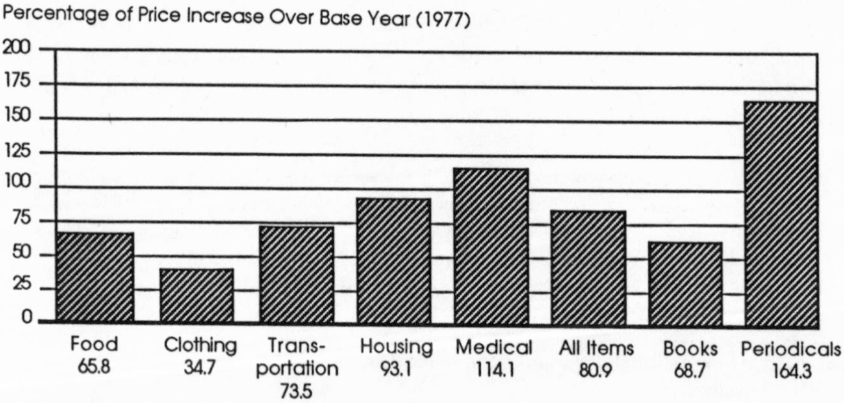

Percentage of Price Increase Over Base Year (1977)

| | Food 65.8 | Clothing 34.7 | Trans- portation 73.5 | Housing 93.1 | Medical 114.1 | All Items 80.9 | Books 68.7 | Periodicals 164.3 |

[1]*Source:* Leach, Ronald G. "Library Materials Price Update." *Library Issues: Briefings for Faculty and Administrators* Nov. 1987: 3.

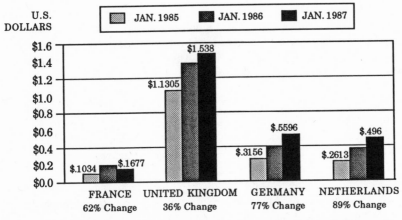

Figure 2. Change in Foreign Exchange Rates for Selected Currencies

higher education have responded to this new environment by becoming smaller, going out of business, or merging or consolidating (Cameron 359), when in fact the real answer may lie in strategic planning.

Leaders in higher education generally have not been able to cope with this new milieu (Riggs 9). Kotler and Murphy (470) have noted that:

> Most colleges and universities are not set up with strategic planning capacity. They (the managers) are basically good at operations, that is efficiently doing the same things day after day.

This new environmental demand has caused educational leaders to react conservatively (Riggs 9). Cameron (361) has listed three reasons for this reactive stance:

> First, the experience of most administrators and managers has largely been in responding to conditions of growth nearly universal during the 1950s, 1960s and early 1970s. Educational leaders from this era are simply not equipped with the appropriate skills for this new environment. Sadly, we know little about how to handle decline and exactly what new skills are required for survival.

"Second," Cameron continues, "the values and ideology of our culture emphasize growth and expansion as being indicative of effectiveness." Managers have been rewarded positively if they produced more, obtained a larger budget, or expanded their organizations. "Finally," Cameron concludes, "most current organizational theory is based on assumptions of growth." In other words, educational administrators have been trained to ignore problems of decline. Rather, they have come to assume that the more uncertain and turbulent the environment, the more their organizations should expand and grow. In fact, traditional organizational theory allows only for management of growth. Theorists in the field of organizational behavior such as Boulding (8) have based their perspectives on assumptions of growth. These theorists have concluded that decline has either been ignored as a possibility or is being treated as a temporary condition.

Library administrators also fit this pattern (Riggs 6). Managers' attitude toward declining economic conditions have led Rubin (211) to comment, "Educational organizations are doing basically less of the same." De Gennaro agreed (1) when he stated, "The library is buying an ever-decreasing percentage of the rapidly growing output of the world's publishers." Stanford University's Weber (14) concurred, warning, "Stanford will never have more than a modest proportion of what is needed." This orientation toward conservation and efficiency may not be in the best long-term interests of higher education. This defensive posture has reduced the overall operation of the organization and tended to ignore the realistic and assertive approach prescribed by the proponents of strategic planning (Cameron 367).

Reasons for this bias toward efficiency and conservation fall into six categories (Cameron 362). First, organizational effectiveness has been extremely difficult to define. Because efficiency is more easily measured, especially in organizations like colleges and universities, administrators have largely ignored measures to improve effectiveness.

Second, the stress from facing conditions of decline has compelled individuals to engage in conservative and self-protective behavior. According to Cameron (363), a common side effect of decline is personal stress among managers; and research has shown that the consequences of this decline-induced stress are (1) engaging in anxiety-reducing behaviors at the expense of problem-solving behaviors, (2) reducing the risk of mistakes (which are more visible under conditions of decline) by becoming conservative, (3) restricting the communication network, (4) reducing the number of participants in decision making, (5) enforcing rules more closely, (6) more readily rejecting disconfirming or contrary information, (7) perceiving tasks and decisions to be more difficult, and (8) being prone to "groupthink" dynamics.

Third, administrators have tended to pursue strategies that succeeded in the past—during times of abundance and growth—even though they are inappropriate under current conditions of decline. Administrators often view conditions of decline as beyond their control; thus they are not likely to suggest proactive responses (Cameron 363).

Fourth, colleges and universities are frequently structured as loosely coupled systems governed by committees and semiautonomous units. With multiple constituents to satisfy, each with vested interests, good decisions are not likely. Loose organizational structure cripples managers in post-secondary education, preventing them from making good strategic responses (Cameron 364).

Fifth, creative and innovative individuals are usually the first to leave an organization when decline occurs. These same individuals are, of course, the most likely to receive job opportunities in other organizations. Therefore, those managers left to manage decline are often the more conservative, play-it-safe types (Cameron 363–6).

Sixth, innovation itself can be perceived as a cause of decline. During periods of growth, risk-taking and experimentations with new programs was considered appropriate, but during less stringent times the tendency is toward eliminating non-traditional and innovative programs and to avoid instituting more innovative or creative alternatives. Thus, institutions respond by becoming more conservative (Cameron 365).

Strategic planning techniques, if used, can help libraries react positively in periods of decline. Cameron (368) has suggested that successful business firms have taken an approach that is almost the exact opposite of what post-secondary education has done when faced with conditions of decline. Colleges and universities are often conservative, efficiency-oriented and internally focused. Conversely, successful business firms have been innovative, effectiveness-oriented, and externally focused. Drucker (61) has noted that:

> . . . every institution needs to think through what its strengths are. Are they the right strengths for its specific business? Are they adequate? Are they employed where they will produce results, and what specifically is the market for this particular business both at the present time and in the years immediately ahead?

De Gennaro (3) summed up the situation when he stated:

> Our task is to develop a strategy for maintaining the library's viability in an information society, not just a strategy for further reducing the current inadequate level of library expenditures.

Although libraries would seem to be prime candidates for strategic planning techniques, there are few academic libraries involved in this kind of planning (SPEC). Some important pioneering work has been done by public and medical libraries however (Palmour 88 and Braude).

METHODOLOGY

Observing this apparent lack of formal planning, we designed a study intended to apply strategic planning techniques to a library environment.

The primary purpose of the study was to develop a strategic plan for the Information Services Division of the Harold B. Lee Library (HBLL) at Brigham Young University. A secondary purpose was to produce a strategic planning model for public service units of academic libraries in Utah.

The overall method used in this study involved (1) a literature search of studies concerned with strategic planning in higher education, especially those dealing with libraries, (2) assessing the planning needs of the Information Services Division, (3) constructing and validating of data collection instruments, (4) distributing survey instruments, (5) recording and treating data gathered from the surveys and the results of the workshop activities, (6) summarizing the findings, (7) developing a strategic plan and model, and (8) evaluating the planning process.

NEEDS ASSESSMENT

A strategic planning needs assessment opinionnaire (see Appendix A) was completed during Winter semester, 1985. This instrument was sent to the 15 academic library directors in the state of Utah who are members of Utah College Library Council (UCLC). This opinionnaire included 17 statements designed to determine interest in and potential usefulness of strategic planning models for their libraries. There are 13 usable responses out of a possible 15.

Appendix A lists the responses to the needs assessment instrument for UCLC administrators. As shown in Table 1, most UCLC administrators responded "strongly agree" or "agree" to the benefits of strategic planning. This table also shows the questions grouped into four categories: usefulness of planning, planning knowledge, benefits of strategic planning and control statements.

As expected, the results from this needs assessment instrument (Figure 3) show that, overall, 92 percent of the UCLC library administrators strongly agree or agree that planning generally is a useful activity for libraries. The first statement that "group planning is a vital part of good library operation" scored almost 100 percent.

Responses from the UCLC administrators to the "planning knowledge" group of statements were mixed. Three statements from the survey in this group scored at about the same level: "Most library managers did not learn strategic planning skills in graduate school and, therefore, need additional help in this area," "Even when planning has occurred in the library, decisions are made which do not utilize the plan," and "daily decisions are made in the library without benefit of library planning." Their responses to these four questions demonstrated little understanding of strategic techniques or terminology.

Managers in the Information Services Division of the HBLL were also surveyed to determine what potential value they thought strategic planning techniques would have for their division operation. These participants agreed that since traditional planning techniques had not met their needs, strategic planning would be an acceptable alternative in the future.

Before data collection began, a pre-assessment document based on information developed by Baldridge and Okimi (17) was administered to the planning group to determine their knowledge of strategic planning concepts (see Appendix B). This instrument encompassed eight planning areas. Respondents were asked to identify each of three statements as characteristic of Strategic Planning (SP), Conventional Planning (CP), or Neither (N).

DATA COLLECTION

To begin gathering data for the development of a strategic plan, we selected a planning group to review the current mission statement of the Lee Library. In doing so, they were to identify areas of that document that specifically dealt with the Information Services Division (Donnelly 3). Then, we asked the planning group to suggest as many new potential mission statements as possible (Edinger 332). They compiled a list of 24 potential statements, which they grouped into eight cluster statements. Then, we held individual meetings with the planners in which we asked them to rank order these clusters. Using these results, the planning group agreed upon a tentative mission statement.

Our next data gathering activity focused on defining "environmental factors." Braude (27) defines these factors as "those forces over which an organization has little or no control." We used his environmental analysis questions to collect the data. Again, we asked the planning group to brainstorm for ideas on each of six external and internal environmental factors—users, service demands, technology, competition, economics and political. Following this activity, we reviewed all suggested ideas with each participant individually.

Next we asked the planning group to identify current library programs in their specific work areas. Again, we used Braude's (27) workbook as a source for our questions. We assigned values 1–5 to each item, with 1 being the most important and 5 the least important, then tabulated the results to get our data.

Another phase of data collection we used was the WOTS-UP activity as outlined by Steiner (16). We used Weaknesses, opportunities, threats, and strengths as major categories. We asked the planning group to list as many items as possible in each category—keeping in mind previous environmental factors. The list they produced, however, did not add substantially to data previously collected.

In the next step of the planning process, we asked participants once again to evaluate the mission of their division and suggest revision of the tentative mission statement developed earlier. This evolutionary process followed the model illustrated in Appendix C.

Using Braude's workbook (34) as a guide, we prepared a definition sheet (see Appendix D) for participants, who we then requested to identify goals and objectives that would support one of the two parts of the mission statement. In the workshop setting each planner shared their goals and objectives with the others in the group (Gallanger 27 and Oldman 464). We also prepared a handout

Table 1. Opinionnaire on Planning UCLC Administrators N = 13

Area	Strongly Agree		Agree		Undecided		Disagree		Strongly Disagree	
	No.	%	No.	%	No.	%	No.	%	No.	%
USEFULNESS OF PLANNING										
Planning is a vital part of good library operations	9	69.23	4	30.77	0	0	0	0	0	0
Knowing how to plan effectively is an important skill for library managers	8	61.53	4	30.77	1	7.70	0	0	0	0
Library leaders are generally in need of strategic planning skills	3	23.07	8	61.54	2	15.39	0	0	0	0
PLANNING KNOWLEDGE										
Planning documents are only useful when applied to daily operations	3	23.07	2	15.38	4	30.77	2	15.39	2	15.39
The primary focus on planning is the "process"	1	7.70	3	23.07	0	0	7	53.84	2	15.39
Most library managers did not learn strategic planning skills in graduate school and, therefore, need additional help in this area	4	30.77	8	61.53	1	7.70	0	0	0	0
Even when planning has occurred in the library, decisions are made which do not utilize the "plan"	0	0	13	100	0	0	0	0	0	0
Daily decisions are made in the library without benefit of library planning	2	15.38	11	84.62	0	0	0	0	0	0

46

Statement	N	%	N	%	N	%	N	%	N	%
Generally speaking planning is done to appease administrators but has little or no practical value to actual operations of the library	0		1	7.70	2	15.38	3	23.07	7	53.85
The primary focus on planning is the final document or "plan"	1	7.70	3	23.07	0	0	7	53.84	2	15.39

BENEFITS OF STRATEGIC PLANNING

Statement	N	%	N	%	N	%	N	%	N	%
Utah libraries could benefit by learning strategic planning techniques	6	46.15	7	53.85	0	0	0	0	0	0
Knowing how to use strategic planning is important for library managers	4	30.77	8	61.53	1	7.70	0	0	0	0
Our staff could benefit from knowing how to use strategic planning techniques	3	23.07	8	61.53	1	7.70	1	7.70	0	0
Strategic planning skills should be taught as a part of inservice training	2	15.40	8	61.53	3	23.07	0	0	0	0
A strategic planning model would be helpful for my library	4	30.77	7	53.84	2	15.39	0	0	0	0

CONTROL STATEMENTS

Statement	N	%	N	%	N	%	N	%	N	%
Planning has nothing to do with effective library operations	0	0	1	7.70	1	7.70	3	23.07	8	61.53
Strategic planning is just another gimmick like Planning, Programming, and Budgeting System (PPMS), Management by Objectives (MBO), Program Evaluation Research Task (PERT), and Management Information System (MIS)	0	0	3	23.07	2	15.39	4	30.77	4	30.77

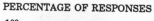

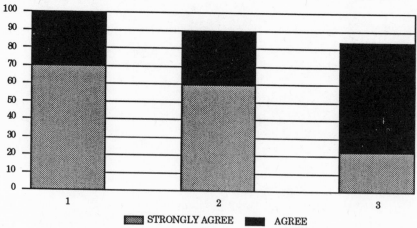

Figure 3.   Usefulness of Planning—N = 11

for each participant that summarized the environmental factors they had earlier identified (see Appendix E) and asked them to be realistic as they were developing a plan (Braude 27).

Riggs (47) speaks of "operating strategies" as those strategies that "deal with the more specific departmental activities of the library." In this light, we asked the planners to attach specific "operations strategies" to their objectives. We developed an outline for this purpose using ideas from Braude (38) and Riggs (47–48). See Appendix F for a copy of the handout.

We also administered a post-test and an evaluation instrument requesting participants to determine whether the data gathering process they had just completed was in fact characteristic of strategic planning and whether the participants had gained any understanding of strategic planning terminology or techniques. Items missed by 40 percent or more of the participants indicated a need for further instruction.

DEVELOPMENT OF A STRATEGIC PLAN

Pre-assessment Instrument

We administered a pre-assessment document (Appendix B) to the 11 members of the planning group. One hundred percent of the planning group was present and participated in this activity. We asked the respondents to identify from a list statements that were characteristic of strategic planning (SP) with other choices on each set of statements including: conventional planning (CP), Neither (N), Both (B) and Don't Know (DK). We tabulated the number of incorrect responses and considered an item missed by 40 percent or more of the participants a valid

PERCENTAGE OF RESPONSES

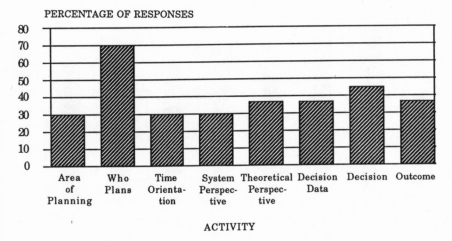

ACTIVITY

Figure 4. Strategic Planning Pre-Assessment

reason for teaching the concept during subsequent planning activities. Figure 4 shows the complete results of the pre-assessment. As demonstrated by the graph in Figure 4, ''Who Plans'' and ''Decision'' were the two areas needing greatest attention during subsequent planning sessions. Using this same instrument, we tested the planning group's knowledge of strategic planning concepts at the conclusion of the planning activities. As a group, the participants did not score below 80 percent on any item (Figure 5). Applying the same criteria as used for the first administration, we considered that they had mastered strategic planning concepts. Figure 6 presents a comparison of both pre-test and post-test results.

PERCENTAGE OF RESPONSES

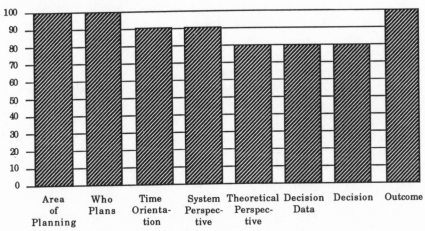

Figure 5. Strategic Planning Post-Assessment

PERCENTAGE OF RESPONSES

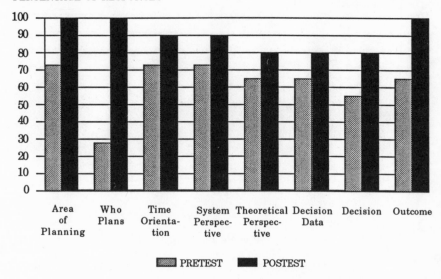

Figure 6.   Strategic Planning Pre-Test/Post-Test Comparison

Mission Statement

The mission statement was developed through several revisions. First attempts by the planning group to identify potential mission statements resulted in the following eight clusters of statements:

Group 1:   Document delivery, Faculty book delivery, Quick access, Referral services, Cooperative networking;

Group 2:   Career opportunities, Professional contributions, Continuing education;

Group 3:   Effective use of resources, Acquisition and selection of materials, Cataloging of information, Technology advances;

Group 4:   Provide scholarly study environment, Accessibility to information, Provide information;

Group 5:   Administrative structure and responsibility, Accountability;

Group 6:   Provide training in library use;

Group 7:   Maintenance of collection, Collection security;

Group 8:   Counseling, Communication and public relations skills, Build rapport, Interpreting information.

Figure 7 shows how proposed mission statements were rated by members of the planning group. Participants grouped these statements into eight analogous categories in the first brainstorming session. As noted in this figure, groups 1 and

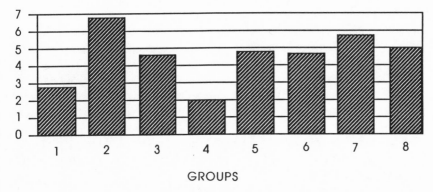

GROUPS

Figure 7. Perceived Value of Various Mission Statements by Selected Information Services Personnel

4 were rated highest with 2.8 and 2.0 respectively. We determined the values of the groups by averaging the number of ones each group received. As can be seen in Appendix C, the final mission statement was the result of several earlier revisions by the planning group. It reads as follows:

> The mission of the Information Services Division of the Lee Library is twofold: (1) to provide knowledgeable, efficient reference and information service to all patrons, and (2) to provide appropriate formal and informal library use instruction to help patrons become self-sufficient in their use of the library.

Environmental Analysis

Results of the environmental analysis activity indicated a variety of elements that in the opinion of the planning group did or could influence libraries. Each participant listed as many "environmental" factors as possible under the following six categories: users, service demand, technology, competition, economics and politics. We collected these data under individual categories. A summary of these data shows the following:

1. Twenty distinct user groups were identified. The main groups were university students, university faculty and staff, townspeople (especially genealogists) and church of Jesus Christ of Latter-day Saints (LDS) Authorities. Each of these groups requires unique responses from the library; i.e, students need to be taught library skills as well as supplied with information, while university faculty and LDS church authorities need only to be provided with the information they seek.

2. Forty "service demands" were identified; however, one main theme emerged—the demand for information and reference service was high. Two subsets of this broad category were "rapid or quick access to information" and "reliable assistance."

3. Issues related to technology and the library were raised. Three received repeated emphasis:
   a. The effects of technology on library operations, staff and patrons
   b. The funding of the new technology
   c. Using the new technology to improve access to information

4. The participants worried about competition with the library from other providers of information, e.g. other libraries, private individuals and information brokers.

5. The analysis of economics elicited concerns about the library's ability to compete with other areas of the university for sufficient funds to (a) make effective use of technology and (b) provide personnel required.

6. The political factors affecting the ability of the library to accomplish its plan included:
   a. Understanding (by division personnel) of the informal and formal political structure of the library.
   b. Support and cooperation of university faculty and departments to further library programs.
   c. The perceived power of the Technical Services Division to control decisions related to the use of technology for public services.

Present Programs

Another important element of strategic planning is "program analysis." The planning group identified existing library programs in their areas. Table 2 displays each item and its average value. This value was computed by adding all ratings of the participants and dividing by the same number. It also shows the number of times each item was mentioned by the group. Of highest value and most often mentioned by the planners was instruction orientation and reference." Another item valued highly was "faculty consultation."

WOTS-UP Analysis

George Steiner's WOTS-UP Analysis was the next planning activity. The initials in this acronym stand for:

W = Weaknesses
O = Opportunities
T = Threats
S = Strengths
U = Underlying
P = Planning

Although the planning group listed 39 items through this activity, all had already been mentioned in the earlier steps of this planning process.

Table 2. Times Mentioned and Average Value
Assigned to Present Programs

Item	Times Mentioned	Average Value
Instruction/Orientation	6	1.40
Reference	6	1
Faculty Consultations	5	1.60
Bibliographic Information	4	1.33
Computer Research	4	1.40
Circulation Development	3	3
Collection Development	3	2
Personnel	3	1.66
Training in House	3	1.66
Information About Periodicals	2	1.33
Reserve	2	1.50
Shelving	2	1.50
Technical Services	2	2.50
Access: Current periodicals	1	1
Access: Newspapers	1	1
Budgeting Dilemma	1	2
Building Security	1	3
Cataloging	1	1
Children's Book Reviews	1	2
Depository Collection	1	1
Exit Control	1	3
Indexing	1	2
Locker/Carrel Issue	1	5
Materials Charge/Discharge	1	1
Microform Storage	1	1
Orientation	1	1
Professional Development	1	3
Provide quiet study	1	1.50
Recalls	1	4
Refers to other sources	1	2
Renewals/Holds	1	4
Special Collections	1	5
Strong Townspeople Mix	1	2
Traces (missing books)	1	4
Volunteer Staffing (free)	1	3

The Plan

Using the results of an earlier mission statement, the environmental analysis, a look at current programs and a revised mission statement, we asked each participant to produce one or more strategic plan for their program area. They followed the worksheet (Appendix F) and completed the form for at least one objective in each planner's program area.

Each planning group member related a specific objective in their program area to a concept in the finalized Mission Statement (See Appendix C). Documents from Brown Library (1985) and Lee Library (1979) containing examples of goals and objectives served as models for starting this activity. Finally, each participant developed strategies for accomplishing these objectives.

Evaluation of the Process

We asked the planning group to evaluate the planning process using a "Strategic Planning Evaluation Form" (See Appendix G). The planning group responded to 14 statements regarding their judgment of the planning process they had just been involved in. All 11 members of the group rated each statement as *I strongly agree, I agree, I am undecided, I disagree*, and *I strongly disagree*. We hypothesized that questions one through nine, eleven and twelve would score high in the *strongly agree* and *agree* categories and that statements four and eight would score significantly lower than the other statements in that grouping. These data are presented in Figure 8.

Respondents should have rated statements 10, 13 and 14 *disagree* and *strongly disagree* categories because a negative response would indicate their understanding of strategic planning concepts. Figure 8 shows all three statements above 70 percent. The planners understood that strategic planning was external, an art form and that the process of planning was more important then the plan.

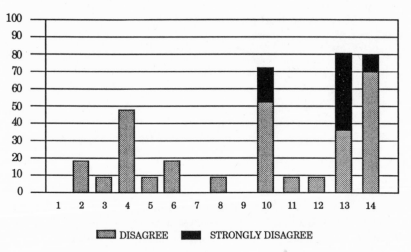

PERCENTAGE OF RESPONSES

Figure 8. Strategic Planning Process—Evaluation

INTERPRETATION

Analysis of the data showed that librarians in the Information Services Division, library administrators and outside consultants generally agreed that a strategic plan was needed for the Information Services Division of the Harold B. Lee Library. Respondents from the UCLC group of library administrators also supported the need for a model. Table 3 illustrates the model developed by this study. Although few libraries had strategic planning models, authors such as Riggs, Braude, and Wood provided models that could be applied to libraries or other non-profit organizations.

The planning group scored lower than anticipated on their understanding of strategic planning concepts. One possible explanation is that the language used in the instrument contained too much unfamiliar jargon. The results of the survey to UCLC administrators showed little understanding of strategic planning concepts. Again, use of terminology peculiar to this type of planning and therefore unfamiliar to the planners might be an explanation why scoring was not higher.

Table 3.   Model of the Planning Processes for the Development of a Strategic Plan for a Public Services Unit of a Library

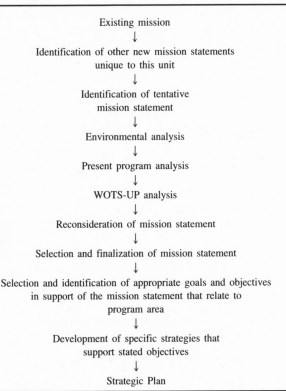

Existing mission
↓
Identification of other new mission statements
unique to this unit
↓
Identification of tentative
mission statement
↓
Environmental analysis
↓
Present program analysis
↓
WOTS-UP analysis
↓
Reconsideration of mission statement
↓
Selection and finalization of mission statement
↓
Selection and identification of appropriate goals and objectives
in support of the mission statement that relate to
program area
↓
Development of specific strategies that
support stated objectives
↓
Strategic Plan

SUMMARY

Strategic planning techniques are recognized by some library leaders and others as one significant way libraries can meet the challenges of the future. Donald Riggs (3–4) has commented that because strategic planning looks at an organization very systematically it may well be that conservative organizations such as libraries can benefit greatly from it. Naisbitt (299), Riggs (6) and others have observed that libraries must plan more carefully as they seek to satisfy the needs of their patrons in an information age. If they use strategic planning practices, libraries can respond in a flexible, positive way to a rapidly changing environment (Riggs 3–4).

Short-range and medium range planning has not been effective for the Information Services Division of the HBLL. Although managers have written and adopted conventional plans, most library personnel cannot locate these documents to make use of them. A needs assessment conducted of division personnel and UCLC administrators showed a clear need for alternate kinds of planning. We identified strategic planning techniques as a good alternative to past conventional-type planning.

According to Wood (15–20), libraries must consider adopting business concepts such as marketing and strategic planning if they want to survive the challenge of the eighties. Most predictions about the future of colleges—and libraries in particular—include conditions of decline. The literature clearly suggests that if organizations want to successfully deal with this crisis, they will need to employ alternative planning systems.

This research effort was a direct response to the "crisis" facing libraries and the anticipated problems that will probably confront the HBLL. Using the data collected in the study, we devised a viable strategic plan. Furthermore, we developed a model of strategic planning that could be adapted to public service units. The process we used to develop our strategic plan followed established strategic planning concepts. Mission, clarification, environmental analysis, present program analysis, assessment of strengths and weaknesses, assignment of strategies, and implementation were strategic planning activities that provided data for developing a plan for the HBLL Information Services Division. In our planning process, we used tested planning techniques. Mechanisms for frequent staff interaction and guidance were provided in problem-solving techniques. The organization's mission and patrons were of prime concern during the planning stages. The "process" of planning rather than undue emphasis on the "plan" itself was kept in clear perspective. The cooperative efforts of the planning team, library administrators and UCLC member libraries, resulted in a strategic plan for the Information Services Division and a model of strategic planning for public service units of academic libraries.

APPENDIX A

Utah College Library Council Opinionnaire

The following statements represent opinions. Your agreement or disagreement will be determined on the basis of your particular beliefs. Kindly check your position on the scale as the statement first impresses you. Indicate what you *believe* rather than what you think you should believe.

SA = I strongly agree
A = I agree
U = I am undecided
D = I disagree
SD = I strongly disagree

	SA	A	U	D	SD
1. Planning is a vital part of good library operations.	9 69.23%	4 30.77%	0 0.0%	0 0.0%	0 0.0%
2. Knowing how to plan effectively is an important skill for library managers.	8 61.53%	4 30.77%	1 7.70%	0 0.0%	0 0.0%
3. Planning documents are only useful when applied to daily operations.	3 23.07%	2 15.38%	4 30.77%	2 15.39%	2 15.39%
4. Planning has nothing to do with effective library operations.	0 0.0%	1 7.70%	1 7.70%	3 23.07%	8 61.53%
5. Library leaders are generally in need of strategic planning skills.	3 23.07%	8 61.54%	2 15.39%	0 0.0%	0 0.0%
6. The primary focus on planning is the "process."	1 7.70%	3 23.07%	0 0.0%	7 53.84%	2 15.39%
7. Utah libraries could benefit by learning strategic planning techniques.	6 46.15%	7 53.84%	0 0.0%	0 0.0%	0 0.0%

	SA	A	U	D	SD
8. Most library managers did not learn strategic planning skills in graduate school and, therefore, need additional help in this area.	4 30.77%	8 61.53%	1 7.70%	0 0.0%	0 0.0%
9. Strategic planning is just another gimmick like Planning, Programming, and Budgeting System (PPMS), Management by Objectives (MBO), Program Evaluation Research Task (PERT), and Management Information System (MIS).	0 0.0%	3 23.07%	2 15.39%	4 30.77%	4 30.77%
10. Even when planning has occurred in the library, decisions are made which do not utilize the "plan".	0 0.0%	13 100.0%	0 0.0%	0 0.0%	0 0.0%
11. Knowing how to use strategic planning is important for library managers.	4 30.77%	8 61.53%	1 7.70%	0 0.0%	0 0.0%
12. Daily decisions are made in the library without benefit of library planning.	2 15.40%	11 84.62%	0 0.0%	0 0.0%	0 0.0%
13. Our staff could benefit from knowing how to use strategic planning techniques.	3 23.07%	8 61.53%	1 7.70%	1 7.70%	0 0.0%

	SA	A	U	D	SD
14. Generally speaking, planning is done to appease administrators but has little or no practical value to actual operations of the library.	0 0.0%	1 7.70%	2 15.39%	3 23.07%	7 53.85%
15. The primary focus on planning is the final document of "plan."	1 7.70%	3 23.07%	0 0.0%	7 53.84%	2 15.39%
16. Strategic planning skills should be taught as part of inservice training.	2 15.40%	8 61.53%	3 23.07%	0 0.0%	0 0.0%
17. A strategic planning model would be helpful for my library.	4 30.77%	7 53.84%	2 15.39%	0 0.0%	0 0.0%

APPENDIX B

Strategic Planning Pre-assessment/post Test

Strategic Planning is different in significant ways from conventional planning. This exercise is designed to evaluate your understanding of the differences between these two types of planning. Information gathered from this instrument will be used to organize effective planning activities. Please write in the line to the right of each statement whether the statement is characteristic of Strategic Planning (S), Conventional Planning (CP) or Neither (N).

Activity

Arena of Planning:

Wide range of issues, non-routine and routine _____
Specific to non-routine issues _____
Organization's destiny, market _____

Who Plans:

Top-level officer _____
Planning office _____
Lowest level workers _____

Time Orientation:

Medium/short-range   _____
Long-range   _____
Short-range   _____

System Perspective:

External, environmental   _____
Internal, organizational   _____
External, organizational   _____

Theoretical Perspective:

Closed system   _____
Combination closed and open systems   _____
Open systems   _____

Decision Data:

Qualitative   _____
Both quantitative and qualitative   _____
Quantitative   _____

Decision:

Exact science   _____
Simple art form   _____
Complex art form   _____

Outcome:

Crystallized goals   _____
Stream of critical decisions   _____
Plan, blueprint   _____

APPENDIX C

Evolutionary Development of the Mission Statement

Statements taken from existing library mission documents: Phase I (March 11)

- . . . and make available for use a collection of the recorded knowledge of mankind in support of the goals of the university, to assist patrons in finding and using these resources and information resources elsewhere, and to foster and encourage learning and scholarship.

- Formalize effective programs for short- and long-range planning and budget support based on established priorities and annual reviews to meet the changing needs of teaching research.

- Where an approved branch has been established, such as the law school library, provide for maximum cooperation and coordination to minimize the duplication of resources and to make the materials and services effectively available to the entire university community.

- House services and resource in space that assures proper conditions and security of the collections, provide for the comfort and study requirements of users, promote efficient staff operations, and enhances general library operations.

- Use new advances in technology and automation in library operations as their development promises efficient, significant improvement in making needed resources readily accessible.

- Provide effective and efficient library patron services so that library users will have maximum ready access to library information and materials they need.

Statement developed from "brainstorming" session with planners: Phase II (March 18)

- The mission of the Information Services Division of the Lee Library is to service the user by expediting his/her access to information in a manner that is consistent with the Christian values of Brigham Young University. The responsibility to provide information which most precisely meets the user's need also entails instructing patrons in library use.

Statement developed after planners had completed several activities— environmental analysis, program analysis, and WOTS-UP analysis: Phase III (April 8)

- The mission of the Information Services Division of the Lee Library is twofold: (1) To provide knowledgeable, efficient reference and information service to all patrons according to their needs, and (2) To provide appropriate formal and informal library use instruction to help patrons become as self-sufficient in library use as necessary.

Final statement adopted by planning group and approved by University Librarian. Phase IV (April 15)

- The mission of the Information Services Division of the Lee Library is twofold: (1) To provide knowledgeable, efficient reference and information service to all patrons and (2) To provide appropriate formal and informal library use instruction to help patrons become self-sufficient in their use of the library.

APPENDIX D

Criteria for Goals and Objectives

Goals should be broad, general statements that reflect results necessary to accomplish the mission. There are usually several goals for each program area. Goals should be a description of the desired future.

Goals should

be broad in scope,
extend over the maximum foreseeable future, 3–5 years,
be action-oriented; start with "to" do something

Criteria for objectives should be specific in order to produce results. Again, the major element is the ability to measure the objective. Types of objectives are:

Operation	Do more
	Do same
	Do things efficiently
	Discontinue
	Maintain organization (survive)
Effectiveness	Innovate
	Improve quality

Objectives should be developed for key result areas:

For whom—users
What—improve, expand, add new, phase out programs
How—collaboration, advocacy, participation
With what—finances, current funds, facilities and equipment, personnel

They should identify in each program area the most important results which are expected. They should avoid just listing functional requirement or responsibilities, e.g., collect more books, circulate more items. Though vital to efficient functioning, they are not directly related to achievement of programs or library operational goals.

Source. Robert Braude. *C.E. 258 Planning: Strategic and Tactical*, 1983.

APPENDIX E

Summary of the Environmental Analysis Activity

The importance of environmental factors in planning cannot be over-emphasized. Braude (1983: 27) notes that:

> Planning begins with a realistic understanding of existing conditions. There are both external and internal forces affecting all organizations. These should be assessed and evaluated in order to provide a firm base for setting organizational goals and objectives and developing a plan for future action.

What follows is a synthesis of the data collected in each category.

Users

Although at least 20 separate "users" were identified, the main service groups were university students, university faculty and staff, townspeople (especially genealogists) and LDS Church authorities. Each of these groups requires unique responses from the library—e.g., students might need to be taught library skills as well as supplied with information, whereas university faculty and church authorities usually need only information.

Service Demand

Approximately 40 "service demands" were identified. One main theme emerged, however: the demand for information and reference services. Two subsets of this broad category were "rapid or quick access to information" and "reliable assistance."

Technology

The three most pertinent concerns the group raised were:

1. The effects of technology on the library
   a. Patterns of operation
   b. Effects on people
2. How to fund the new technology
3. How to use the new technology to improve access to information

Competition

The question of competition to the library generated the smallest list of items. It seems evident that with the application of technology to the world of information, i.e., individual access to online databases and the appearance of "information brokers" several not so subtle threats to the library are also raised: (1) how will technology change the librarian as an information provider? and (2) how much information will the library provide its competitors?

Economic

An overriding concern in this category was a lack of sufficient resources to (1) make effective use of new technology and (2) provide the unique personnel needs required. While the group noted that a minimal number of library programs would likely continue, they were concerned that new dollars to support uses of technology, i.e. new hardware and software that support library purposes, would be difficult to obtain through conventional channels. One solution to this problem that they suggested was the "tapping" of foundation monies for their purposes.

APPENDIX F

Program Area:

Mission:

Goal:

Objective:

	Operating Strategies	Person Responsible	Date Due
1.			
2.			
3.			
4.			
5.			

Sources.   Robert Braude, *C.E. 258 Planning: Strategic and Tactical,* 1983 and Donald Riggs, *Strategic Planning for Library Managers,* 1984.

APPENDIX G

Strategic Planning Process Evaluation Form

The following statements represent your best judgement. Kindly check your position on the scale as the statement first impresses you. Indicate what you *believe* rather than what you think you should believe.

SA = I strongly agree
A = I agree
U = I am undecided
D = I disagree
SD = I strongly disagree

	SA	A	U	D	SD
1. Mechanisms were provided for frequent staff interaction.	8 72.72%	3 27.28	0 0%	0 0%	0 0%
2. Guidance was provided in problem-solving techniques.	2 18.18%	7 63.64%	0 0%	2 18.18%	0 0%
3. Organization's destiny and market were of prime concern during the planning activities.	4 36.36%	6 54.54%	0 0%	1 9.10%	0 0%
4. Normal operating procedures were relaxed.	1 9.09%	4 36.36%	1 9.09%	5 45.46%	0 0%
5. Appropriate top-level officers in the library were involved in the planning.	3 27.28%	6 54.54%	1 9.09%	1 9.09%	0 0%
6. Appropriate in-house training was provided for group interaction.	2 18.18%	7 63.64	0 0%	2 18.18%	0 0.0%
7. Communication was encouraged betweeen staff and management.	4 36.36%	6 54.54%	1 9.09	0 0.0%	0 0.0%

	SA	A	U	D	SD
8. Adequate support was provided for the decisions reached.	1 9.09%	5 45.45%	4 36.37%	1 9.09%	0 0%
9. Planning activities revolved around a medium to short-range timeframe.	4 36.36%	7 63.64%	0 0.0%	0 0.0%	0 0.0%
10. Emphasis of the planning was internal and organizational rather than external and environmental.	1 9.10%	2 18.18%	0 0.0%	6 54.54%	2 18.18%
11. Planning process was typified more by an open system than a closed system.	2 18.18%	8 72.72	0 0.0%	1 9.10%	0 0.0%
12. Decisions arrived at during the planning were both qualitative and quantitative.	2 18.18%	7 63.64%	1 9.09%	1 9.09%	0 0.0%
13. Planning proved to be an exact science rather than an art form.	0 0.0%	0 0.0%	2 18.18%	4 36.36%	5 45.46%
14. A perfect plan was produced by this group.	0 0.0%	0 0.0%	2 18.18%	8 72.72%	1 9.10%

REFERENCES

Baldridge, Victor J. and Patricia H. Okimi. "Strategic Planning in Higher Education." *AAHE Bulletin* 35 (Oct. 1982): 15.
Boulding, Kenneth E. "The Management of Decline." *Change* 7 (June 1975): 8–9.
Braude, Robert M. *C.E. 258 Planning: Strategic and Tactical.* Omaha, Nebraska: 1983.
Brown University Library. *The Brown University Library: Goals and Objectives for the Eighties.* Providence, Rhode Island: 1985.

Cameron, Kim. "Strategic Responses to Conditions of Decline." *Journal of Higher Education* 54 (July/Aug. 1983): 359–377.

De Gennaro, Richard. *Library Support: The Invisible Crisis: A Report of the Director of Libraries University of Pennsylvania, 1980–81*. Philadelphia: n.p., 1981.

Donnelly, Robert M. "Strategic Planning for Better Management." *Managerial Planning* 30 (Nov./Dec. 1981–82): 3–6.

Dougherty, Richard M. *Maintaining the Library's Excellence: When the Past Will Not Be Prologue*. Ann Arbor: University of Michigan, 1982.

Drucker, Peter F. *Managing in Turbulent Times*. New York: Harper and Row, 1980.

Edinger, Joyce A. "Marketing Library Services: Strategy for Survival." *Marketing Library Services* 41 (1980): 329–332.

Gallinger, George W. "Strategic Business Planning." *Managerial Planning*, 31:41–44. July/August, 1982–83.

Kotler, Philip and Patrick E. Murphy. "Strategic Planning for Higher Education." *Journal of Higher Education* 52 (Sept./Oct. 1981): 470.

Leach, Ronald G. "Library Materials Price Update." *Library Issues* Nov. 1984: 2–3.

————."Library Materials Price Update." *Library Issues* Nov. 1987: 2–3.

Lee Library, Brigham Young University. *Collection Analysis Project: Interim Report*. Provo, Utah: 1979.

Naisbitt, John. *Megatrends*. New York: Warner Books Inc., 1982.

Oldman, Christine. "Marketing Library and Information Services." *European Journal of Marketing* 11 (1977): 461–474.

Palmour, Vernon E., Marcia C. Bellassai and Nancy V. DeWath. *A Planning Process for Public Libraries*. Chicago: American Library Association, 1980.

Riggs, Donald E. *Strategic Planning for Library Managers*. Phoenix: Oryx Press, 1984.

Rubin, I. "Retrenchment, Loose Structure, and Adaptability in the University." *Sociology of Education* 52 (1979): 211–212.

Sandler, Mark. "Where Did all the Money Go? Libraries Face Severe Economic Realities." *Library Issues* Jan. 1988: 1–4.

SPEC. "Strategic Planning in ARL Libraries." *Spec Flyer*. 108 Oct. 1984: 1–2.

Steiner, George A. *Strategic Planning: What Every Manager Must Know*. New York: The Free Press-MacMillan, 1979.

Weber, David. "Libraries Must Emphasize Interdependence in Future Years." *Campus Reports* 28 Oct. 1981: 14.

Wood, Elizabeth J. "Strategic Planning and the Marketing Process: Library Applications." *The Journal of Academic Librarianship* 9 (Mar. 1983): 15.

MANAGEMENT ISSUES IN SELECTION, DEVELOPMENT, AND IMPLEMENTATION OF INTEGRATED OR LINKED SYSTEMS FOR ACADEMIC LIBRARIES

Elaine Lois Day

INTRODUCTION

Despite the volume of literature on library automation, few sources bring together the available data on planning strategies, design, technical specifications, cost analysis, implementation, and changes in staff operations. An overview of these issues from a managerial perspective may be useful in assessing criteria for choosing and implementing online library systems.

While this paper provides a general overview of library automation, and

Advances in Library Administration and Organization,
Volume 8, pages 69-111.
ISBN: 0-89232-967-X

specific examples from design specifications and case studies, no attempt is made to determine the relative merits or costs of existing installations, and no recommendations of specific systems or system features are offered.

PROBLEM STATEMENT

Librarians face important decisions when purchasing or developing integrated systems, or adding additional components to existing automated systems. The pace of technological advance in bibliographic control, sluggish in the 1960s when library budgets were strong, has rocketed ahead of our ability, under budgetary constraints of the 1980s, to experiment casually with new and interesting options. The possibilities for library automation are diverse, costs are staggering, and the technology is as yet too young to offer clear choices of one system or set of standards over others. While librarians share the fascination of students, faculty and the general public with the speed and power of computers; economic constraints, coupled with the size and complexity of bibliographic databases, require an informed, pro-active approach to the long-term commitment of resources for automation of any library.

Anticipating the leadership qualities and pragmatic orientation required for effective decisionmaking in planning for library automation, William Axford (1979) called for stronger leadership and management within the library, and greater attention to the cost-effectiveness of innovations as they relate to fulfilling the library's humanistic mission:

> We are no longer a cottage industry and cannot continue so to regard ourselves unless we wish to see library management infiltrated by persons from other professions who have managerial credentials but may have no understanding of the need to employ advanced technology in a manner consistent with the library's historically humanistic role (p. 171).

Determining appropriate applications of technology within the library's historical role may first require reaffirmation of that role in a culture that seems to question the value of libraries in current and future educational and economic systems. Beyond role definition, choice or design of library technologies requires systematic linking of institutional goals to specific automation decisions. To refine the process even further, these decisions are ideally informed by empirical analysis of patron needs and behavior, technical operations, and site-specific cost projections.

Axford's plea for analysis of cost-effectiveness is a call heard repeatedly in library literature, and one which is very difficult to answer. How does one determine the cost-effectiveness of a service, the value of which has not been defined by the academic community? How much are rapid online response time, comprehensive catalog coverage, and professional reference service worth? As is the case with services of other not-for-profit institutions, the value of library service is actually determined by how much the administration, trustees, and legislature or benefactors of the university are willing to pay for it. Consequently, when librarians discuss the "cost-effectiveness" of library technology, we are usually referring to the "affordability" of various options that we have prioritized within the context of a particular budgetary climate. This point is especially pertinent as libraries move from an emphasis on automation of technical processes, which are quantifiable, to automation of patron access, which is essentially qualitative.

In an time when fiscal accountability and quantification of costs and benefits are greatly stressed, a significant challenge faced by automation planners is that of relating the additional costs of automation to the scholarly and educational goals of the university. Fussler (1973, p. x, preface) observed that, while our society, our research programs, and our educational systems are clearly dependent upon efficient access to literature and information, "satisfactory techniques for economic analysis of the benefits of access to recorded knowledge or information are conspicuously lacking." Most information access by scholars and students occurs outside of the marketplace economy, and is therefore difficult to analyze in cost-benefit terms.

Despite inherent difficulties in quantification of benefits, the prevalent motivation and justification for automation of library processes is expansion of services and enhanced access to resources, rather than anticipated cost reduction of technical processing. Saffady (1987) interviewed administrators and automation specialists at 55 integrated system sites. Interviewees stated a variety of reasons for automation, including: (a) efforts to upgrade the institutional image within the community and compete more effectively for new students, (b) a library building project, which facilitated related innovations, and (c) a desire to expand library services without increases in staff. Saffady comments:

> Several interviewees explicitly stated that cost reduction was not a motive for library automation, and that the decision to implement an integrated system was intended to expand and improve services rather than save money (p. 734).

System selection, development, and implementation require systematic analysis of service goals and financial resources, patron needs, operating requirements, organization, and personnel. Clearly stated objectives and readiness to "expect the unexpected" in terms of both beneficial and undesirable effects of automation are necessary elements of successful planning as reflected in the case study literature.

"PRIMARY" QUESTIONS

Beyond the exercise of wisdom and caution in selection of existing systems, librarians have the opportunity and the responsibility to participate in the design of new technologies, shaping library services to meet the future needs of patrons, rather than accepting the innovations of others and adapting library services to random technological change. Winner (1986), noting that new technologies have been frequently embraced with little attention to long-term consequences and side effects, proposes a new area of inquiry, a "philosophy of technology," which would examine primary questions on the purpose and probable effects of innovation:

> . . . we are seldom inclined to examine, discuss, or judge pending innovations with broad, keen awareness of what those changes mean. In the technical realm we repeatedly enter into a series of social contracts, the terms of which are revealed only after the signing (p. 9).

Consideration of primary questions relating to the purposes and effects of library automation is fundamental to budgetary justifications and rational design; for example:

1.   How will an online library catalog advance the scholarly and educational goals of the university? Will it answer the expressed or apparent needs of individual patrons? For example, will all disciplines be well served by the coverage and indexing language of the system? Will keyword searching, rapid response time, and remote access capabilities increase the quality and pace of education and research?

2.   Is the online library catalog a democratic or an authoritarian technology (Adams, 1988)? Can quality access for different groups of users be achieved within the same system? Will the system be directed and shaped by persons sympathetic to and knowledgeable about the values and functions of librarianship and scholarship, or will librarians and patrons be expected to adapt their behavior to rigid and less than appropriate technologies?

3.   Will an integrated system improve the efficiency and accuracy of technical processing and the quality of reference services? For example, is it highly desirable to integrate access to multiple resources and multiple subsystems from the same terminal, even though online access may provide somewhat homogenized or abbreviated records compared to those of manual files or printed bibliographies?

4.   Will automation improve or inhibit staff interaction and communication between patrons and librarians? For example, will staff members accustomed to control of separately housed manual files be comfortable with shared responsibility for a single database?

5.   Will automation handicap library materials and operating budgets? Will it draw the support of additional funding sources? Or, will it prove cost-effective at current funding levels?

6.   What additional burdens or benefits may result as side effects of automation? For example, the ability of patrons to view order status online may create a

rush of traffic in the technical services department and necessitate a new priority system for cataloging based on patron requests. If several patrons are in the same week alerted to a recently acquired title, a "funnelling" effect could conceivably direct more readers to the same item, thus affecting both scholarship and the need for acquisition of multiple copies.

The overwhelming consensus in the literature of libraries and automation is that all of these concerns may be addressed to the satisfaction of patrons, librarians and administrators. There is nothing inherent in computers or in automation which is inimical to democratic access to information or to the traditional humanistic values of scholarship and librarianship. The manner in which technology is designed and implemented will determine its ultimate benefits and costs. Concerns of privacy, equal access, staff cooperation, user education and cost containment, among others, will be addressed in the development process of any well-designed library system.

POLITICS, PERSONNEL, AND FINANCE: ENVIRONMENT OF THE DECISION PROCESS

When planning major internal change, library administrators consider overall institutional objectives. long-range funding, accountability to trustees and state legislators, as well as effects on library staffing and organization. Plans for local control of materials processing and patron access must be coordinated with norms for inter-institutional resource sharing, which require adherence to technical and intellectual (i.e., cataloging) standards set by the Library of Congress, national and international library associations, OCLC, and other bibliographic utilities. The cost of sophisticated online searching and in-depth indexing must be weighed against the need to complete retrospective conversion of manual records, incorporate non-book formats into the catalog, reduce cataloging backlogs, and anticipate the cost of future telecommunications upgrades.

A significant factor, often noted in the literature, is the lack of precedent in libraries for funding of automation. Will long-range funding come from special grants? From trimming of existing library materials and operating budgets? Or, will university administrators recognize the need to institute and adequately fund a separate budget for the automation infrastructure? Saffady (1987) illustrates the magnitude of these expenses relative to the traditional library budget, estimating that the annual $100,000 allocation required to amortize the initial implementation costs a typical integrated system is "equivalent to at least 50 percent of the annual book budget for almost half of the North American integrated system installations."

Saffady's interviewees report that they routinely followed relevant professional literature, attended automation conferences and workshops, and viewed product demonstrations for several years before purchasing an integrated system. Success in obtaining approval and funding was often precipitated by events marginally related to the system itself, including for example, the hiring of a new library director who is committed to automation, budgeting for construction or refurbishing of library buildings, and general upgrading of centralized processing facilities. Funding sources included special university accounts designated for automation projects, external funding from state government grants for automation, state grants obtained through political influence, national and local foundations, and funds donated by local business and other organizations. One academic library in Saffady's study was permitted to assess a special student registration fee to cover the costs of its integrated system. Saffady cautions that libraries receiving nonrecurring appropriations for automation are often forced to draw on their annual budgets to fund ongoing operation of the system.

Hirshon (1986) conducted in-depth telephone interviews with representatives of 12 ARL libraries that had implemented integrated systems. Questions covered pre-purchase design decisions, responsibilities for system implementation and operation, and expectations for the future. Methodologies for selection and design reflected the libraries' general decision-making processes. Although committees were employed for both general review and for writing of specifications, decisionmaking was frequently kept at an administrative level. Consultants were employed by a minority of the libraries surveyed. They provided specifications for purchase or design, wrote broad outlines of system architecture, evaluated design concepts, and validated the work of other consultants.

The degree and quality of staff participation in the decision process depends upon the institution's history of staff involvement; however the library automation literature stresses the importance of open communications between planners and those staff members who will be responsible for implementation and operation of the system. Librarians and support staff in a decision-making or advisory capacity can benefit from awareness of technical, political, social, and economic realities, as well as patron needs and usage patterns relating to online catalogs. Axford (1979) advocated diffusion of management attitudes throughout the entire organization, stating that:

> . . . important issues, such as automated cataloging, should be discussed within the context of empirically derived cost-benefit data rather than be settled by the enthusiasms and anxieties generated by the prospect of impending change'' (p. 171).

Accurate documentation of empirical data and reduction of staff anxieties and staff resistance in the planning and implementation processes require good communications among staff at all levels. In addition to their cooperation in data collection, planning, and implementation, staff can offer individual expertise in automation, and experiential knowledge of patron needs, characteristics, and behavior.

GOAL DEFINITION

Initial Motives for Library Automation

Automation of library processes was initially designed and justified by the need for efficient control of "housekeeping" functions; for example, cataloging, serials control, accounting, and interlibrary loan. Indeed, those systems which have been most successful as public access catalogs—for example, Northwestern University's NOTIS/LUIS and UCLA's ORION—evolved gradually from serials or other technical processing subsystems.

Current Motives for Library Automation

Integrated library systems facilitate local control of bibliographic databases. Storage of full MARC records is favored over continued dependence on bibliographic utilities for repeated access to records for locally held items. Once MARC records are loaded into the local database, the library and the online catalog user may manipulate them in a variety of ways.

Martin (1984) suggests returning to a type of controlled decentralization which will satisfy local needs while maintaining standardized MARC formats for resource sharing. Bibliographic networks, dependent upon hard-pressed libraries for their revenues, can survive the decentralization movement if they provide financial and technical service to libraries in the use of small computers. This is, of course, exactly what OCLC and WLN have done in marketing software and dedicated systems such as OCLC's LS/2000. Moran (1984) notes that the future of centralized versus distributed processing may depend largely on changes in telecommunications costs—an excellent example of the need for librarians to be aware of the environment outside the library and the university.

Current design objectives emphasize maximum patron access to locally controlled bibliographic databases, via comprehensive integrated or linked computerized systems. There is an extensive literature on access to online catalogs, identifying technical and intellectual changes needed to convert the static card catalog record to the versatile "perspective" of the online catalog (Crawford, 1987, p. 3). As early as 1982, an overwhelming percentage of library patrons expressed positive attitudes toward online catalogs (Ferguson, 1986). As these enthusiasts gain in experience and expertise, they demand more and better service from the automated catalog. Following are some of the options discussed by patrons, reference librarians, and system designers:

- Access to more terminals
- Printers connected to the terminals
- Faster response time

- Online circulation and order status information
- The ability to place holds and ILL requests online
- Logical sorting of retrievals (e.g., chronological, alphabetical, etc.)
- Better access to the subject searching vocabulary
- Online lists of related terms
- Keyboard and boolean searching
- The ability to expand or narrow a search
- Automatic correction of input errors
- Online see/see also references
- Inclusion of older monographic materials, serials, newspapers, and government documents
- Indexing of journals
- Online bibliographic instruction
- Access to online databases (BRS, DIALOG) through the library catalog

Operational Efficiency

Perhaps the most frequently discussed and most public goal of operational efficiency is rapid response time. While it is unproven that most online systems are significantly faster than, for example searching the card catalog, or manually checking in journals, time spent sitting before an unresponsive video screen may be more stressful than an equal period spent purposefully striding between physical files, or fingering cards. This enforced inactivity, together with the users' knowledge that technology could be employed to alleviate the situation, makes improved response time a universally popular objective. Gorman (1979, p. 251) stresses, however, that the value of library automation reaches far beyond the ability to perform traditional functions more quickly. Referring to the use of computers simply to speed up traditional technical processes as a "perversion of technology." Gorman calls for a complete reconsideration of all library systems and examination of the nature and purpose of each procedure. In support of this argument, he cites three main benefits of library technology:

1. Improvement of the efficiency of service to library patrons; by, for example, increasing the levels of access and the number of access points.
2. More efficient use of limited resources; for example, using a machine to sort entries, thereby freeing staff for other, less redundant and repetitive tasks.
3. Improving the quality of technical services employment, by eliminating much of the drudgery and busywork in libraries.

While their chief advantage in terms of access to materials is the ability to perform multi-level searches through a wide variety of access points, the primary operational advantage of integrated systems is not speed, but rather elimination of repetitive searching and data entry through the creation of a single database which may be converted into various screen formats and shared throughout the library system. For example, UCLA's ORION is constructed around an authority file and a bibliographic file. Any change to the form of entry for an author can be made globally to all records linked to that author. Even the less advanced first generation online catalogs provide a single "record level" description for multiple copies of a work, and for access from various search keys, eliminating the need to produce, file, and correct card sets recording each occurrence of an name, title or subject.

Efficiency is also achieved from the viewpoint of the catalog user when works of an author can be presented in chronological rather than alphabetical order; when brief descriptions can be scanned for relevance, and complete descriptions called up on demand; when search terms and results can be printed or saved to a disk; and, when it is possible to quickly browse subject indexes for useful headings. This efficiency is achieved without repetition of the same data elements in varied formats, but rather by re-organizing the presentation of centrally stored data elements.

Lessening redundancy also suggests the possibility of improving the accuracy and reliability of catalog records, a goal of any good library technology. Repetition and duplication naturally increase the possibility of error. For example, a public access printout of serial holdings may have information which contradicts that in the manual serials check-in file; a card-based name authority file can be updated to reflect the correct form of entry for an author, but staff may neglect to insert appropriate cross references in the card catalog. Some managers have expressed concern that eliminating manual files might cause library staff to become less conscientious, or to take less pride in the accuracy of their records; however, the opposite appears to be the case. The visibility of each worker's contribution to the central database, and the increased inter-departmental cooperation required to build automated records heighten each individual's sense of involvement and commitment to quality control.

Good response time and operational efficiency cannot be provided in an automated catalog without adequate processing power, hardware, and telecommunications. The literature on automation stresses the importance of planning more than adequate technical support for computer operations, with attention to power, compatibility, and the potential to upgrade equipment and standards. When the system does fail, backups for the database serve two purposes: (a) preservation of institutional records—usually on archival tapes, and (b) public access to the catalog—usually on microform or CD-ROM.

An Adaptable System

Technical specifications of computer hardware and telecommunications are rapidly advancing; for library systems software there is as yet no ideal system or fixed standard. An important goal of library automation is, therefore, to maintain a flexible position for future development. Storage of records in USMARC or MARC-compatible formats, purchasing or leasing hardware of proven reliability from vendors who provide regular equipment upgrades, and allowing for future expansion in the number of terminals, records, and online transactions to be supported are strongly advocated in the literature. Careful examination of processing procedures and standards in light of the new technologies is also warranted.

Advocates of utility and economy contend that much of the information encoded on catalog records is so arcane that it is not understood by either patrons or reference librarians; and worse yet, that the unnecessarily complex code is continually changing, requiring libraries to invest in expensive retrospective conversion of existing records in order to participate in bibliographic networking. Administrators, frustrated over the high cost of retrospective conversion, often question cataloging and classification practices. An example frequently cited is bracketing of dates that do not appear on the chief source of information. Matthews (1985), noting the high cost of card catalog storage and maintenance, reported the following statistics from a 1969 Library of Congress report:

> 12 percent of all catalog cards need to be changed within 5 years.
> 22 percent of all catalog cards will be modified in 10 years.
> 42 percent of all catalog cards will have been altered at least once within 30 years (p. 7).

This report did not anticipate the massive changes resulting from the adoption of AACR2 in 1980, at which time the Library of Congress went online, closing its card catalog.

Conventions of entry and punctuation designed for catalog cards are unnecessary for online searching and display. For example, although analogous conventions may be developed for local screen formats, it is not necessary in an online display to follow each subject tracing with a full stop (period) or to separate the edition statement with double dashes. Abbreviations are also less desirable in online catalogs than on $3'' \times 5''$ catalog cards.

The complex punctuation and subfield tagging of MARC formats, originally designed to facilitate international sharing of bibliographic resources by reducing the need for translation, had little initial utility, as European libraries were not able to afford UNIMARC tapes and other costs of library automation. The subfield designations are however invaluable for local indexing and masking elements in the online record. It may be surprising that MARC formats, developed in the mid-1960s, long before the availability of online public access catalogs or integrated library systems, can be used in communicating bibliographic data within the new technologies. This is, however, a direct result of the application of relational and network database principles to the pre-existing MARC record. The MARC record—though not an ideal structure for relational databases, due to its hierarchical organization—does subdivide the main elements of the catalog record by indexable fields, subfields, and records. Once this structure is imposed and the records are entered, the data may be presented or reindexed in a variety of ways limited only by the level of detail inherent in the field/subfield structure.

The primary catalysts of retrospective conversion—(a) growth and change in the classification of knowledge, (b) open shelving of library materials by subject (a practice that requires a linear classification scheme), and (c) change in bibliographic technology—seem unavoidable in most settings. The potential for cost effectiveness of automated library systems lies in the ability to initiate global changes in the format of a machine readable database. Hafter (1986) suggests that a flexible code is needed for online catalogs, and that boolean and keyword searching, and inclusion of tables of contents may increase subject access without adding to the intellectual work of cataloging.

A Functional System

A library catalog in any form is a means to an end—that of identifying and locating works and specific items available in the library or through services of the library. As Patrick Wilson (1983) has noted, the typical library catalog does not provide access to all works in a collection, but only to the broad subject descriptions and partial contents of physical items. The catalog record is nevertheless a reasonably useful and affordable indicator of the intellectual content of library materials, and serves as a link between holdings and their physical descriptions and location codes.

An integrated system has the potential of providing multi-level access, reducing duplication of effort, and maximizing the sharing of information. To be truly functional and cost-effective, the new system must also eventually supplant the library's card catalog, serials cardex, and manual order file. As an illustration of problems with dual catalog systems, younger students, trained in online catalog use, may be reluctant to learn the concepts and strategies required for effective card catalog searching (Popa, et al., 1988). Older students and faculty may avoid the online catalog as long as some relevant citations can be retrieved from the card catalog. If the online catalog contains records for items acquired since 1980, and the card catalog is no longer updated, patrons who search effectively only in the closed card catalog and those who search effectively only in the online catalog will each lack access to a significant portion of the collection. Similarly, requiring library employees to operate parallel manual and automated technical services systems will likely result in wasted effort and uneven work quality.

Hernon and McClure (1986) applied unobtrusive reference testing methods in a study of 26 academic and public federal depository libraries. Proxies approached the reference department with bibliographic questions, all of which could be satisfied by reference to that library's government documents collection. Staff often failed to recognize the titles as government publications or to provide referrals to alternative sources; the use of online aids, such as OCLC, by reference staff attempting to answer the test questions was rare. In addition, the study revealed an over-dependence on the library's general catalog for comprehensive information on holdings:

> Apparently, many public service personnel assume that an online, microfiche, or card catalog includes all the library's holdings. . . .
> The extent of staff dependency on a general catalog provides a rationale for why such catalogs should provide a comprehensive record of the holdings of a library (p. 40).

Ideally, an integrated library system will provide access to all library resources and automated processes from the same database. Adding government documents to the automated database might be prohibitively expensive; however, the library can provide online pointers—for example reference data files (Hildreth, 1987)—to additional catalogs and indexes. In addition, the library's journal holdings and book orders may be viewed online via linked or integrated serials and acquisitions subsystems. Some libraries have attempted to integrate indexing of journal articles by importing online database services to terminals of the online catalog. For example, the University of California's MELVYL system provides access to *Magazine Index*, which covers one hundred popular journals.

The functional advantages of linkage and integration can be further extended by access from private homes and offices. Microcomputers allow users to download bibliographic records on personal computers or local area networks, and manipulate them via database management systems or citation software packages such as BiblioLinks/ProCite. The resource sharing first enjoyed by libraries with the advent of MARC formats and access to OCLC database has evolved to include a seemingly limitless potential for local control and customized presentation of bibliographic records. Concurrently, national level cataloging standards and resource sharing opportunities continue to improve with the development of the National Coordinated Cataloging Program (Avram, 1988) and the Linked Systems Project (Avram and Wiggins, 1987; McCallum, 1987). Perhaps the greatest practical benefit of machine readable catalog records is that libraries will no longer need to dispose of the old catalog as it becomes outmoded. With vigilance in maintaining coding and communications standards, libraries may readily convert existing machine readable records to new catalog technologies as they evolve.

RESEARCH QUESTIONS

Control of form and cost, enhancement of access and reference service, efficient and accurate processing, good working relationships, and adaptability are common goals of library automation projects. The remainder of this paper will be devoted to an examination of the specific questions which an orderly, empirical evaluation of automation planning might address:

Access

What qualities are (a) essential, and (b) desirable in a library catalog? What kind of information do patrons want from the catalog, and how do they seek it? Which searching features do they want? Which will they use? Which are most effective? How should name and subject authorities be managed?

Operations Analysis

What are the automation requirements of library operations? What data elements, screen formats, and operations are required for processing in collection development, acquisitions, cataloging, serials, circulation, interlibrary loan, etc.? How can these needs be met by automation design?

Design

Rather than purchasing a fully integrated library system, is it better to choose the best available subsystems (i.e., circulation, acquisitions, cataloging, etc.) and link them together? Will the system be operated by the library on its own dedicated computer, or by the university computing center on a fixed or variable fee basis? Will the system offer adequate protection of users' privacy? Will the system itself be protected against possible abuse?

Hardware and Telecommunications Requirements

How will technical specifications of hardware, software and telecommunications affect the future cost and viability of a particular system?

Selection and Procurement

Should the library establish an automation department with primary responsibility for planning and implementation decisions, or should a systems librarian be appointed to coordinate planning and implementation, with research responsibility and decision authority distributed among existing departments? How can planning and implementation of the system be informed by knowledge of local requirements for effective operations and access? In other words, how can the understanding that staff members have of local operations and library patrons be incorporated into planning decisions? What other information resources, such as consultants, case studies, site analysis, and reports of colleagues, are available to librarians planning automation projects?

What is the history of online library catalogs and related subsystems? What is their current state of development? What systems are commercially available, and what do they have to offer? What are the prospects for future advances?

Cost Estimation

How can the costs and benefits of various components be measured and prioritized? How can the costs of installation be estimated for a particular site? What will be the long range costs of maintenance and future upgrades? Can the library devote the programming time and financial investment required to develop a system to its own specifications, or should it purchase and adapt an integrated system developed elsewhere?

Conversion and Implementation

How will the system affect staffing, work flow, and organizational relationships? Will the library staff enthusiastically accept the prospect of an automated system, or will they fear possible staff reductions and loss of job satisfaction? What efforts will be needed to instruct staff members and patrons on the use of terminals, on input and searching techniques? Will some employees and patrons be unable to understand conceptual changes in organization and access that are basic to relational databases? How will the system affect operations, workflow, and working relationships?

ACCESS ISSUES

Standards of utility for the library catalog are generally measured against *Cutter's Rules for a Dictionary Catalog* (reprinted in Carpenter and Svenonius, 1985) which require that the catalog:

- enable a person to find a book of which either the author, title or subject is known,
- show what the library has by a given author, on a given subject, or in a given kind of literature,
- assist in the choice of a book as to its edition, or its character (p. 67).

The first generation of online catalogs failed to meet these basic requirements. Known-item searching was possible by author or title, provided the patron was able to enter the appropriate search key in the precise form required by the system. Bibliographic records were displayed in abbreviated form without adequate clues to relevance, and without keys for additional searching. When subject searching was added, the absence of cross references and internal authority control required a degree of familiarity with the Library of Congress Subject Headings not possessed by most library patrons. The rate of searches failed or quickly terminated on these systems was quite high.

Authority files, boolean and keyword searching, online help, and custom screen displays, have recently brought many online catalogs up to Cutter's standards. Linked or integrated subsystems now provide online access to materials in circulation, on order, and those received but not yet cataloged or shelved. For example UCLA's ORION provides circulation and order status information. NOTIS allows patrons to request interlibrary loans online.

As the library's bibliographic database has begun to resemble those of commercial online database vendors, there is a trend in the literature to emphasize development of online public access catalogs with user-controlled subject searching protocols similar to those of DIALOG and BRS. In a related trend, some librarians and patrons suggest indexing or displaying terms from the table of contents and index of each item cataloged. There are however significant differences between library catalogs and online services in content, structure and user expertise.

First, because online databases cover specific subject literatures (Biology, Law, etc.) or communication media (e.g., popular magazines), the controlled vocabulary utilized by each database is selected for a particular group of users or for a specific subject area. In contrast, the language of the academic library catalog is universal in scope and must be accessible to users in all specialties and with varying levels of expertise. Both the controlled and free text vocabulary of the library catalog are therefore very much larger than those of a single online service, compounding the problem of narrowing a search to a few relevant retrievals.

Secondly, commercial online databases provide abstracts to enable users to evaluate the relevance of searches and narrow the number of retrievals; as this practice is not feasible for libraries, users must assess relevance from the title and subject headings of the bibliographic description, again making it more difficult to narrow a large retrieval set resulting from a keyword or boolean search.

Finally, search protocols for the commercial online services have been developed for expert searchers and are beyond the interest and skill levels of most library users. Even end-user searching aids such as MEDLINE'S "Grateful Med" and "Paperchase" require multiple steps to recover a set of relevant citations. Library catalogs must be accessible to both the expert searcher who will desire both efficiency and precision, and to the first time user who may be satisfied with any available edition or with the first accessible work on a general topic.

How do library users search for information, and what do they expect from the catalog? Will users accustomed to making one pass at the catalog in search of a single item or information on a single subject term have the interest and perseverance required to perform sophisticated, multi-step searches? Most recent literature on use of online catalogs refers to a 1982 use study conducted by the Council on Library Resources and reported by Matthews, Lawrence, and Ferguson (1983). Findings from a survey of 17 online systems in 29 libraries showed that over half of users wanted access to more terminals; many also requested printers for use with the terminals. With regard to special features, Lawrence (1986, p. 9) reports that most of the additional features requested by users related to subject searching: (a) a list of related subject terms (45 percent), (b) the ability to search a book's table of contents or index (42 percent), and (c) subject keyword searching (24 percent). Circulation information was desired by 37 percent of respondents. Other improvements requested included identifying the physical locations of books, changes in screen displays, limiting by publication date or language, and call number searching. Lawrence reports that OCLC and the University of California analyzed transaction logs of seven online catalogs, and found that sophisticated searching features, such as limiting, index browsing, and saving and linking sets, are not used by searchers.

A significant finding of use studies has been that most users do not persist in searches long enough to achieve the control required for successful free text searching of tables of contents and indexes. Most searches terminate after one operation; significantly increasing the number of retrievals per search through keyword and boolean searching on tables of contents and/or indexes requires the patron to perform a complex set of searching refinements for satisfactory results. A possible alternative use of tables of contents displays may be as non-searchable displays for assessing relevance of particular records.

Keyword searching can be more easily applied to the Library of Congress Subject Headings (LCSH) or other controlled vocabulary. Use of LCSH as an online access tool is addressed by Chan (1986), who concludes:

> The Library of Congress subject headings system is a viable subject access tool in the online environment. Many of its current recognized shortcomings are mitigated, not exacerbated, by the properties of online information processing systems (p. 367).

Several sources indicate that reference librarians and other online catalog users do want and use enhanced subject access, provided it includes online help and browsing of subject heading lists (Markey, 1984; Hildreth, 1987). Matthews (1985, pp. 7–8) summarizes results of four card catalog use studies, conducted between 1968 and 1973: Of all persons coming into the library, 41 percent did not use the catalog at all; of the 59 percent who used the catalog, 48 percent searched for known items by author or title, with a success rate of 66 percent; the remaining 52 percent of card catalog searches were for unknown items (approached by subject), and had a 50 percent success rate. Markey (1986, pp. 42–43) cites an online catalog subject searching rate of over 40 percent (as compared to author/title searches) for 7 out of 8 systems studied in 1983, with a range of 34 percent to 65 percent.

Markey (1984) has written extensively on subject access through online catalogs. She identifies a "known-item bias" in systems development. Known-item searching, with book (or order slip) in hand is the only type of access required for technical processing. Administrators and systems designers tend to underestimate the amount of subject searching actually attempted by catalog users, while overestimating the user's ability to choose the correct form of entry for these searches. With the emphasis now on public access through automated systems, Markey anticipates a "paradigm shift" (first identified by Cochrane, 1983, p. 89), from known-item searching to subject access, with appropriate authority controls, and multiple access points.

In a recent article, Adams (1988) evaluates the online catalog from the perspective of the humanities reference desk. Due to the broad range of materials required, and the retrospective nature of their sources, researchers in the humanities have been the group least well served by currently available automated catalogs. Adams states that patrons want uniform search strategies across systems, inclusion of government documents, newspapers, journals, dissertations, and older books; distributed terminals for greater privacy; and protection of transaction logs from unauthorized personnel.[1]

Fussler (1965) warned against the tendency of research libraries to isolate materials in non-Western languages by creating separate catalogs and repositories. Integration of materials in non-Western languages with related subject literatures will serve the area specialist by providing specific subject access points for all materials within a subject group. Large quantities of materials may be located in Government Documents, Manuscripts, and Serials departments; Technical Services may have a backlog of uncataloged materials. Isolation of these resources by format, rather than integration by subject, complicates selection and access, undermining the advantages of indexing languages and online technology. In the case of rare books and manuscripts, where physical isolation is necessary, the online catalog can never-the-less integrate bibliographic access to these materials with similar subject matter in the main collection. As Fussler stated, "subject control and analysis of all kinds of research materials need to be drastically improved. If they are improved enough, the physical arrangement of books will be of less and less consequence" (p. 357).

Classification, may, however, be useful beyond the collocation of books on the shelf. There has been much discussion in the literature on classification as an online access point. DeHart and Matthews (1986) coordinated subject catalog searching and shelflist searching in research on 16 subject queries. The specificity and length of the classification number were found to compliment subject headings in narrowing searches to the desired topic. DeHart and Matthews emphasize that despite the current availability of sophisticated searching software, searching will most likely be performed on databases inherited from previous catalogs. They note that patrons may prefer browsing to boolean searching, and they urge catalogers to emphasize the logical association of subject headings and class numbers for online browsing.

Local control of the database and enhancement of cataloging records is perceived by librarians as an improvement to patron access. A public library may find it necessary to simplify and compress Library of Congress subject headings for easier access and consistency. A special library or special collection may add analytical entries for access to topics that are more specific than that of the work as a whole. Other examples of locally controlled subject access include the following:

1. Added entries for local history or biography.
2. Analytic subject headings derived from tables of contents and indexes.
3. Added subject headings which make it more likely that a particular item will be retrieved.
4. Establishment and maintenance of name and subject authorities to reduce the number of failed online searches.

A survey conducted recently by this author (Day, 1988) confirms findings in the literature of subject access problems in online catalogs. Reference librarians at a public library site commented that the online catalog could be improved by adding additional access points; reference librarians at an academic library, referring to the OCLC LS/2000 system, reported that subject searching was often difficult for patrons, because they could not identify the appropriate Library of Congress subject headings; because it is difficult to narrow a search; or because subject headings have to be entered in a precise format.

Despite some calls for additional cataloger-supplied subject headings, economic concerns and the malleable nature of the automated catalog seem to favor subject analysis defined by the user, through free-text searching of various fields (for example, title, notes, imprint) over the static, perhaps biased, and certainly conservative analysis provided by subject catalogers. The question remains as to whether patrons can be encouraged to employ sophisticated searches, and whether libraries can afford to store additional indexes and impose authority control on the additional name and subject variants found in those fields. The technology for optical scanning of tables of contents and indexes in various formats and type fonts is becoming available; debate continues as to whether storage and searching of these sources is really practical.

Authority Control vs. Free Text Searching

Although recognizing the drawback of storage cost, Hildreth (1987) does not find that lack of authority control will negate the value of searching tables of contents and indexes—hit or miss keyword access to these sources is better than none. In this regard it should be noted that online databases (e.g., BRS and DIALOG) do not have name authority controls, although a controlled subject vocabulary usually functions together with slower and less reliable free text searching. Hildreth's proposal should perhaps be qualified with the understanding that the controlled subject headings of the catalog record will still be linked to automated authority files. Jamieson, et al. (1986) compared success in keyword searching with that of controlled vocabulary searching, and found that keyword, while a powerful retrieval technique, did not compensate for lack of database structure.

Avram (1984) defines the role of authority work in library catalogs as the task of identifying distinct forms of headings and of showing relationships among headings with the purpose of allowing patrons to retrieve individual items, particularly works, or particular versions of works. The burden of authority work, if not assumed by the librarian or accomplished with shared information from other libraries, will necessarily default to the patron. Avram stresses the importance of online authority control, noting the distinction between the intellectual component of creating authority headings, and the computerized linkages—equivalent to typing cross references for the card catalog—that are required to make authorities accessible online.

According to Paterson (1987), authority control in an online catalog can mean (a) the availability of cataloger-created authority records on computer tape, or (b) tape loaded authority records with automatic validation of incoming headings by comparison with an existing database. Paterson defines three levels of sophistication for automatic validation of headings. These may be summarized as follows:

1.   Incoming headings are automatically compared to headings currently in the catalog. The existing headings serve as an authority file, and exceptions are tagged for cataloger review. This facilitates internal consistency, but not "correctness" in relation to national-level (e.g., Library of Congress) authority control.

2.   Incoming headings are validated against the local database. In addition, local cross references are created, and blind references to headings not currently used by the library are removed in a process called 'deblinding.'

3.   In addition to automated cross-references and deblinding, the system provides validation of incoming headings against a secondary source such as Library of Congress authority records, rather using the local catalog as an authority file. Wherever incoming headings match the LC file, local catalogers need not verify their accuracy.

Potter (1986) advocates the use of authority records to protect the integrity of the bibliographic database, and automated cross references to enhance ease of searching:

> It is preferable that cross-references be unobtrusive and not punitive. If readers enter a variant form of an author's name or a subject heading, they should not be punished by being told to enter the correct form. Rather, the system should execute a search on the correct form with only, perhaps, a gentle mention of the correct form to avoid confusion (p. 128).[2]

OPERATIONS ISSUES

Highsmith (1986) compared nine integrated systems, evaluating (a) basic processing functions provided for record-creation and maintenance, (b) system flexibility, and (c) ease of use. All systems use archival tapes to load records into the database initially. Some continue to update the local database with weekly tape loads. This method may be advantageous or necessary when the systems staff is small. Most systems, however, make use of an online interface whereby records can be transferred from the utility directly into the local system as they are encountered during bibliographic searching. Lag time is still a factor as records are often received in a local edit file and later batch loaded into the public catalog.

A few systems offer screen to screen transfer from utility to local system, giving the cataloger an option to edit the record either on the utility before transfer or on the local system immediately after transfer. Editing within the context of the local database facilitates authority work and shelf listing. NOTIS, BLIS, and LIAS utilize a MARC match technique, allowing the institution to maintain its own subscription to the MARC database, thus bypassing the utilities. Highsmith notes the following advantages of MARC match for retrieval and local editing of bibliographic records:

1. Reviewing records within the context of the local catalog increases the likelihood that editions of a work will be correctly classified and that all titles can be fitted logically into the existing collection.
2. Direct access to MARC tapes increases the currency of bibliographic information for local use.

Error checking in batch or online cataloging may include automatic verification of ISBN and ISSN numbers, bar codes, OCR numbers, and MARC formats. Most systems examined by Highsmith were weak on error checking for batch tape loading. Online shelflisting is hampered in many systems by an inability to browse the shelflist both forward and backward. Some systems provide a post-production call number list that tags duplicate call numbers produced in batch mode.[3]

Highsmith also notes the importance of profiling, or masking, catalog records by selective exclusion of unneeded MARC fields or subfields. She concludes that MARC match and system support for local editing are positive steps in the direction of linked systems, standardized formats for shared cataloging, and fully customized local environments.

Hudson (1986) observed cataloging operations at six university libraries that had implemented automated systems. Results show a tendency to align acquisitions and copy cataloging in the same department. Davis (1987), discussing the use of NOTIS at Indiana State University, explains that where an integrated system reflects titles on order and in process, most of the copy cataloging and local access decisions have already been made at the time an order is placed. Where pre-order cataloging provides access points for materials not yet received, bibliographic searching, receiving, and copy cataloging must be closely coordinated. In a related development, online database maintenance, utilizing systems and catalog management staff is an increasingly important responsibility with integrated systems. As a result, collection management is often coordinated with systems support. Other examples of administrative reorganization will be discussed below.

DESIGN ISSUES

The literature on subject access is abundant with references to a traditional monographic bias in library automation (Markey, 1986; Flecker, 1988). Systems development favors known-item searching because it has been the only means of access required for cataloging and processing from network databases; books are the format favored by online catalogs because they are the focus of traditional catalogs, and of most shared cataloging efforts. Dale Flecker (1988), Associate Director for Planning and Systems at the Harvard University Library warns of another bias, "OCLC centrism"—the assumption in system design that all records are and will be acquired from OCLC. A well designed system should be able to retrieve bibliographic data from a variety of sources. The Linked Systems Project, connecting the databases of the Library of Congress, OCLC, the Research Libraries Information Network, and the Western Library Network will eventually provide this type of access (Fenly and Wiggins, 1988; Avram, 1988).

Flecker stresses the importance of building full USMARC formats directly into the local system; even though there may be no current use for each of the fields and subfields, future flexibility and resource sharing require storage of a complete and standardized MARC record. Bland (1986) also stresses the importance of maintaining the integrity of MARC records. There are fields specifically designated for local data; others should be left intact. Local suppression, or masking, of unwanted fields will achieve the same result as truncating the stored MARC record.

Hildreth (1987, p. 647–648) notes that the online catalog stands apart from earlier catalogs because it is "*interactive*, infinitely *expandable*, and *public*"; able to communicate with the patron; "responsive and informative at a given time to a given need." In addition, the online catalog is "fence resistant" in the sense that its form does not inhibit its development and modification. Access points, search strategies and display formats can be added or easily changed; the system itself may be expanded through linkages to online subsystems. Finally, patron search strategies and access needs may be assessed through analysis of transactions logs.

Hildreth (1987) is responsible for the classification of "first, second, and third generation" online public access catalogs (OPACS). First generation OPACS were known-item finding tools, "crude attempts to replicate the card catalog," providing few access points, and displaying short, non-standard bibliographic records. They lacked subject access and cross-references, and they offered patrons little or no online assistance:

> Without subject access, authority-based searching with cross references, and meaningful browsing facilities, first-generation online catalogs were understandably criticized as inferior to traditional library catalogs (p. 650).

Hildreth's second-generation OPACS include browsing and subject searching analogous to that provided by card catalogs together with the keyword and Boolean strategies of online database searching. Many systems offer the ability to limit searches by date of publication and language. Features such as right-hand truncation, and masking of stopwords and ambiguous punctuation also increase recall with second-generation catalogs.

Hildreth cautions, however, that unlike commercial online databases, online public access catalogs must be usable by inexperienced searchers. Also, there are no abstracts in the library catalog, and subject headings are relatively sparse, complicating assessment of relevance for large retrieval sets. Finally, in contrast to the well-defined subject coverage of specialized online databases, most library catalogs are universal in terms of the intellectual scope of materials indexed, thereby increasing the complexity of vocabulary control and the need for specificity in search strategies.

Hildreth advocates common sense, not artificial intelligence in the refinement of second-generation and design of third-generation online public access catalogs, placing particular stress on the need for online help and interactive features to reduce the number of failed searches, resolve users' confusion about what to do next, and provide easier access to the subject vocabulary, Keyword searching of titles and pre-coordinated subject headings (i.e., LCSH) will increase retrievals without bringing them beyond the number which a typical user can successfully limit without the aid of online abstracts. Online display of related terms (such as that provided by WILSONLINE) would apparently satisfy many users; those who wish to employ boolean techniques will need extensive online help in refining search strategies. Browsing of keyword lists, display of full bibliographic records, including subject headings, on the first screen of records displayed, and retrieval of citations in chronological or alphabetical order are suggested by Hildreth, and by Crawford (1987). A two-tiered system of menu-driven searching—for beginning users—and command-driven searching—for experienced users—seems to serve well in the University of California's MELVYL catalog (Rocke and Ross, 1985).

How do patrons approach the online catalog? How can they be encouraged to persist in carrying searches out to their most productive conclusion? Exploratory searching can be facilitated by online help messages, index browsing, and links to additional search keys. Hildreth (1987) and Rice (1988) advocate online catalog designs which will promote exploratory searching and serendipitous discovery. As Hildreth notes:

> Online catalog users display no desire to search in the disciplined, highly-structured, linear manner of trained search intermediaries who aim to produce a well-defined list of citations for an end user (p. 657–658).

Rice compares browsing online indexes with the "holism" achieved by fingering through large numbers of catalog cards. In addition to author, title and subject indexes, some OPAC users may browse the shelf list or even browse Dewey numbers in some LC databases. The accidental discovery of new information by "bridging" from one bibliographic record to another can be facilitated by online catalogs. Rice notes the advantage of online catalogs in storage of large authority and cross-reference files. Authority files may be linked to bibliographic records, allowing automatic updating and creation of related terms lists.

As an example, ORION, UCLA's integrated online library system employs an expensive, but highly efficient and access-oriented design (Fayollat and Coles, 1987). ORION originated in the 1960s with an automated serials processing system for the UCLA Biomedical Library, and has since added cataloging, acquisitions, online catalog, circulation/inventory, fund accounting, and authority control modules. The system serves the main library, branches, departmental and off-campus collections. Access is available via dedicated terminals in the libraries and campus offices, and by dial-up access from home microcomputers.

ORION's stores records in alphabetical order by main entry in all files. More computer resources are required to add new records than would be the case with the more commonly used random storage and access methods, however the pre-sorted contents of this database dramatically speed retrieval, and enable search results from several files to be presented to the patron in a single alphabetical listing. The system is MARC-compatible and very current—all record updates are done online. Authority files are linked to bibliographic records and are in synchrony with the bibliographic files at all times.

The system includes four browse files: name and subject authorities, serials titles, and call numbers. Changes to headings in bibliographic records or the addition of new bibliographic records trigger immediate update of the authority files. Catalogers may also directly alter headings in the authority files; the changes immediately proliferate to the linked bibliographic records.

Hildreth's third generation of online catalogs will include online periodical holdings, and access to commercial databases, such as *Magazine Index*—now available through the MELVYL system. Online lists of related terms, optical scanning of tables of contents, a richer vocabulary, and a better user-system interface will enhance subject access and patron satisfaction. Optical scanning of title pages will permit automatic retrieval of MARC records for additions to the database. Online reference data files will supplement the catalog file, directing users to other print of machine readable information sources.

System design should address the access and processing needs defined in automation planning, but should not burden the library with rigidly structured operating procedures. Flecker (1988) urges a balance between specificity and generality in system design. Referring to the lack of specificity in design of a proposed subsystem for North Carolina's Triangle Research Libraries Network Bibliographic Information System (BIS), he notes:

> There is the potential for a great deal of misunderstanding given the current specification. A large number of designs could satisfy the specifications as they exist; all would not be equally acceptable to library staff.

Design specifications should be detailed enough to avoid ambiguities; however, system functions should not be too finely specified. Flecker recommends that the BIS acquisitions system be designed to provide a few very generalized processing functions. Flexibility in design reduces programming cost, while allowing for future procedural changes.

HARDWARE AND TELECOMMUNICATIONS ISSUES

Potter (1986) emphasizes the importance of adequate computing power and telecommunications. The choice of a system must be informed by awareness of hardware compatibility and confidence in the ability of the hardware manufacturer to provide future upgrades and expansion. A common error is installation of hardware that is not powerful enough to meet the demands of everyday use, and the expanded use which inevitably accompanies increased efficiency. Potter suggests that vendors be selected based upon their reputations for support of upgrades and expansion; for example, IBM and Tandem consistently provide more powerful systems, compatible with existing equipment. Hardware that cannot be expanded or replaced may eventually require extensive reprogramming, and may even result in inability to support the current online system.

Allowances must be made for increases in database size and the number of terminals served. Many institutions intend to provide dial-up access for users in academic offices and homes, and for interlibrary loan; keyword and boolean searching will also require considerable amounts of power. Inferior or inadequate hardware and telecommunications design will result in slow response time when additional terminals, ports, and indexing features are added. Saffady (1987) reports that most interviewees in his survey "attributed their hardware upgrades to either an inadequate original equipment configuration or to an expansion of application requirements" (p. 748).

Downtime and equipment failures were significant factors for automated systems of the 1960s and 1970s, prompting fears that, should the system crash after the card catalog is closed or discarded, irreplaceable data could be lost, and patrons would be denied access to the catalog for hours or days at a time. Operating procedures normally require daily backup of data on archival tapes, usually stored off-site. Public access back-up catalogs are available in microform and CD-ROM. Moreover, as Saffady's study documents, the reliability of computer equipment has improved significantly in the last five years, and few libraries with fully operational systems report hardware failures:

> Some equipment failures are to be expected during initial system installations. For opera-
> tionally stable systems, however, the libraries interviewed reported few, if any, incidents of
> downtime attributable to hardware malfunctions (p. 757).

Integrated systems are commonly run on dedicated minicomputers or shared mainframes. The dedicated minicomputer may be located in the library, or in a central computer facility. Saffady identifies a trend in favor of centralizing institutional data processing sites. Even where the library system operates on a dedicated minicomputer, there are advantages in locating that computer in the university computing center rather than the library:

1. The library need not allocate its own space and resources for site preparation.
2. The computing center can more easily attract and afford experienced operators.
3. Computing center personnel often have prior experience with the hardware and operating systems on which the library's system will run.

Migration of library systems to the computing center, and particularly the difficulty of attracting to the library qualified operators and staff who are experienced with specific hardware and software configurations, raises interesting questions—probably best left for a future paper—about the role of computer science within the library profession. Perhaps computing should be considered a consulting or support service of resource access—much as accounting provides support to library acquisitions—rather than a subset of the library profession, ever striving with the university computing center for recognition and comparable pay. This is not to suggest that librarians should be reluctant to specialize in the study and construction of databases and design of systems. It is useful, however, to distinguish between the elements of database structure which are unique to bibliographic control and patron access—and should therefore be designed by information scientists in libraries—and the "database engine" (Crawford, 1987), the wiring, terminals, central processing unit, and operating system that allow the system to function electronically and logically—which should be designed and controlled by information scientists in computing centers.

SYSTEM SELECTION AND PROCUREMENT

Selection and Procurement Process

Information resources available to automation planners include case studies, use studies, library committees, automation consultants, system documentation and marketing information, and site visits to other institutions. For widely used systems such as NOTIS and VTLS, comparison with other institutions using the same system is especially useful, although many aspects of operation and cost analysis are specific to a particular location.

Saffady (1987, p. 737) describes the classic approach to system procurement as detailed analysis of operations and requirements, followed by preparation of a formal request for proposals (RFP). The RFP represents system specifications and is sent to as many vendors as possible.[4] Disadvantages of the RFP method reported by Saffady's (1987, p. 738) respondents include the following:

1. Implementation was delayed for nine months to one year during formal evaluations and negotiations.
2. Committee meetings interfered with daily work routines and created wish lists which could increase costs and delay implementation.
3. Proposals of different vendors were often difficult to compare and did not always distinguish currently available projects from those under development or merely under consideration.
4. Although RFPs were widely publicized and sent to as many vendors as the library could identify, most interviewees indicated that less than half of the vendors actually responded with proposals.
5. Concern for compatibility with existing hardware configurations often carried more weight in the decision than did a process of open bidding.

Among the most significant selection criteria, interviewees in Saffady's study (1987, p. 740–741) cited the following: (a) the availability and effective integration of OPACs, circulation control and other desired modules, (b) a good interface between the system and the user; (c) rapid response time, (d) compatibility with other local systems for resource sharing, (e) specification of hardware that is expandable and on which a variety of competitively available software packages can be run, and (f) availability of in-house expertise and experience with the system's hardware and operating system.

The importance of staff involvement in planning, selection and implementation can be stressed on several levels: (a) effective communications to keep staff members informed on the progress and characteristics of automation, and to provide a sense of involvement in and responsibility for planning and implementation; (b) directly involving staff members or committees in planning and implementation of automated processes specific to their library activities; (c) drawing on specific areas of technical expertise possessed by individual staff members and, (d) critiques of the system by staff members responsible for its operation.

Shaw (1986, p. 145) reports positive and stable staff reactions to automation over a one year period at Indiana State University. Understanding and positive attitudes were attributed to the use of written news memos, general meetings, and specialized subcommittees, which provided staff with opportunities to expand their knowledge and contribute to the automation process.

Overview of Systems

An online public access catalog is the most common addition currently planned for automation at college and university libraries. Sitts (1985) reported the following summary of library automation in 92 ARL institutions:

Among operational systems, the five most-often-reported uses for automation are:

- database searching (92)
- cataloging/utility (89)
- administrative (85)
- interlibrary loan (87)
- serials/union list (57).

Of libraries planning to automate functions, the five most frequent responses are:

- online catalog (58)
- serials check-in/claim (43)
- reserve room (39)
- cataloging/local (30)
- circulation (29).

When libraries report on modifying systems, they most often reported:

- acquisitions (10)
- circulation (8)
- cataloging/local (6). (p. 4)

Additional automated functions include collection development (27), bibliographic instruction (10), and telefacsimile transmission (14).

Camp, et al. (1987) surveyed 201 (137 small, 55 medium, and 18 large) academic libraries at four year institutions. Respondents reported plans for implementation of online systems for the following functions:

- Online public access catalog   57.1 %   (120)
- Circulation   51.4 %   (108)
- Serials control   48.6 %   (102)
- Acquisitions   40.5 %   (85)
- Interlibrary loan   32.8 %   (21)
- Integrated systems   53.9 %   (96)

Potter (1986) identifies three types of automated library systems by source: turnkey systems, from commercial vendors; locally-developed, marketed systems; and, "home-grown" systems. Turnkey systems were originally designed for small to medium size libraries, and offered many features of integrated systems. The most commercially successful of these, CLSI's LIBS 100 system, includes integrated circulation, public access catalog, acquisitions, cataloging, and interlibrary loan modules. A CLSI upgrade, called CL-CAT, includes browsing, menu-driven keyword searching, and command-driven boolean and keyword access to most parts of the catalog record. Maintenance and reprogramming are performed by the vendor, so that it is unnecessary for the library to employ a programmer or systems specialist.

Potter notes that the market for turnkey systems in the early 1980s was highly competitive, and some vendors had difficulty meeting contractual commitments. Other vendors were criticized for trying to service too many sites, and consequently falling behind in systems development. Walton and Bridge (1988) report, however, that in 1986 and 1987, the market for these systems grew dramatically. As hardware costs dropped and more libraries were able to automate, 14 American and Canadian turnkey vendors installed 263 systems. The distinction between vendor-marketed and locally developed, marketed systems, such as NOTIS and VTLS, is also beginning to blur as both NOTIS and VTLS have incorporated—NOTIS, as a wholly-owned subsidiary of Northwestern University—and established independent marketing/systems development facilities. Turnkey vendors have also installed systems in large libraries; the largest served by Data Research Associates, Los Angeles County Public Library, holds 4,193,000 volumes and has 430 online terminals. OCLC has been very successful in marketing its LS/2000 system to medium size academic libraries.

Of marketed systems popular with large university libraries, Northwestern's NOTIS, and the VTLS system of the Virginia Polytechnic Institute are the most successful. CARL, a system, developed by the Colorado Alliance of Research Libraries, and marketed by Eyring Research Institute of Salt Lake City, Utah, is a simple and powerful system, featuring keyword "name" and "word" searches. It has been installed by the Pike's Peak Library District as MAGGIE III (Potter, 1986).

NOTIS has been installed in more than 80 libraries, about half of which operate the system on a dedicated minicomputer, and half on a mainframe in the university's computing center. Installation of a system such as NOTIS requires local decisions about compatible hardware and telecommunications, and employment of a full-time programmer or systems librarian for local adaptation and maintenance (Corey, 1988).

In-house development of integrated library systems requires a very significant long-term investment in programming time and funding. ORION's first subsystem was in development in the 1960s; NOTIS started in the 1970s. LCS, at Ohio State University, the oldest online library system, now provides circulation status/information. The University of Illinois at Urbana-Champaign has linked LCS to Western Library Network (WLN) software, providing a full online catalog with WLN authority control, plus circulation status and the ability to place online interlibrary loan requests (Potter, 1986, p. 124). MELVYL, serving nine campuses of the University of California, is distinguished by its powerful telecommunications features, and already included boolean and keyword searching at the time of the CLR national online catalog use study in 1982.

Linked and Integrated Systems

Potter (1986, p. 126) defines an integrated system as one that supports two or more library functions by sharing common files and programs, and a linked system as one for which pathways between individual systems have been established so that information from each system can be viewed from the same terminal.

Within an integrated system, all information pertaining to an item can be viewed from one terminal, and, as illustrated by the previous description of ORION, all records pertaining to a bibliographic item can be updated simultaneously. Integrated systems, such as ORION, NOTIS and MELVYL are seen as the ideal in much of the literature, however Hirshon's (1986) survey of 12 institutions found few purely integrated systems. Potter argues that the advantages of integrated systems can be achieved through linkages which avoid some of the pitfalls of integration. He notes three disadvantages of integrated systems: (a) An integrated system is tied to a single source, vendor or systems office, for upgrades and new subsystems. (b) All subsystems of the integrated system may not be of equal quality; linking allows one to choose the best available system for each function. (c) Functions of the integrated system may be so closely related that the demands which one operation places on the computer may degrade the operation of another; linked systems operate separate programs, so that interference of one with another is unlikely, even though they may be run on the same computer. Examples of linkage in addition to that of WLN and LCS at the University of Illinois, are several systems which link Innovative Interfaces' INNOVACQ microcomputer acquisitions system to their online catalogs (Potter, 1986). The F.W. Faxon MICROLINX serials control system can also be linked to a number of other library systems, including NOTIS and VTLS (Walton and Bridge, 1988, p. 43).

SITE-SPECIFIC COST ESTIMATION

Cost estimates for adaptable systems such as NOTIS, and especially for local systems development, are not practical without consideration of local conditions such as campus geography, computing center fees, and the previous level of automation. For example, if bibliographic records are already in MARC-compatible format, the conversion will be much less expensive and lengthy than retrospective conversion of printed catalog cards or machine readable, but incompatible records. Also, telecommunications costs for wiring several or many campus libraries will exceed those for a single centralized library.

A report prepared by James F. Corey (1988) for Duke University Libraries on the cost of installing NOTIS provides some general guidelines. In April 1987, the University's Internal Audit Department concluded that Duke could have a fully-integrated system, using a purchased software package, for less than the cost of participation in the BIS system of the Triangle Research Libraries Network. Adjusting the auditors' figures for anticipated increases in database size, workload, growth in the number of supported terminals, and the costs of indexing improvements, Corey estimated start-up and initial five-year expenses for purchase and operation of the NOTIS system under two possible configurations: (a) on a dedicated computer located in and maintained by the library, and (b) at the Duke University Computing Center for a monthly cost based on the Center's current fee structure. Corey's estimate for purchase, installation, and operation of a dedicated system over the first five years is $1,734,000. The estimated cost for purchase, installation, and operation at the Duke University Computing Center is estimated at between $3,431,000 and $3,962,000 over the first five years.

The estimates were based on data from the currently operating NOTIS sites which most closely resemble the Duke Libraries. Corey suggests that the estimates for operation at the University Computing Center could be refined via analysis of a month's worth of NOTIS activity from Auburn University or Clemson University, and comparison of the tape with the fee structure of the Duke University Computing Center. Corey's report recommends the dedicated system, noting, however, that hidden costs include provision of space and operations responsibility at Perkins Library, and that costs for the second option could be reduced, as they have been at other institutions, by agreeing to a flat monthly fee for operation of NOTIS at the University's computing center.

Corey emphasizes the need for adequate telecommunications, especially where addition of keyword and boolean searching capabilities is anticipated. Cross references, keyword, and boolean searching are expensive in terms of power usage and response time. Software controls in NOTIS do, however, provide options for limiting the amount of keyword and boolean searching, thus controlling cost impacts. Corey's estimates included software, hardware, installation, training, travel, and local programming (a position upgrade for the systems librarian), but excluded network upgrades, file upgrades (bibliographic authorities, and serials conversion), local enhancements of NOTIS, and costs to allow searching of the database by other institutions.

The most commonly mentioned pitfalls in cost estimation are (a) underestimating the number of man-hours needed for programming in local systems development, and (b) underestimating the degree of in-house systems support that will be required to operate a leased or purchased system. On the issue of cost projection for local development, Flecker (1988) cautions against over-reliance on initial estimates:

> Most obvious is the need to emphasize that we are discussing estimates and that initial estimates are necessarily imprecise. Development estimating should be an iterative process, with the precision of the estimate increasing over time as the system comes to be more fully understood and the inevitable pitfalls perceived.

When local systems development is contemplated, site-specific factors such as physical distribution of branch collections, user characteristics, and data processing support are compounded by potential changes, over the years needed for system design and programming, in administration, personnel, salary requirements of programmers, hardware costs, and in the technology itself. Some of these changes—technological advances, for example—are beneficial; others, such as higher salary requirements for programmers, or difficulty in attracting and retaining qualified personnel, may increase costs and slow development. It is not possible to predict all of these factors at the outset. However, flexibility in finance and design will allow libraries to embrace unforeseen advantages while coping with difficulties.

CONVERSION AND IMPLEMENTATION: EFFECTS ON LIBRARY OPERATIONS AND SERVICE

Freedman (1984) and Harrington (1986) describe the impact of integrated systems on library technical services divisions. Manual operations in acquisitions, cataloging, circulation control, and other departments produced physical files, which, except for the card catalog, were usually accessible only to the personnel maintaining them. With automation, everyone in the library has access to the same information, ending isolation and specialization based on control of bibliographic information. Freedman predicts that future working relationships among library departments will be based on shared knowledge and professional skills. Stevenson (1983) also notes problems with the traditional isolation and over-specialization of technical services, and sees the advantages of integration, with technical and public services both participating in bibliographic instruction, and reference librarians suggesting subject headings and access features for online catalogs.

Several factors specific to shared cataloging began to alter the management of technical services even before the advent to integrated library systems:

1. Work flow became dependent upon the availability of network terminals. For maximum efficient use of hardware and telecommunications costs, terminals were designated for batch input and copy cataloging.
2. Items having no OCLC record, or inadequate records, were sent to original cataloging or to the backlog; most current items were processed by copy catalogers.
3. Telecommunications charges and network downtime, rather than local factors, often determined optimal work hours.
4. Cataloging quality was evaluated, and error reports issued, by network personnel and "master catalogers" at other institutions in addition to cataloging department heads and colleagues in the department.

Hafter (1986) identifies the increased network visibility of each cataloger's work, and the isolation of original catalogers from the normal work flow of the technical services division as factors profoundly affecting the work and professional orientation of catalog librarians at large universities. Her study, one of the few based on empirical research, consisted of in depth interviews with original catalogers and administrators at research universities, and with representatives of the OCLC, RLIN and the Western Library Network. Hafter found that original catalogers are often isolated from other library activities. They have limited or no access to terminals for the online catalogs to which they contribute, and, because they work with the 'dregs'—materials not acquired by the Library of Congress, or so specialized that they are not available elsewhere—each cataloger, isolated from the current literature being processed through copy cataloging, must cover a subject range so broad that he or she cannot keep up with terminology or maintain a subject specialization.

Several institutions have attempted to counteract the negative aspects of automation by decentralizing technical processes. For example, Hugh Atkinson, at the University of Illinois at Urbana-Champaign (Williams, 1987), experimented with physically decentralized subject units incorporating subject-oriented selection, original cataloging, and reference; the Virginia Technical Institute has organized cataloging "teams" including original and copy catalogers who work together to organize all materials in a specific subject literature; other institutions have created separate units for collection development, acquisition, and cataloging of literature in Oriental or Slavic languages.

The term, "deprofessionalization" is often associated with automation of technical services. However, not all sources concur with Hafter's gloomy conclusions on professional cataloging. For example, Bishoff's (1987) definition of the role of professional catalogers in the online library may be summarized as follows: The professional contribution to bibliographic control is not equated with narrow-minded adherence to cataloging rules; knowledge of patrons' searching strategies is essential for effective cataloging. Addressing library education, Speller and Burgin (1987) note that there is a need to look more closely at a basic question in librarianship: How do people use information? The traditional cognitive skills of the librarian are needed in conjunction with an understanding of new technologies in order to provide effective intellectual access to information.

Assessing the potential impact on public services, Ferguson (1986) predicts that subject searching online may place a premium on subject specialization for reference librarians. Reference librarians will also need to become familiar with MARC formats in order to exploit them for improvement of databases. Telephone reference interviews may increase with the number of distributed terminals in offices and users dialing-up from home. With increasing sophistication and inclusiveness, online catalogs will allow patrons and reference staff to access more resources within and beyond the walls of the library from a single terminal. Inclusiveness must, however, include completing retrospective conversion of the card catalog as well as access to non-book sources (e.g., manuscripts, sound recordings, videos, etc.). Public services staff should be assured a voice in assessing and prioritizing changes in automation. Additional use studies will assist in system evaluation as patrons gain in searching expertise.

Automation alone does not appear to increase communication and cooperation between technical and public services; it may however increase awareness of access problems and aid in documentation. Interdependence may be facilitated in smaller libraries or operational units within a library. A pro-active attitude in favor of communication, and a mutual understanding of cataloging and reference functions in relation to patron access seem necessary to effect change. Anderson (1986) notes the dynamic relationship of personal reference service to the online catalog: the catalog is not intuitive, and cannot stand alone; patrons will continue to seek interaction with professional staff members for assistance in the retrieval, interpretation and assimilation of knowledge resources.

Visibility of work quality becomes apparent throughout the library with the adoption of an integrated system. Bibliographic records, serials holdings, circulation status, and acquisitions records are centrally stored on a machine readable database and visible at distributed terminals. Each department cooperates with others to build a single central file, and each staff member must share responsibility for the quality of the database. This required shift in staff attitudes from protection of locally created and maintained files, to cooperation, responsibility and accountability in the creation and maintenance of shared files is illustrated in McKinley's (1985) description of conversion to the ORION serials control subsystem at UCLA and at the University of California at Irvine:

> In an attempt to apportion responsibility for maintenance of the online records, both serials managers attempted to divide responsibility for various portions of an automated record among specialists on their staffs—ordering, binding, check-in and so forth—and found this to be an impossible task.
>
> Independently, serials managers in both libraries reached the same conclusions. The staff would have to learn to work together in creating and maintaining records. They would have to accept responsibility for all aspects of record creation and maintenance (p. 57).

Rhine (1986) and Sandore and Baker (1987) discuss personnel issues in automation, each stressing a theme repeated throughout the literature, the need to inform employees on all levels about how their role in automated processes will serve organizational goals, and to solicit input from employees in the planning process. McKinley's (1985) description of contrasting experiences at UCLA and the University of California at Irvine illustrates this point: At UCI, the serials department staff and management were involved in planning from the outset of the selection process, and actively participated in planning and monitoring implementation of the ORION serials control module. Processing delays and staff frustration were minimized by the cooperative efforts of personnel responsible for planning, implementation, and operation of the system. At UCLA, on the other hand, an independent department was established to plan serials automation. Poor communication between this systems unit and the Serials Department later resulted in substantial ordering and processing delays.

Henn and Sellberg (1987) report that much of the early planning for reorganization prior to implementation of IO at the University of Indiana, Bloomington took place in confidential meetings. The absence of open communications at this stage had unfortunate consequences for morale and system implementation:

> The appearance of secrecy and the lack of staff involvement during the early stages of reorganization planning hindered implementation and affected the morale of some employees. It would have been preferable to discuss the need for reorganization with all the staff and then ask for their specific recommendations in building the plan (p. 32).

Is organizational change really necessary with automation? As McKinley reports, the UCLA and UC Irvine serials managers concluded that it is not:

> The jobs that were performed at typewriters or with pen and pencil are now done at terminal keyboards. After carefully considering various possibilities, the serials managers at UCLA and UCI decided that no organizational changes were necessary simply as a result of having replaced a manual operation with an automated one . . . While there may be isolated exceptions, workers who typed or wrote on cards are happily typing on keyboards and speaking the new jargon. No organizational changes have been necessary because of individual reluctance to change (p. 58–60).

While organizational change is rarely required as a result of staff resistance to automation, or from the inability of employees to learn new technologies, Horny (1987) reports that organizational streamlining of Northwestern University library operations following the development of NOTIS has resulted in elimination of 2.5 professional positions, 5.53 support staff positions, and in upgrading of several support staff positions.

Reorganization at Northwestern (Horny, 1987) seems to reflect the transition from a departmentalized personnel structure and fragmented set of manual files, to functional organization around a shared bibliographic database. A systems analyst was hired in 1967; in 1970, mail services were transferred from the Technical Services division to the Administrative Services division. In anticipation of a serials record conversion project and online serials control, a Serials department was created in 1970; concurrently, a Search department was created to serve both the Order department and the Catalog department with unduplicated bibliographic searching information. A librarian and several typists and other employees in the Search, Order, and Catalog departments moved to positions in the Library's Data Center, a newly formed department under Technical Services. By 1978, it was decided to merge Search and Order as sections of a new department, Acquisitions. The Bindery and Marking departments were eventually converted to subsections of the Cataloging department; non-serials binding was transferred in 1982 to a newly created Conservation department within the Collection Management division. In short, operations related to intellectually creating order and cataloging records; physically receiving and labeling new materials; and electronically providing access to the online database were consolidated and retained under Technical Services, while preservation and inter-office mail, which are functionally unrelated to acquiring and organizing the collection, were re-allocated to more appropriate divisions.

At Indiana University (Henn and Sellberg, 1987), monographic acquisitions and copy cataloging were aligned to streamline redundant activities and free personnel for the task of online catalog implementation and database cleanup. Administrative reorganization prior to implementation of the IO system at Bloomington resulted in creation of a small catalog management department responsible for coordination of automation planning and database management. No additional positions were created. Initial advantages of a small systems staff cited by Henn and Sellberg (1987, p. 28) include (a) facilitating development of new procedures and workflows, (b) freeing supervisors to provide maximum attention to each employee as new procedures are learned, and, (c) freeing the department head to coordinate plans for database development.

The most common organizational change associated with library automation is probably that of appointing a systems librarian or establishing a systems office. Open communication and cooperation with other departments is essential for successful functioning of a systems operations whether they are coordinated by a newly-created office for automation or by a catalog management department organized from the existing Technical Services structure.[5]

CONCLUSIONS

Long-range Planning and Funding:

The cost of computer hardware is declining, enabling more institutions to go online or expand and update existing systems. However, the choice of certain types of searching and indexing features may profoundly affect computing and telecommunications costs. In addition, planners are advised to budget telecommunications and computer support to exceed considerably the initial demands of the system. The diversity of available programs and equipment shows no immediate prospect of lessening. Libraries face many choices and risks in planning integrated systems, and must therefore concentrate on long-range planning and cost-benefit estimations.

Long-term funding of automation through a budget independent of those for library materials and operations is important for maintenance and future conversion to more advanced systems. Initial procurement and implementation are often made possible by a special institutional or external grant. Allocations for library systems are sometimes coordinated with expansion of the university computing center, or they may accompany a change in library administration or administrative philosophy. It should be emphasized that bottom line estimates from vendors, and cost comparison with other installations are grossly insufficient and inadequate. There are many site-specific factors to be considered, for example, the number of libraries served and their geographic distribution, anticipated growth of the database, and fee structures of the computing center.

In the planning process, access and operational needs can be defined and systematically compared to available system features. The relative advantages of linked and integrated subsystems should be considered. The choice between a dedicated minicomputer, to be located in the library or the computing center, or a shared mainframe in the computing center will depend on existing hardware configurations, fee structures of the computing center, and the degree of in-house control desired by the library.

Planning and Implementation Resources:

Directors should identify and mobilize planning and implementation resources, including staff, university administrators, the university computing center, consultants, colleagues, and private or governmental sources for automation grants. Planners should be aware of state-of-the-art developments in library automation, and should anticipate future trends, maintaining a flexible position for expansion and eventual reconversion to an alternate system.

Early involvement of employees in the planning process will improve the quality and viability of the system, as well as the morale and enthusiasm of librarians and support staff. Staff on all levels may offer specific areas of expertise and detailed knowledge of operating requirements. Plans to include systems positions within previously existing departments may be more success-ful and cost-effective than creation of a separate management structure for automation. Systems responsibilities can be linked to traditional areas of biblio-graphic control, for example, catalog maintenance and access services.

Equal Access:

A decade of research and experience with online public access catalogs has demonstrated their popularity and success in providing the basic information functions expected of a library catalog. Dramatically enhanced depth of index-ing, together with index browsing, and boolean and keyword searching, provide a level of access not possible with previous catalog technologies. In addition, the online catalog has been integrated with other library information systems to the extent that both patrons and staff may view and utilize the same bibliographic records, authority files, indexes, and circulation/order information. Duplication of effort has been largely eliminated. The catalog is available from remote locations, and at times when the library building is not staffed.

As Adams (1988) notes in her review of "democratic" and "authoritarian" aspects of online catalogs, now is the time to study and assess the diversity of systems and patron access features which have been developed and proposed. Future standardization may reduce the possibilities for making full use of this technology to provide complete and equitable intellectual access to library materials. Carefully prioritizing optional features will aid in decisionmaking. Consultation with colleagues at other automated libraries, and with outside experts in cost analysis and systems development seems more than justified.

Knowledge of patron behavior and research needs is basic to system design. User and staff surveys, transaction log analysis, circulation studies, and analysis of terminology and bibliographies in various subject specialties may contribute to this understanding. Interactive features, indexing languages, and files should be designed or selected to meet the needs of a variety of patrons, from undergradu-ates to scholars conducting advanced research. If a suitable level of detail cannot be achieved in the main catalog, access to specialized resources in the reference department can be facilitated via pointers from the online catalog to reference files.

Cost-effectiveness:

Should library automation plans be initiated for purposes of cost reduction and stream-lining technical processes, or for enhanced patron access to information and integration of reference resources? Upon beginning this research, the author assumed this to be a valid either/or question.

First, there is little evidence in the literature to support claims of cost reduction in materials processing. Many sources imply or demonstrate that personnel costs are reduced as support staff assume responsibility for cataloging the 90 odd percent of items located on the OCLC database; however, the cost of automation has so far appeared to outweigh these savings. For example, Horny (1987) documents significant savings in the technical services personnel budget following automation at Northwestern; she does not however attempt to allocate substantial automation and hardware and costs among divisions, stating simply that the benefits of the integrated system and its costs are distributed throughout technical and public services. Secondly, despite the efficiency and volume of production afforded by copy cataloging units, most large universities still have backlogs of uncataloged materials, and bibliographic records are often divided between the card catalog and the online catalog database.

Design and applications indicate that benefits of automation related to the quality and cost-effectiveness of traditional library functions such as acquisitions, cataloging, reference, bibliography, and accounting will result not from processing speed, but rather from (a) reducing duplication of effort when inputting or searching data, (b) the integration and sharing of information resources, and (c) depth of indexing and new access methodologies. As the library's database is shared by patrons and library staff, and as both perform searching and input processes, the economy of effort and enhanced access afforded by the new technologies should theoretically benefit public and technical services in equal measure.

The current emphasis in the library literature favoring patron access as the over-riding justification of expenditures for automation, is, in the opinion of this author, somewhat misguided, and possibly a reaction to the failure of previous assurances that automation would prove its worth in quantitative measures of volume and speed. Operational advantages of automation are more likely to be found in qualitative measures of economy of effort, accuracy, flexibility, and depth of access to processing information. Whether these benefits will result in measurably greater efficiency for library operations or patron research efforts remains to be demonstrated. The methodology of such a test is a topic for further research.

Effects on Library Service and Library Employment:

The functional distinctions between patron and librarian appear to be changing—librarians have less responsibility for repetitive clerical functions, manual retrieval of exclusive information, and coordination of disparate catalog resources. Both patrons and librarians have new responsibilities to acquire computer skills, comprehend a new way of organizing information, and interpret and manipulate records through an interactive system. Patrons are assuming a more active and self-sufficient role for retrieval of citations and materials. In other words, access to library information is becoming less a mysterious activity reserved for the specialist, whose primary public responsibility is to interpret the system for the patron and deliver the requested material.

Will access of patrons and librarians to the same user-friendly database mean that librarianship will in the future be less important or challenging? On the contrary, case studies in automation and the literature on library education indicate that freedom from clerical and finding tasks will enhance the intellectual challenge and professionalism of librarianship. Reference librarians know that patrons do not look for books and journals, but for answers to questions and solutions to problems. Access to books, articles, microforms, and documents will often satisfy patron inquiries, and many computer-competent users may never approach a librarian except to ask directions to the rest room or to report problems with computer hardware. However, professional reference research, and help from librarians in formulating research strategies and interpreting information are essential to the pursuit of knowledge for many patrons. Catalog technologies serve to simplify the bibliographic surrogate and its retrieval, they do not clarify the value and meaning of recorded knowledge. The intellectual and educational role of academic librarianship will be enhanced as finding and processing tasks are deprofessionalized.

Patrons benefit also from the intellectual and professional efforts of librarians who establish cataloging and classification codes and local procedures, formulate subject headings, structure bibliographic databases, and format screen displays. The educational role of librarians in the academic community is further enhanced by development of bibliographic instruction programs and cooperation with faculty to structure library research into the undergraduate curriculum.

This paper has identified those factors in library automation which management must continue to examine carefully, both from the perspective of library operations and the perspective of patron access. The decisions to be made are neither simple nor inexpensive. However, planning and expenditures will be more effective when they are based on relevant statistical data, specific comparison of design specifications, and case studies in cost analysis, personnel, implementation, and maintenance. Decisions considered within the context of long-range institutional goals, with a keen understanding of research and education, economic realities, political resources, and local conditions, will reap the greatest long-term benefit for the library, the scholar, the college, and the university.

NOTES

1. Addressing issues of privacy and protection in design of library systems, Crawford (1987) notes that a good system protects the patron from the system, the patron from other patrons and agencies, and the system from the patron. In view of the success which law enforcement agencies have had in obtaining hard copy circulation records, librarians must be vigilant in opposing any automated system which would store a permanent record of searching or circulation information linked to patron names or identity numbers.

2. For a description of various authority control programs offered by bibliographic networks and library automation software vendors, see Taylor, et al. (1985).

3. Automated quality control is also addressed by Morita (1986).

4. Matthews (1986a, pp. 6–8) outlines the basic elements of a request for proposal for automated systems.

5. Post and Watson (1983) and Sessions and Post (1986) discuss these and other issues in relation to conversion from one online system to another at the University of California, Chico.

REFERENCES

Adams, Judith A. (1988, February 15). The computer catalog: a democratic or authoritarian technology? *Library Journal, 113*, 31–36.

Anderson, Rosemary. (1986). The online catalog and the library manager. [Paper presented at the ALA Conference in Los Angeles, June 1983.] In Joseph R. Matthews, (Ed.), *The impact of online catalogs* (pp. 71–80). New York: Neal-Schuman Publishers.

Auld, Larry. (1982, October/December). Authority control: an eighty-year review. *Library Resources and Technical Services, 26*(4), 319–330.

Avram, Henriette D. (1984, January). Authority control in its place. *Journal of Academic Librarianship, 9*(6), 331–333.

Avram, Henriette D. and Wiggins, Beacher. (1987, May). The role of the Linked Systems Project in cooperation and resource sharing among libraries. *Libraries and computing centers: issues of mutual concern, 2* (insert of the May 1987 *Journal of Academic Librarianship*).

Avram, Henriette D. (1988, January). The National Coordinated Cataloging Program. *Library Resources and Technical Services, 32*(2), 111–115.

Axford, H. William. (1979). The great rush to automated catalogs: will it be management or muddling through? (Paper presented at a 1977 conference on management issues in automated cataloging, sponsored by the Associated Colleges of the Midwest) In Gore, Daniel, Kimbrough, Joseph, and Spyers-Duran, Peter (Eds.), *Requiem for the card catalog* (pp. 169–180). Westport, CT: Greenwood Press.

Bishoff, Lizbeth J. (1987, September). Who says we don't need catalogers? *American Libraries, 18*(8), 694–696.

Bland, Robert. (1986, Winter). Quality control in a shared online catalog database: the Lambda experience. *Technical Services Quarterly, 4*(2), 43–58.

Busch, B. J. (editor). (1985). *Automation and reorganization of technical and public services* (Spec kit 112). Washington, DC: Office of Management Studies, Association of Research Libraries.

Camp, John A., et al. (1987, July). Survey of online systems in U.S. academic libraries. *College & Research Libraries, 48*(4), 339–350.

Carpenter, Michael and Svenonius, Elaine. (1985). *Foundations of cataloging: a sourcebook.* Littleton, CO.: Libraries Unlimited.

Chan, Lois Mai. (1986). *Library of Congress Subject Headings: Principles and Application.* 2nd ed. (pp. 333–369). Littleton, CO.: Libraries Unlimited).

Chang, Roy. (1987, Summer). Relational database management systems: a review. *Technical Services Quarterly, 4*(4), 85–93.

Cochrane, Pauline A. (1983). A paradigm shift in library science. In, *Redesign of catalogs and indexes for improved online subject access: selected papers of Pauline A. Cochrane* (pp. 89–90). Phoenix, AZ: Oryx Press, 1986. Reprint of: Guest Editorial: a paradigm shift in library science. *Information Technology and Libraries* (March 1983), 2(1), 3–4.

Corey, James F. (1988, March 28). Cost estimates to use NOTIS at Duke University. Unpublished report.

Crawford, Walt. (1984). *MARC for library use.* White Plains, NY: Knowledge Industry.

Crawford, Walt. (1986). *Technical standards: an introduction for librarians.* White Plains, NY: Knowledge Industry.

Crawford, Walt. (1987). *Public Access: Issues for Online Catalogs.* Boston: G.K. Hall.

Davis, Betty Bartlett. (1987. Managing the online bibliographic database for an integrated library system. *Technical Services Quarterly, 5*(1), 49–56.

Day, Elaine. (1988). Automation of library services: a survey of change in library catalogs and staff interactions at a public and a college library. Unpublished MS.

DeHart, Florence E. & Matthews, Karen. (1986, Fall). The catalog department's legacy to OPAC subject searchers. *Technical Services Quarterly 4*(1), 3–10.

Fayollat, James and Coles, Elizabeth. (June 1987). Database management principles of the UCLA library's ORION system. *Information Technology in Libraries, 6*(2), 102–115.

Fenly, Judith G. and Wiggins, Beacher (compliers). (1988). *The Linked Systems Project: a networking tool for libraries.* (OCLC library, information, and computer science series; 6) Dublin, Ohio: OCLC Online Computer Library Center.

Ferguson, Douglas K. (1986). Reference and online catalogs: reflections and possibilities. [Paper presented at the ALA Conference in Los Angeles, June 1983.] In Joseph R. Matthews (Ed.), *The Impact of Online Catalogs* (pp. 25–33). New York: Neal-Schuman Publishers.

Flecker, Dale P. (1988, March 25). Unpublished letter from the Associate Director of Planning and Systems, Harvard University Library, to Jerry D. Campbell, Vice Provost and University Librarian, Duke University.

Freedman, Maurice J. (1984, June 15). Automation and the future of technical services. *Library Journal, 109*(11), 1197–1202.

Fussler, Herman H. (1965, October). Discussion of The general research library and the area-studies programs by F. H. Wagman. *Library Quarterly, 35,* 355–360.

Fussler, Herman H. (1973). *Research libraries and technology.* Chicago: University of Chicago Press.

Genaway, David C. (1984). *Integrated online library systems: principles, planning and implementation.* White Plains, NY: Knowledge Industry.

Gorman, Michael. (1979). Cataloging and the new technologies. In M. Carpenter and E. Svenonius, *Foundations of cataloging: a sourcebook* (p. 242–252). Littleton, CO.: Libraries Unlimited, 1985. Reprinted from Maurice J. Freedman and S. Michael Malinconico (Eds.), *The Nature and Future of the Catalog* (pp. 127–136). Phoenix, AZ: Oryx.

Gorman, Michael. (1987). The organization of academic libraries in the light of automation. In Hewitt, Joe A. (Ed.), *Advances in library automation and networking, Volume 1* (pp. 151–168). Greenwich, CT: JAI Press.

Grossman, George S. (1984-85). The totally online library: Northwestern's integrated library system. *Law Library Journal, 77*(1), 47–57.

Hafter, Ruth. (1986). *Academic librarians and cataloging networks: visibility, quality control, and professional status.* New York: Greenwood Press.

Harrington, Sue Anne. (Winter, 1986). The changing environment in technical services. *Technical Services Quarterly, 4*(2), 7–29.

Henn, Barbara and Sellberg, Roxanne. (1987, Summer). Midway to automation: reorganizing technical services prior to online catalog implementation. *Technical Services Quarterly, 4*(4), 21–32.

Hernon, Peter and McClure, Charles R. (1986). Unobtrusive reference testing: the 55 percent rule. *Library Journal, 111*(7), 37–41.

Highsmith, Anne L. (1986, December). Library processing systems and the man/machine interface. *Information Technology and Libraries, 5*(4), 267–279.

Hildreth, Charles R. (Spring, 1987). Beyond boolean: designing the next generation of online catalogs. *Library Trends, 35*(4)647–685.

Hirshon, Arnold. (1986). *Automated library systems in ARL libraries* (ARL Spec. Kit, no. 126). Washington, D.C.: Office of Management Studies, Association of Research Libraries.

Horny, Karen L. (1987, January/March). Fifteen years of automation of technical services staffing. *Library Resources and Technical Services, 31*(1), 69–76.

Hudson, Judith. (1986, March). Cataloging for the local online system. *Information Technology and Libraries, 5*(1), 5–27.

Jamieson, Alexis J., Dolan, Elizabeth and Declerck, Luc. (1986, November). Keyword searching vs. authority control in an online catalog. *Journal of Academic Librarianship, 12*(5), 277–83.

Lawrence, Gary S. (1985, January/March). System features for subject access in the online catalog. *Library Resources and Technical Services, 29*(1), 16–51.

Lawrence, Gary S. (1986). Online catalogs and systems designers. [Paper presented at the ALA Conference in Los Angeles, June 1983.] In Joseph R. Matthews (Ed.), *The Impact on Online Catalogs* (pp. 1–14). New York: Neal-Schuman Publishers.

Logan, Susan L. (Spring, 1987). The Ohio State University's Library Control System: from circulation to subject access and authority control. *Library Trends, 35*(4), 539–551.

Markey, Karen. (1984). *Subject searching in library catalogs: before and after the introduction of online catalogs.* (OCLC Library, Information, and Computer Science Series; 4) Dublin, Ohio: OCLC Online Computer Library Center.

Markey, Karen. (1986). Users and the online catalog: subject access problems. [Paper presented at the ALA Conference in Los Angeles, June 1983.] In Joseph R. Matthews (Ed.), The Impact of Online Catalogs (pp. 35–69). New York: Neal-Schuman Publishers.

Markey, Karen and Miksa, Francis. (October/December 1987). Subject access literature 1986. Library Resources and Technical Services, 31(4), 343–344.

Martin, Susan K. (1984, June 15). The new technologies and library networks. Library Journal, 109(11), 1194–1196.

Matthews, Joseph R. (1985). *Public access to online catalogs: a planning guide for managers* (2nd ed.). (Library automation planning guides series; no. 1) New York: Neal-Schuman Publishers.

Matthews, Joseph R. (1986). The online catalog and technical services. [Paper presented at the ALA Conference in Los Angeles, June 1983.] In Joseph R. Matthews (Ed.), *The Impact of Online Catalogs* (p. 15–24). New York: Neal-Schuman Publishers.

Matthews, Joseph R. (1986a). *Guidelines for selecting automated systems.* Chicago: Library and Information Technology Association, American Library Association.

Matthews, Joseph R., Lawrence, Gary S., and Ferguson, Douglas K. (editors). (1983). *Using online catalogs: a nationwide survey.* New York: Neal-Schuman Publishers.

McCallum, Sally H. (1987). The Linked Systems Project: implications for library automation and networking. In Hewitt, Joe A. (Ed.), *Advances in library automation and networking, Volume 1* (pp. 1–20). Greenwich, CT: JAI Press.

McDonald, David R. (1987, July). MARC: the foundation of library automation. *Libraries and Computing Centers: Issues of Mutual Concern, 3* (Insert of the July 1987 *Journal of Academic Librarianship*).

McKinley, Margaret. (1985, Winter). Management of serials automation: two libraries in transition. *Drexel Library Quarterly 21*(1), 50–61.

McKinley, Margaret. (1986, Summer). Serials automation at UCLA. *The Serials Librarian,* 10(4), 13–24.

Meyer, James. (1985). NOTIS: The System and its Features. *Library Hi Tech, 3*(2), 81–90.

Mitev, Nathalie Nadia. (1986, April). Users and ease of use: online catalogues' raison d'etre. *Program, 20*(2), 111–119.

Moran, Barbara B. (1984). *Academic libraries: the changing knowledge centers of colleges and universities.* (ASHE-ERIC Higher Education Research Report No. 8) Washington D.C.: Association for the Study of Higher Education.

Morita, Ichiko. (1986). Quality control of online catalogs: automation vs. human control. In Nitecki, Danuta A. (Ed.), *Energies for Transition: Proceedings of the Fourth National Conference of the Association of College and Research Libraries, Baltimore, Maryland, April 9–12, 1986* (pp. 44–46). Chicago: Association of College and Research Libraries.

Paterson, Judy. (1987, December). Preparing for the automated catalog. *Colorado Libraries*, *13*(4),17–19.

Popa, Opritsa D., Metzger, Deborah A., and Singleton, James A. (1988, May). Teaching search techniques on the computerized catalog and on the traditional card catalog: a comparative study. *College and Research Libraries, 49(3), 263–274.*

Post, William & Watson, Peter, (editors). (1983. *Online catalog: the inside story.* Chico, Calif.: Ryan Research International.

Potter, William Gray. (1986, April). Online catalogs in North America: an overview. *Program,* *20*(2), 120–30.

Potter, William Gray. (1988, May). Library automation: hitting the links. In, *Libraries and Computing Centers: Issues of Mutual Concern, 8.* (Insert in the May 1988 *Journal of Academic Librarianship.*)

Rhine, Leonard. (1986). Effects of the adoption of an integrated online system on a technical services department. *Library Hi Tech*, Issue 16, 89–92.

Rice, James. (1988, February 15). Serendipity and holism: the beauty of OPACs. *Library Journal*, 113(3), 138–141.

Rocke, Hans J., and Ross, Johanna C. (1985, Spring/Summer). Online catalogs for and by librarians. *Technical Services Quarterly, 2*(3/4), 1–10.

Saffady, William. (1987, September, October). Integrated systems installations: characteristics and experience of integrated library systems installations. *Library Technology Reports, 23*(5).

Sandore, Beth and Baker, Betsy. (1987, Fall). Changing concepts of motivation and productivity in the library. *Illinois Libraries, 69*(2), 122–125.

Sessions, Judith, and Post, William. (1986). Moving from a first generation to a second generation online catalog database. In Danuta A. Nitecki (Ed.), *Energies for Transition: Proceedings of the Fourth National Conference of the Association of College and Research Libraries, Baltimore, Maryland, April 9–12, 1986* (pp. 236–238). Chicago: Association of College and Research Libraries.

Shaw, Debora. (1986, Summer). Staff opinions in library automation planning: a case study. *Special Libraries, 77*(3), 140–151.

Sitts, Maxine K. (1985). *The automation inventory of research libraries. Washington, D.C.: Office of Management Studies, Association of Research Libraries.*

Speller, Benjamin F. Jr. and Burgin, Robert. (1987, Summer). Library education in a telecommunications environment: a North Carolina perspective. *North Carolina Libraries, 45*(2), 70–72.

Stevenson, Gordon. (1983, Fall/Winter). Current issues in technical services. *The Reference Librarian, 9,* 31–41.

Taylor, Arlene G., Maxwell, Margaret F., and Frost, Carolyn O. (1985, April/June). Network and vendor authority systems. *Library Resources and Technical Services, 29*(2), 195–205.

University of California. Division of Library Automation. (1983, October). ORION: The UCLA Library's Online Information System. *DLA Bulletin, 3*(2,5), 10–11, 20.

Walton, Robert A. and Bridge, Frank R. (1988, April 1). Automated system marketplace 1987: maturity and competition. *Library Journal, 13*(6), 33–44.

Williams, James W. (1987, Summer). The decentralization of selected technical services at the University of Illinois at Urbana-Champaign. *Technical Services Quarterly, 4*(4), 5–19.

Wilson, Patrick. (1983, January/March). The catalog as access mechanism: background and concepts. Library Resources and Technical Services, 27(1), 4–17.

Winner, Langdon. (1986). *The whale and the reactor: a search for limits in an age of high technology.* Chicago: University of Chicago Press.

ACQUISITIONS MANAGEMENT:
THE INFRINGING ROLES OF ACQUISITIONS LIBRARIANS AND SUBJECT SPECIALISTS— AN HISTORICAL PERSPECTIVE

Barbara J. Henn

INTRODUCTION

After 30 years in library service in the United States, the position of subject specialist/bibliographer in academic research libraries remains a topic on which librarians have strong and varied opinions. One area of difference centers on the management responsibilities of the subject specialist and the points of overlap with the management duties of the acquisitions librarian. This study takes a close look at several areas of possible conflict in those duties.

To begin this examination, it is important to define the term subject specialist or bibliographer. Many nouns are used interchangeably when discussing such a

Advances in Library Administration and Organization,
Volume 8, pages 113-129.
Copyright © 1989 by JAI Press Inc.
All rights of reproduction in any form reserved.
ISBN: 0-89232-967-X

position. They include collection developer, area specialist, selector and manager. In this review such a role means that the individual works in an academic research library and spends at least 50 percent of the time in book selection duties.

This review first looks at the development of the role of subject specialist in academic libraries in the United States. It contrasts the original duties and place in the organizational structure with current practices. Next it scrutinizes the historical role of acquisitions librarians and the administrative duties allotted to those positions. The section which follows then discusses those areas where the role of each appears to infringe on the other. Finally, the study examines automation and other trends which impact on the future of research libraries and the anticipated effect of those trends on the positions and duties of both the subject specialist and acquisitions librarian. Proposals to alleviate the conflict and subjects for future study conclude the review.

ROLE OF THE SUBJECT SPECIALIST

Academic and research libraries in modern Europe grew out of monastery collections and the donation of collections from benefactors. These benefactors were usually men of wealth who had assembled significant special, private collections. Germany was the first country to develop the use of subject specialists to work with and continue to enlarge these distinct holdings. Those subject specialists were scholars in their own right.

The idea of the subject specialist position was developed in Germany in the last century. Branch libraries with specific book selection duties in a subject had been functioning for some time. Biskup discusses the *Fachreferent* or *Referent* as dating "back to the early years of this century, while the idea behind the system—placing of book selection in specific fields in the hands of library staff with high academic qualifications—may be traced to the Napoleonic era."[1] While Germany is cited as the place where the idea of librarians as subject specialists became prominent, other European countries also advanced this pattern. Subject specialists in other European libraries are listed in Danton's writing about national and university libraries.[2] These countries do not appear to place the same emphasis on the positions as is done in German libraries. The libraries of Great Britain developed the use of subject specialists in a time period similar to that of the development in the United States. Scrivener points out that the specialization has a short history in the British university library.[3]

John Hopkins University is identified as the first university in the United States to place an emphasis on research, similar to that which was done in German universities. The establishment of that university in the late 1800s had a major impact on the future direction of other university libraries and collections in this country. While the position of librarian did not change immediately, collecting patterns and goals to gather research materials became important to faculty and trustees. The growth of university libraries generally has run parallel to the economy of the United States. As the economy expanded in the 1920s, university libraries also flourished. The depression of the 1930s caused cutbacks in the programs of research libraries. During the 1940s and World War II, libraries were lucky to maintain the status quo. After this period university libraries in the United States started down a path of rapid change. This change included the development of the position of subject specialist. Duino has identified the period at the end of World War II as the time when these specialists began to appear in both Britain and America.[4]

The advent of Sputnik in 1958 initiated the increase in U.S. federal funding for education.[5] Sputnik alarmed the country and the Congress. It demonstrated that education, particularly the sciences, needed help to meet the challenge presented by Russia's launching of Sputnik. One approach by the Congress was to increase the federal funds for universities and their libraries. The early sixties, then, were a time when libraries had more of everything—bigger budgets, increased staff, more space, more technology, and more problems. The emphasis on increased research matched a growth in book production. Area studies were rewarded with federal monies. Universities had more enrollment and more administrators. The Higher Education Act of 1965 with its title IIC grants added to the growth in libraries' materials budgets. The first use of subject bibliographers in U.S. libraries was for interdisciplinary and area studies. These specialists were "familiar with the languages of the area in which intensive and interdisciplinary studies were beginning or were being greatly increased."[6] Haskell points out, though, that the positions were limited to those libraries which were large and building comprehensive collections in a variety of languages and subjects.[7] By the late sixties, a number of large university libraries had transferred selection responsibilities to specialists. These included Columbia, Cornell, Harvard, Indiana, Michigan, Stanford, UCLA, and Washington (at Seattle).[8] Even though the federal dollars disappeared in the early seventies, the shortage of librarians to deal with the changed environment continued.

One of the results of the shortage of librarians was the variety of tasks assigned to a new subject specialist. Besides the primary duty of selection, these bibliographer/subject specialists have had a mixture of additional responsibilities. The supplementary duties usually include advanced reference for graduate students and faculty and liaison with the departments and faculty for those subjects under their jurisdiction. Byrd lists other tasks: "They are sometimes required to serve in the general reference department; they regularly consult with public service and technical departments for advice and information; they can search for a lost book, show visitors around the library, serve on committees, and, in brief, in all ways conduct themselves as librarians whose objectives are service to patrons in need. These multiple assignments may include teaching formal courses in bibliography and cataloging."[9] Baatz's review revealed that area specialists"who deal with exotic language—Chinese, Japanese, Slavic, South and Southeast Asian, African, Hebrew—often supervise the acquisitions and cataloging of their materials, or actually do some or all of the cataloging. They also may suggest dealers to be used in procuring materials, and they may assign priorities for handling or cataloging volumes.''[10] The numerous responsibilities require that the subject specialist know the clients, the subject, and the library well, including problems and special proficiencies in each category. This allows the specialist to be a problem solver or "trouble shooter" for the clients served.[11]

The educational background of a subject specialist customarily includes courses at the university level on those subjects for which he or she will have collection responsibility. Some bibliographers complete a doctoral program in their field. Management experience is usually not a major part of the qualifications or employment history. In addition there is the opportunity for continuing education in the subject by taking courses at the university where they are employed and choosing workshops, seminars, and other limited programs offered by scholarly and professional associations. On-the-job training appears to be an underdeveloped area for some subject specialists. Knowledge of local technical service routines and policies may not be formally addressed. Public service procedures in interlibrary loan, computerized databases and general reference work may not seem to be significant for such a position. This lack of emphasis on in-house instruction may be the foundation for the philosophical and organizational difficulties which appear inherent in many such positions.

Subject specialists carry out these multiple assignments in a variety of organizational structures. When Sloan studied the organization of collection development in the early seventies, three types of functional units were in use:

1.   Specialists as part of a larger, functional unit,
2.   Specialists in a separately created unit, and
3.   Specialists in a temporary, separate unit.[12]

The third unit, one which is both temporary and separate, would seem the least desirable for effective collection development. Directors believed that collection development activity should be more closely coordinated with administration and reader services, rather than closely linked to the acquisitions unit.[13] Bryant's study, in the 1980s, listed seven different organizational configurations for collection development when in small academic, public, school, and special library systems.[14] Haskell summarizes these patterns, listing three areas of reporting as most typical—in acquisitions, reference, or a separate independent unit which reports to an assistant director of collection development.[15] The organizational structure of this group should depend on whether the focus is oriented to the book trade and processing or oriented to the client and his needs. If the former is true, then the logic is to structure the unit of subject specialist with technical services. If the second approach is the chosen route, then a structure within the public service area is most appropriate according to Smith.[16] The study of seven different academic libraries by Cline and Sinnott pictured this diversity of organization among the seven profiled. Subject bibliographers were structured anywhere from a separate department within technical services to a completely separate unit reporting directly to the Dean of University Libraries.[17] A recent survey by Sohn of the 93 academic libraries which are members of the Association of Research Libraries concluded that no specific organizational pattern was predominant in these libraries.[18] "More than half of the respondents (57.1 percent or 40 respondents) indicated that collection development is a separate unit within the library, while 17.1 percent (12) of the libraries have placed it in technical services and 14.3 percent (10) have placed it in public services."[19]

The conflict of the specialist's role as scholar versus that of manager compounds the confusion of organizational structures. The various assignments have both scholarly and managerial requirements. The balance needed for special, scholarly activities and the imprecise, managerial activities would seem to be in direct opposition for the bibliographer's time and ability to complete such tasks. These opposing needs can easily add to any morale problem which originates from the organizational structure. The growth in publishing and in the variety of formats takes additional selection time. While the subject specialist usually has the autonomy to concentrate on each aspect as he or she chooses, that same autonomy can be the source for further frustration. As Dickinson points out, "an individual who is and must be granted a great deal of freedom in the prosecution of some of his duties will very likely insist on at least as much freedom in carrying out other duties assigned to him, in spite of the fact that the collateral duties may and probably will be such as to require substantially more standardization, coordination, and control that is desirable or possible in collection development activities alone."[20] Likewise Scrivener argues that one of the disadvantages of subject specialists positions in the tendency toward "the establishment of a variety of individual systems—less compatible as time goes by."[21] This can make the subject specialist a focus of strife as his responsibilities overlap with both technical and public service units of the library. Add to this Smith's assertion that "perhaps, most important of all, however, has been the marked tendency, among specialist librarians, to expand their own range of activities."[22] When these attitudes and frictions are focused on the process of acquisitions, the situation becomes unpleasant for both the subject specialist and the acquisitions librarian.

ROLE OF THE ACQUISITIONS LIBRARIAN

Acquisitions work has been done by a variety of people during the brief history of university libraries in the United States. Selection for purchase was done by committees of trustees in the early years at some universities. From that group it passed to the faculty before being transferred to librarians. The lack of regular funding for purchases in the early years of university libraries resulted in donations being the predominant source for additions to the collection. Some funds were provided for purchases by monies from endowments, the sale of duplicates, student fines and fees, and other miscellaneous activities. Exchanges were another method for acquiring materials for the collection.

The acquisitions librarian historically has had administrative responsibility for the ordering and delivery of materials for the library's collection. The role has many facets to it. As Tuttle remarks, "I have always assumed that the bibliographer-selector came into existence because one person could not stretch time enough to both administer the acquisition function and coordinate selection."[23] Before this development, the position of acquisitions librarian plausibly grew out of the head librarian's lack of time to administer all the library's functions and oversee the purchasing process. Librarians in the colonial period of university libraries were prominent men. Sometimes they administered the libraries as part of their presidential duties. Others went on to be named presidents of their colleges and universities.

As the academic library staff became more professional in the 1920s, both the number of staff and the size of the collections increased. Women became part of this picture in increasing numbers at the same time. In some libraries the head of technical services had the responsibility for directly overseeing acquisitions. The growth in libraries and staff raised the idea of an assembly line format for acquisitions work by the 1940s. The multiple dimensions of the acquisitions role are expressed by Grieder's statement, "The acquisitions librarian should, ideally, possess the wisdom of Solomon, the patience of Job, the learning of J. S. Mill, and the charm of Alcibiades."[24]

The ten standard operations of an acquisitions unit are listed by Magrill and Hickey:

1. Obtaining information about proposed acquisitions,
2. Initiating the purchasing process by
    a. Selecting the vendor
    b. Preparing the order
    c. Encumbering the money,
3. Maintaining records on items ordered,
4. Receiving and checking materials,
5. Authorizing payment,
6. Clearing order records,
7. 'Special treatment' handling for continuations, gifts, and exchange,
8. Solving problems of claims, credits, and rushes,
9. Integrating the requirements of cooperative and special systems, like blanket orders and approval plans, into the regular order routines, and
10. Developing and analyzing performance statistics.[25]

Considering the administration of these operations, Reid and High have identified the tasks of the librarians who manage acquisitions, specifically excluding
collection development, as:

1. Designing and evaluating work flow,
2. Determining the format of order information files (including serials
   control),
3. Establishing and evaluating exchanges,
4. Monitoring expenditures,
5. Evaluating vendor performance,
6. Setting guidelines for:
   a. Searching and verifying,
   b. Selecting vendors,
   c. Authorizing payment,
   d. Disposing of unwanted materials,
7. Resolving issues not covered by guidelines.[26]

Others might add to this list such tasks as the establishing and evaluating of
out-of-print acquisitions policies and procedures and the coordination of solicited
and unsolicited gift processing. Any one of these activities could be the worthy
subject of a book, yet all of them are considered part of the day-to-day administrative activities of the acquisitions librarian. Grieder has another telling comment about all of these responsibilities. "And any acquisitions librarian will soon
discover that many fellow librarians outside his realm are very little better
informed about the nature of Acquisitions than are faculty and students."[27]

The business aspects of acquisitions always have placed heavy demands on the
acquisitions librarian. Wulfekoetter noted that the local regulations and restrictions of the accounting unit caused acquisitions departments of various libraries
to be less similar than other departments of the same libraries.[28] These financial
complexities have not diminished. Magrill compared the order activities in a
research library to those of a medium-sized business and believes they demand
sophisticated controls.[29]

The acquisitions librarian, unlike the subject specialist, has no clear pattern of
formal education as preparation to manage such a medium-sized business as
pursuing acquisition of library materials. Library schools typically offer a course
in technical services that devotes one or two sessions to the discussion of
acquisitions. If an acquisitions librarian has no previous business experience, the
first one or two years may prove to be a difficult and exhausting learning
experience. Even with a business background, learning local practices and lore is
time consuming, but basic to being an effective acquisitions librarian. In fact the
new acquisitions librarian generally will be trained by the staff in the department
about local idiosyncrasies. Taking accounting courses or other business courses
may be beneficial, but each university's accounting policies and practices are

unique and must be learned and understood before an acquisitions librarian can function adequately. Additional formal courses in management, budgeting, and administration are helpful along with workshops and specialized acquisitions conferences. All of these programs will help the acquisitions librarian find his or her place in the overall university structure.

The organizational structure of acquisitions is well defined. Schmidt's survey of the acquisitions departments of the Association of Research Libraries revealed that 82.4 percent of those responding report to the heads of technical services, Five, however, do report to the collection development officer.[30]

Librarians in acquisitions units today are closely involved in evaluation and planning. These are two chores which are fundamental to good management "no matter how small the staff or how few the materials obtained."[31] Magrill and Hickey describe two other important developments. "Contemporary emphasis upon economy in technical services has fostered two trends in acquisitions work: data processing and computer-based systems, to streamline the record keeping routines, and increased reliance upon cooperative and centralized organizational structures, to minimize duplication of effort in library systems."[32]

INFRINGING ROLES AND TASKS

Writers who discuss the activities of subject specialists and acquisitions librarians give contradictory counsel about a number of tasks. While the responsibility for selection seems to fall clearly under the jurisdiction of a subject specialist, Edelman expands on this by saying that "selection functions are not separable from acquisitions, cataloging and reference functions." He also states that standardization of procedures may not contribute to the quality of services or collections.[33] When selection extends to buying trips, vendor contacts, and vendor selection, the acquisitions processes may be made to endure inefficiencies or even suffer breakdowns. The buying trip has been supported by subject specialists according to Stueart's survey. "Most bibliographers, 93 percent, felt that it was desirable for the area bibliographers to make buying trips to his 'area' of the world. At the same time, both administrators and faculty reacted neutrally to this activity. About one-third of each of those groups felt it was unnecessary."[34]

The use of approval plans is a unique type of vendor contact, where the selection of materials is done by the vendor's staff after working out a selection profile with the library and its subject specialists. This type of contact is also one that many subject specialists oppose. Selecting with the book in hand may seem practical to some, but it lacks the opportunity to compare critical reviews about the material. Sewell offers another reason for opposition. "It may be that librarians have some fear of developing such profiles because they are far more significant and detailed than the often pious oaths of collection development statements."[35] Acquisitions librarians, on the other hand, see approval plans as an efficient, cost effective method to acquire materials. Approval plans will bring in materials that would ultimately be firm ordered, and such plans assure the library has a copy before a title becomes out of print. Also, staff can do most of the processing and free librarians, in both categories, for other use of their time. One other difficulty is the reluctance of a bibliographer to deal with interdisciplinary works which come on such broad plans. While the subject specialist readily agrees that the title is a valuable addition for the collection, he or she is reluctant to have the expense charged to 'his fund' since it is inter-disciplinary. If the subject specialists or collection development officer would agree to one fund for approval plan charges, this disagreement and many other time consuming inefficiencies would disappear from approval plan processing.

The more standard type of vendor selection is the point at which opinions diverge widely over which type of librarian should be responsible. Kennedy describes the whole area of contact with the book trade as "somewhat murky."[36] Two publications offer support for vendor contacts as a responsibility for subject bibliographers. Haskell lists this activity among their duties, emphasizing the book trade of foreign countries.[37] The Collection Management and Development Committee from the Resources and Technical Services Division of the American Library Association recently has produced a *Guide for Writing a Bibliographer's Manual*. This is the second support for vendor contact by subject specialists. It lists "maintaining appropriate contact with vendors" as an obligation of a collection development officer.[38] Later, though, the *Guide* identifies this activity differently. "Bibliographers may have responsibility for maintaining relations with vendors and booksellers ranging from knowing the existence of specialized dealers (particularly for locating retrospective materials), through contacting booksellers at conferences to choosing and evaluating vendors for all their orders."[39] Those writers discussing acquisitions activity uniformly list vendor selection as a responsibility of the acquisitions librarians. In the older work by Wulfekoetter it is listed as one of the activities comparable to a business office.[40] Ford takes the same approach in his list of functions of an acquisitions department—"selecting dealers or other sources for the purchase of materials, typing, and mailing orders, . . ."[41] Curley and Broderick describe selecting the dealers to be used and preparing and forwarding orders to them as a typical acquisitions functions, one which is so important that it is second only to the selection of the book itself.[42] Reid and High parallel the establishment of guidelines for vendor selection and the assessing of a vendor's performance as crucial tasks for acquisitions librarians.[43] This activity of vendor selection seems to be a new or enlarged responsibility for subject specialists since Stueart's survey did not reveal that supervising the ordering was felt to be an important activity by area bibliographers.[44]

Many other areas of acquisitions activity have been discussed by acquisitions librarians and subject specialists. Subject specialists may see a need for changes

within processes, particularly focusing on more decentralization for a process
and more specialized individual processes. The acquisitions librarian tends to
emphasize the centralization of processes. These contrasting points of view can
be confusing to the staff in acquisitions. "The staff specialists are not always
content to function without a measure of formal authority, and their efforts to
improve production or services are not necessarily welcomed by the line people."[45] Some subject specialists may prefer separate, specialized acquisitions and
cataloging units for the handling of their selections. This approach has been
rejected by acquisitions librarians in written statements for nearly 50 years.
Coney is one of the earliest recorded. "Thus it appears that, with increase in
volume, functional workers in a material unit may as well be assigned to
functional departments."[46] Wulfekoetter commented on this practice of separate
units as ineffective, at least for acquisitions.[47] The benefits of a centralized
process are that "a centralized operation can provide assembly-line processing
and specialists who can perform the work faster, do better work, and achieve a
coordination of effort that would be impossible in a decentralized situation."[48]
Other advantages which are available through centralized purchasing are:

1. Coordination and standardization of bibliographic searching,
2. More intelligent and economical purchasing because of both a broader
    and more intimate knowledge of the book trade, and
3. Better discounts and service, based on volume.

Acquisitions librarians deal with these practicalities daily, but often find it
necessary to enumerate the benefits for subject specialists and collection development officers.

Gifts are another topic which impacts both categories of librarians. Acquisitions librarians frequently are responsible for the initial processing of gift materials for a library's collection. While members of the library community have
advocated aggressive gift collecting since before World War II, few subject
specialists appear to put much time into such exercises. As a library's budget
grows at a slower rate or even stabilizes, gifts can become a major factor in
building the collection. Even when unsolicited gifts arrive, some bibliographers
are reluctant to spend much time selecting from them.

Exchanges can be used very successfully to add to a library's treasury. The
bibliographer must be willing to spend some time in making contacts and
working out procedures with acquisitions staff. The countries of the Third World
and Eastern Europe are prime sources for such programs. Regular purchases in
these areas are problematic, and exchanges are one of the best ways to deal with
those materials. Aggressive exchange, including duplicates, has been advocated
also for many years.

Out-of-print titles are an area where differences occur, and librarians from
each sector believe their methods are more valid. As the U.S. publishing patterns
have changed over the last decade, titles appear to go out of print at a more rapid

pace. Acquisitions librarians are concerned that a title be ordered in a timely manner to assure the securing of it for the library. A subject specialist may defer ordering until a favorable review pattern emerges. If that pattern of reviews is delayed, or the bibliographer is delayed in noting them, the whole acquisitions process may collapse. Going to the out-of-print market, then, makes acquisition uncertain and definitely more time consuming and costly.

All these infringing responsibilities and viewpoints appear to evolve from different philosophies or views of library management. The subject specialist appears to focus more narrowly—on a single title and individual subjects. The responsibility for a subject collection seems to take precedence over the general library collection and the most efficient policies and procedures needed to build the collection and serve all the patrons. The acquisitions librarian, on the other hand, must focus on the total collection and establishing routines that will serve the general good in order to acquire materials from everywhere for everyone. Examples of these different outlooks are reflected in their different approaches to the school year. The subject specialist is closely tied to the academic year, since that is when the faculty liaison work is most practical. Vacations often are taken in conjunction with school recesses. The acquisitions librarian has a far different pattern. While a surge in work is anticipated for reserves for each new semester, particularly the Fall one, it is important and more efficient to have a steady workload throughout the fiscal year. When a subject specialist takes vacation in June, that time usually becomes the most critical in acquisitions work. That is the time to resolve problems, settle issues, and generally complete transactions to bring the fiscal year to a successful close. These differing perspectives can readily lead to divergent opinions or even disagreements on library operations.

To reduce or avoid such conflicts, close coordination between subject specialists and acquisitions librarians and staff is important. Evans says that poor coordination results in wasted effort, slow response time and high unit costs, and he believes that all parties involved must understand the processes, problems, and utility of each other's work to achieve the desired coordination.[49] This coordination should assist the subject specialist in the liaison function with faculty and students. The need for cooperation is a concept that all agree is necessary. The *Guide* recommends "a statement of extent to which liaison function extends to non-collection development and management concerns (e.g., patron questions related to processing)."[50] Such a statement is the more formal resolution. "Whatever its place in the chain of command, a bibliographic department must have a close, if not formal, liaison with acquisitions because it must know about and work within the established routines of this department."[51]

FUTURE DIRECTIONS

Automation and the use of computers is the most obvious trend impacting libraries. Their influence on collection development and acquisitions is already great and continuing to grow. The major bibliographic utilities make the resources of research libraries widely known. The other online services and databases provide more current information and do so quickly. There has been a shift toward the purchase of more technology, software and access to data. Access, rather than the material itself, may have a significant affect on the expenditure of a library's information resources budget, formerly labeled the library's materials budget. The use of such databases, whether bought or simply used, may require specialized knowledge and training to implement successful search strategies.

The use of automation for internal processing—online public catalogs, circulation, acquisitions and cataloging—should provide new and valuable management data. It should reduce the confusion and eliminate the number of manual files maintained by subject specialists and acquisitions staff. Such technology well may continue to require more uniformity in procedures and processing.

The updating and formalization of collection development policies is also clearly aided by automation technology. These policies may be more sharply defined in order to increase the ability to exchange statements with other libraries as an aid to resource sharing. The statements could have a strong role in the uncertain future of collection development budgets. The collection development statements could aid also in the growth of approval plans and blanket orders by assisting in the preparation of plan profiles. Osburn describes library operations as evolving "from a book-centered service to a journal-centered service to a technology-centered service."[52]

The development of expert systems could have enormous impact on collection development and day-to-day selection work. Expert systems "use data, a knowledge base, and an inference mechanisms to solve problems in narrow subject domains."[53] Sowell developed a prototype called the Monograph Selection Advisor which modeled the item-by-item decisions that a subject specialist made in selecting monographs in the field of classical Latin literature. This program was used against a small group of citations successfully enough to plan for a future study in mass communication law. While some see such expert systems as useful in training new subject specialists, their greatest potential would appear to lie in reviewing the machine-readable bibliographic information of vendors and utilities to make selections based on current library collection practices. This method of selection would free bibliographers to spend more time with faculty and students or in performing other tasks.

Opinions differ sharply on how all these changes will affect the role of subject specialist. Humphreys believes that the technology will diminish the need for book selectors.[54] Michalak takes the opposite view that "in an era of budgetary stagnation and retrenchment, subject specialist librarians should be able to make additional contributions."[55] Some librarians believe a subject specialist is necessary for collection development only when a library is acquiring materials that are esoteric and difficult to find. Other librarians take the position that in-depth subject knowledge is not necessary when a library is purchasing only a core collection or is trying to procure everything for an extensive collection. This second view then extends to the supposition that a subject specialist is best used to set up a program and establish a collection development policy and to select when funds are moderate and decisions must be made about how many items to add beyond the basic tools. Dickinson states that the reduced economic conditions and shrinking buying power both counterbalance the need for a balanced collection and the need for subject specialists, and these factors may extend indefinitely into the future. In fact, the relatively high salaries of subject specialists could be considered part of the problem.[56]

Personnel in all areas of library operations will be impacted by automation and economics. More personnel may be shifted to public services. Both acquisitions librarians and subject specialists would be affected if the library takes advantage of the developing capabilities of jobbers to service blanket orders/approval plans, the increasing interest in publication on demand, and the spreading systems of library cooperation. Resource sharing through cooperative collection development and interlibrary loan are two growth areas for academic libraries. The complex area studies collections probably will continue to need the support of an area specialist for full development.[57] This view of reduced numbers of personnel as selectors or bibliographers, however, also is supported by Cline.[58]

Humphreys takes a positive view of the possible reduction in selection activity by subject specialists. "In my view therefore, the future of the subject specialist must inevitably lie in the field of reader service. It would seem to me, too, that the developments in the technology of information services will increase rather than diminish his importance."[59] Another variant is the changing curriculum and the new subjects or interdisciplinary approaches which could be added. The impact of such changes is difficult to measure.

All of these elements are part of the emerging accountability focus of the public, the university, and the library. "As libraries move into an age conditioned by a thirst for information and raised expectations for service, it is logical that a dominant environmental factor for collection development will be that of accountability to the community."[60] One evidence of this is the use of responsibility center budgeting or resource management programs in a number of private and public universities. Responsibility center budgeting is a type of accounting in which all actual costs of operation are assigned to organizational units. The assumption is that units have revenues to offset such costs. Each organizational unit then should be able to control both costs and revenues to its advantage. Some libraries within both public and private universities have been able to use this system or some semblance of it to their advantage. As the citizens demand such accountability of all agencies, it seems clear that libraries must be able to demonstrate efficiencies of operation in order to be considered successful.

Added to this list for the future is the complex issue of the library's place in relation to the campus computing center. The center is one more piece of the growing information technology which the library must address. Failure to take the lead as an information and service broker could doom the library and staff to a maintenance role, subordinate to those who do assume the lead in such roles.[61]

Summing up possible changes and trends, Haro believes that all changes in the library system must be flexible enough to allow the subject specialist to deal with all levels of staff and with all the service units.[62] And in acquisitions, Magrill sees three trends in dealing with decreased budgets as the most significant—greater selectivity in new acquisitions, more emphasis on efficient procedures, and increased reliance on other libraries.[63]

CONCLUSION

After reviewing all these divergent opinions on this significant area of library service, the need to reach a consensus on responsibilities and lines of authority is clear. The two groups, subject specialists and acquisitions librarians, should be able to function more effectively and overall library services should be improved. It is incumbent on these groups and leaders within the research library community to extend the dialogue on these issues. At individual libraries the priorities and goals of that library should give direction to the organizational structure and to the accountability of persons and departments. There will always be a need for internal communication and coordination of services offered by the library.

As libraries incorporate automation and the new technologies into their existing services, libraries will need to be adaptable and mature in facing the future. More information should be gathered to supplement and reinforce the positive attitudes of librarians facing an uncertain future. Additional research and analysis on organizational structure and efficiency should assist in demonstrating accountability to the library's community.

If the role of subject specialist continues, these bibliographers must forge communication networks with scholars; they need to know about research in progress. Subject specialists and acquisitions librarians must be allies, not adversaries. Both are educators training other staff, librarians, and users. "Acquisitions and collection development indeed have a symbiotic relationship, which must be recognized and nurtured if library collections are to continue to flourish."[64]

NOTES

1. Peter Biskup, "Subject Specialists in German Learned Libraries: Impressions from a 1975 Visit to the Federal Republic of Germany," *Libri* 27 (1977): 137.

2. J. Periam Danton, "The Subject Specialist in National and University Libraries, with Special Reference to Book Selection," *Libri* 17 (1967): 51.

3. J. E. Scrivener, "Subject Specialization in Academic Libraries: Some British Practices," *Australian Academic and Research Libraries* 5 (1974): 113.

4. Russell Duino, "Role of the Subject Specialist in British and American University Libraries: A Comparative Study," *Libri* (1979): 16.

5. R. D. Stueart, *Area Specialist Bibliographer: An Inquiry into His Role* (Metuchen, N.J.: Scarecrow Press, 1972), 23.

6. Rose Mary Magrill and Mona East, "Collection Development in Large University Libraries," in vol. 8 of *Advances in Librarianship*, ed. M. J. Voigt (New York: Academic Press, 1978), 5.

7. John D. Haskell, Jr., "Subject Bibliographers in Academic Libraries: An Historical and Descriptive Review," in vol. 3 of *Advances in Library Administration and Organization*, ed. Gerard B. McCabe and Bernard Kreissman (Greenwich, Conn.: JAI Press, 1984), 74.

8. Robert P. Haro, "The Bibliographer in the Academic Library," *Library Resources and Technical Services*, 13 (1969): 165.

9. Cecil K. Byrd, "Subject Specialists in a University Library," *College and Research Libraries* 27 (1966): 193.

10. Wilmer H. Baatz, "Collection Development in 19 Libraries of the Association of Research Libraries," *Library Acquisitions: Practice and Theory* 2 (1978): 113.

11. E. R. Smith, "Impact of the Subject Specialist on the Organization and Structure of the Academic Research Library," in *Academic Library: Essays in Honor of Guy R. Lyle*, ed. Evan Ira Farber and Ruth Walling (Metuchen, N.J.: Scarecrow Press, 1984), 71–74.

12. Elaine F. Sloan, *The Organization of Collection Development in Large University Research Libraries* (Ann Arbor, Mich.: University Microfilms, 1974), 59–61.

13. Ibid., 81–82.

14. Bonita Bryant, "The Organizational Structure of Collection Development," *Library Resources and Technical Services* 31 (1987): 117.

15. Haskell, "Subject Bibliographers in Academic Libraries," 80.

16. Eldred R. Smith, "The Specialist Librarian in the Academic Research Library," in vol. 2 of *Seminar on the Acquisition of Latin American Materials. Final Report and Working Papers*, ed. Jane Garner (Washington: Pan American Union, 1975), 107.

17. Hugh F. Cline and Loraine T. Sinnott, *Building Library Collections: Policies and Practices in Academic Libraries* (Lexington, Mass.: Lexington Books, 1981), 33–68.

18. Jeanne Sohn, "Collection Development Organizational Patterns in ARL Libraries," *Library Resources and Technical Services* 31 (1987): 123.

19. Ibid., 126

20. Dennis W. Dickinson, "Subject Specialists in Academic Libraries: The Once and Future Dinosaurs," in *New Horizons for Academic Libraries: Papers Presented at the First National Conference of the Association of College and Research Libraries, Boston, Mass., Nov. 8–11, 1978*, ed. Robert D. Stueart and Richard D. Johnson (New York: K. G. Sauer, 1979), 441.

21. Scrivener, "Subject Specialization in Academic Libraries," 119.

22. Smith, "Impact of the Subject Specialist," 73.

23. Helen Welch Tuttle, "An Acquisitionist Looks at Mr. Haro's Bibliographer," *Library Resources and Technical Services* 13 (1969): 170.

24. Theodore Grieder, *Acquisitions: Where, What and How: A Guide to Orientation and Procedure for Students in Librarianship, Libraries, and Academic Faculty* (Westport, Conn.: Greenwood Press, 1978), 12.

25. Rose Mary Magrill and Doralyn J. Hickey, *Acquisitions Management and Collection Development in Libraries* (Chicago: American Library Association, 1984), 53–54.

26. Marion T. Reid and Walter M. High, "The Role of the Professional in Technical Services," *RTSD Newsletter* 11 (1986): 59.

27. Grieder, *Acquisitions: Where, What and How*, 5.

28. Gertrude Wulfekoetter, *Acquisitions Work: Processes Involved in Building Library Collections* (Seattle: University of Washington Press, 1961): 3.

29. Magrill, *Acquisitions Management*, 57.

30. Karen A. Schmidt, "The Acquisitions Process in Research Libraries: A Survey of ARL Libraries Acquisitions Departments," *Library Acquisitions: Practice and Theory* 11 (1987): 37.

31. Magrill, *Acquisitions Management*, 59.

32. Ibid., 52.

33. Hendrik Edelman, "Subject Specialist and Job Requirements: Notes, Comments, and Opinions from an Administrative Viewpoint," in vol. 2 of *Seminar on the Acquisition of Latin American Materials. Final Report and Working Papers*, ed. Jane Garner (Washington: Pan American Union, 1975), 212–213.

34. Stueart, *Area Specialist Bibliographer*, 103.

35. Robert G. Sewell, "Managing European Automatic Acquisitions," *Library Resources and Technical Services* 27 (1983): 402.

36. Gail A. Kennedy, "The Relationship Between Acquisitions and Collection Development," *Library Acquisitions: Practice and Theory*, 7(1983): 230.

37. Haskell, "Subject Bibliographers in Academic Libraries," 79.

38. *Guide for Writing a Bibliographer's Manual*, compiled by the Collection Management and Development Committee of the Resources and Technical Services Division of the American Library Association, chaired by Carolyn Bucknall (Chicago: American Library Association, 1987), 11.

39. Ibid., 17–18.

40. Wulfekoetter, *Acquisition Work*, 6.

41. Stephen Ford, *The Acquisition of Library Materials* (Chicago: American Library Association, 1978), 20.

42. Arthur Curley and Dorothy Broderick, *Building Library Collections* (Metuchen, N.J.: Scarecrow Press, 1985), 264 and 271.

43. Reid, "The Role of the Professional," 59.

44. Stueart, "Area Specialist Bibliographer," 97.

45. Biskup, "Subject Specialists in German Learned Libraries," 149.

46. Donald Coney, "Administration of Technical Processes," in *Current Issues in Library Administration*, ed. Carleton B. Joeckel (Chicago: University of Chicago Press, 1939), 175.

47. Wulfekoetter, *Acquisition Work*, 9.

48. Ford, *The Acquisition of Library Materials*, 27.

49. G. Edward Evans, *Developing Library and Information Center Collections*, 2d ed. (Littleton, Colorado: Libraries Unlimited, 1987), 213.

50. *Guide*, p. 19.

51. Grieder, *Acquisitions: Where, What and How*, 25.

52. Charles B. Osburn, "Toward a Reconceptualization of Collection Development," in vol 2. of *Advances in Library Administration and Organization*, ed. Gerard B. McCabe and Bernard Kreissman (Greenwich, Conn.: JAI Press, 1983), 178.

53. Steven L. Sowell, "Expanding Horizons in Collection Development with Expert Systems: Development and Testing of a Demonstration Prototype." (Paper delivered at the Seventy-ninth Annual Conference of the Special Libraries Association, Denver, Colorado, June 11–16, 1988), 1.

54. K. W. Humphreys, "Subject Specialists," in *University Library Problems: Proceedings of a Symposium in Library Science on the Occasion of the 350th Anniversary of the Uppsala University Library Together with the Programme and Speeches at the Jubilee Celebration* (Uppsala, Stockholm: Almqvist and Wiksell, 1975), 49.

55. Thomas J. Michalak, "Library Services to the Graduate Community: The Role of the Subject Specialist Librarian," *College and Research Libraries* 37 (1976): 264.

56. Dickinson, "Subject Specialists in Academic Libraries," 439 and 441.

57. Ibid., p. 442.

58. Cline, *Building Library Collections*, 13–14.

59. Humphreys, "Subject Specialists," 49–50.
60. Osburn, "Toward a Reconceptualization," 179.
61. Ibid., 183.
62. Haro, "The Bibliographer," 169.
63. Magrill, "Collection Development," 40.
64. Kennedy, "The Relationship Between Acquisitions and Collection Development," 231.

REFERENCES

Fleming, Thomas P. and J. H. Moriarity. "Essentials in the Organization of Acquisition Work in University Libraries." *College and Research Libraries*. 1(1940): 229–234.

Goldstein, Harold, ed. *Milestones to the Present: Papers from Library History Seminar V*. Syracuse, N.Y.: Gaylord Professional Publications, 1978.

Hamlin, Arthur T. *The University Library in the United States: Its Origins and Development*. Philadelphia: University of Pennsylvania Press, 1981.

Harris, Michael H. *History of Libraries in the Western World*, Compact text ed. Metuchen, N.J.: Scarecrow Press, 1984.

Randall, William, ed. *The Acquisition and Cataloging of Books*. Chicago: University of Chicago Press, 1940.

Shores, Louis. *Origins of the American College Library 1638–1800*. Hamden, Conn.: Shoe String Press, 1966.

DEVELOPMENT AND USE
OF THEATRE DATABASES

Helen K. Bolton

INTRODUCTION

Wherever and whenever humans have progressed beyond the mere struggle for physical
existence, the gods and recreation and self-expression, there has been theatre in some sense:
an inevitable place for acting, dancing, dialog, drama, in the ordered scheme of life (Cheney,
1958, p. 1).

Archaeological evidence suggests that rituals were performed more than 20,000
years ago. Egyptian myths date from 2800 to 2400 B.C. Comedy as an art form
received official recognition from the Greeks in 487–486 B.C. (Brockett, 1977).
Some aspects of theatre have been shown to exist in all cultures at all times;
others are uniquely characteristic of each community of people and appear to

Advances in Library Administration and Organization,
Volume 8, pages 131-144.
Copyright © 1989 by JAI Press Inc.
All rights of reproduction in any form reserved.
ISBN: 0-89232-967-X

have developed interactively with special beliefs, customs and events. Historian and author, Sheldon Cheney, suggests that

> If one could spread out a picture of the world's stages, if the entire pageant of their activities could be momentarily fixed in a magic canvas, the spectator would know at once that no definition ever can be broad enough, elastic enough, to snare in words, the elements and the modes of art, the facets and the directions of theatric-dramatic life (Cheney, 1958: 1).

Theatre bridges all time periods and national boundaries, and encompasses a vast panorama of theories, methods, playwrights, directors, costumes, architecture, special effects, management, audiences and criticism. The lack of definition for this complex concept has not discouraged civilizations from creating and treasuring records of theatre thought and activity. Millions of volumes of theatre-related materials provide rich descriptions of both the past and present. The concept does however, present towering challenges to ardent scholars who need parameters by which to identify and organize theatre information for storage and retrieval. Theatre-related materials exist in a host of different disciplines, under a seemingly endless variety of subject headings, and indexed by an array of synonyms, including numerous forms of "drama." Theatre researchers face the present day information explosion with the need to formulate search strategies as complicated as the topic of theatre itself. A growing number of creative scholars are now turning to computer technology for help. Some have taken the bold initiative to develop specialized databases devoted exclusively to theatre materials, while others search for theatre information included in many already established databases.

It is the intent of this paper to explore the present state-of-the-art of computer-assisted theatre research, describe the specialized databases being developed, and examine the readily available commercial systems that are useful sources of theatre-related information. Because very little has been published on this topic, current facts were supplied through database directories, and telephone conversations and correspondence with librarians and the directors of theatre research centers. A few statistics were compiled by the writer from recent computer searches. A discussion of observations and trends comprise the conclusion.

The need for research of theatrical materials can take place at many levels and for very diverse purposes. Although many theatre fans are simply interested in what movies or plays are playing in area theatres, more serious devotees seek reviews of plays of the past or present, and an in-depth understanding of the development of theatre art forms or works of a chosen playwright. Theatre professionals involved with the project of putting performances together require staging plans, necessary equipment, and items with which to develop desired sets. Scholars immerse themselves in theories, and use the wealth of theatre materials to prove or disprove a point or opinion. Because of these diversities, databases must vary greatly to serve an amalgam of purposes.

PRIVATELY DEVELOPED THEATRE-SPECIFIC DATABASES

Privately developed, theatre-specific databases are a valuable yet scarce and fragile species. Their development is hindered by the fact that they serve a considerably smaller and generally less computer-oriented segment of the population than do the thriving business and scientific databases. Indeed, it is observed that, ". . . humanists have an ingrained opposition to computing based on ignorance of how and where the machine can help them" (Schneider, 1974: 16). Very few people have comprehensive knowledge of both theatre and computer systems. The health of these databases is plagued further by a lack of ready funds. Although the National Endowment for the Humanities contributes substantially to the development of several private American databases, the funds do not cover the enormous costs of database production and must be supplemented with matching amounts from private institutions, foundations, and personal gifts. Nonetheless, a handful of courageous theatre scholars battle these odds to create extremely complex and fully automated reference sources.

Dr. Ben Ross Schneider, Jr., an English professor at Lawrence University, became interested in automation when, to prove a theory he faced the prospect of a manual search through all 11 volumes (and more than 8,000 pages) of the newly published *London Stage, 1660–1800*. Dr. Schneider was convinced by a colleague that a computer-readable version of this monumental work would make a month long project a mere afternoon's effort. Unfortunately, the *London Stage* did not then exist in computer-readable form. Thus, the *London Stage Information Bank* (LSIB) was conceived: a full-text database and a service to provide searches to scholars in history, theatre, economics, linguistics and social history (Schneider, 1974).

In *Travels in Computerland or Incompatibilities and Interfaces: A full Account of the Implementation of the London Stage Information Bank*, Dr. Schneider humorously details the trials and tribulations of his experience producing a private database on a limited budget in the late 1960s and 1970s. Developed on magnetic tape (the only option available to Dr. Schneider at that time), the *London Stage Information Bank* (LSIB) is best described by the full title of the work from which it was produced: *The London Stage, 1660–1800, A Calendar of Plays and Afterpieces, Together with Casts, Box-receipts, and Contemporary Comments, Compiled from the Playbills, Newspapers, and Theatrical Diaries of the Period*. At its completion, this database was searchable with Boolean logic for ". . . comprehensive information on performances by date, casting, plays, roles, actors, authors, musical pieces, dances, songs, place names, and historical persons appearing in the sources." (*Encyclopedia of Information Systems and Services* (EISS), 1988: 1227). The data could be sorted to indicate trends in such topics as ticket prices and popularity of plays; and to explore stage careers, royal patronage and role histories (Falk, 1981: 265). In 1979, seven years after the birth of LSIB and $200,000 later, a printed *Index to London Stage* was produced from this database. Published by the Southern Illinois University Press, this index contains 500,000 references to 25,000 titles and names (Schneider, 1979: xv).

Sadly, the LSIB is not accessible to anyone at present. Advances in computer technology have made its present form incompatible with the computer systems now used at Lawrence University. Dr. Schneider turned his project over to the Harvard Theatre Collection which now has the responsibility to determine the future of this valuable reference source (personal communication, March 11, 1988). Dr. Schneider continues to list LSIB in the *Encyclopedia of Information Systems* . . . and is exploring the possibility of producing *London Stage* . . . on CD-ROM.

At the University of Massachusetts, Amherst, Professor Joseph Donohue is in the process of creating a machine readable database entitled *The London Stage 1800–1900: A Documentary Record and Calendar of Performances*. Mount Holyoke College, Eastern Michigan University, the University of Texas, Austin, and the Readex Microprint Corporation are also affiliated with this project (EISS, 1988: 907). Playbills and programs, play texts, monographs, newspaper and journal articles, contemporary and modern theatrical and bibliographical references, letters, diaries and theatre records are being compiled into data banks of which the subjects include: a census of archives, a checklist of newspapers and periodicals, a bibliography, a biographical dictionary, a directory of theatres, a catalog of iconography, and a calendar of performances. Although Professor Donohue and his colleagues began *The London Stage, 1800–1900* . . . with a main frame computer, several years ago they started working with a microcomputer and a commercial database called Revelation. Supplemented with a Bernoulli Box, the present computer has a storage capacity for 20MG of information on two 10MG hard-disk cartridges (Herbert, 1986: 176).

Both of the London Stage databases were developed as a response to American scholars' needs for retrospective research. In Munich, Dr. Heinrich Huesmann and the staff at the Deutsches Theatermuseum are presently developing TANDEM, a computer system to provide answers to queries on both historical and current productions in Germany and in cities of other countries. Using the IBM *Stairs* database software on a neighboring IBM 3081 host computer, TANDEM addresses such questions as: When did a play open? Who was in it? At what other theatres has it been performed? And, in which theatre collection can the costume designs be found? Play texts, programmes, and performance reviews will also be available (Edwards and Herbert 1985: 149).

Because TANDEM is expected to develop as an international system of interlinking information, Dr. Huesmann devised a detailed set of rules by which all entries must be processed consistently. A production card is first developed that sorts all information into almost 100 fields (i.e., dramatist, designer, composer, etc.), and assigns appropriate field numbers. Casting data is compiled on a supplementary card, and a bibliography card records similar information on a play text or a piece of music. Details of an object from a theatre collection are listed on an object card.

The complex nature of theatrical material has inspired the developers of TANDEM to create a "tree" of information. Entries are held in six searchable banks of data. On one side, the Search-Title File holds the common names under which a play or opera is known. This file and a Work-Catalog File (a list of all versions and translations), direct the computer to the Work-Title File of original titles. Three files of information concerning the dates, places and facts involved with specific productions are stored on the "other" side of the tree but linked to the Search-Title file. Production Data is the main file. All the "parts" in a production are maintained in a subfile of roles. Information on objects related to productions are kept in another subfile. The work involved in entering all this information is tremendous, and the developers have found that translations, accents and transliterations from non-Roman alphabets pose especially challenging problems (Edwards and Herbert, 1985).

The principles of classification developed by TANDEM have been used to create a checklist of productions from both Germany's Reinhardt Archive and the Theatre Museum in the United Kingdom. Italy and Scandinavia are adopting similar initiatives. TANDEM's grand goal is to have information on any production, past or present, available anywhere in the world "at the touch of a few buttons" (Edwards and Herbert, 1985: 151).

At a 1985 conference on international theatre research held in London, Dr. Huesmann reported that 13,000 documents from a number of contributing countries had been entered into the file of theatre productions, about 5,000 entries existed in the Search-Title file, over 1,000 original titles were established in the Work-Title file, and that an unspecified number of object entries had been included in the Object-Catalog from the Theatre Museum in London. At this conference, Londoners were able to access the database through the Munich central storage computer (Herbert, 1986: 175–6). Currently, TANDEM is being funded by the European Economic Commission. However, in the future, 50 percent of its costs will have to come from state sources in order to maintain prices at a rate that the average user can afford. It is hoped that some parts of the operation, like publishing, will become self-financing.

Here in the United States, secondary materials about the theatre are being organized in a bibliographic database by Dr. Irving Brown, at the Theatre Research Data Center (TRDC), Brooklyn College, City University of New York. Conceived by the American Society for Theatre Research in 1980, the TRDC computer readable reference source is designed to allow theatre scholars to use keywords to retrieve bibliographic information and annotations of articles from periodicals, books, microfilms and other forms of media. Although a demonstration given at the previously mentioned 1985 conference permitted conference members to access TRDC from London, at present, just TRDC staff use this database. Approximately 12 searches have been run to date on personal requests, and fees have not yet been established (R. Wang personal communications, March 11, 1988). It is hoped that powerful and sophisticated IBM search techniques will eventually make theatre information available not only to the American public, but also to European researchers through TANDEM. Indeed, it is anticipated that TRDC will actually be thought of as a further TANDEM file. To this end, the Theatre Research Data Center and Deutsches Theatermuseum have agreed to work in parallel and not overlap each other. "Books and journals will be recorded on the TRDC database, but plays and reviews will be kept on TANDEM" (Herbert, 1986: 175), and the IBM "SPIRES" software used by the TRDC is compatible with TANDEM's "STAIRS" (Edwards and Herbert, 1985:152).

Financed by the National Endowment for the Humanities, the Rockefeller Foundation and Brooklyn College, the Theatre Research Data Center currently uses its database to produce the *International Bibliography of Theatre (IBT)*, a series of extensive theatre-specific indexes. The research and editorial work is done by a group of distinguished scholars at TRDC, and the entries are developed by a network of approximately 70 volunteer field bibliographers (Edwards and Herbert, 1985). Reviews of the 1982 and 1983 *IBT* texts are very favorable, and reflect well on the quality and scope of the database from which they are derived. For *ARBA*, reviewer Colby H. Kullman (1987: 513) states:

> *IBT:1983* will greatly assist theatre scholars in locating information about playwrights, composers, directors, performers, critics, and thousands of other topics related to all aspects of theatre: writing, composing, performance, production, management, design, technology, and history.

IBT:84 has 852 pages of references to over 3,500 theatre articles and books and 18,000 subject index entries. They are listed under broad subject headings with many subdivisions. Separate indexes are featured for document authors and countries. Main entries include a document number, time and place dealt with and full bibliographic information. A brief annotation is given when titles are vague. Foreign titles are translated. Twenty nations contributed directly to the contents of *IBT: 1984* and 124 nations are represented by entries. *IBT: 1984's* Periodical List now numbers 805 journals, each of them annotated with original publishing dates, frequency of issue, publication addresses and language used. These periodicals range from the very scholarly *Shakespeare Quarterly* to the *Village Voice*. The TRDC database is enlarging so rapidly that a double issue is planned for *IBT: 85–86*. The staff at TRDC are presently concerned with locating more computer storage space.

London Stage Information Bank, *London Stage 1800–1900*, TANDEM and TDRC are just a sample of the many international privately developed databases which are specifically for theatre research. Four other databases which are theatre-specific, but have been developed commercially, also deserve mention. Theatre Link-Up, produced by Gwynn Williams Viewdata, uses the British Prestel interactive videotex system. Subscribers can "call up" formatted information on a television screen via a telephone. Data records concern the "availability of theatres to producing managements, and productions that can be brought in by the theatres." (Herbert, 1986: 176–7). A more widely used database, also part of Viewdata, lists the productions playing throughout London and the United Kingdom. The French Mirabel-Acte is a similar set-up that contains a databank of more than 2,500 plays, 80 percent of which are unpublished. Scripts can be ordered by electronic mail. *Theatre Crafts* magazine in New York is setting up Access, another overseas database that computerizes directories of theatre suppliers and college theatre programs. It will also index *Theatre Crafts*. The United States Institute for Theatre Technology is joining in this venture (Herbert, 1986).

COMMERCIALLY DEVELOPED THEATRE-RELATED DATABASES

Because access to theatre-specific databases is yet extremely limited, theatre scholars must look to broader based, commercially prepared systems for computerized theatre information. Fortunately there is considerable theatre-related, secondary material provided through major vendor services. Since theatre has developed as an expression of human experience, a rich coverage of a variety of theatre aspects may be found in humanities databases.

In the United States, perhaps the most familiar source of theatre literature is *MLA Bibliography*, an online version of the printed *MLA International Bibliography of Books and Articles in the Modern Languages and Literatures*. Joyce Duncan Falk (1981) alerted theatre scholars to the usefulness of MLA seven years ago, when she counted 77 different journals or series with specific content on drama, plays or theatre indexed by MLA. The journals were deemed scholarly in nature and offered appealing depth in foreign coverage. In a recent search, this writer used truncations of theatre and drama in the title and descriptors fields, and drew 38,042 records.

MLA is published by the Modern Language Association and accessible through DIALOG, Knowledge Index and Wilsonline. It currently holds an overall total of about 770,000 citations compiled from approximately 3,500 regularly published journals, books and essay collections. Coverage begins from 1966 and is updated monthly. MLA plans to gradually extend its coverage back to 1921 (File 71: MLA Bibliography, 1987: 71–4).

MLA offers a variety of convenient search features and a few noteworthy idiosyncracies. It is indexed by subject, author, name, journal name, document type, year of publication of the original document, the entry number in the printed MLA, historical period, language and several other types of data. Information in these indexes fields may be searched separately or in any combination with appropriate prefix or suffix codes. Editors, translators and compilers are included with authors in the author field. The basic Subject Index includes all words in titles of the original documents, brief notes occasionally added by MLA editors, and the subject index descriptors. Descriptors for records indexed from 1981 forward are derived from titles and headings in both the Classified and Subject Indexes (File 71, 1987: 71–8).

According to Ms. Falk (1981: 267), "it is MLA policy to index as drama only those items that are *about* drama and not to index items on individual authors with the genre designation." Individual names must be used with "drama," "theatre," and "theater" to draw relevant citations. Specific terms, such as burlesque, vaudeville or circus, etc., further pinpoint retrievals. The fact that MLA does not provide abstracts, however, limits the chances of these words being found.

Titles are indexed in full as they appear in the original source and are not translated. Index descriptors and words used in the "notes" are in English. In title field searching, a "complete" search would include foreign words. Citations in non-Roman alphabets are transliterated according to the Library of Congress System (File 71, 1987: 71–2).

Dissertation Abstracts Online (DAO) is another fertile source for serious theatre research. This scholarly database corresponds to *Comprehensive Dissertation Index*, *Dissertation Abstracts International*, and *American Doctoral Dissertation and Masters Abstracts*. It claims to hold virtually all doctoral dissertations accepted at accredited American institutions from 1861 to date, many from Canada and a few from overseas (EISS, 1988: 884). Falk (1981: 268) found that 7578 of 700,000 entries (1980) included a form of the words "theatre," "theater," or "drama" in the title or descriptor fields. A search done by this writer in 1988 yielded 9,159 items from the database's 900,000 records. Updated monthly, this database adds approximately 30,000 entries each year.

Available through DIALOG, BRS, INC., BRS AFTER DARK, BRS/BRKTHRU, DAO can be searched not only for subject terms in the title and index descriptors, but also by author, name of the university at which the thesis or dissertation was written, the type of degree awarded, and the year the dissertation or thesis was completed. Because each entry is usually assigned only one very general subject heading that relates to a university department, Falk (1981) recommends that search statements should include specific names or terms with appropriate synonyms that might likely be used in titles. Citations can be printed in several different formats, and they can be alphabetically or numerically sorted by author, title, university degree or year of completion.

Rich coverage of a wide variety of theatre aspects also may be found in such historical databases as *American: History and Life* (AHL) and *Historical Ab-*

stracts (HA). Corresponding to the printed publications with the same names, both of these databases are available on DIALOG. *American History and Life* spans the history of the United States and Canada from prehistory to the present. It also provides interdisciplinary studies of historical interest and history-related topics in the social sciences and humanities. Citations refer researchers to information on current affairs, area studies, ethnic studies, folklore, historiography and methodology, international relations, oral history, prehistory, government and political science, popular culture, urban affairs and teaching history. Approximately 2,000 journals including local, state and special interest publications are indexed, abstracted or annotated. Book reviews from 134 historical journals and the text of *Dissertation Abstracts International* are included. Several classic theatre history journals, such as *Theatre Survey* and *Revue d'Histoire du Theatre* are indexed in this scholarly reference source. Currently, the database includes approximately 200,000 records dating from 1964 to the present, and it is updated six times per year. Researchers can access AHL by classification code, abstract number, author/editor name, title in original language, English translation of a title, bibliographic references, abstract, abstractor's name, chronology, and indexing terms (EISS, 1988).

The basic index of AHL is composed of all words in the titles, abstracts or annotations, and index descriptors of the bibliographic entries. The fact that abstracts are included greatly improves the chance of retrieving theatre material on specific or unusual topics. The subject index terms are ". . . as specific as the subject matter of the original article, book or dissertation." This feature facilitates more precise searching, as does the ability to access entries published 1974 and later by both general or specific historical periods. Prior to 1974, all documents were articles. Falk found searching AHL ". . . especially advantageous" as it provides ". . . the ability to search almost instantaneously through 17 volumes of abstracts for instances of the words theatre or drama . . . and retrieves entries that would not be found using the printed indexes . . ." She warns though, that in AHL, "theatre" can bring false drops for military theatres (1981: 269). This writer treated "theat???" with "(not) military" and found the number of retrievals was reduced by only one.

Historical Abstracts is a companion database to AHL. It excludes the United States and Canada and covers world history from 1450 to the present. Like AHL it offers a rapid method to scan numerous volumes of materials. HA abstracts and annotates almost 2,000 journals published in 90 countries in some 40 languages. It contains more than 250,000 records beginning from 1973 and online updates occur quarterly with about 25,000 new citations added per year (EISS, 1988: 20). Searchable in the same fields as AHL, HA has the same capacity to retrieve very specific items.

HA allows access to journals not represented in MLA but "ones in which articles on theatre are occasionally published. Falk (1981: 270) comments that ". . . searching foreign language items in AHL and HA is more accurate and

complete than in MLA because all non-English titles have English translations.''
Even though MLA and HA cover a number of the same articles, Falk explains
that the two sources use different selection criteria. HA excludes purely literary
articles and has different cut off dates. Researchers can first identify a topic by
searching for specific terms (i.e., puppets, music halls, masques, mesmerism,
etc.), and then limit the search to certain geographical areas, time periods, or
both. Several of the titles retrieved from international history and social science
journals in Falk's sample search give an idea of the interesting subjects and wide
wide scope of the uniquely interesting articles available: "Taking Melodrama
Seriously" from *History Workshop Journal*; "Victorian Music Hall Entertain-
ment in the Lancashire Cotton Towns" from *Local Historian*; "The Origins of
the French Popular Theatre" from *Journal of Contemporary History*; "Shakespearean Contradictions and Social Change" from *Sciences and Society*; "Theatre in Siberia in the 18th and Early 19th Centuries" from *Istoriia USSR*; and "The
Theatre in Manchu China" from *Asian Affairs* (1981: 270).

A citation index developed by the Institute for Scientific Information offers a
different but equally effective type of database in which to search for records not
only on theatre, but also film, television, and radio. *Arts and Humanities Search*
(AHCI), available through BRS, Inc., BRS AFTER DARK, BRKTHRU and
INSTRUCTOR, is composed of over 500,000 bibliographic citations from 1,300
journals in art, film, history, literature, music, philosophy, religious studies and
other related fields; 5,600 journals covered in other ISI databases are also
selectively indexed. A relative newcomer, AHCI covers materials published
from 1980 to the present (Plum, 1987: 1384).

Plum (1987: 1384) reviewed this database for *CHOICE* and was pleased with
the relevant citations received in sample searches. AHCI not only identified
reviews of film and theatre productions, but also "substantial critical studies in
journals outside the film area that would otherwise have been difficult to find.''
More expensive than other humanities databases, AHCI is updated biweekly and
offers access to cross-disciplinary topics through the title-keyword index and
related citations listed under author entries.

The absence of abstracts in AHCI complicates search techniques and strategies. However, entries can be accessed through journal subject categories, cited
references, type of publications, language, author and author affiliation. Plum
(1987) recommends combining cited primary or secondary references with title
keywords. The AHCI guide cautions that without paragraph qualification the
entire record is searched. The use of the document-level operator and "and"
may bring together keywords from widely separated fields which are not logically related. In full text searching, it is therefore recommended that the
positional operations "same," "with" and "adj" be used.

Useful, interesting theatre information can also be found in specialized humanities databases such as *ARTbibliographies Modern* (ABM) and the music-

oriented *RILM (Repertoire International de Litterature Musicale) Abstracts.* Both are made available through DIALOG.

Providing abstracts and indexes to current literature on 19th and 20th century are and design, ABM scans books, dissertations, exhibition catalogs and approximately 300 periodicals. It holds 106,000 records that date from 1974 to the present. Updated online twice a year, approximately 8,000 entries are added annually. Information on theatre architecture, furniture, stage and costume design, art performances, art of the dance and art of the theatre can be specifically retrieved with computer-convenient search techniques (EISS, 1988). Searches by this writer in 1988 yielded 246 records for the term "stage (w) design???." "Theat??? (w) architecture or building" yielded 5,416 records.

RILM offers similar possibilities with a music emphasis. EISS (1988: 1124) lists RILM as holding 50,000 records, retrospective to 1971 and updated three times a year. DIALOG, however, provides access only to records from 1971 to 1981. Falk (1981: 271) found that searches for authors, composers, musicians, titles of operas, characters or myths could be effectively accomplished.

To research current materials of a general, critical or technical nature, theatre scholars and students will find a host of relevant articles, editorials, news reports and reviews of theatre productions in *Magazine Index* (MI). This very large database offered by DIALOG, all BRS, Inc. services, Knowledge Index and Mead Data Central, is updated monthly and adds 144,000 records per year. It presently includes 2,260,309 records from 1959 to date (NAOD, 1987: 72). *Dance Magazine*, *Drama*, *News*, *Encore*, *Plays*, *Theatre Crafts*, and *Variety* are among the 400 North American journals indexed by MI. In addition to many traditional search options, MI has a few especially useful features. Reviews can be retrieved separately from other types of citations and come graded according to the reviewer's evaluation. A "Named Person" index identifies the persons responsible for the artistic aspect of a production being reviewed, such as author, actor, director, designer and producer.

Falk (1981) reports enthusiastically on the retrieval rate for material on contemporary issues. In some instances MI brought in four to five times the citations found in other databases. For example, her search with the index term "popular culture" retrieved entries on Eskimo drama and a satirical play on Pierre Trudeau.

Finally, the very latest in theatre news can be located through the *New York Times Index*. Updated daily with the full text of the final *New York Times Late City Edition*, this database provides access to "local newspapers" at the heart of the American theatre world. Approximately 98,000 records have been added annually since 1980. Vended by NEXIS, *New York Times Index* is a logical source for theatre reviews, the status of current and planned productions and news stories concerning theatre personalities and production executives and staff (NAOD, 1987: 83).

OBSERVATIONS, DISCUSSION AND CONCLUSIONS

There is a striking dearth of published information about computerized theatre materials and retrieval methods. More articles like the extremely informative and useful ones that inspired this paper are needed to keep abreast of the constant changes in computer technology. An exploration of the literature published since 1986 failed to reveal more recent studies. If "quantity of published data" equates to "awareness or interest level," then only a marginal number of theatre scholars appear to be actively involved in computer-assisted research.

Online reference sources for theatre information do exist and are developing. An exclusively-convenient, commercially-prepared database is not presently available for the vast and complex term "theatre", but the realization of this goal comes closer with the burgeoning of such ambitious enterprises as the Theatre Research Data Center, the TANDEM system and the *London Stage: 1800–1900*. Hopefully, the *London Stage Information Bank* will soon find an avenue for new life and join these other projects. Meanwhile, several databases that benefit from the financial backing of broader support bases provide considerable access to theatre materials published from the early 1960s and 1970s to the present. Theatre researchers, however, do not seem to be taking advantage of this convenience.

Automation apathy is evidently characteristic of humanists as a group. Puzzled by the fact that requests for bibliographic searching from faculty and students in the humanities represented only 4 percent of the total searches made in 1982–83, the staff of the University of Rhode Island Computer Access (URICA) service launched a campaign to attract their attention. Told that humanists in general had no idea of what was involved in online searching, and were either unaware of the service or opposed to the fees charged, URICA's director obtained a grant to promote and conduct free sample searches. The results were interesting. Although a few stated that they would search online again only if it was free, all participants indicated they would continue to use the service if the costs were less. Despite the retrospective limitations to in-depth researching, 60 percent said they would search online again. Approximately 25 percent indicated that their interest depended totally on the cost factor, and 15 percent preferred to wait until more databases were available. A majority found that, indeed ". . . computer searching does save time, and is faster and more convenient than the manual search method. Everyone was impressed by the fact that a complete and printed bibliography was produced instantly (Krausse and Etchingham, 1986: 93). A follow-up study would be valuable to determine if the percentage of requests from humanists increased as a result of this project.

D. Crawford (1986: 570) suggests that humanists shrink from technology for several reasons. He feels they tend to be ". . . timid by nature when it comes to technology, intimidated by gadgets, afraid of looking silly, . . . and perhaps snobbish about old-fashion ways.'' He also senses that humanists ''. . . don't trust the sensibilities of those who are urging them to jump into the fray.'' Additionally, the jargon of the media documentation and manuals is often a turn-off. Crawford quotes a letter from a friend: ''[What is needed is] a kind of discourse accessible to many humanists that combines the authority of tone and clarity of expression that will catch his or her imagination.''

It would seem then, that computerized humanities searching (theatre research included) is stymied by the ''which comes first, the chicken or the egg'' dilemma. Available, efficient, and cost effective online services promote user loyalty. Yet, a ready interest in and broad support of online databases is necessary to assure the development of such projects. Extensive, good public relations is needed to convince theatre scholars that there is an advantage to automated searching.

Perhaps reassurance that online searching is indeed a cerebral activity would elicit more enthusiasm from the ranks of the hard-core skeptics. Surely some might be both reassured and enticed by the reality that all the knowledge they can bring to bear on a search (i.e., related terms, synonyms, names, dates, and times), as well as their familiarity with professional literature, is extremely valuable for a truly productive research effort.

It may take time to convince the humanists that automation can enhance their access to information, and, yes, even be worth the cost. This writer optimistically foresees that the inevitable reality of computers in daily life will erode resistance, develop facility, and heighten the demand for computer accessible theatre materials. With building enthusiasm and advances in computer technology, the trend toward national and international database networking should continue. Although no definition ''. . . ever can be broad enough, elastic enough . . .'' to adequately describe the concept of ''theatre,'' perhaps computer-readable databases will eventually become the ''magic canvas'' with which this colorful pageant can be viewed and small pieces captured for theatre study.

REFERENCES

Brockett, O. G. (1977). *History of the theatre*. Boston: Allyn and Bacon, Inc.

Cheney, S. (1958). *The theatre: Three thousand year of drama, acting, and stagecraft*. New York: David McKay Company, Inc.

Crawford, D. (1986, November). Meeting scholarly information needs in an automated environment, a humanist's perspective. *College and Research Libraries*, 47, 569–574.

Edwards, C. and Herbert, I. (1985, March). Computer databases for the performing arts: TANDEM and International Bibliography of the Theatre. *Theatre Notebook*, 39, 149–152.

Encyclopedia of Information Systems and Services. (1988). Detroit, Michigan: Gale Research Company.

Falk, J. D. (1981, February). Theatre ex machina: Using the computer for theatre. *Theatre Journal*, 33, 265–274.

File 71: MLA Bibliography. (1987) In DIALOG. [loose leaf instructions]. Palo Alto, California: DIALOG Information Services, Inc.

Herbert, I. (1986, June). Computer databases for theatre studies. *New Theatre Quarterly.* 2, 175–180.

Krausse, S. C., and Etchingham, J. B., Jr. (1986, April/June). The Humanist and computer-assisted library research. *Computer and the Humanities*, 20, 87–96.

Kullman, C. H. (1987). [Review of International Bibliography of Theatre: 1983] In B. S. Wynar (Ed.), *American Reference Books Annual* (p. 513). Littleton, Colorado: Libraries Unlimited.

The North American Online Directory: A directory of online information products and services with names and numbers. (1987). New York: R. R. Bowker Company.

Plum, S. H. (1987, May). [Review of *Arts and Humanities Search*]. *Choice*, 24, 1384.

Schneider, B. R., Jr. (1974). *Travels in computerland or incompatibilities and interfaces: A full account of the implementation of the London Stage Information Bank.* Reading, Massachusetts: Addison-Westley Publishing Company.

Schneider, B. R., Jr. (1979). *Index to the London Stage: 1660–1800.* Carbondale, Illinois: Southern Illinois University Press.

THE ACADEMIC LIBRARY
AND THE LIBERAL ARTS
EDUCATION OF YOUNG ADULTS:
REVIEWING THE RELEVANCE OF THE
LIBRARY-COLLEGE IN THE 1980s

Peter V. Deekle

INTRODUCTION

The formal education of young adults in the 1980s has reflected a trend toward increased student enrollments in specialized, occupationally-oriented under-graduate curricula, such as business administration, computer science, and high-technology disciplines. A 20 year report (1966–1985) of the Cooperative Institu-

Advances in Library Administration and Organization,
Volume 8, pages 145-169.
Copyright © 1989 by JAI Press Inc.
All rights of reproduction in any form reserved.
ISBN: 0-89232-967-X

tional Research Program, the nation's largest and oldest empirical study of higher education, documents this migration away from the traditional liberal arts.

Despite the recent shift in undergraduate studies toward career training, many educators have begun to recognize that rapid changes in the modern work environment warrant the pursuit of a broad liberal education (Zemke and Zemke, 1981). John Naisbitt, for example, has advocated a foundation in the liberal arts as a basis for flexible career decision making and other important life choice (Naisbitt, 1984).

This paper is derived from the author's doctoral study on the role of academic libraries in the liberal education of young adult undergraduates (Deekle, 1987). It acknowledges the viability and compatibility with liberal arts curricula of the adult education humanistic principles formulated by Malcolm Knowles (Knowles, 1984). Through an assessment of attitudes towards a library-centered undergraduate curriculum among educators and students in Pennsylvania colleges and universities, this paper includes references to the Library-College movement and its relevance in the 1980s for life-long learning.

FUNDAMENTAL BASES OF THE STUDY

The purpose of this research study was to identify and assess the perceptions of Pennsylvania liberal arts college faculty, administrators, librarians, and undergraduate students concerning their understanding and acceptance of the fundamental Library-College principles which most closely reflect the premises of adult education expressed by Malcolm Knowles. Toward this end, the study assessed the historical impact nationally of the Library-College concept on American higher education since 1973. The reader is referred to the end of this paper for a brief explication of library-centered instruction (the Library-College model) and the Knowles' postulates examined in this study.

HYPOTHESES

The author's original study of attitudes from the academic community confirmed seven stated hypotheses about differences and similarities in population group perceptions. This paper, derived from the study, reports the pertinent research data and assess the study's research questions and hypotheses as they may relate to prevailing perceptions throughout American higher education.

A SURVEY OF ATTITUDES

The author developed a questionnaire using the key tenets of the Library-College and Knowles' learning principles to investigate the attitudes of Pennsylvania's academic community. The questionnaire was distributed by direct mail to the chief academic officers, library directors, and bibliographic instruction librarians at 33 liberal arts institutions. The on-campus mail service at eight cooperating institutions of the total group provided the means of distribution for questionnaires to 400 full-time undergraduate students and 160 full-time faculty. There were 380 total returns, constituting 58 percent of the respondents.

The highest return rate came from bibliographic instruction librarians (33 total; 23 returns; 70 percent), followed by library administrators (33 total; 21 returns; 64 percent) and undergraduate students (400 total; 239 returns; 60 percent).

The questionnaire sought respondents' years of professional experience (except for students), age, academic background (except for students), academic discipline of present assignment or study (except for administrators and librarians), class standing (students only), most recent year of formal study (except for students and faculty), and type of institution (public or private). Each of these variables, it was postulated, might be significant for an individual's attitude toward library-centered liberal education.

THE AGE OF RESPONDENTS

The author was interested in how adults perceived the role of libraries as active contributors to a liberal education. Therefore, it was important to determine the age of respondents from all groups of the sample. Of the 364 returns, 158 (43 percent) were from respondents between the ages of 18 and 20 years; 57 of the respondents (16 percent) were age 20 to 30 years. These two age categories comprised the largest percentage of returns, as expected, because the largest group in the sample was undergraduate students (n = 400).

PROFESSIONAL EXPERIENCE OF RESPONDENTS

Students were not asked to define the extent of their work experience. Of the 113 responses to this survey item, 75 (63 percent) of the respondents had 16 or more years of related educational experience. The next highest percentage (13.3 percent, 15 respondents) had fewer that five years of experience.

RECORD OF FORMAL STUDY

Faculty respondents (n = 160) were asked to record the dates of their formal study and earned degrees. Questionnaire returns identicated that 15 persons (26.3 percent) pursued formal study within the past five years. The next highest percentage (24.6 percent) was associated with the 14 respondents whose latest formal study occurred between 11 and 15 years ago, followed by responses from 11 persons (19.3 percent) who completed formal study within the most recent 5 to 10 years.

DEGREES EARNED BY RESPONDENTS

All participant groups except students were asked to complete a questionnaire item for earned degrees. Of the 131 responses to this item, 72 persons (55 percent) held doctoral degrees. A single masters degree or a second masters degree (or advanced study) was held, respectively, by 29 and 30 of the respondents. A higher percentage (77.9 percent) of the respondents continued to pursue an advanced degree or further study than those who stopped with a single advanced degree (22.1 percent).

TYPE OF ACADEMIC INSTITUTION

Two-thirds (n = 250) of the survey respondents represented private institutions. This finding was expected because of the large number (five out of eight) private institutions contained in the sample of students and faculty.

THE ACADEMIC DISCIPLINE OF RESPONDENTS

Both student and faculty survey groups were asked to identify their primary academic fields of study. Of the 305 respondents to the survey, 77 persons (25.2 percent) were associated with business curricula, 76 (24.9 percent) with arts and humanities, and 63 (20.7 percent) with the social sciences. There were 69 respondents (22.6 percent) who represented the combined fields of mathematics and engineering. The data, therefore, was at relatively comparable levels among four primary discipline categories.

CLASS RANK OF STUDENTS

Only students (n = 400) were asked to state their class rank. Nearly two-thirds (n = 143) of the 231 respondents were lower division undergraduates (freshman or sophomore level). Junior and senior level respondents comprised 38 percent (n = 68) of the total returns.

RETURNS OF RESPONDENT GROUPS

The total number of returns from the chief academic officers, library administrators, and bibliographic instruction librarians was considerably smaller than for either faculty or students; this was attributable to the smaller size of the subsamples for each of the three former groups. Therefore, a judgment call was made; the three respondent categories were grouped together to form one category: librarian. This judgment was based on the essentially non-instructional and administrative responsibilities of the three groups. The resulting "librarian" groups consisted of 50 persons. Students (239) represented the majority of the respondents to the survey, with faculty (81) comprising the second largest respondent group.

ANALYSIS OF THE SURVEY RESULTS

The principal question to be answered by this study was whether there were significant differences between the perceptions of college undergraduates, faculty, and non-teaching professionals regarding the instructional role of academic libraries and librarians. The primary elements of this role have been expressed in the Library-College model.

Seven hypotheses were stated for testing by statistical analyses of the survey results. The reader of this report is referred to the original study for details on the stated hypotheses and their analysis (Deekle, 1987). Each hypothesis was tested through the calculation of chi-squares or one-way analyses of variance. In every case, the independent variable was group membership, and the dependent variable was the score for the designated questionnaire item. The questionnaire items were scored on a five-point Likert-type scale with a positive rating (5) of ALWAYS and a low score representing a negative rating (1) of NEVER.

Results of the survey indicated that there were significant differences among the attitudes of respondent groups ($<.05$) for 10 of the questionnaire items. The survey findings for these items have been reported below. The reader may refer to the sample questionnaire at the end of this publication.

For this report, the hypotheses have been expressed as research questions. The survey findings for each of the questions have been summarized following each stated question.

CONSIDERING THE QUESTIONNAIRE ITEMS

The first questionnaire item ("Undergraduate programs offer many opportunities for self-directed learning, recognizing the maturity of students and their increasing ability for independent study."), taken from principles of adult learning, sought to characterize the control which a student has in a standard liberal arts program of study. Responses to this item illustrated a significant difference in group perceptions. Students (with a group mean score of 3.51) were much more willing to accept this principle than faculty (mean score, 3.21) or librarians (mean score, 3.42). Faculty were the least likely, therefore to recognize the maturity of undergraduates as readiness for independent study. This finding suggested that prior to the successful implementation of a library-centered curriculum or program with self-directed exercises, considerable effort toward securing favorable faculty support would be needed.

Questionnaire item 2 ("The liberal arts learning mode should, realistically, emphasize lecture-text-recitation over students' independent inquiry and critical thinking.") defined traditional methods of instruction, minimizing the student's independence. The student sample (mean score, 2.59) accepted this teaching mode more readily than either faculty (mean score, 2.25) or librarian (mean score, 2.25) groups.

One interpretation of the findings for item 2 was that undergraduate students, while desiring more opportunities for self-directed study, generally felt the need for more formalized instruction in prescribed skill areas.

For questionnaire item 4 ("In undergraduate education there should be greater emphasis on the process of learning, thinking, and expression of thought rather than on the memorization of factual information.") an active rather than passive learning mode is advocated. Student respondents (mean score, 4.21) were less favorable toward this position than faculty (mean score, 4.35) or librarians (mean score, 4.54); the results suggested that, while all three groups generally favor a more active student role, students as a group were less convinced of their readiness to pursue such a role.

The student response (mean score, 2.78) to item 5 ("For undergraduates in any field of study the principal text should be a library's unique organization of resources in a network of bibliography, classification, indexes, and catalogs rather than assigned subject textbooks.") was significantly lower than that for faculty (mean score, 2.83) or librarians (mean score, 3.16). This questionnaire expressed the fundamental Library-College opposition to textbook instruction. Students, and to a lesser degree, faculty, were less willing than librarians to abandon the convenience of a comprehensive text as a basis for undergraduate instruction. The scores indicate, however, that none of the groups strongly advocated the centrality of a library collection over a standard text in any field of study.

Item 10 ("Undergraduate learning modes can be successfully library-centered in most disciplines [focusing on the universe of knowledge] rather than classroom-centered.") advocated a curriculum focused fully on the active use of libraries. Recognizing the extensive collaboration between librarians and faculty required in this instruction, faculty (mean score, 2.91) and students (mean score, 2.81) were significantly less favorable toward this position than librarians (mean score, 3.54). Clearly, this non-traditional mode was both an unfamiliar and untested option for many respondents. Again, the results demonstrated, however, that all of the groups responded to a moderate (SOMETIMES) implementation of this principle.

The accommodation of library-centeredness in the role of undergraduate instructors was defined in questionnaire item 11 ("An instructor of undergraduates should be considered essentially a cross between a library-oriented teacher and a teaching-oriented librarian."). This role, originally explained in the models of the Library-College, presumed that the central teaching function of libraries and librarians would be generally accepted within the academic community. However, the results of the survey indicated that student (mean score, 2.71) and faculty (mean score, 2.80) groups were much less favorably disposed toward this concept than librarians (mean score, 3.53). The patterns of group responses for items 10 and 11 (each of which treated related concepts of the library-centered teaching) were similar.

Questionnaire item 12 ("Both generalists and subject specialists as instructors should be more committed to encouraging and motivating, rather than informing and directing students.") received strongly favorable responses from each of the three primary groups. The mean score (3.37) for students, however, was significantly lower than those for faculty (mean score, 3.72) or librarians (mean score, 3.77). Faculty and librarians were readier than the undergraduate students themselves to accept the qualities in teachers which encourage student independent inquiry.

The next questionnaire item receiving group responses of statistically significant differences was item 14 ("For undergraduates, information resources in all their print and nonprint forms should be the principal media for communicating information."). While faculty (mean score, 3.33) and librarians (mean score, 3.34) did not markedly differ on their generally moderate acceptance of this principle, students (mean score, 3.11) tended to be less certain of the value of multiple information formats. A possible explanation for this student reticence could be their lack of familiarity with the breadth of information media types.

Students (mean score, 3.71) were much more accepting of item 15 ("In every course experienced by undergraduates, instruction should always include faculty-constructed syllabi, bibliographies, guides, and reading plans, supplemented by individual conferences, group seminars and occasional inspirational large-group lectures.") than faculty (mean score, 3.10) or librarians (mean score, 3.18).

The final numbered questionnaire item for which there were statistically significant differences among the group mean scores was item 18 ("The primary objective of an undergraduate education is to prepare students to enter the workplace or pursue graduate study, rather than to prepare for a lifetime of learning."). Students (mean score, 3.11) agreed (SOMETIMES) with this much more readily than faculty (mean score, 2.06) or librarians (mean score, 2.09); the latter two groups ranked this concept at not more than SELDOM applicable. The student response could have been attributable, in part, to a tendency among undergraduates toward valuing the immediately tangible and career-oriented objectives of education, rather than the long term preparation for a lifetime of learning.

The questionnaire contained four final statements concerning the occupational roles of college librarians which the survey participants were asked to rank ("1" being most preferred and "4", the least preferred). The results of statistical tests on the data indicated that one item ("College librarians can be of most value as resource agents for individual students [providing reference and information services related to the student's specific needs].) was ranked of significantly less importance by librarians (mean score, 2.35) than by students (mean score, 1.59) or faculty (mean score, 1.75). This traditional service role was least acceptable to librarians, but most familiar and acceptable to both faculty and students.

The other questionnaire statement concerning roles of college librarians ("College librarians can be of most value as contributors in the instructional process [meeting periodically with students to introduce and explore the use of various information resources].") with which librarians most strongly agreed (mean score, 1.79) also received statistically significant responses. Faculty rankings for this statement (mean score, 2.58) and student rankings (mean score, 2.80) reflected only moderate approval for this more active instructional role.

It was clear, from an analysis of survey data by participant group, that faculty and students tended to accept a more traditional service and research role for librarians. The latter, however, preferred a collaborative role with faculty in the teaching process. The role preferred by librarians was closer to that advanced by the Library-College, and consistent with the tenets of a program of study centered on an academic library.

CONSIDERING THE HYPOTHESES

As previously stated, the author restated the seven hypotheses as research questions which could then be answered affirmatively or negatively in this paper. Based on the survey's statistical evidence, the following conclusions were made.

Question 1

Were there significant differences among the perceptions of the groups concerning the importance of research skills for college students? This was an important question because a learner's bibliographic skill was critical for effective use of a library, and for a lifetime of independent learning.

There were significant differences among the responses. (Student scores for questionnaire items 5 and 10 [those items most directly related to this question] were significantly higher than faculty or librarian response scores.

Question 2

Were there significant differences between the perceptions of faculty and librarians concerning student readiness for independent study research [as defined by the Library-College]? Questionnaire items 1 and 2 most directly concerned this question.

Again, there were significant differences. For item 1 student and librarian scores were significantly higher than those for faculty, more strongly advocating the appropriateness of independent study. For item 2 the results showed librarian and faculty mean scores significantly lower than student scores, documenting support from the former two groups for student independent study and critical thinking.

Question 3

Were there significant differences between the perceptions of faculty and librarians concerning the instructional role of college teachers [as defined by the Library-College]? This research question was important for two reasons. It embodied the original conception of the Library-College teaching norm; it also solicited evaluation by traditionally non-teaching groups of the role of college faculty, a topic typically reserved for consideration by the faculty themselves.

Significant differences among the responses were observed. Questionnaire items 11 and 12 most appropriately concerned the role of an instructor of undergraduate students. In both instances, the lower mean scores of the student group support their acceptance of a more pedantic role for faculty than that defined by faculty and librarian responses.

Question 4

Were there significant differences among the perceptions of the groups concerning the importance of adult learning principles? The value of lifelong learning advanced by Malcolm Knowles was compatible with a library-centered liberal arts program of study. Perceptions of this research question, therefore, were important determinants of the degree of acceptance for this basic principle.

There were significant differences in perceptions among the survey group. Item 18 considered the fostering of a positive attitude among undergraduate students toward lifelong learning.

Question 5

Were there significant differences between the perceptions of faculty and librarians concerning the role of teachers (as defined in the Library-College conceptual model)? How college faculty perceive their instructional role in respect to the one defined by a library-centered liberal arts model was critical to this study. The degree to which this perception differed from that of librarians was also important.

The perception differences of the survey groups were significant. Items 11 and 12 expressed qualities of this role. The statistical test results reported significantly lower mean scores for students, supporting their acceptance of a more pedantic role for teachers than that favored by faculty and librarians; faculty responses (mean score, 2.80) were not, however, as high (favorable) as librarians' (mean score, 3.53) for item 11.

Question 6

Were there significant differences among the perceptions of all groups concerning the importance of humanistic adult learning principles? The author queried survey participants in their acceptance of a basic liberal arts position on formal education: the preparation for lifelong learning. Determining the degree of acceptance among and between groups helped to characterize the amount of support for a library-centered liberal arts curriculum.

There were significant differences among group responses to Item 18 (the questionnaire item which stated the prominence of career preparation as a primary aim of formal education). Both faculty and librarians were closely allied in their low ranking of this tenet, while students ranked the educational aim of career preparation considerably higher.

Question 7

Were there significant differences among the perceptions of all groups concerning the importance of lifelong learning? There were no significant differences among group responses to items 6, 7, 9, or 17, each of which introduced aspects of the lifelong learning concept.

The results of the survey indicated no significant differences among the group responses. For this research question there was uniform agreement and strong support for its importance.

Question 8

Were there significant differences between the perceptions of faculty and librarians concerning the curricular conditions required for the successful implementation of an undergraduate library-centered program?

The survey results indicated that differences in group mean scores were statistically significant. Faculty and student mean scores for item 10 were significantly lower than for librarians, reflecting a reluctance by the former to reject a classroom oriented instructional mode.

Group mean scores for item 14 were significantly higher for both librarians and faculty than for students, suggesting for the two former groups the importance of information in all its formats. For item 15 the student mean scores were significantly higher than for librarians or faculty, indicating the student interest in a variety of instructional functions performed by the teacher and prescribed by the Library-College.

Question 9

Were there significant differences among the perceptions of all groups concerning the instructional role of academic librarians? Previous research questions sought to clarify group attitudes toward the faculty's instructional role. This question addressed the librarian's role as instructor in a liberal arts library-centered environment.

Questionnaire items 20 through 23 concerned attitudes toward librarians as instructors. The first two items (20 and 21) were ranked by participants with resulting significant differences among the responses.

OTHER ANALYSES OF SURVEY DATA

Differences in responses to the questionnaire items as a function of the demographic variables (age, academic discipline, group membership, etc.) were determined. The information about response frequency (associated with selected variables) provided support for some of the conclusions found at the end of this report.

The data suggested that perceptions of respondents were affected by their GROUP membership, AGE, and DISCIPLINE assignments. The GROUP membership (student, faculty, librarian) and the AGE category of the survey respondents were identified as significant variables for items 1, 2, 10, 14, 15, and 18. A third variable associated significantly with two (item 5 and 15) of the questionnaire items was the student or faculty academic DISCIPLINE.

Questionnaire item 1 concerned the importance of self-directed learning and independent study in an undergraduate curriculum. This item recognized the maturity of students as an important element in the learning process. A generally positive (OFTEN or ALWAYS) rating was recorded for 55.6 percent of the student respondents and 50.8 percent of the librarians. However, only 38.2 percent of the faculty rated this as a typical or preferred condition of undergraduate curricula.

The AGE of respondents in relation to responses for item 1 indicated strong positive ratings for accepting student maturity and a self-directed study mode of learning among both younger (under 18 through 30 years) and older (51 years and up) respondents. Middle aged respondents (31 through (31 through 50 years) were considerably less positive in their rating of this item. Respondents between the ages of 31 and 50 years comprised 25.3 percent of the total survey population.

Percentage of Responses to Item 1
by Age Category
(For Ratings of "Often Agree"
or "Always Agree")

Less than 18 years	66.6 %
18–20 years	51.2 %
21–30 years	59.6 %
31–40 years	33.3 %
41–50 years	40.0 %
51–60 years	56.2 %
60+ years	83.3 %

Item 2, which asked respondents to characterize the preferred learning mode of a liberal arts program, received a high percentage of negative (SELDOM or NEVER) responses from each group. These ratings reflect a preference for student independent inquiry and critical thinking. Faculty (67.5 percent) and librarians (65 percent) rated this item considerably higher than students (51 percent).

The AGE variable, when considered in relation to responses for item 2, reflect the fact that students (those respondents predominently found in the under 18 through 30 years group) were much less likely than faculty or librarians to positively rate item 2. For respondents to this questionnaire item, students comprized 62.1 percent of the survey population.

Percentage of Responses to Item 2
by Age Category
(For Ratings of "Seldom Agree"
or "Never Agree")

Less than 18 years	44.4 %
18–20 years	55.1 %
21–30 years	43.8 %
31–40 years	72.0 %
41–50 years	64.0 %
51–60 years	68.7 %
60+ years	33.3 %

Item 10 stated the position, advocated by the Library-College, that the learning mode for most fields of study can be library-centered. All three groups generally rejected this position. The librarians rated the position most positively, with 43.3 percent expressing agreement (OFTEN or ALWAYS). The faculty were much less positive (23.7 percent giving positive ratings). Students contributed the lowest positive ratings for this item, 15.9 percent.

The AGE variable was significant in analyzing the survey responses for item 10. It was apparent that middle aged respondents were much less likely than other age groups to negatively rate (SELDOM or NEVER) the library-centered learning mode. The table below reports the data.

Percentage of Responses to Item 10
by Age Category
(For Ratings of "Seldom Agree"
or "Never Agree")

Less than 18 years	27.7 %
18–20 years	40.5 %
21–30 years	23.2 %
31–40 years	19.0 %
41–50 years	18.0 %
51–60 years	31.2 %
60+ years	33.3 %

Survey item 14 stressed the importance of using all information formats in the instruction of undergraduates. The Library-College "generic book" concept advanced this position. Among the librarian group, 44 percent rated this concept positively (OFTEN or ALWAYS), compared to only 36.8 percent of the faculty respondents. Students were less positive about this concept (29.1 percent rated OFTEN or ALWAYS).

Item 5 presented the varied resources of a college library as the principal text for liberal arts students. The Library-College advocated the use of a library's entire collection over the selection of a single textbook for any course of instruction. Only 17.5 percent of the faculty responded positively to this concept (OFTEN or ALWAYS); 36.2 percent responded that they "seldom agreed." Only 20.6 percent of the student respondents agreed with this concept. 35.5 percent of the librarian group rated this item positively.

Considering the DISCIPLINE variable (only found in student and faculty questionnaires) the survey data confirmed that persons associated with the arts and humanities or the social sciences were less negatively disposed to use of the library over single texts (31.5 percent and 31.7 percent, respectively, SELDOM or NEVER agreed) than their business or mathematics and technology counterparts (51.3 percent and 46.3 percent).

Item 15 defined the responsibilities of the instructor in a liberal arts undergraduate curriculum. Using the Library-College model, this item required the instructor to address the learning needs of both groups and individual learners. Student respondents were generally very positive toward this concept (62.1 percent OFTEN or ALWAYS agreed). Librarians and faculty were, however, much less positive (35.5 percent and 40.7 percent, respectively).

From the perspectives of those associated with academic disciplines (students and faculty) the instructor's responsibilities defined in item 15 were generally rated positively. Arts and humanities (60.5 percent), social sciences (58.7 percent), and business-related respondents (57.1 percent) expressed the strongest agreement ratings. Mathematics and technology students and faculty, however, were considerably less positive (only 48.5 percent) toward this definition of an instructor's responsibilities.

The emphasis on a lifetime of learning is a fundamental concept in the liberal arts Library-College model. Item 18 asked survey participants to determine what the ultimate end of an undergraduate liberal arts education should be. Negative ratings (SELDOM or NEVER) for this item represented acceptance of the lifelong learning principle; positive ratings (OFTEN or ALWAYS) reflected agreement with an ultimate educational goal of career readiness or post-graduate study. Students were much more concerned with the satisfaction of immediate needs (career preparation). Only 30.6 percent SELDOM or NEVER agreed with the career training role of a liberal arts curriculum. The faculty and librarian groups, however, strongly endorsed the lifelong learning role of an undergraduate education; they responded 70.3 percent and 71.6 percent in the negative to this survey item.

FINDINGS FOR THE HYPOTHESES

The previous sections of this report documented elements of the statistical analysis of survey data. Each of seven hypotheses was stated in this report as a separate research question.

Hypothesis 1.   There **were** significant differences among the perceptions of all groups concerning the importance of research skills for college students. The librarian group responded much more favorably (3.16 mean score) to the use of library collections over single textbooks (questionnaire item 5) than did faculty (2.83 mean score) or students (2.78 mean score). Similarly, item 10, concerning instruction centered around the library rather than the classroom, the librarian group mean score (3.54) was substantially higher (more positive) than the faculty mean (2.91) or student (2.81). However, the chief academic officers (among the librarian group) contributed more negative ratings for library-centeredness than library administrators or bibliographic instruction librarians.

The survey findings were interpreted to suggest that:

1.   Teaching faculty continue to prefer the traditional mode of textbook instruction.
2.   Textbook instruction continues to be a predominant mode of teaching on the undergraduate level.

3. The acceptance by undergraduate students of textbook instruction may be attributed to their familiarity and comfort with this traditional mode of teaching.
4. Undergraduate curricula continue to be largely content-centered with a focus on the acquisition of a specified body of information; they are less characterized by interdisciplinary study with an emphasis on individualized study and research.
5. The negative faculty and student ratings for item 10 may reflect the influence of a content-centered and textbook based teaching mode.

Hypothesis 2. There **were** significant differences between the perceptions of faculty and librarians concerning student readiness for independent study and research. Students were more positive (3.21 mean score) toward the proposition that student maturity warranted increasing opportunity for self-directed learning (item 1) than librarians (3.51) or faculty (3.42). Persons less than 18 to 30 years of age (predominantly students) strongly favored this concept. For faculty and librarians (found in the 31 to 50 years group) there were fewer ratings of OFTEN or ALWAYS agree and for the 23 respondents over 50 years (who were strongly positive).

For item 2, a negative response (SELDOM or NEVER) indicated support for independent study and critical thinkings. Fifty-eight faculty were strongly negative toward this item, followed by 39 librarians. One hundred twenty-one students were also strongly negative. AGE variable findings for item 2 contributed nearly parallel negative ratings.

The survey findings were interpreted to suggest that:

1. Librarians and students may be considerably more satisfied than faculty that the current prevailing learning mode offers sufficient opportunities for self-directed learning.
2. The lack of a strongly positive faculty response to item 1 may suggest that faculty are less likely to recognize a student's maturity and ability for independent study.
3. Faculty, and librarians to a lesser degree, appear to advocate more student guidance and direction as part of the undergraduate learning mode.
4. Despite the content-centeredness of faculty attitudes in this survey, there is a strong opposition to a traditional mode of learning. Faculty and librarians, more than students, emphasized the importance of independent inquiry and critical thinking.
5. Faculty responses indicated a preference for a less traditional lecture-textbook-recitation learning mode, while reinforcing their belief in the need for teacher-directed rather than student-directed learning.

Hypothesis 3. There **were** significant differences between the perceptions of faculty and librarians concerning the instructional role of college teachers. Item 11 from the questionnaire described the requisite bibliographic skill of instructors while item 12 contrasted a teacher's motivational role favored by the Library-College with the more traditional directive role. The GROUP membership of respondents was found to be the variable which most significantly affected perceptions. For item 11, although more than 58 percent of each group responded positively (SOMETIMES, OFTEN or ALWAYS), the strongest positive ratings came from the librarian group (29 respondents). Within this group, only three respondents (chief academic officers) OFTEN or ALWAYS agreed with the position, closely paralleling faculty responses. Students were not strongly positive (only 41 responded OFTEN or ALWAYS).

Ratings by GROUP membership for item 12 were also predominantly positive, with more than 80 percent of each group selecting responses of SOMETIMES, OFTEN or ALWAYS. Forty from the librarian group selected the highest two positive ratings; within this group, 13 chief academic officers were strongly positive for this proposition. In comparison, while a majority of the faculty (49) selected the highest positive ratings, fewer than half the student sample was highly positive.

The survey findings were interpreted to suggest that:

1. An undergraduate instructor's knowledge of the literature of an academic discipline and the skill to access information related to the discipline is generally favored by all groups.
2. Librarians (both library administrators and bibliographic instruction librarians) are much more likely than members of the other groups to value the importance of bibliographic expertise for undergraduate instructors.
3. All groups favor an instructional mode which is characterized by student-teacher collaboration; instructors in this mode encourage and direct students toward greater degrees of independent learning.
4. Undergraduate students, in contrast to other groups, are less likely to strongly advocate the collaborative and encouraging role for teachers identified above.

Hypothesis 4. There **were** no significant differences among the perceptions of all groups concerning the importance of adult learning principles. Questionnaire items 6 and 17 most directly defined principles of adult learning as expressed originally by Knowles. More than 75 percent of the respondents from each group OFTEN or ALWAYS agreed with item 6. These responses supported the adult learning principle of actively using student life experience as an element of instruction.

For item 17, which stated that adult learners are primarily motivated to learn through identification with the solution of particular problems or issues relevant in life, group responses were generally positive.

The survey findings were interpreted to suggest that:

1. There is general agreement among all groups that a primary motivation to learn among young adult undergraduates is the satisfaction of a need to solve particular intellectual problems, rather than master a body of classified knowledge.
2. The problem-centered learning mode supports a library-centered approach to study because the student will identify and define the intellectual problem in terms of certain issues which require further research (and, therefore, use of the library).

Hypothesis 5. There **were** significant differences among the perceptions of all groups concerning the importance of lifelong learning. Questionnaire item 18, concerning the importance for all groups of lifelong learning, received statistically significant responses for which both GROUP and AGE variables were important. Negative responses (SELDOM or NEVER) for this item supported the rejection of career training and the acceptance of the lifelong learning objective for undergraduate education. Forty-three respondents of the librarian group and 57 faculty endorsed the lifelong learning objective. However, 73 students rejected the career training objective, demonstrating significantly lower positive support for this proposition.

Regarding the AGE variable, 75 persons less than 18 to 30 years (predominantly students) rejected the career training proposition. Among persons between the ages of 31 and 50 years, 92, a strong majority for this age group, rejected this proposition; 26 respondents over 50 years of age responded similarly.

The survey findings were interpreted to suggest that there were significant differences between the attitudes of students and both the faculty and librarian groups concerning the importance of lifelong learning as a principal objective of undergraduate education. Students and other respondents under 31 years of age valued a more immediate application of learning (for career or post-graduate study) than did faculty or librarians.

Hypothesis 6. There **were** significant differences between the perceptions of faculty and librarians concerning conditions necessary for the implementation of a library-centered program of instruction on the undergraduate level. Questionnaire items 14 and 15 most directly related to this research question. For both items, the GROUP membership and AGE variables were significant in association with the responses.

Item 14 asserted the primacy of the Library-College "generic book" (information in all its formats) for communicating knowledge. The source of these formats for undergraduate learning was identified as the academic library. The strongest approval rating (OFTEN or ALWAYS) for this item came from library administrators (47.7 percent or 10 respondents). Among members of the librarian group as a whole, 26 respondents selected the two highest positive approval categories, compared with only 28 faculty. Students expressed the lowest positive approval for this position (only 68 respondents). More than 60 percent of each group selected SOMETIMES, OFTEN or ALWAYS for item 14.

Item 15 described primary faculty instructional responsibilities as defined for a Library-College. These responsibilities were associated on the questionnaire with every course of study. Faculty respondents (27 persons) rated this position more negatively (SELDOM or NEVER), while students (31 respondents) contributed the lowest negative rating. Twelve respondents from the librarian group negatively rated this item. Young adults (under 31 years of age) were the most positive (142 persons); followed by persons 31 to 50 years (38 respondents); 39.5 percent of those respondents over 50 years of age contributed positive ratings.

The survey findings were interpreted to suggest that:

1. In order to successfully implement a library-centered curriculum, librarians, more readily than any other group, advocate the primacy of information resources (the "generic book") in all formats as a basis for learning.
2. Students are the most likely group to favor prescribed instructional tasks from instructors, regardless of the course of study; faculty, however, are the most resistant to prescribed instructional responsibilities and tasks for them or their students.

Hypothesis 7. The final four questionnaire items (not numbered) related to perceptions of an academic librarian's instructional role. The first two of these received the most statistically significant differences in respondents from the survey participants. The first item (twentieth on the questionnaire) presented the most traditional role of the librarian as a reference service and information resource agent. The second item (twenty-first on the questionnaire) presented the librarian's role as an active contributor to instruction (working directly with individual students and groups). The strongest ranking (1 on a 4-point scale of 1 to 4) was assigned by faculty (1.75 mean rank) and students (1.59 mean rank) to the traditional resource agent role. Members of the librarian group, however, preferred (1.79 mean rank) the active contributor role.

Although the twenty-second and twenty-third items on the questionnaire also addressed variations in a librarian's instructional role, no group ranked these role variations as strongly as they did the first two.

The survey findings were interpreted to suggest that:

1. Librarians may see their instructional role as more directly centered on meeting student and faculty information needs than on forming an instructional partnership with faculty.
2. The service orientation rather than active instructional role is a more readily accepted distinction for faculty and students than for librarians; librarians tend to identify these role distinctions as inseparable.
3. The traditional faculty-associated curriculum development role continues to be generally accepted by both librarians and students.
4. Faculty and students identify academic librarians most often as non-instructional service agents rather than as instructional professionals.

The findings from this study demonstrated that a library-centered instructional program like that advocated in the Library-College concept was not a current reality in American higher education. Many of the primary elements of such a program (see their description as questionnaire items), however, had been positively perceived by participants in this Pennsylvania survey of students, faculty, and non-instructional personnel.

THE FINDINGS CONSIDERED

One important conclusion drawn from this study's findings was the apparent distinction between positive faculty attitudes toward traditional modes of instruction and their contrasting strong advocacy of a student learning mode which fostered more critical thinking and independent inquiry. This conclusion differed from Jordan's (1986) assessment of present conditions. The difference between surveyed perceptions and assessed conditions support a the favorable implementation of an interdisciplinary, library-centered, liberal arts education.

Both Pearson (1980) and a Carnegie Foundation study (Major Carnegie recommendations, 1986) strongly advocated the importance of professorial knowledge of the literature in their field of study and strong research and bibliographic skills. This study concluded that such requisite skills were equally valued by each group of respondents. However, the call for improved faculty bibliographic expertise cited by Lubans (1970) and McCarthy (1985) was championed most strongly by the members of the librarian group.

The content-centeredness of current undergraduate curricula identified by Robinson (1976) and Jordan (1986) was contrasted with the prevailing attitudes measured in this study. All groups accepted the proposition that problem-solving was a strong motivation for student learning. This problem-centered perspective reflected Robinson's assertion that education's value was found in the nurturing of a student's ability to resolve intellectual problems.

The findings of this study also supported the conclusion that faculty and librarians had strong positive attitudes toward an undergraduate education's preparation of students for a lifetime of learning. This conclusion paralleled an important Carnegie Foundation recommendation (A House divided, 1986). However, the survey for this study also documented, in contrast to the importance of lifelong learning, the substantially greater student interest in immediate application (career preparation or post-graduate study) of learning as a primary aim of an undergraduate education.

A major building block of the Library-College and a central element of library-centered education was the concept of the "generic book." The centrality to liberal arts of information resources in all formats was articulated by MacGregor and McInnis (1977); it was most strongly supported in this study by librarians.

A principal focus of this study concerned the faculty, student, and librarian perceptions of the librarian's major instructional role in undergraduate education. Benson (1981) advocated a central curriculum development role for academic librarians, similar to that advanced by the Library-College. The findings of this study, however, reinforced the prevalence of traditional attitudes among faculty and students toward the librarian as a key reference resource and research agent, rather than as a full partner in the instruction of undergraduates. Terwilliger's (1975) recommendation (advanced education beyond the professional degree in library science) could counteract the exclusion of librarians from the instructional ranks.

RECOMMENDATIONS

This study of attitudes and perceptions in the American academic community resulted in conclusions which formed the basis for the following recommendations. Further study is needed to increase the detail and focus of these recommendations. For example, a future study using a program evaluation method jointly developed by librarians and faculty should be conducted to systematically assess the impact on the quality of student academic performance in a library-centered program of study.

It is recommended that library-centered elements identified in this study be incorporated in the general undergraduate curriculum. The Library-College model is an ideal which initially identified and advocated the application in undergraduate education of these elements.

It is recommended that bibliographic skills and library-centered instruction be introduced in the first year of undergraduate study. This recommendation is based on supportive faculty attitudes toward the early introduction of these skills. Such skills and their early and continual application within the first year of study can contribute to a student's more successful and extensive use of the academic library. Early bibliographic instruction and skill use also can foster an undergraduate course of study which is more interdisciplinary and problem-centered, and less reflective of the traditional lecture-textbook-recitation teaching mode.

It is recommended that there be greater articulation of bibliographic instruction programs between lower division (first two years of undergraduate study) and upper division programs. This articulation can foster the integrated use of bibliographic skills throughout the introductory and advanced levels of undergraduate study.

It is recommended that the concept of the "generic book" be expanded to include advancing computerized information retrieval options essential to all educated persons. This recommendation reinforces an appropriate active instructional role for the academic librarian, recognizing the current and growing prevalence of computerized database services in libraries.

It is recommended that there be increased levels and varieties of duties for library support staff members. This may free librarians from many repetitive but complex tasks which may appropriately be performed at a paraprofessional level; the resulting benefit would be the opportunity for librarians to apply a higher degree of effort to the instructional process. Support for this action should be sought from both the Association of College and Research Libraries (American Library Association) and the Council on Library-Media Technical Assistants.

It is also recommended that results of this and similar studies concerning the instructional role of librarians in liberal arts education be disseminated to members of the teaching faculty and chief academic officers in order to increase their awareness of the academic library and librarians as valuable instructional resources.

The study suggested that there is a general acceptance among all academic groups of the principles of adult learning as associated with an undergraduate liberal arts education. However, the survey also confirmed the prevailing faculty and student preference for a more directive, teacher-centered rather than teacher-student instructional mode.

There exist today undergraduate programs, such as those associated with the work of Evan Farber at Earlham College, which represent an effective library-centered curriculum. It is hoped that the recognition of these programs in conjunction with this study provides an enhanced understanding and acceptance of the academic librarian's role in the instruction of young adult undergraduates, particularly as this role fosters independent inquiry and critical, problem-centered thinking.

REFERENCES

Allen, D. Y. (1982). Students need help in learning how to use the library. *The Chronicle of Higher Education, 24* (June 9), 56.

Along the L-C way. *Learning Today, 9*, 1 (Winter 1976), 14.

American Library Association, Association of Colleges and Reference Libraries; College and University Postwar Planning Committee. (1946). *College and university libraries and librarianship: An examination of their present status and future development.* Chicago, IL: American Library Association.

Association of College and Research Libraries; Committee on Standards. (1959). Standards for college libraries. *College and Research Libraries, 20* (July), 278.

Astin, A. W. (1986). *The American freshman: Twenty year trends, 1966–1985.* [Summary]. Los Angeles: University of California, Higher Education Research Institute.

Benson, S. H. (1979). *Administering course-related library instruction programs in selected academic libraries* (Doctoral Dissertation, University of Oklahoma, 1979).

Benson, S. H. (1981). Has education ever gotten so little for so much? *Learning Today, 12* (1), 40–46.

Berdie, D. R., Anderson, J. F. and Neibuhr, M. A. (1974). *Questionnaires: Design and use.* Metuchen, N. J.: The Scarecrow Press, Inc.

Bevan, J. M. (1978). Faculty resource pool: Mark of an innovative institution (Address presented at the NCLA conference, 1977). *North Carolina Libraries, 35,* (Winter), 33–41.

Bird, C. (1975). Where college fails us. *Signature, 10,* 60.

Boorstin, D. J. (1974). *Democracy and its discontents; Reflections on everyday America.* New York: Random House.

Breivik, P. S. (1978). Leadership, management, and the teaching library. *Library Journal, 103* (October), 2048.

Brown, B. et al. (1978). Covering culture gulch (A personalized study of journalism). *Learning Today, 11,* (Summer-Fall), 34–48.

Bryson, E. M. and Kelly, W., ed. (1982). *Library research manual: History.* ERIC (ED229011).

Buddy, J. W. (1982). Orientation to the university library: The missing link. *NASSP Bulletin* (December), 99–102.

Cammack, F. M. (1980). Chance of a lifetime; Independent education. *Hawaiian Library Association Journal, 37,* 3–20.

Cammack, F. M. (1979). Leeward Library offers learning licenses. *Community and Junior College Journal, 49* (April), 32–35.

Carlson, D. H. and Miller, R. H. (1984). Librarians and teaching faculty: Partners in bibliographic instruction. *College and Research Libraries, 45* (November), 483–491.

Checke, R. A. (1980). It's definitely more than rhetoric! (A review of literature on implementing Library-College). *Learning Today, 13* (Summer), 40–58.

Clayton, E. R. (1981). Measuring effects of a liberal education. *Nursing Outlook, 29,* 10 (October), 582–587.

Clayton, H. (1978). Conversation on the Library-College between Lucious Dimkopf, Williston Wallingford, Ernest Youngblood. *Learning Today, 11* (Winter), 28–46.

Clayton, H. (1978). Scholiast (The Library-College experimenter). *Learning Today, 11* (Summer-Fall), 8–10.

Clayton, H. (1976). What is this Library-College business? *Learning Today, 9,* 36–71.

Clayton, H. and Jordan, R. T. (1971). Library College. In *The Encyclopedia of Education* (Volume 5, pp. 608–613). New York: Macmillan.

Dameron, J. R. (1978). The generic book in action. *Learning Today, 11* (Summer-Fall), 73–75.

Deekle, P. V. (1986, August). [Interview with Robert and Kathy Jordan]. Alexandria, Virginia.

Deekle, P. V. (1986, August). [Interview with Gloria Terwilliger]. Alexandria, Virginia.

Deekle, P. V. (1987). *The Impact of Library-College Centered Instruction on the Formal Education of Liberal Arts Students.* (Doctoral Dissertation, Temple University, 1987).

DeHart, F. (1970). The Library-College and graduate library education. *Journal of Education for Librarianship,* 298–301.

DePriest, E. R. (1977). Wanted: A rational for the academic library. *Improving College and University Teaching,* xxv (Summer), 173–177.

Draft: Standards for college libraries; 1975 revision. (1974). *College and Research Libraries News, 35* (December), 284–305.

An evaluation checklist for reviewing a college library program. (1979). *College and Research Libraries News,* (November), 305–319.

Fishbein, M. and Ajzen, I. (1975). *Belief, attitude, intuition and behavior: An introduction to theory and research*. Reading, MA: Addison-Wesley.

Fitzpatrick, K. (1978). Caldwell '78 (Workshop on the Library-College concept). *Learning Today, 11* (Spring), 19–20.

Ford, J. E. (1982). The natural alliance between librarians and English teachers in course-related library use instruction. *College and Research Libraries*, (September), 379–384.

Ford, N. (1979). Towards a model for library learning in educational systems. *Journal of Librarianship, 11* (October), 247–260.

Gavryck, J. (1986). Information research skills: Sharing the Burden. *Wilson Library Bulletin, 60*, 22–24.

Givens, J. (1974). The use of resources in the learning experience. In *Advances in librarianship, 4* (pp. 149–174). New York: Academic Press.

Gossage, W. (1975). The American Library-College movement in 1968: The library as curriculum, and teaching with books. *Education Libraries Bulletin, 18* (2), 1–21.

Grady, M. P. and Harvey, Sr. J. (1980). Teacher is a learner (St. Louis University Open Learning Area). *Learning Today, 13* (Fall), 38–44.

Guskin, A. E., Stoffle, C. J., and Boisse, J. A. (1979). The academic library as a teaching library: A role for the 1980s. *Library Trends, 28* (Fall), 281–296.

Gwinn, M. E. (1980). Academic libraries and the undergraduate education: The CRL experience. *College and Research Libraries, 41* (January), 5–16.

Gwinn, N. E. (1978). The faculty-library connection. *Change, 10* (September), 19–21.

Harkins, M. T. (1975). Evaluation of Library-College methods. *Learning Today, 8*, 4 (Fall), 66–68.

Harris S. (Ed.) (1986). *Accredited institutions of postsecondary education: 1985–86*. Washington, D. C.: American Council on Education.

Hatt, F. (1978). Library instruction, individualized learning and independent learning (Paper presented at ARLIS seminar on user education held at Leeds Polytechnic Institute, 7–8 April, 1978). *Art Library Journal, 3* (Winter), 5–16.

Haworth, D. E. (1982). Library services to the off-campus and independent learning: a review of it. *Journal of Librarianship, 14* (July), 157–175.

Haywood, C. R. (1978). *The doing of history; A practical use of the Library-College concept*. Norman, OK: The Library-College Associates, Inc.

A House divided: Prologue. (1986). Washington, D.C.: The Carnegie Foundation for the Advancement of Teaching.

Hover, L. M. (1979). *The independent learner and the academic library: Access and impact*. Saur Verlag (pp. 545–549).

It just goes on and on; Teaching reading through the Library-College concept (1980). *Learning Today*, (Spring), 78–79.

It's all right here (1978). *Learning Today, 11* (Winter), 22.

It's all in the method; Teaching through the Library-College (1980). *Learning Today, 13* (Spring), 74–76.

John, you don't say! (Reply to "Educating the user") (1978). *Learning Today, 11* (Spring), 28–29.

Jordan, R. T. (1980). Academic libraries and undergraduate education (Letter in reply to N. E. Gwinn). *College and Research Libraries, 41* (May), 245–246.

Jordan, R. T. (1986, August). [Interview with Robert T. Jordan, Alexandria, Virginia].

Kathman, M. D. (1983). National invitational conference on independent scholarship. *College and Research Libraries News, 3* (March), 75–77.

King, D. N. and Ory, J. C. (1981). Effects of library instruction on student research: A case study. *College and Research Libraries, (January)*, 31–41.

Kinney, L. C. (1977). Librarians as educators. *Community and Junior College Journal*, 10–11, 27.

Knowles, M. S. and associates. (1984). *Andragogy in action; Applying modern principles of adult learning* San Francisco, CA: Jossey-Bass, Inc.

Kuhlman, A. F. (1938). *College and university library service: Trends, standards, appraisal, problems* (Papers presented at the 1937 Midwinter Meeting of the American Library Association). Chicago, IL: American Library Association.

Labaw, P. J. (1980). *Advanced questionnaire design*. Cambridge, MA: Abt Books.

Lehman, A. E. (Ed.) (1985). *Guide to four-year colleges: 1986*. Princeton, NJ: Peterson's Guides.

Library user instruction in academic and research libraries (1977). *ARL Management Supplement, 5* (September), 1.

Lipschutz, D. (1984). A practical approach to teaching library skills to freshmen. *Journal of College Student Personnel, 25* (November), 560–561.

Lubans, J. (1970). On non-use of academic libraries: A report of findings. In *Use, mis-use and non-use of academic libraries* (pp. 47–72). New York Library Association, College and University Libraries Section.

Luckenbill, W. B. (1983). Learning resources and interactive learning principles. *Drexel Library Quarterly, 19* (Spring), 91–116.

McCarthy, C. (1985). The faculty problem. *Journal of Academic Librarianship, 11* (July), 142–145.

McCrum, B. P. (1937). *An estimate of standards for a college library: Planned for use of librarians when presenting budgets to administrative boards*. Lexington, VA: Journalism Laboratory Press, Washington and Lee University.

MacGregor, J. and McInnis, R. G. (1977). Integrating classroom instruction and library research. *Journal of Higher Education, 48* (January), 17–38.

Major Carnegie recommendations to improve the undergraduate experience [Summary]. In, *College: The undergraduate experience in America* (1986). New York: Harper and Row.

Melom, C. (1979). *The Library-College program at Long Beach City College*. Master's thesis, University of California, Los Angeles. ERIC (ED172887).

The mission of an undergraduate library (Model statement). (1979). *College and Research Libraries News, 10* (November), 317–318.

Muldoon, J. P. (1985). Library skills: A lifelong necessity. *NASSP Bulletin* (April), 98–99.

Naisbitt, J. (1982). *Megatrends*. New York: Warner Books.

Nobody's asking for a revolution: An interview with Samuel B. Gould. (1980). *Learning Today, 13* (Spring), 38–45.

Norman, A. (1977). Central Tech adopts lab learning approach. *Nebraska Library Association Quarterly, 11* (Summer), 25–26.

Oppenheim, A. N. (1966). *Questionnaire design and attitude measurement*. New York: Basic Books.

Palmer, S. E. (1983). Teaching students to do research: Professors get help from libraries. *The Chronicle of Higher Education, 26*, (May 18), 27–28.

Pearson, L. (1978). What has the library done for you lately? *Improving College and University Teaching, 26* (Fall), 219–221.

Pearson, L. (1980). Curriculum-integrated library instruction. *Liberal Education, 66* (Winter), 402–409.

Pearson, P. and Tiefel, V. (1982). Evaluating undergraduate library instruction at The Ohio State University. *Journal of Academic Librarianship, 7* (January), 351–357.

Person, R. (1981). Long-term evaluation of bibliographic instruction: Lasting encouragement. *College and Research Libraries*, (January), 19–25.

A personnel program for selected faculty employments in Pennsylvania State Colleges and University. (1969). Chicago, IL: Public Administration Service.

Piagetian catechism on Library-College thought. (1980). *Learning Today, 13* (Fall), 46–54.

Rader, H. B. (1986). The teaching library enters the electronic age. *College and Research Libraries News, 47*, 6 (June), 402–404.

Roberts, A. (1978). *A study of ten SUNY campuses offering an undergraduate credit course in library instruction*. Washington, D.C.: Council on Library Resources.

Robinson, T. E. (1976). *The teacher: Key to library-centered instruction*. Norman, OK: The Library-College Associates, Inc.

Scherdin, M. J. (1984). A marriage that works: An approach to administrative structure in curriculum centers. *College and Research Libraries, 45,* 2, 140–147.

Schiller, A. (1968). *Characteristics of professional personnel in college and research libraries.* Urbana, IL: University of Illinois Research Center.

Schuster, Sr. M. (1977). *The library-centered approach to learning.* Palm Springs, CA: ETC Publications.

Seeing the light: When students do library-centered study they learn on their own. (1978). *Learning Today, 11* (Winter), 23–24.

Sellen, M. K. and Jirouch, J. (1984). Perceptions of library use by faculty and students: A Comparison. *College and Research Libraries, 45* (July), 259–267.

Shaw, M. E. and Wright, J. M. (1967). *Scales for the measurement of attitudes.* New York: McGraw-Hill Book Co.

Sheehan, H. B. (1976). The student and the Library-College. *Learning Today, 9,* 2 (Spring), 30–45.

Sheppard, S. (1976). Selling the Library-College. *Library-College Experimenter, 2,* 10–14.

Sheppard, S. (1981). New experimenter [Independent study]. *Learning Today, 14* (Winter), 65–68.

Siepmann, C. (1973). The ubiquitous and the absurd. *Learning Today, 6,* 33–40.

Smalley, T. N. (1977). Bibliographic instruction in academic libraries: Questioning some assumptions. *Journal of Academic Librarianship, 3* (November), 280–283.

Smith, B. J. (1980). The state of library user instruction in colleges and universities in the United States. *Peabody Journal of Education, 58,* 15–21.

Spencer, R. C. (1978). The teaching library. *Library Journal, 103* (May 15), 1021–1024.

Standards for university libraries. (1979). *College and Research Libraries News, 4* (April), 101–110.

Terwilliger, G. H. P. (1975). The library-college: A movement for experimental and innovative learning concepts: Applications and implications for higher education (Doctoral Dissertation, University of Maryland, 1975). *University Microfilms International.* (Order No. MAC73–08446).

The unity of becoming: A mini-explanation of the Library-College concept. (1983). *Learning Today, 16,* 46–47.

Waples, D. (1936). The library. *The evaluation of higher institutions* (Vol. IV). Chicago, Il: University of Chicago Press.

Weigand, W. A. (1977). Toward the Library-College . . . step . . . by . . . step. *Learning Today, 10,* 42–49.

Werking, R. H. (1976). *The library and the college: Some programs of library instruction.* U. S. Department of Health, Education, and Welfare, National Institute of Education. ERIC (ED127917).

Whoever would have thought it? [The Library-College workshop]. (1980). *Learning Today, 13,* 22–25.

Why ideas fail [Committee discussion of the Library-College concept]. (1978). *Learning Today, 11* (Spring), 22–24.

Williams, B. R. (1977). *The Library-College in higher education: A survey of five of its structural components.* ERIC (ED180486).

Williams, B. R. (1980). Will the critics ever learn? *Learning Today, 13,* 2, 50–53.

Winter, D. G. et al. (1981). *A new case for the liberal arts.* ERIC (ED208764).

Wood, R. J. (1984). The impact of a library research course on students at Slippery Rock University. *Journal of Academic Librarianship, 10* (November), 278–284.

Yerburgh, M. R. (1979). The utilization of academic librarians as classroom teachers: Some brief observations. *Academe, 65,* (November), 441–443.

You expect what of me? [An interview with Richard Sacksteder, Shoreline School, Seattle]. (1978). *Learning Today, 11* (Spring), 36–48.

Zemke, R. and Zemke, S. (1981). 30 Things We Know for Sure about Adult Learning. *Training, 18* (June), 45–46, 48–49, 52.

COLLEGE LIBRARIES:
THE COLONIAL PERIOD
TO THE TWENTIETH CENTURY

Eugene R. Hanson

INTRODUCTION

The role of the college and university library in early America was largely determined by the philosophical, social, economic and cultural levels of our society at that time. During this period, education in general was at a premium, being reserved largely for those who were gifted with sufficient economic resources and social stature.

Although many of the first settlers had been dissatisfied with the religious, economic and political opportunities of the old country, most of them had accepted the status quo of the educational institutions and attempted to emulate them in America. The means of education varied from one colony to another because of the concepts and demands regarding educational needs (Good, 1947:

Advances in Library Administration and Organization,
Volume 8, pages 171-199.
Copyright © 1989 by JAI Press Inc.
All rights of reproduction in any form reserved.
ISBN: 0-89232-967-X

374). The northern colonies were settled primarily by working classes while the southern areas were dominated by the aristocracy who adopted the plantation system. Social classes and religious fevor both had a definite impact on the development of basic and higher education.

During the early colonial period the literacy rate was not easily determined but it was probably in the 25 percent range. In 1870, illiteracy was 20 percent thus substantial progress had been made in the last century (*Historical Statistics*, 1975: 382). Educational efforts within the 13 colonies were primarily concerned with the training of apprentices who eventually would become tradesmen, religious instruction which required rudementary knowledge of reading and writing, and the education of clergy and landed gentry who attended colleges and later universities. Education during this early period was viewed as the responsibility of the parents who relied heavily upon a variety of institutions. Apprentices received instruction primarily in the workplace while religious training and basic instruction in reading and writing were the responsibility of the churches, missionary societies, charity schools, locally supported neighborhood schools and private schools or tutors. A very limited system of public education existed before the mid-nineteenth century in most parts of America and was primarily concerned with the members of the poor and lower classes. Although many leaders professed support for universal education, the question of who should establish, develop, and support educational institutions at all levels was of major concern. The church traditionally retained responsibility for imparting the basic skills necessary for religious practices.

Basic or elementary education was the most pressing issue because of the need for a labor force and an educated citizenry who would be able to read and comprehend the principles of religion and the capital laws of the land. Early efforts by the colonies supporting elementary school, known by various names, were augmented by an increasing number of state and local laws.

By the last decade of the eighteenth and the first half of the nineteenth a spirit of republicanism, a wide acceptance of French deism, and a belief in the value of a literate citizenry were influencing social and educational demands.

Undoubtedly the paucity of educational opportunities may be attributed to a general lack of need for extensive education because of the limited level of technological development within our society at that time. Our economy until the middle of the nineteenth century was primarily dependent upon agrarian pursuits with the majority of the citizenry concentrating upon obtaining the necessities of life while the more humanistic ideals were expressed through the formation of the few existing colleges.

Some colonies were very progressive in defining the role of the government in educational matters. A unified state supported system of common schools developed very early in Massachusetts and New York while the Middle Atlantic and Southern states relied more heavily upon parochial and private until a later period. It was almost an unwritten law that wherever there were no elementary and secondary schools, a college would develop (Rudolf, 1965: 48). With the passage of the first compulsory attendance law in Massachusetts in 1852 a definite pattern of common school growth began which eventually was followed by other states so that by 1890 nearly one-half of the states has such laws (Good, 1947: 450).

After their establishment, the development of secondary education paralleled that of the elementary or common schools. A form of secondary education intended to train young men for college, was manifested in the Latin or grammar schools which were both privately and publicly supported. The latter were generally established in the eighteenth century and tended to offer more courses which were more widely in demand rather than the classical literary curriculum. Both prospered for several decades but were eventually replaced by a newer form, the academy which at first tended to be located in the larger cities during the middle of the eighteenth century. Although primarily concerned with preparing students for college, they provided general and vocational education and trained teachers for the common schools. Many of the academies eventually became colleges. The English classical school was another type of secondary education which was established in Massachusetts as a replacement for the academy.

Once legislation was in place by the middle of the nineteenth century the rapid expansion of secondary education at public expense followed the pattern of development so prevalent in Massachusetts, Connecticut, Rhode Island and New York. The ratification of the Constitution in 1789 reaffirmed the responsibility of each state for the development of a system of public education. Thus the efforts made by many of the northern colonies served as a firm basis for further growth. By 1890 approximately 2,500 public high schools were operating in the United States plus a number of programs combining the last two years of high school with the first two years of college (Kandel, 1930: 449).

The need for a college education was primarily limited to those of economic means and those seeking entry into the ministry, medicine, and politics. Reading and learning for the professional person were associated with the day to day activities while for the common individual it was most closely associated with spiritual well being and the earning of a living.

Collegial education was also at a minimum level with an estimated one out of every 1000 colonial citizens in 1775 having attended college at one time or another (Greene, 1943: 123). In all of the colonies at this time there were approximately 2,500 living college graduates (Thwing, 1906: 165). A survey of a group of Yale graduates revealed that during the early seventeen hundreds over seventy percent of the graduates became clergymen although subsequent years indicated a gradual decline: 37 percent by 1761, 22 percent by 1801, 30 percent by 1836, 20 percent by 1861, 11 percent by 1881, and 6 percent by 1900 (Hofstadter and Hardy, 1952: 7). A concern for spiritual matters permeated not only the atmosphere and programs of the denominational institutions but also those supported by public revenue. An ambivalence toward temporal and scholarly learning undoubtedly was the result of colonial America's economic and social orientation in which the Puritan philosophy was blended with the rugged individual and the realization that hard physical work was necessary in most cases in order to earn a living in a frontier setting.

As the population increased, the standard of living rose, technological and industrial development became common, and the demand for specialized education and training increased. As noted in the case of secondary education, the need for strictly a classical education at the levels beyond basic education gave way to greater interest in general, scientific, and vocational subjects.

A similar change was taking place within the colleges and universities as indicated by changing aims and goals of higher education. The objectives of American higher education have frequently been characterized as diverse and confused undoubtedly because of its attempted response to the forces in society. Studies of the literature of higher education indicated that approximately 28 aims and objectives were mentioned by various authors between the period 1842 to 1860 (McKenna, 1963: 120–23). During the early period from 1842–1876, the major purpose (63 percent) was upon moral and religious development, liberal education and mental discipline. By 1909–1921, emphasis on this purpose had decreased to 39 percent and by the 1925–1939 it dropped to 8 percent only to rebound to 27 percent in the 1947–1952 and 19 percent in the 1956–1960 period. Although the purpose of "mental discipline" had disappeared completely by the late period, interest in the traditional liberal arts objective of higher education decreased somewhat during the last quarter of the nineteenth century although it continued to be a strong contender. By the end of the century, the objectives of higher education seemed to be shifting from the broad general goals to the more specific and pragmatic ones pertaining to "civic and social responsibilities." Later such aims as "development of scholarly aims and ambitions, adjustment to the modern world, and development of the individual as a person" were widely supported.

The curriculum of the typical college prior to 1850 had been based on the liberal arts. This classical approach centered around the trivium (grammar, rhetoric, and logic) for the undergraduates and the quadrivium (geometry, arithmetic, music and astronomy) for the more advanced student. The latter was often referred to as the three philosophies of Aristotle and consisted of mental, moral, and natural philosophy. The first was a combination of psychology and logic; the second, contained ethics, law, and politics with a smattering of economics; and the third was physics and some biology. All of these were in turn based on a knowledge of Latin, Greek, and some Hebrew.

Between 1780 and the Civil War, the college curriculum slowly responded to the changing conditions within society by adding subjects outside the classical realm such as mathematics, the natural and physical sciences and modern languages. The change, however, was laborious as Koch theorized that curriculum at Harvard had experienced practically no change in its first two centuries of existence (Koch, 1924: 18). The origins of the elective system allowed students to pursue a wider field of study. Between 1795–1850 it was estimated that over 15 colleges had some kind of experimental curriculum such as the parallel course of study or the direct addition of scientific and practical courses (Hofstadter and Hardy, 1952: 23). Many colleges were establishing separate technical schools such as the Scheffield Scientific School at Yale and Lawrence Scientific School at Harvard in 1847 (Hofstadter and Hardy, 1952: 27). Engineering was added to the liberal arts courses of Union College as early as 1846. The composition of the governing boards was radically changing from a predominance of clergymen to professional men. By 1860 only 30 percent of the college trustees were clergymen, dropping to an all time low of 7 percent in 1930 (Hofstadter and Hardy, 1952: 33). The philosophy of mental discipline was slowly giving way, to serving the needs of the people. American colleges up to 1800 were graduating less than sixty bachelor's degrees a year, compared to over 400,000 by the middle of the twentieth century (Dobler, 1963: 4).

The period following the Civil War was characterized by a large number of factors which had a decided affect upon higher education. A few of these were:

1. Decline of sectarian influence
2. Morrill Act, 1862, authorizing the establishment of the Land Grant universities.
3. Demand for graduates with practical training rather than only classical knowledge
4. Growth of the university particularly those derived and supported by state legislative action
5. Growth of manual and vocational colleges and technical schools
6. Expansion of the elective system
7. Expanded curriculum with emphasis on social science, science, and applied arts
8. Rise of professional schools
9. Establishment of normal schools
10. Establishment and growth of women's colleges
11. Newer methods of teaching such as seminar, laboratory, and independent study
12. Increased enrollment in secondary schools
13. Philanthropic donations for educational institutions
14. Rise of professional administrators such as Eliot of Harvard and Harper of Chicago
15. Increase in college enrollment, doubling by the end of the nineteenth century (resulting as a consequence and a cause of curricular change)

German universities exerted considerable influence upon American education. As early as 1815 George Ticknor and Edward Everett were championing the German emphasis in the sciences and the social sciences. Both practical studies and pure scholarship moved forward in the form of education for specialists.

The goals of the colleges and universities during the Civil War period were expressed by the achievements in "mental discipline, liberal education, religious training, speech and manners" while those of the latter decade of the century were aimed at: "civil and social responsibility, morality and character, domestic responsibility, training for leadership, occupation or pre-professional training, knowledge for its own sake, development of scholarly interest and ambition, training for life's needs, recreational and aesthetic aspects, selection for higher education, and exploration and guidance (Koos, 1921: 499–509).

The establishment of Johns Hopkins in 1876 ushered in the age of the American University with its emphasis on scholarly research which was to continue to exert tremendous pressure on the curriculum, faculty, and facilities such as laboratories and libraries. Improved methods of instruction were beginning to replace textbook-recitation which had persisted so long. Reading courses, independent study, and other forms of research necessitated the use of printed materials. The growth of the scientific method, the proliferation of printed material, the rise of professional librarians, increased financial support, influences of the federal government, and the rising enrollment all exerted considerable influence upon the place of the library in the structure of higher education. Hofstader and Hardy summarized the change and evolution of higher education at the beginning of the twentieth century:

> The old college, noble as its goals were, had been hampered by meagre support and by its own inflexibility. Its curriculum had been inadequate, its teaching unimaginative, its tone dogmatic. The university era brought decided improvements, but it carried most colleges to opposite extremes in an effort to eliminate old failings. The straitjacket curriculum was abandoned, but too often in favor of a disorganized elective system. The classics were divested of their monopoly, but the value of classical culture was almost forgotten. Excellent new methods of teaching came into use, but in large institutions they were swamped by the exigencies of mass education. Theology and dogma were largely displaced, but education lost too much of its emotional and spiritual content. Science won a larger place, but science teaching was too often given a sharp preprofessional slant to the neglect of its broader intellectual possibilities. The idealistic old college gave way to a new one with an excessive vocational bias (Hofstadter and Hardy, 1952: 56).

AVAILABILITY AND CONTENT
OF PUBLISHED MATERIALS

The content of the collection was limited to a great degree during this period by the types of material which were available for purchase and donation. Until the Revolution, the majority of the books were imported from England with the local colonial presses serving primarily to supply functional or practical materials such as pamphlets, school texts, newspapers and business or legal forms. Evans listed some 34,000 titles including newspapers, almanacs, and assembly laws and proceedings which were issued by the English Colonial Press in America from 1639–1791 (Evans). Between 1640 and 1776 it was estimated that an average of about 60 books a year emanated from the printing presses in this country until the development of national literature in 1820 (Growoll, 1939: i). Benedict found that the subject content of the total production of the colonial press from 1639 to 1763 was theology 37 percent, law 19.5 percent, literature 19.5 percent, political science 6.5 percent, social science 4.5 percent, history 4.5 percent, education 3.5 percent, science 1.5 percent, economics 1.5 percent, applied science and art 1.0 percent, philosophy .5 percent, and bibliography .5 percent (Lehmann-Haupt, 1939: 31). Material imported from England allowed a great variety although the number of religious titles remained comparatively high as reported in the *Port Folio*, published in Philadelphia in 1800 (Growoll, 1939; xi).

The first American attempt at a trade bibliography issued by a number of Boston Booksellers in 1804, listed 1,338 American publications in print (*Catalogue of Books Printed in the United States* in *Growoll*, pt. II). The catalogue was arranged in six divisions plus a short listing of 32 Bibles and 19 omissions which fell in several categories. The most titles occurred within the miscellanies section which was composed of 796 titles including literature, political science, natural and physical science, mathematics, history, rhetoric, moral science, etc.; second was divinity which consisted of 259; third were school books with 110; fourth, physics with 63 titles; fifth, law with 34; and last, singing books with 25.

During the last quarter of the eighteenth century domestic book production increased substantially and there seemed to be a greater balance between secular and ecclesiastical titles. In 1778 a total of 461 titles were in print in this country with 37 in theology, 17 in literature, 15 in social science, 12 in political science, 8 in music, 7 in medicine and the balance in the miscellaneous (Lehmann-Haupt, 1939: 102). By 1798 a total of 1801 were reported with 244 in theology, 203 in literature, 143 in political science, 62 in social science, 38 in medicine, 16 in music, and the balance were miscellaneous (Lehmann-Haupt, 1939: 102). The highest multiple of increase had been recorded in the area of political science and literature although the production of titles in theology remained high. There appeared to be a shifting of intellectual interests from those closely confined to theology to more broadly based cultural endeavors particularly in literature and political science. The influence of a more stable society, expanded physical growth and experimentation with political idealism was having more impact upon the demands of American readers.

During the period between 1830 and 1842 book production remained limited with Tebbel estimating approximately 100 books being produced by domestic publishers; but increasing to 879 in 1853; 1,092 in 1855 and 1,350 in 1859/60 (Tebbel, 1972/81: V. 1, 221).

The total number of books which had been published in America from 1820 to 1852, including reprints and original works, was over 24,000 according to *Bibliotheca Americana* (Roorbach). Book production in the United States by 1853 increased with an estimated 733 new works of which 278 were reprints of English books and 35 were translations of foreign authors (Tebbel, 1972/81 V. 2, 23). The *American Catalogues* listing titles between 1861–1871 indicated 11,307 in the first volume and 18,000 in the second (Kelly).

Coupled with rapid economic growth of personal wealth and more leisure time for many, a wide spread decrease in the restrictions of rigid religious orthodoxy, a spirit of optimism with regard to the inevitable progress which lies ahead for America, and an increased interest in learning and reading. By the end of the half century a revolution in book publishing had occurred with demand and improved production methods stimulating publishing to a high level. The reprinting of English works, however, remained a more profitable venture than those written by American authors.

Book production between 1880 and 1899 was reported by the *Publishers Weekly*, although the statistics given are not totally accurate largely because of the lack of cooperation from publishers (Tebbel, 1972/81: V. 2, Appendix A, 675–92). The annual output of titles ranged from 2,076 in 1880 to a high of 5,469 in 1895 with each intervening year except 1885, 1887, 1889, 1894, 1897, 1898 recording some increase over the previous. Fiction accounted for the largest production of annual titles for each of the 20 years ranging from a high of 1132 including new editions in 1893 to a low of 292 in 1880. Juvenile ranked second for three years, third for eight years, fourth for four years, fifth for two years and sixth for three years. Theology and religion never ranked as the most prolific subject although it ranked second for seven years, third for eight years, fourth for three years and fifth for two years. Law proved to be a popular subject ranking second for nine out of the 20 years, third for four years, fourth for three years, fifth for two years, and eleventh and thirteenth for one year each. Education ranked third for one year, fourth for six years, fifth for 11 years and sixth for two years. Literary history and miscellany ranked second for one year, fourth for two years, fifth for two years, sixth for five years, seventh for one year, eighth for two years, ninth for three years, tenth for one year and eleventh for three years. Poetry, biography, political history, travel and fine arts were also popular subjects among the publishers, ranking from fifth to fifteenth place. Medical science ranked fifth to twelfth places during the 1880s but production decreased during the 1890s. Physical science, mathematics, and the useful arts ranked from ninth to sixteenth place with production of both increasing in the 1890s.

In addition to monographic works serial publications became an increasingly important commodity in the college library after the first quarter of the nineteenth century. During the early period very few periodicals other than newspapers were issued in the Colonial America and frequently the survival rate was 50 percent or less. During the period 1800–1825, Mott estimates probably 500 or

600 periodicals other than newspapers were published in the United States (Mott, 1957/68: V. 1, 121). This included less than 100 in 1825 and about 600 titles in 1850 (Mott, 1957: V. 1, 342). He noted that the life expectancy of many titles was approximately two years. During the period 1850–1865, 2,500 periodicals other than newspapers were issued (Mott, 1957: V. 2, 4). This was comprised of 685 periodicals or magazines in 1850 but by 1860 the number had diminished to 575. He estimated these had an average life span of approximately four years. The latter half of the century, 1865–1885, found 8,000–9,000 periodicals or magazine titles being published, reflecting the rapid growth of information, the rise of associations and the increased specialization of business, educational and professional groups (Mott, 1957/68: V. 3: 5). This included 700 periodicals in 1865; followed by 1,200 in 1870; 2,400 in 1880 and 3,300 in 1885.

Cost of Materials

The cost of printed materials was and remained a constant problem for libraries. Until the rise of newer printing technology in the late nineteenth century, printing was slow and comparatively costly. Lehmann-Haupt concluded "that the cost of books to the eighteenth century American reader was not greatly different, relative money values considered, than to his descendants of the present day" (Lehmann-Haupt, 1939: 39). Although it is impossible to estimate average costs at various periods, a few examples and comparisons will denote the magnitude of expenditures required. The typical cost of a novel or book of poems during the colonial period was from $1 to $2 depending upon the type of paper used in the edition. When related to earning power at that time, it would require a laborer one days' work for the inexpensive version which was also the amount needed to purchase five loaves of bread, one third of a gallon of brandy or 12 pounds of beef (Bradsher, 1913: 862–66). In 1834, the average retail cost of a work of an American author was $1.20 while English and other foreign reprints were 75 cents each (Tebbel, 1972/81: V. 1, 23). By the latter part of the nineteenth century novels such as Bellamy's *Looking Backward* and Stockton's *The Dusantes* were retailing for a low of 50 to 75 cents while those nonfiction titles of more limited sales potential such as Cromer's *Modern Egypt* were listing for $6.00 (Tebbel, 1972/81: V. 2, 49, 69). The average price of 130 fiction titles in the first part of the twentieth century was $1.40 (Tebbel, 1972/81: V. 2, 33). This modest increase during the nineteenth century was vastly overshadowed by the inflationary increases occurring by the middle of the next century.

Subscriptions for periodicals during the early period were comparatively high reaching record levels in more recent times. In the eighteenth century, titles such as Franklin's *General Magazine* sold for an equivalent of $2.00 annually which would require a farm laborer four or five days of work in order to purchase (Mott, 1957/68: V. 1, 33). After the Revolutionary War subscription prices rose slightly but results of surveys made in 1788–91 and 1926–29 indicated only slight change in rates (Mott, 1957/68: V. 1, 33–34). The average price of $3.00 for a periodical during the 1850s undoubtedly proved to be a substantial barrier to college libraries with their limited budgets. Certainly a working family earning a mechanics' wage of $1.00 per day or a clergyman receiving considerably less than $500 per annum were unable to expend such an amount.

From these statistics the trend toward increased production of a wider variety of secular titles continued during the eighteenth and nineteenth centuries. Assuming from the variety of titles being issued by American publishers, public interest in theology and religion continued only now it was accompanied by a strong growing interest in belle letters, political science, history, biography, useful arts, fine arts and other subjects associated with our economic and social life. The demand for imported books followed a similar trend particularly after the development of a national literature during the first half of the nineteenth century in the United States. Periodical titles became an important part of college library collections after the first few decades of the nineteenth century. As would be expected the cost of materials was and continued as a problem to most college libraries then as today.

COLLECTION

The book collection of the colonial college library was extremely small and limited in scope when compared with present day standards. This exiguous character clearly reflected the educational philosophy, the narrow classical curriculum, and the extremely limited method of instruction of the period. The paucity of published materials in America during the seventeenth and eighteenth century, particularly books and periodicals, as previously noted, was further complicated by comparatively high prices and a lack of available funds to purchase items which were viewed as useful but non-essential supplements to the textbooks commonly used. The pattern of growth undoubtedly denoted utmost concern for the surety of the library collection which was augmented by a frugal program of financial aid stemming primarily from direct appropriations, student fees for using the library, endowments, rentals of materials, and sale of duplicate materials. It is estimated that direct purchase probably provided less than 10 percent of the books in the colonial college collections from 1636 to 1800 (Shores, 1934: 109). The bulk of the collections were acquired through donations from private benefactors in the colonies and abroad. As late as 1851 Jewett complained that:

> Our colleges are mostly eleemosynary institutions. Their libraries are frequently the chance
> aggregations of the gifts of charity; too many of them discarded, as well nigh worthless, from
> the shelves of the donors. This is not true of all our college libraries; for among them are a few
> of the choicest and most valuable collections in the country, selected with care and competent
> learning, purchased with economy, and guarded with prudence, though ever available to
> those who wish to use them aright (Jewett, 1851: 39).

Libraries founded before the middle of the nineteenth century generally followed the familiar pattern of originating with a small gift collection which was slowly augmented by further donations of materials and endowment funds. The increasing demand upon the libraries, created by the changing educational concepts of the latter half of the nineteenth century, stimulated an increase in more than the token support. Many of the state supported colleges from 1860–80 were extremely destitute for library material and in keeping with existing teaching methods perpetuated the earlier period by relying extensively upon textbook instruction.

Size

Harvard's embryonic collection of approximately 300 volumes had grown to the most extensive one in the colonies by 1764, boasting 5,000 volumes accumulated after 125 years of collecting, only to be almost totally consumed by fire during the same year. The growth of the library after this disaster was much more pronounced, resulting in a collection of approximately 12,000 volumes by 1790 and 30,000 in 1830 (Rhees, 1859: 122).

Of the nine colonial colleges founded before the Revolution, all had less than 15,000 volumes by 1750, indicating a very slow rate of growth. From the colonial era to 1799, 25 permanent colleges had been established in the 13 colonies which were later the United States (Tewksbury, 1932: 4).

The period from 1800 to 1850 was marked by nominal growth of collections but a proliferation of colleges which caused keen competition for donors willing to provide books or endowments. Publishing in the United States was in its beginning, producing a very limited number of titles and the bulk of the imported materials was subject to a very high duty. In 1824, Thomas Jefferson wrote Francis Gilmer, who was on a buying and recruiting mission to Great Britain, that he was concerned about the importation of books belonging to faculty members servicing at the University of Virginia because "our duties on books in English are almost a prohibition . . ." (*American Higher Ed.*, 1961: V. 1, 230). By 1836 Harvard ranked first in the number of volumes held with 47,500 which was certainly optimum rather than typical for the period (U.S. Bureau of Ed., 1876: 764). In 1851 only the collections of the Library of Congress, the Boston Athenaeum, the Philadelphia Library, Harvard, and Yale (only by counting student society libraries which were housed in the main library) contained over 50,000 volumes each. One hundred and twenty six college libraries had a total aggregate of 586,912 volumes with almost one fifth of them located at Harvard, Yale, and Princeton (Jewett, 1851: 190).

The sluggish growth of the collections before the latter part of the nineteenth century was apparent. Jewett (1851) and Rhees (1857) presented a rather dismal picture regarding the number of books added and library expenditures. There was such a wide variation in number of volumes added per annum for a 10 year period, 1840–49, that no pattern could be established as the number ranged from a few scattered donations to a high of 2040 at Harvard. The lack of appropriations was frequently cited as the primary reason for an absence of systematic acquisitions. Washington College at Lexington, Virginia reported that in 60 years, 1776–1837, the college had acquired only 700 volumes in a very "shattered condition" (Jewett, 1851: 144). University of North Carolina reported that their collection, now numbering 3,501, was being increased with "little effort" as the shelves of the rooms had been more than full for some time, "among other reasons;" suggesting that a systematic effort would be made after the erection of a new building during the next year" (Jewett, 1851: 148–49). Geneva College, New York indicated that the average increase was 70 or 80 volumes which were mostly gifts (Jewett, 1851: 83). The expenditures of Bowdoin College for its library supposedly never exceeded $200.00 for over 80 years (Carlton, 1907: 69).

In an effort to create a typical library of the nineteenth century, Brough selected 33 libraries from Jewett's *1851 Report*, containing the most complete data and ranging in size from 86,000 volumes (Harvard) to 1,000 volumes (Norwich University in Vermont). Estimated acquisitions per annum for a 10 year period 1840–1849 were 2040 for Harvard with 30 for Maryville College in Tennessee. A composite typical library of the period was one having a total collection of 10,300 volumes (combined college and society), and adding approximately 200 volumes annually at a cost of $200.00 (Brough, 1953: 12). It is readily seen that probably a considerable number of the 200 additions were donations as $200.00 would not buy the indicated amount of books even in 1851. The statistics used to create this fictitious library, contained a disproportionate share of the stronger libraries of the period, thus presenting a much more glowing picture than actually existed. By the turn of the eighteenth century, institutions such as Harvard, Yale, and about half a dozen others had elevated their libraries to a more visible position while the majority of the colleges at the mid-century could be characterized as small, inadequately supported, limited acquisitions, relatively inaccessible to students, and playing no vital part in the education program.

The next 25 years found a marked increase in the library collection with a new emphasis on an expanded curriculum, the elective system, the graduate schools, and newer methods of teaching. The collection at Harvard for each decade between 1856 to 1876 increased at an average rate of 63 percent compared with an average of only seven and one-half percent in each decade, 1776 to 1856. By 1875 the library was adding 6,000 to 8,000 volumes annually (U.S. Bureau of Educ. 1876: 79). Yale's collection stood at 38,000 in 1860; 55,000 in 1870; 78,000 (excluding society collections) in 1875 to which must be added at least 25,000 pamphlets. Its average annual growth was a little more than 3,000 from 1860–1870 which increased to 4,500 between 1870–1875 (U.S. Off. of Educ. 1876: 66). This growth, however, was not typical of all collections; but it does indicate the growing emphasis placed on the library because of faculty demands which were being supported by more realistic financial resources.

Prior to the Civil War graduate education as known today was non-existent, although a Master of Arts was given after a resident period of generally three years. Organized study in a field of concentration was limited to those planning to enter a profession. Yale initiated formal graduate work in 1846, granting the first American Ph.D. in 1861 (Hofstadter and Hardy, 1952: 62). Columbia and Harvard followed suit by establishing graduate departments in many areas. The last three decades of the century found many colleges blossoming into universities, thus further stimulating a need for greatly expanded library resources. Harvard was probably the only institution which possessed some semblance of a collection strong enough to support such a move.

In 1869 Charles Kendall Adams offered the first seminar at the University of Michigan (*American Higher Educ.*, V. 2, 667). The idea quickly spread to Cornell, and other graduate schools, reaching its zenith for the period in the founding of Johns Hopkins in 1876. The seminar method was not an American innovation, but rather originated in Germany where it was supported by an almost autonomous system of strong seminar libraries maintained at the expense of the central collection. This idea did not have the same impact upon libraries in the United States where a more loosely formed system of making books available in special subject alcoves and limited seminar room collections were frequently within the library. Strong departmental collections did develop within some of the larger institutions such as Harvard. It was not until the twentieth century that libraries were organized by broad subject divisions and by level of students such as undergraduate and graduate.

In 1876 Harvard had the largest university collection in the country with 227,650. Yale was second with 114,200, while six others tallied between 30,000 and 45,000 (U.S. Bureau of Educ., 1876: 125–26).

Most college libraries of the last five decades of the century did not fare very well. The proliferation of many small colleges created too many institutions which were lacking sufficient financial resources to support an adequate program. The library was generally the first to feel the "pinch" of pecuniary shortages. The closing decade found over 454 colleges with widely varying collections as to size and quality.

By the end of the nineteenth century the typical small college library could be characterized as containing 6,000 to 20,000 volumes comprised mainly of donations. Emphasis was primarily on supporting the curriculum rather than research. University libraries held considerably larger number of volumes ranging from almost 500,000 at Harvard to 135,000 at the University of Pennsylvania. Libraries at this level were supporting not only curriculum needs but also in department research in many graduate programs.

The effectiveness of the smaller collections would be seriously questioned today in view of the standards suggested by the Association of College and

Research Libraries and other accrediting agencies and collection size formulas which have been developed. Although collection size and annual growth do not necessarily guarantee quality, it does indicate the probability that if the college or university is willing to expend large sums of money for materials it will concentrate on selecting those of suitable quality. Fremont Rider concluded after careful study that a direct correlation existed between the educational effectiveness of the educational institution and the growth of the library. He further suggested that on an average the collections of college and university libraries between 1831 and 1925 had doubled in size every 15 years for the past 200 years (Rider, 1940: 566–69).

Content

The colonial college library was largely comprised of theological works supplemented by the classics and standard treatises in philosophy, logic, and history. A lack of current materials was very evident, although this seemed to have little impact on the narrow curriculum of theological and classical studies. President Clapp of Yale reported in 1765 that "We have a good library consisting of about four thousand volumes, well furnished with ancient authors such as the Fathers, Historians, and Classics. Many valuable books of Divinity, History, Philosophy, and Mathematics, but not many authors who have wrote within these thirty years" (U.S. Bureau of Educ., 1876: 29).

The printed catalogs of 1773 and 1790 at Harvard indicated a similar coverage. Three-fourths of the entries in the former were in the fields of theology, history, literature, and science. (Kraus, 1961: 248)

The second, a manuscript catalog of 1790, contained about 50 percent religious works. Its 350 pages had 100 devoted to theological tracts, 50 to theological books, three and one-half to Bibles, four to books of travel, 10 to Greek and Latin authors, three-fourth to periodicals, and an undetermined number to polite literature (English and French authors) (U.S. Bureau of Educ., 1876: 25).

America's growing nationalism after the Revolution tended to create an increased discussion of what constituted a satisfactory academic library. George Ticknor, after a trip to Germany in 1816, compared the 200,000 volume holdings of the Gottingen University with the 20,000 at Cambridge, pointing out the latter was 50 years behind in size, expenditures, and accessibility of books because of an overconcern with buildings and faculty. He surmised that "we have not learned that the library is not only the first convenience of a University, but it is the very first necessity,—that it is the life and spirit,—and that all other considerations must yield to the prevalent one of increasing and opening it, and opening it on the most liberal terms to all who are disposed to make use of it" and concluded by referring to the ". . . parsimonious administration of the Cambridge Library" (*American Higher Educ.*, 1961: V. 1, 256–57).

Edward Everett in 1849 echoed the criticism of Ticknor by pointing out that the collection at Harvard was well supplied with standard classic works which were never antiquated, but was sadly lacking in current books in the areas of science, literature, travel, statistics, etc. He attributed the deficiency to the meager expenditure of only $800.00 a year for library materials. (*American Higher Educ.*, 1961: V. 1, 382–83).

In 1851 Henry Tappan of the University of Michigan in a work entitled *University Education* believed that the first step in creating a university would be

> . . . a choice, varied, and ample library, second to none in the world in books to aid students in attaining ripe scholarship, and in promoting investigation in every department of knowledge—a library distinguished more for valuable and directly available resources of scholarship than for curious and antiquarian collections estimated rather by character than the number of its volumes (*American Higher Educ.*, 1961: V. 2, 504).

The president of the University of Pennsylvania referred to the library at his institution as a "miserable excuse" for a literary institution (Jewett, 1851: 129). At Amherst there was meagerness in "even the standard works of science" (Jewett, 1851: 18) Dartmouth held "many rare and valuable items" but had a deficiency in current books (Jewett, 1851: 13). Jewett substantiated many of these criticisms by pointing out that America in 1851 was deficient in ". . . the appliances for thorough study, for original research, for independent investigation" (Jewett, 1851: 41).

Allegheny College, Meadville, Pennsylvania represented a typical small library of the period. The library, although comprised of 8,000 donated volumes, was considered an outstanding collection if the preface of its printed catalog was to be taken literally:

> In the catalog, the intelligent will perceive that there is an extensive range of the best editions of the Greek and Roman classics, and the ancient Fathers of the Christian Church; that there are books in thirty different languages, ancient and modern, with lexicons and grammars, and elementary books for studying most of them; and that in history, ancient and modern, in belles-lettres, and other branches of literature and service, there is a most excellent collection (Jewett, 1851: 111).

Works in modern languages were becoming more popular during this period. Several well known collections of modern foreign languages were: 4,000 French books at St. Louis University; 6,000 German books at the Union Theological Seminary in New York; 600 Spanish books at the College of Nva Sva de Gaudelupe at Santa Ines, California and other modern language collections at Georgetown College and Smithsonian Institution at Washington, D.C. (Rhees, 1859: XXII).

The collection at the University of Indiana, as revealed through its 1842 catalog, consisted of an unusually fine group of less than 5,000 volumes which had been ". . . specifically selected for the needs of the curriculum as well as for information and cultural reading" (Lowell, 1961: 424). Reference material such as lexicons, dictionaries, and concordances along with current historical and literary works considered necessary by the trustees had been provided.

The University of Vermont, University of South Carolina, Brown University, and the Theological Seminary at Andover, Massachusetts were all satisfied their books were well selected and were of great benefit to faculty and students especially those of the upper classes. Vermont was depicted as ". . . one of the few libraries in the United States selected with competent bibliographical knowledge and with good judgment and purchased with economy" (Jewett, 1851: 16). Two-thirds of the works were in English while the balance consisted of an almost complete set of the best editions of Greek and Latin authors.

Marietta College, Marietta, Ohio, contained the ". . . general works of literature, a valuable collection of philological works, procured in Europe as well as a large collection of textbooks which were 'furnished at a trifling percentage' for nearly all the preparatory and college courses" (Jewett, 1851: 173).

Indiana State University supposedly possessed a choice collection augmented by a recent purchase of about $2,000. It contained "Greek, Latin, French, and English classics, the best standard works on history, biography, and the sciences, together with a selected variety of miscellaneous literature" (Jewett, 1851: 175).

Wellesley College was proud of its cases enclosed by glass doors which housed a striking collection of works of outstanding "external dress" with the greater extent bound in calf and morocco. All were selected with great care as to tasteful binding, best edition, and reflected the objects of the college. It was further depicted as a "serviceable working library" with "no accumulation of rubbish" (Jewett, 1851: 93).

South Carolina College at Columbia was considered one of the best selected collections in the country, rich in Egyptology and books with outstanding bindings. "The collection is far more valuable than many twice its size. The legislature of South Carolina has abundant reason to be proud of its liberality, and satisfied with the manner in which it has been seconded by the officers of the college" (Jewett, 1851: 155).

In 1868 Charles A. Cutter, one of the most distinguished librarians of the century, wrote that colleges no longer consisted of two departments (classical and theological) but rather were made up of two dozen or more and that very few of them possessed a library which could be called well-selected by the professors. "The truth is, it will not do for a library to depend on gifts. They are valuable helps, but they rarely supply what is most needed." He further noted that although the library at Harvard was strong in religion and the classics, it was weak in natural history, science, astronomy, law, medicine, recent theology, moral philosophy, education, social science, geology, paleontology, engineering and technology (Cutter, 1868: 580).

Collections of this century clearly emphasized the tempo of the times. By the 1870s many changes had occurred in higher education which influenced collection development. Some of the most influential factors were:

1. The expansion and development of the curriculum to embrace a wide range of subjects with a growing interest in the pure and applied sciences and social sciences.
2. The rise of the elective system with students exercising more liberty in selecting courses as well as programs of study.
3. The growth and demand for scientific information with an emphasis on newer methods, research, independent investigation, and thorough study. The rise of the graduate schools aided substantially in supporting scientific inquiry and research.
4. Faculty members demanded more preparation by students with outside readings growing in popularity.
5. An intellectual awakening stimulated by advanced methods of book production, periodicals, and newspapers resulted in the liberalization and increased use of library facilities.
6. A vastly increased number of book and periodical titles available.

All of these were to have a profound influence on the libraries of the latter half of the nineteenth century. Although the roots of many could be traced back to the Revolutionary era, a steady growth began after the Civil War and gathered momentum as the value of education was more fully recognized. The rise of professional librarians such as Justin Winsor, Charles Cutter, and Melvil Dewey, who advocated such innovations as the merger of books and students, were welcomed by conscientious faculty members of many more progressive institutions. In addition educational administrators were recognizing the logic of paying more than lip service to the concept advanced by an unknown author writing in the *North American Review* in 1818 who believe "the library was the heart or soul of the institution idea" ("Literary Institutions," 1818: 193). The best way to support such a theory was to first employ a professional librarian which was not done by institutions such as at the University of Illinois until 1894 (Thurber, 1945: 351). Second, the provision of adequate financial support which resulted in such drastic increases as 2,000 percent for library expenditures at Indiana from 1875 to 1903 (Lowell, 1961: 426). Third, the construction of suitable quarters which in many cases didn't exist until the closing days of the century or well into the next.

The goals were clearly in mind as many fine collections were in the beginning stages of development, encompassing not only the subjects of the curriculum but also recreational materials, foreign language publications, specialized scientific works, source materials, periodical literature, and ephemeral material such as reports and pamphlets which were so eagerly sought by some of the foresighted librarians of the day. The collections of the research libraries were no longer bound by the narrow confines of the curriculum, but were beginning to recognize the responsibility of collecting adequate materials to support increasing research needs as required by expanding graduate schools.

By the end of the nineteenth century small libraries typically had small miscellaneous collections of standard works of reference and ordinary books of common branches of science, literature and arts. University libraries contained a broader range of secondary and primary materials which supported instructional and research programs. A growing need for access to other collections by these libraries prompted greater interest in the development of union catalogs, cooperative acquisitions and interlibrary loan. "The ideas of those who use it are generally bound, not by the horizon of the subject which they are considering, but by the literature which is accessible" (Ambrose, 1893: 114).

ADMINISTRATION

The collections of the colleges of the nineteenth century existed primarily for their own sake as provisions for their utilization were very limited until newer educational methods and concepts evolved. The ineffectiveness of the library was largely due to the traditional ideas regarding teaching and learning and limited personnel and financial support. This in turn was influenced by a number of additional factors.

Housing, Arrangement, and Catalogs

The physical facilities of the libraries of the eighteenth and nineteenth centuries were generally a room or two located in the main building near the chapel. The size was inevitably smaller than $38' \times 50'$.

Books were generally arranged by size, donor, subject or author in wall cases frequently isolated from the average patron. Subject arrangement was prevalent, becoming more refined, standardized, and widely adopted with the publishing of the Dewey Decimal Classification scheme in 1876. The library was intended only as a storage room and lacked suitable provisions for study until the latter part of the nineteenth century. The library at Marietta College represented a typical situation:

> A brick building, 65 feet by 53, and three stories high, has just been completed. On the first floor are the laboratory, room for philosophical apparatus, and recitation room for the senior class. On the second floor, the library, the cabinet, and Hildreth cabinet, and the rhetorical-room, used at present as a chapel. In the third story are two large rooms for the societies, with recesses for the libraries . . . The library room is, say 53 by 25 feet, and 14 feet high . . . Dr. S. P. Hildreth has lately presented his valuable cabinet to the college. This cabinet contains more than 4,000 specimens in the various departments of the natural history arranged in cases and drawers, labeled, numbered, and entered in a catalogue under their respective heads (Jewett, 1851: 172–73).

In addition to the mineralogy cabinet many libraries had extensive collections of coins, sculpture, paintings, and relics which indicated an emphasis upon preservation rather than the multiplicity of educational materials.

Separate library buildings were non-existent until 1841 when Gore Hall at Harvard was completed followed by similar independent structures at Yale, Williams College, and Dartmouth. In 1870, these were the only colleges having separate buildings devoted exclusively to library purposes. The architecture of these were very ornate, copied from medieval chapels or imposing temples with primary concern for exterior appearance rather than functional interior qualities. Preference seemed to be given to those of curious shapes such as octagons, circles, and crosses (both conventional and Greek) so that by the end of the century, library buildings clearly reflected the intellectual tastes of college planners and benefactors rather than knowledgeable librarians. Mammoth reading rooms abounded with little concern for individual study areas, acoustics, proper ventilation, and expansion. Collections slowly became more accessible to the students which at first was achieved by establishing reading rooms with limited collections and later by allowing liberal access to the stack areas through a system of permits. Free access was not widely accepted until the twentieth century in the small college library while the large university frequently adhered to a limited system of admittance.

The catalogs of the early libraries were inevitably in a book format arranged by subject with author, title and donor index. They were, however, costly to compile and difficult to keep up-to-date. In 1862 Harvard began to use an improved approach, a catalog of author and subject on $2'' \times 5''$ cards, which was quickly adopted by the majority of libraries in the United States during the next decade although with frequent minor variation (Weber, 1964: 26). By 1876 the popularity of the book catalog had been surpassed by that of the card catalog only to be revived during the next century through the advent of unit record and photographic equipment and computers.

Financial Support

Early library collections were supported principally by donated materials. It soon became apparent, however, this was insufficient in most instances because of a flourishing publishing industry and burgeoning demands by faculty and students. Some institutions such as Brown, Harvard, and Yale were fortunate in soliciting many gifts and endowments. The publicly supported institutions were generally granted appropriations by the state legislatures while those in the private sector relied most heavily upon philanthropic resources. If college wide funds were available, there was still the problem of convincing governing boards and college officers of the role and the needs of the library. A few of the libraries were fortunate in having reasonable funds available, but generally it was an exception rather than a rule. Washington College at Chestertown, Maryland, had "no yearly appropriation for the increase of the library, as yet, ". . . as the board was devoting all efforts toward the erection of a new building (Jewett, 1851: 137). St. Louis University in Missouri reported that "no special fund is set aside for library purposes, but grants for the purchase of books are made annually by the faculty. Nearly all books have been purchased with funds thus obtained (U.S. Bureau of Educ., 1876: 96). To alleviate the situation many of the colleges devised a system of library fees, assessed from the student on a yearly or term basis. Generally these fees ranged from 40 cents to $5.00 a year. The College of New Jersey (Princeton) used a student tax of $1.00 per term for over 70 years of the nineteenth century as the sole revenue for support of the library (U.S. Off. of Educ., 1876: 100). Amherst employed a system of charging students four or five cents per each item checked out. The librarian reported that about 200–300 books were usually out at one time to the faculty while students utilized few because of the charge (Jewett, 1851: 17). The library of the Medical College of Georgia at Augusta devised a most positive system for conserving books by requiring a $10.00 deposit as security for the return of each volume taken out (Jewett, 1851: 157).

The former criticisms of Jewett were echoed again in the 1870s when collections were described as consisting ". . . largely of voluntary gifts of many individuals, and hence are usually of a miscellaneous character. It is apparent ". . . few colleges have possessed funds to build up libraries on a scientific plan" (U.S. Bureau of Educ. 1876: 62). Library fees supported by more liberal appropriations were more common by 1875 when a few selected libraries reported the following funds: Harvard $169,000; Yale $65,500; College of New Jersey $40,000; Trinity College $35,000; College of the City of New York $30,000; Wesleyan University $27,000; Madison University $20,000; as compared to $44,340 for the Library of Congress (U.S. Bureau of Educ., 1876: 62). These amounts seem meager by today's standards but they did represent substantial expenditures at that time. More realistic and systematic budgetary planning did not materialize until the next century.

Hours

The exiguous hours of the early academic library clearly reflect its minor place in the educational life of the student. The meager collections were protected from wear and loss by formidable regulations. The library served primarily as a storehouse with short designated periods allowed for the return and withdrawal of books. An early rule at the University of Alabama library stipulated that ". . . the books shall ordinarily be received at the door without admitting the applicant into the library room (Koch, 1924: 23). The situation was frequently complicated by restricting the use of books within the library, without regard for the meager hours they were open. Thus the use of books both within and outside the library were seriously hampered because of the amount of time available and the restriction as to where they could be used. The students generally had no choice but to follow the practice of textbook study or seek the aid of the many more flexible society libraries which were developing in response to student needs.

Jewett's *1851 Report* clearly indicated the problems faced by potential library users. A sampling of 46 of the 126 libraries surveyed in 1849 revealed regular periods of opening ranging from one hour every two weeks to a half an hour once a week to "several hours daily." This at best resulted in "18 to 20 hours a week for six of the colleges, while half of them could claim only the minimum" (Stories, 1945: 242).

The latter part of the century found some improvement in many of the larger libraries. Cornell in 1875 was ". . . open throughout the year (except Sundays) from 8 o'clock in the morning till 5 o'clock in the afternoon, or till sunset when that is before 5;" (U.S. Bureau of Educ., 1876: 108). This reference to sunset was very important as most libraries were not open after dark because of inadequate lighting with many forbidding the use of an open flame in the building because of the fire hazard. The development of the electric light by the end of the century exerted a favorable influence upon extended hours for libraries. Students no longer were required to end their library activities at sundown.

By the close of the century, a marked progress in the accessibility of library materials and in the removal of illogical barriers preventing the ready handling and use of books was apparent.

Use of Material

Provisions for the use of academic libraries presented a patchwork series of regulations ranging from almost complete exclusion of student usage to free access by the end of the century. Many of the early collections were accessible only to faculty, college officers, and to the junior and senior class members. The prevailing philosophy in many institutions seemed to be that the library was primarily for consultation by advanced students and faculty. In 1850 the Universities of Rochester and Cornell both regarded the library for this purpose with Cornell still clinging to this concept as late as 1875. St. Mary's College of Baltimore sometimes loaned books out to read, but this had been discontinued ". . . at present on account of former abuse of the privilege" and Yale reported that "books are lent out but consultation in the library is encouraged in preference" (Jewett, 1851: 133, 71). As late as 1885–86 the librarian at the University of California was lamenting the loss of 24 books, and ". . . could see no means of preventing this as long as students enjoyed unrestricted access to the shelves" (Thurber, 1945: 352). The end of the century found a few colleges still restricting students to reference use of the library only, but generally home use was widespread. The number of volumes which could be checked out was regulated by many libraries.

William Frederick Poole in 1912 substantiated the students lack of access to the library at an earlier period when he said:

> To those of us who graduated thirty or forty or more years ago, books outside of textbooks used, had no part of our education. They were never quoted, recommended, or mentioned by

instructors in the classroom. As I remember it, Yale College Library might as well have been in Wethersfield, or Bridgeport, as in New Haven, so far as the students were concerned (Koch, 1924: 25–26).

The lending of books outside the college community itself was allowed by many in spite of the restrictions placed on student use. Oglethorpe University at Milledgeville, Georgia reported ". . . the laws allow of the books being lent, within a mile of the college, at the discretion of the president" (Jewett, 1851: 158). Maryville College at Maryville, Tennessee allowed free use by clergymen educated at the college living within 100 miles of the college (Jewett, 1851: 164). Other colleges indicated this privilege was available upon application to college officials.

Many of the libraries in Jewett's *1851 Report* indicated the number of volumes "taken out" or lent from the library. The number circulated varied greatly and as a whole was very limited. Bowdoin and University of Virginia reported annual circulations of about 3,000 volumes each although the latter indicated 275 had consulted the library without taking books. The number of people consulting in the library was small with Virginia's estimate being typical rather than an exception until after the 1870s.

The U.S. Bureau of Education *1876 Report* reflected the growing pattern of free access to the shelves by students. The concept that the collection was to be utilized rather than stored as a treasure for the future indicated a changing philosophy of the role of books and periodicals in higher education. Librarians were admonished to become capitalists rather than misers ". . . constantly using his accumulated wealth for the encouragement of further production" (U.S. Bureau of Educ., 1876: 60).

By the end of the century students were enjoying the benefits of longer hours and greater access to library resources as the use of a variety of materials became a recognized part of the instructional process.

Personnel

Duties of early librarians varied greatly from the complex activities which prevail today. The early "keeper of the books" was primarily concerned with seeing that all items were available for the annual physical check or inventory by the visiting committee of the overseers. His attentions were principally concerned with entering new books upon the list of accessions, keeping the library open for a short time so that faculty and students could withdraw and return books, retrieving loaned books from faculty and students, and concern regarding the similarity of the student's textbooks with material in the library. Occasionally an interested librarian would go beyond these mundane clerical tasks and attempt to improve the collection through a systematic buying program which first had to be supported by the college leaders or he would compile a more elaborate catalog than was actually required for inventory purposes. At the other extreme, a few who boasted about turning part of the money appropriated for books back to the trustees. Frugal compensations and part-time assignments for those in charge of the library mitigated against an effectively administered library. The major change in the library concept came after 1876, when trained library personnel began to influence library practices by applying newer techniques of organizing materials and in promoting usage. Faculty and librarians were beginning to recognize that students must use books readily and continuously in order to derive the greatest benefit and that the role of the librarian was not one of keeper or protector but rather that of an interpreter who willingly offers personal assistance. By the end of the century, the problem of an inadequate number of trained personnel continued to be an important factor in contributing to minimal library service. In 1893 it was estimated that only one-third of the colleges had full time librarians whose chief duty was to direct the library (Ambrose, 1893: 115). The pattern of a part-time "library keeper" had persisted in many American academic institutions for over 250 years. The effect of this joint appointment was apparent with the energy and best effort being placed in the classroom where the needs were most immediate. Faculty pleas, exemplified by that of the professor-librarian at the University of Michigan in 1894 who expressed an urgent need for a trained librarian and catalogers to process the materials, were typical during the waning years of the century (Thurber, 1945: 351).

As the century drew to a close, the benefits to be derived from employing a trained, full-time librarian as well as adequately trained supportive personnel were apparent as the library was now recognized as more than a store-house. The issue of the qualifications of a librarian had been ably described by an unknown author as early as 1868 who concluded that a librarian should be trained much the same as a lawyer or a doctor. The library should not be a place for ". . . some old fossil, who has exhausted his best energies in another business ". . . or for a young clerk but rather relegated to an active individual who knows literature, methods of use in learning, and library organization ("Libraries," 1864: 486–87).

The recognition of these traits, when supported by an adequate college education and specialized course in librarianship aided in providing a working cadre of librarians. Tradition, lack of administrative and faculty concern, and a paucity of funds, however, continued to be the greatest obstacles to optimum library service.

SOCIETY LIBRARIES

During the latter part of the eighteenth century, student literary societies were frequently established because of the lack of library response to student needs. They served as a center for discussion, debate, and self-improvement and were free from many of the inhibitions experienced when trying to use the typical college library. Collections of materials formed an integral part of these societies, reflecting a greater concern for up to date, popular, and periodical literature and more liberal hours, reading areas, and ready accessibility and checkout. The societies were generally allowed to use a room in a college building; but were expected to provide furniture, periodicals, books, and supervisory personnel. Financial support was drawn from the members of the society and allocated for the purchase of materials such as: fiction, essays, plays, poetry, voyages, and travels, American history as well as periodicals which were typically not available in the college library.

Frequently the society libraries were large, well selected, and carefully arranged serving as a supplement to the textbooks and as a source of material for essays and debates which were a fundamental part of the activities of the society. The collections were generally of a more popular and less scholarly nature than those of the college library, serving primarily as a working collection. In later years they frequently contained the works of the standard authors of the day and the leading literary reviews.

The heyday of the society library was during the 1830s which was marked by an era of exiguous growth for most college libraries. Society libraries had been established in nearly 80 percent of the existing colleges by 1830 with approximately 50 percent of them larger in size than the regular college library collection (Stories, 1945: 241). In 1851 Jewett reported 142 student society libraries containing 254,639 volumes or almost half as many as contained by the college libraries of that year (Jewett, 1851: 191). Yale and Dartmouth had truly outstanding society libraries which were later transferred to their general libraries during the 1870s. The demise of the society libraries was attributed to the many changes in the college curriculum, new extracurricular interests rather than literary discussions and debate, increase in periodicals and competing forms of communication, cost of maintenance borne by members, and more realistic management of the college libraries by dedicated full-time librarians (Harding, 1959: 105–108). The society collections had successfully served to fulfill part of the functions of the college library which had been neglected by apathy and the lack of money. It is ironical that the students recognized the needs and took steps to correct them while the institutions tended to accept the status quo until the latter part of the nineteenth century. Frequently the college libraries eventually became the beneficiary as many of the old society collections passed into their possession.

The founding of the American Library Association in 1876 and the influence of the growing number of "professional librarians" exerted a positive influence in allowing the academic community to develop improved library collections and services. In addition, the establishment and growth of other associations and pseudo-professional groups focused attention on growing information needs. In any event, the student society libraries were examples of student ingenuity in resolving a very pressing problem and undoubtedly focused attention on the need for a logical approach to the question of the accessibility of library resources.

CONCLUSIONS

The development of academic libraries has been an evolutionary process. During the early colonial period the focus of most members of the society was primarily to survival and to earn a living. Education in general was unorganized and viewed primarily as the responsibility of the parents. Slowly the dominate efforts of the colonial period by private, religious and charitable groups as seen in the common schools, Latin schools, academies and colleges, gave way to a more organized system based upon local support. The Constitution clearly authorized local and state legislation which provided the states with the means to develop and support a system of their own design. Later support from the Federal government would further augment the availability of funds.

The middle of the nineteenth century was marked by greater attention to educational concerns and a proliferation of general and scholarly literature. After the Civil War, the localized economic patterns based upon a cottage type, artisan technology burgeoned into a "self generating industrial economy" (Edelman and Tatum, 1976: 222). Paralleling this growth was the proliferation of institutions of higher education which evolved through a period of classical traditionalism to an era of greater flexibility and the development of strong undergraduate and graduate programs in not only the humanities but also in the social and pure sciences.

The change in the academic library during the last half of the nineteenth century was slow but identifiable. The necessity for preserving the cultural heritage through books had been recognized from the very beginning with Harvard and Yale both having collections donated in advance of the formation of each college. The storehouse or "state of inconsequence" as Ticknor described it, kept these collections in virtual isolation for many years largely because of the scarcity of printed materials and simply an apparent lack of need for them in teaching courses within the early curriculum. In the United States, the adherence to traditional methods of instruction had stifled library growth. It is apparent that the libraries were frequently just what many faculty members expected and what trustees could or were willing to support. The idea that an adequate library was necessary in order to revolutionize the methods of higher education was true when one considered the advanced state of European universities during the nineteenth century and the role of their extensive collections numbering several hundred thousand. Although the scientific revolution occurred much later in the United States than in Europe, the last quarter of the nineteenth century was marked by substantial growth in the philosophy, the methodology, the products, and the dissemination of scholarship in higher education. A definite shifting from the repeated reading of a few staple works to the need for accessibility to a broad number of monographs and serial publications slowly elevated the library to a more essential position.

By the end of the nineteenth century, the inadequate services and resources of the past and the need for revitalization were vividly described by such leaders as President W.R. Harper of the University of Chicago.

> A quarter of a century ago the library in most of our institutions, even the oldest, was scarcely large enough, if one were to estimate values, to deserve the name of library. So far as it had location, it was the place to which the professor was accustomed to make his way occasionally, the student almost never. It was open for consultation during perhaps one hour a day for three days a week. The better class of students, it was understood, had no time for reading. It was only the 'ne'er do well,' the man with little interest in the class-room textbook, who could find time for general reading. Such reading was a distraction, and a proposition that one might profit by consulting other books which bore upon the subject or subjects treated in the text-book would have been scouted. All such work was thought to be distracting. The addition of one hundred volumes in a single year was something noteworthy. The place, seldom frequented, was some out-of-the-way room which could serve no other use. The librarian— there was none. Why should there have been? Any officer of the institution could perform the needed service without greatly increasing the burden of his official duties (Koch, 1924: 24– 25).

In a later article, he contended that the library and the laboratory had revolutionized the methods of higher education. The library was now the center of educational activities and referred to it as the "most learned faculty—certainly the most influential." He hypothesized that departmental libraries must be close at hand for ease of consultation with students studying in the "midst of books" (Harper, 1902: 457–58). Thus after its dubious function for over two centuries, the role of the library was being recognized by leading academic administrators as a key factor in the process of higher education.

With the rise of the "new education," the library underwent many changes although three were particularly outstanding. First, the library user constituency changed from primarily faculty and upperclassmen to potentially all students and faculty who required a wide range of readily accessible materials. Faculty members and administrators, in the best institutions, were undoubtedly supporters of extended library resources and services. The very nature of the new instruction rested upon a "working collection" of suitably selected titles while research needs called for comprehensive collections or at the least ready access to them. Second, the rise of effective library management was in part a result of the first. Library development was no longer left to chance. The "new librarians" tended to "sluff off" the old traditional rules aimed at conformity, replacing them with regulations encouraging the use of books. With an organized program of library development, directed by one or more individuals working closely with the faculty, the objectives of the curriculum were clearly translated into appropriate resources, services, and facilities. Financial support was no longer a matter of chance but rather a carefully planned procedure being necessary for the overall instructional and research program. Library personnel were trained and organized to go beyond the mere processing of materials, providing aid in interpretation and bibliographic advice. Administration became more of a planned and carefully developed process rather than one based upon intuition and position. Programs were broadened to include all phases of the student's education through the diversified materials which began to be commonplace in the library. Third, the growing amount of material being printed in the United States and in other countries required a systematic approach to its identification, acquisition, preservation, and accessibility. Although collection development goals had traditionally been based on self-subsistence rather than cooperation, attempts to develop and maintain collections capable of supporting undergraduate and graduate curriculums were needed. Larger libraries, feeling the need for comprehensiveness, recognized the need for cooperative programs, particularly in such areas as accessibility, collection development and cataloging.

The library was a product of the total pattern of higher education, developing a posture which supported and responded to the demands of the academic community. This, of course, was subject to all kinds of variables such as egocentric individuals, periods of financial depression, rising costs for personnel and materials, the weight of popular opinions, ability to adapt to new technology and newer curricular demands, and the establishment of its role in the instructional and research process. The success or failure of an academic institution, then as now, depended largely upon the integration of: the faculty functioning as curricular and research leaders; librarians serving as consultants; library administrators planning, coordinating and evaluating the overall operation; and campus administrators and trustees being providers.

REFERENCES

Ambrose, Lodilla. "A Study of College Libraries," *Library Journal*, 18 (April, 1893), 113–19.

American Higher Education: A Documentary History. Edited by Richard Hofstadter and Wilson Smith. Chicago: University of Chicago Press, 1961. 2 V.

Bradsher, Earl L. "Early American Book Prices," *Publishers Weekly*. (March 8, 1913) 862–66.

Brough, Kenneth. *Scholar's Workshop: Evolving Conceptions of Library Service*. (Illinois Contributions to Librarianship, No. 5), Urbana: University of Illinois Press, 1953.

Carlton, W. N. Chattin. "College Libraries in the Mid-nineteenth Century," *Library Journal*, 31 (November, 1907): 479–96. (Reprinted in *Contributions to American Library History*. Edited by Thelma Eaton. Champaign: Illini Bookstore, 1961.)

Catalogue of Books Printed in the United States. Boston, 1804. Reprinted in Adolph Growell. *Book Trade Bibliography in the Nineteenth Century*. New York: Burt Franklin, 1939, Part II.

Contributions to American Library History. Edited by Thelma Eaton. Champaign: Illini Bookstore, 1964.

Cutter, Charles A. "Harvard College Library," *North American Review*, 107 (1868), 568–93.

Dobler, Richard P. *Campus Planning*. New York: Reinhold, 1963.

Edelman, Hendrik and G.M. Tatum. "Development of Collections in American University Libraries." *College and Research Libraries* 37 (May 1976): 222–45.

Evans, Charles. *American Bibliography. A Chronological Dictionary of all Books, Pamphlets and Periodical Publications Printed in the United States of America from the Genesis of Printing in 1639 down to and Including the Year 1820.* Chicago: Privately Printed for the Author by Blakely Press, 1903–34. 12 V.

Good, Harry G. *A History of Western Education.* New York: Macmillian, 1947.

Greene, Evarts B. *The Revolutionary Generation, 1763–1790.* (A History of American Life, V. 4). New York: Macmillan, 1943.

Growoll, Adolph. *Book Trade Bibliography in the Nineteenth Century* Reprint of 1804 edition. New York: Burt Franklin, 1939.

Harding, Thomas. "College Literary Societies: Their Contributions to the Development of Academic Libraries, 1815–1876," *Library Quarterly*, 29 (January-April, 1959): 1–26; 94–112.

Harper, William Rainey. "The Trend of University and College Education in the U.S.," *North American Review*, 174 (April, 1902): 457–65.

Historical Statistics of the United States Colonial Times to 1970. Bicentennial edition. Washington, D.C.: Bureau of Census, 1975.

Hofstadter, Richard and C. DeWitt Hardy. *The Development and Scope of Higher Education in the United States.* New York: Columbia University Press, 1952.

Jewett, Charles C. *Notices of Public Libraries in the United States.* Washington: Printed for the House of Representatives, 1851.

Kandel, I.L. *History of Secondary Education: A Study in the Development of Liberal Education.* Boston: Houghton Mifflin, 1930.

Kelly, James. *The American Catalogue of Books (Original and Reprints) Published in the United States from January 1861–January 1871.* Compiled and arranged by James Kelly. New York: P. Smith, 1938.

Koch, Theodore W. . . . *On University Libraries.* 2d ed. Paris: Edouard Champion, 1924.

Koos, Leonard V. and Crawford, C.C. "College Aims Past and Present," *School and Society*, 14 (December 3, 1921): 499–509.

Kraus, Joe W. "The Harvard Undergraduate Library of 1773." *College and Research Libraries*, 22 (July, 1961): 247–52.

Lehmann-Haupt, Hellmut. *The Book in America: A History of the Making, the Selling and the Collecting of Books in the United States.* In Collaboration with Ruth Shepard-Grannis and Lawrence C. Wroth. New York: Bowker, 1939.

"Libraries," *Harper's New Monthly Magazine*, 29 (1864): 482–88.

"Literary Institutions, University Library," *North American Review*, 8 (December, 1818): 191–200.

Lowell, Mildred H. "Indiana University Libraries, 1829–1942," *College and Research Libraries*, 22 (November, 1961).

McKenna, David L., Shrum, John W. and Tarratus, Edward A. "Changing Objectives in American Higher Education, 1842–1960," *School and Society* 91: (March 9, 1963): 120–23.

Mott, Frank Luther. *History of American Magazines, 1741–1850.* Cambridge, MA: Harvard University Press, 1957/68. 4 V.

Rhees, William J. *Manual of Public Libraries in the United States and British Provinces of North America.* Philadelphia: Lippincott, 1859.

Richardson, Ernest Cushing. *The Growth of College and University Libraries.* (Occasional Papers, No. 6), Philadelphia: Pennsylvania Library Club, 1899.) (reprinted in *Contributions to American Library History.* Edited by Thelma Eaton. Champaign: Illini Bookstore, 1961.)

Rider, Fremont. "Growth of American College and University Libraries and of Wesleyan's," *Association of American College Bulletin*, 26 (December, 1940): 566–69.

Roorbach, Orville A. *Bibliotheca Americana Catalogue of American Publications, Including Reprints and Original Works from 1820 to 1852, Inclusive* . . . Compiled and arranged by O.A. Roorbach. New York: The Author, 1852.

Rudolf, Frederick. *The American College and University*, New York: Vantage Books, 1965.

Shores, Louis. *Origins of the American College Library, 1638–1800*. Nashville: George Peabody College, 1934.

Stories, Catherine. "The American College Society Library and The College Library," *College and Research Libraries*, 6 (June, 1945): 240–48.

Tebbel, John. *A History of Book Publishing in the United States*. New York: Bowker, 1972/81. 4 V.

Tewksbury, Donald G. *The Founding of American Colleges and Universities Before the Civil War, with Particular Reference to the Religious Influences Bearing Upon the College Movement*. New York: Teachers College, Columbia University, 1932.

Thurber, Evangeline. "American Agricultural College Libraries, 1862–1900," *College and Research Libraries*, 7 (September, 1945): 346–52.

Thwing, Charles F. *History of Higher Education in America*. New York: Appleton, 1906.

U.S. Bureau of Education. *Public Libraries in the United States of America: Their History, Condition and Management, Special Report, Part 1*. Washington: Government Printing Office, 1876.

Weber, David C. "The Changing Character of the Catalog in America," *Library Quarterly*, 34 (January, 1964): 20–33.

LIBRARY ADMINISTRATORS' ATTITUDES TOWARDS CONTINUING PROFESSIONAL EDUCATION ACTIVITIES

John A. McCrossan

INTRODUCTION

A great many continuing professional education opportunities are available to library administrators. Such activities include such personal endeavors as reading professional journals and such group programs as attendance at association meetings or participation in workshops or seminars.

This writer did two studies—one of public library administrators and the other of academic library administrators. The purpose was to find out how library directors and other administrators feel about the importance of various types of continuing education activities in their own professional development. How

Advances in Library Administration and Organization,
Volume 8, pages 201-213.
Copyright © 1989 by JAI Press Inc.
All rights of reproduction in any form reserved.
ISBN: 0-89232-967-X

highly do they rate such activities? Do they feel some types of activities are more useful than others? Do the opinions of public library administrators differ in any considerable ways from those of college and university library administrators?

DEFINITIONS

First of all, what is continuing professional education for librarians? Perhaps the best definition is the one developed by a team of six library and information science leaders who comprised the National Council on Quality Continuing Education for Information, Library, and Media Personnel. It reads as follows:

> Continuing education is a learning process which builds on and updates previously acquired knowledge, skills, and attitudes of the individual. Continuing education comes after the preparatory education necessary for involvement in or with information, library, and media services. It is usually self-initiated learning in which individuals assume responsibility for their own development and for fulfilling their need to learn. It is broader than staff development which is usually initiated by an organization for the growth of its own human resources.[1]

Another useful definition emphasizes these points about continuing education:

1. A notion of lifelong learning as a means of keeping up-to-date with new knowledge and preventing obsolescence.
2. The updating of a person's education.
3. The allowance for diversification to a new area within a field.
4. The assumption that the individual carries basic responsibility for such education.
5. The idea that continuing education activities are beyond those considered necessary for entrance into a field.[2]

One item above which may not apply fully to all the library administrators studied is No. 5. Most college, university, and public library employers require that professionals on their staffs, including library administrators, have completed a Master's program in library science at a school accredited by the American Library Association—the type of preparation considered essential by the library profession. In some instances, however, the Master's in library science is not required. Small public libraries, for example, sometimes employ in professional positions those without such education, giving as justification that they cannot afford to hire library school graduates. Academic libraries will sometimes employ those who do not have a library science degree but have other types of academic preparation. In order that these studies present a complete picture of library administrators attitudes, both those with the library science Master's degree and those who did not have that degree were polled.

In summary, continuing professional education for librarians is any education which has the goal of improving their professional performance and which is undertaken generally after completion of a Master's degree program in library science. Such education is usually initiated by the individual concerned and may include a variety of different types of activities.

Library administrators polled in this study include library directors, associate and assistant directors, department heads, and heads of branch libraries.

PREVIOUS RESEARCH

For the past 20 years or so, a great deal has been written about continuing professional education for librarians. There has been some research on the topic, but most of the writing is descriptive in nature or consists of opinions about the types of education needed. There has been very little research which has focused on librarians' opinions of how important different types of continuing education activities have been in professional development.

Several research studies, however, have provided useful background information and have been helpful in planning and designing this writer's studies. One of the first major scientific studies of continuing education for librarians was Elizabeth Stone's landmark dissertation which was published in 1969. Stone surveyed a large number of librarians, identified a number of different types of continuing education opportunities available to them, and attempted to discover various factors which encourage or discourage them from participating in such activities. She found that a large percentage of them participated very little or not at all, and noted that one of the major reasons for the lack of participation was the absence of encouragement from their institutions. She recommended that library administrators take a much more active role in encouraging development of their staffs, and also made recommendations of various ways in which library schools, library associations, and library planners at the state and national levels could promote staff development.[3]

The National Commission on Libraries and Information Science commissioned a study which would recommend a plan for a nationwide program for continuing education for librarians and information personnel. After polling a large number of professionals, the study recommended the creation of an organization which would provide leadership in continuing education.[4] The organization was named the Continuing Library Education Network and Exchange (CLENE). After functioning as an independent group for a number of years, it later became a unit of the American Library Association—the Continuing Library Education Network and Exchange Roundtable.

The roundtable provides leadership to the profession, including publishing a regular newsletter, sponsoring meetings and workshops, encouraging research, and generally providing a needed forum for members of the library/information community who are interested in continuing education and staff development problems.[5]

James Neal surveyed a 25 percent sample of the 360 professional librarians employed in units of the City University of New York. Part-time and adjunct librarians and library directors were excluded from the study. Respondents were asked to assign a priority to several different types of continuing education activities. The group gave highest priority to (1) interaction with other librarians at conferences and association activities; and (2) self-study programs. Formal course work was rated somewhat lower.[6] In his conclusion Neal writes as follows:

> The librarians at CUNY viewed continuing education as a source of more effective job performance, challenge, creativity, and satisfaction. However, practical concerns, particularly the inability to budget sufficient funds and time, frequently made involvement difficult.[7]

He also concludes that even though some types of continuing education activities are rated low by the majority of librarians, they are still rated high by some. Therefore, he states, "continuing education opportunities must be broad, with freedom of choice and individualized programs ensured."[8]

Edwards and Schon surveyed a randomly selected group of school/library media specialists located in the Phoenix, Arizona metropolitan area and asked them to indicate how important various types of continuing education activities had been in improving their job performance. Questionnaires were sent to 133 media specialists, and 92 (69 percent) were returned.[9] The activity rated most highly was participating in district level library meetings. Eighty-five percent of the respondents labeled that type of activity as "important" or "very important." Professional reading was rated "important" or "very important" by 66 percent of the respondents. Professional association meetings, however, were rated relatively low by the group, in contrast with the high rating given by the academic librarians surveyed in the Neal study discussed above. Only 36 percent of the library media specialists labeled that type of activity as "important" or "very important," and 48 percent rated it as "not important" or "somewhat important."[10] The writers expressed their concern about the low evaluation of library association meetings as follows:

> Even though 68 percent of the school library media specialists are members of associations, only 25 percent actually attend meetings, hold office, or work on committees.
> It is interesting to speculate on why school library media specialists don't take more advantage of the opportunities for development activities and other benefits provided by professional organizations. Is the message not getting out? Are the programs irrelevant? Perhaps, in an attempt to meet the needs of a broad audience . . . professional associations provide less practical help for individuals.[11]

Edwards and Schon conclude by recommending that (1) professional associations need to study ways in which they can provide more meaningful programs for media specialists; and (2) that library schools should "ensure that students are made aware of the need for a personal commitment to professional development and of the variety of development activities available to them as practicing school library media specialists."[12]

PUBLIC LIBRARY SURVEY

A survey of the administrators of Florida public libraries serving populations of 10,000 or more was done by this writer to find out how important they felt various types of continuing education activities were in their professional development.[13] Ideally, this type of study could be done on a national basis. Since time and funds were not available for such an extensive survey, this study was limited to the writer's home state of Florida. Therefore, the sample polled reflects only the opinions of library administrators in that state. It is suggested, however, that they may constitute a representative microcosm of librarians in similar positions throughout the United States.

Several major directories were used to identify that total population for the survey—all those public librarians holding administrative positions in Florida public libraries serving populations of 10,000 or more.[14] A total of 520 administrators were identified. From that total population, a 20 percent random sample was drawn.

A questionnaire was developed which requested administrators' opinions of the value of a variety of different types of educational activities which could assist them in their professional development. Previous research was examined for ideas about questions to pose on the questionnaire. Such previous studies, particularly those discussed above, were especially helpful in developing a list of continuing education activities which librarians pursue. The questionnaire draft was also submitted to several knowledgeable library researchers for comments, and it was also pre-tested on a number of library administrators. Various changes were made as a result of those procedures.

Respondents were asked to rate each of 8 different types of activities on a scale of 1 to 5. A rating of 1 would indicate that a respondent felt a particular type of activity had been very unimportant in his/her professional development. A rating of 5 would indicate the belief that a type of activity had been extremely important, and a rating of 2, 3, or 4 would signify the opinion that the importance of an activity lay somewhere between the extremes indicated by a 1 or a 5.

The types of activities listed, in the order in which they were listed on the questionnaire, are as follows:

* Reading library science publications
* Reading publications of other professions
* Attending meetings of professional library associations
* Attending meetings of other professions
* Attending workshops, courses, or seminars
* Visits to observe other libraries
* Working with other librarians to improve a skill or to learn a new skill
* Writing professional pieces for publication

An open-ended question gave respondents an opportunity to describe 1 or 2 particular activities which they thought had been most useful to them in their professional development.

Seventy-three questionnaires (70 percent of those mailed out) were returned— a very good rate of return for a study of this type. Results of the survey are shown in Table 1. (For purposes of comparison, results of a later survey of academic library administrators are also shown in the table.)

The type of activity rated most highly by the public library administrators was "Attending Workshops, Courses, or Seminars." That activity, listed as number I on the table, received a high rating of 4 or 5 from 66 respondents—90.4 percent of the total. Only two respondents (2.8 percent) gave it a low rating of 1 or 2, and the mean rating was a very high 4.32. "Reading Library Science Publications" and "Working with Other Librarians" also received high ratings of 4 or 5 from a large majority of respondents and a low rating from only a small minority. A considerably smaller proportion gave a high rating to "Attending Meetings of Professional Library Associations" and to "Visits to Observe Other Libraries."

"Reading Publications of Other Professionals" received a high rating of 4 or 5 from only 27.4 percent and a low rating of 1 or 2 from 31.5 percent of respondents. "Attending Meetings of Other Professions" received an even lower rating with more than half of the public library administrators giving that type of activity a rating of 1 or 2. "Writing Professional Pieces for Publication" was rated lowest of all, with only 5.7 percent giving it a rating of 4 or 5 and a large majority of 77.1 percent giving it a low rating of 1 or 2.

Sixty-six of the public library administrators responded to the open-ended question in which they were asked to note one or two activities which they thought had been most useful in their professional development during the past five years. They listed a total of 83 different activities. The type of activity listed most frequently was some type of workshop, course or seminar. Such programs were listed 57 times, or 69 percent of the total. Other types of activities noted included attendance at professional meetings, committee work, working with other librarians, and participating in some kind of community activity.

ACADEMIC LIBRARY SURVEY

After completion of the public library study, this writer decided to do a survey of academic library administrators in order to find out how they felt about continuing professional education and also to determine whether their attitudes differed in any substantial ways from the public library administrators studied. Academic library administrators were identified by using three directories.[15]

Questionnaires were sent to 98 Florida college and university library administrators, and 71 were returned (72.4 percent). Responses indicate that their opinions are generally quite similar to those of the public librarians. However, there are also some interesting differences between the two groups. Most of the differences appear to be too small to be statistically significant and may be due to chance. In any case no statistical tests of significance were done because the two studies were done at different times and are not entirely comparable. Some future research could be done, however, to find out whether there are significant differences between the two groups on certain types of continuing education activities. For example, there were relatively large differences between the two groups in their estimation of the value of "Writing Professional Pieces for Publication" as an aid in professional development.

On Activities I, II, III and VI there appear to be very few differences between the two groups of library administrators. As is shown in Table 1, the mean rating on all four activities for the academic librarians is very similar to the mean for the public librarians. There also are only very modest differences in the percentages of each group who gave a particular rating to those activities. The public library group gave a slightly higher average rating to "Attending Workshops, Courses, or Seminars" and to "Working with Other Librarians" while the academic library group gave a slightly higher average rating to "Reading Library Science Publications" and to "Reading Publications of Other Professions." Basically, however, the two groups seem to have very similar attitudes towards the four different activities.

There are somewhat greater differences between the two groups on Activities IV, V, VII, and VIII. While the mean rating given by both groups to Activity IV—"Attending Meetings of Professional Library Associations"—is not very great, the percentage of each group who rated that type of experience high or low is surprisingly large. Of the academic librarians, 73.2 percent gave "Attending Meetings of Professional Library Associations" a high rating while only 56.9 percent of public librarians gave it a similar rating. On the other hand, more than twice as many of the public librarians gave it a low rating of 1 or 2 as did the academic librarians (20.8 percent compared with 8.4 percent).

Why such relatively large differences? One can only speculate on the reasons, and further research would be needed to gain more information. Could it be that the academic environment provides greater encouragement to participate in one's professional associations than the public library environment? For example, college and university professors in all disciplines are generally encouraged to take part in their professional associations for contacts with others and for purposes of their own continuing professional education. Perhaps academic library administrators thus also feel some obligation to be active in their own associations. Public library administrators, as employees of city or county governments, may not always receive the same degree of such encouragement since the average local government unfortunately often does not place such a high premium on professional development of their employees.

On Activity VII—"Attending Meetings of Other Professions"—there are smaller differences between the two groups. Interestingly, however, almost twice as many academic library administrators, as public library administrators, gave that type of experience a high rating. On the other hand, very similar proportions—more than half of both groups—gave that activity a low rating of 1 or 2. Apparently, most of the library administrators do not consider participation in meetings of other professional groups to be particularly valuable in their professional development.

On Activity V—"Visits to Observe Other Libraries"—the greatest difference occurs in the percentage of each group which rated that activity low. Among the public librarians, 17.8 percent gave that experience a low rating while only 5.7 of the academic librarians assigned a low value to it. Could it be that recent progress in automation has affected academic libraries somewhat more than public libraries and that visits to observe automation projects are perceived as valuable; therefore, elevating librarians' general attitudes towards visits. That is only a guess, however, and further research would be needed to identify reasons for the noted difference in opinions of the two groups.

The academic librarians rated "Writing Professional Pieces for Publication" somewhat higher than the public librarians. Of the academic library administrators, 11.4 percent gave "Writing" a high rating, which only 5.7 percent of the public library administrators did. On the other hand, 77.1 percent of the public librarians gave that activity a low rating compared with 57.1 percent of the academic librarians.

Why do academic library administrators perceive writing for publication as more valuable in their continuing education than public library administrators? Perhaps because, being in an academic environment, the former group are more oriented towards research and writing—a major occupation of the professors and students to whom academic library administrators relate.

Also, in a number of colleges and universities, academic library professionals are required to do at least a minimum amount of writing for publication in order to receive tenure. The local government environment in which public library administrators work rarely provides such encouragement for writing for publication.

It is surprising, however, that the academic library administrators did not rate writing for publication even much higher than they did. The expectation was that, being in a college or university environment, the majority would have given that activity a high rating of 4 or 5. Why did they not do so? Could it be that in recent years the administrators in academic libraries have become so deeply involved in day-to-day management problems that they do not feel they have time nor see the value of research and writing, at least not to the extent that leading college and university library directors did in the past?

As a general comment, it is very sad that library administrators, both public and academic, who are leaders in the library profession, have such a low opinion of writing for publication as a way to develop their own insights and skills. Carefully researching and writing about an activity or idea can lead to great professional growth. Also, library administrators are involved in many, many activities which would be of great interest to other librarians and library science students if they were written and published.

If every librarian, administrator and non-administrator, would write even one short piece for publication every year or two, our professional literature would be immeasurably enriched. Library science professors in library schools are constantly made aware of the dearth of literature in all areas of our profession. This becomes acutely obvious when library science students select topics for term papers. So many students optimistically select interesting topics to research, then a few days later will report that surprisingly there are only one or two, or sometimes no articles of any recency on the topics in library literature.

In summary, the literature of library/information science is quite thin, library administrators have much knowledge and much they could write about, and their writing could contribute a great deal to the advancement of our profession. It is hoped that more administrators of all types of libraries will take the time to put their knowledge and ideas on paper and submit them for publication.

Similar to the public library survey described above, the survey of academic library administrators contained an open-ended question which requested them to note briefly one or two particular activities which had been most useful to them in their professional development. Sixty-two of the 71 academic library administrators returning questionnaires responded to that question. They listed a total of 92 different activities. Some type of workshop, course, or seminar was listed most frequently— 42 times, or 47 percent of the total. Other types of activities listed more than 5 times were as follows:

A variety of other types of experiences were listed by one or more respondents. They included (1) designing a library building; (2) serving temporarily as a dean or an officer in academic affairs; (3) serving on an accreditation team; and (4) writing an article for publication.

These responses are relatively similar to those of the public library administrators polled previously. Both groups listed participation in a workshop, course, or seminar most frequently. Among the academic librarians, however, such participation accounted for only 47 percent of the total, while among the public librarians it accounted for 69 percent. As the public library group, the academic library group also listed attending association meetings and participating in association work fairly frequently, but much less frequently than participation in workshops, courses, or seminars.

CONCLUSIONS

Two studies were done—one of public library administrators and one of academic library administrators—to find out how they perceived the value of continuing professional education activities. There has been a considerable amount of literature about continuing education of librarians, but most of the

Table 1. Library Administrators' Opinions of Different Types of Continuing Education Activities

Type of CEA	Total of Low Ratings (1 or 2)	Extremely Unimportant 1	2	3	4	Extremely Important 5	Total of High Ratings (4 or 5)	Mean	Total Number of Responses
I. Attending Workshops, Courses, or Seminars									
Public Library Administrators	2(2.8%)	1(1.4%)	1(1.4%)	5(6.8%)	32(43.8%)	34(46.6%)	66(90.4%)	4.32	73
Academic Library Administrators	3(4.2%)	0	3(4.2%)	12(17.0%)	17(23.9%)	39(54.9%)	56(78.8%)	4.30	71
II. Reading Library Science Publications									
Public Library Administrators	6(8.2%)	2(2.7%)	4(5.5%)	10(13.7%)	22(30.1%)	35(47.9%)	57(78.0%)	4.15	73
Academic Library Administrators	3(4.2%)	1(1.4%)	2(2.8%)	10(14.0%)	27(38.0%)	31(43.7%)	58(81.7%)	4.20	71
III. Working with Other Librarians									
Public Library Administrators	6(8.2%)	4(5.5%)	2(2.7%)	15(20.5%)	27(37.0%)	25(34.2%)	53(71.2%)	3.92	73
Academic Library Administrators	7(9.9%)	1(1.4%)	6(8.5%)	18(25.4%)	20(28.2%)	26(36.6%)	46(64.8%)	3.90	71

								Mean	N
IV. Attending Meetings of Professional Library Associations									
Public Library Administrators	15(20.8%)	4(5.5%)	11(15.3%)	16(22.2%)	15(20.8%)	26(36.1%)	41(56.9%)	3.67	72
Academic Library Administrators	6(8.4%)	2(2.8%)	4(5.6%)	13(18.3%)	28(39.4%)	24(33.8%)	52(73.2%)	3.96	71
V. Visits to Observe Other Libraries									
Public Library Administrators	13(17.8%)	1(1.4%)	12(16.4%)	21(28.8%)	20(27.4%)	19(26.0%)	39(53.4%)	3.60	73
Academic Library Administrators	4(5.7%)	1(1.4%)	3(4.3%)	21(30.0%)	25(37.7%)	20(28.6%)	45(64.3%)	3.84	70
VI. Reading Publications of Other Professions									
Public Library Administrators	23(31.5%)	8(11.0%)	15(20.5%)	30(41.1%)	17(23.3%)	3(4.1%)	20(27.4%)	2.89	73
Academic Library Administrators	19(26.7%)	5(7.0%)	14(19.7%)	30(42.3%)	18(25.4%)	4(5.6%)	22(31.1%)	3.03	71
VII. Attending Meetings of Other Professions									
Public Library Administrators	39(53.4%)	15(20.5%)	24(32.9%)	26(35.6%)	4(5.5%)	4(5.5%)	8(11.0%)	2.42	73
Academic Library Administrators	39(54.9%)	21(29.6%)	18(25.4%)	17(23.9%)	14(19.7%)	1(1.4%)	15(21.1%)	2.38	71
VIII. Writing Professional Pieces for Publication									
Public Library Administrators	54(77.1%)	37(52.8%)	17(24.3%)	12(17.1%)	1(1.4%)	3(4.3%)	4(5.7%)	1.80	70
Academic Library Administrators	40(57.1%)	25(35.7%)	15(21.4%)	22(31.4%)	5(7.1%)	3(4.3%)	8(11.4%)	2.23	70

211

writing is descriptive in nature and very little reports on research related to librarians' opinions on the topic.

The survey of public library administrators was done first and was published as noted (see Note 13). In order to gather information about academic library administrators, a second survey, previously not published, was also done.

Analysis of responses to the surveys indicates that both public and academic library administrators feel continuing education is very important in their professional development. Moreover, the responses of both groups are quite similar. Both the academic and public library administrators rated several types of activities very highly. Also, their ratings of most of the specific activities were quite similar.

More than 75 percent of both groups gave a high rating to "Attending Workshops, Courses, or Seminars" and "Reading Library Science Publications." Fewer than 75 percent but more than 50 percent of both groups gave a high rating to "Working with Other Librarians," "Attending Meetings of Professional Library Associations," and "Visits to Observe Other Libraries." Fewer than one-third of both groups gave a high rating to "Reading Publications of Other Professions," "Attending Meetings of Other Professions," and "Writing Professional Pieces for Publication."

The similarity of ratings given by the two groups was somewhat surprising. This writer expected there might be greater differences in the perceptions of academic and public library administrators since the former work in a college or university environment while the latter work in a city or county government environment—workplaces which have somewhat different expectations of staff members. However, the fact that both groups have such similar ideas about continuing professional education may lend some evidence to the hypothesis that librarianship is one profession. Perhaps, regardless of the type of library in which one works, one is a librarian and has certain ideas akin to those of librarians in other types of libraries.

There were, however, some interesting differences between the two groups. Further research should be done to explore the reasons for those differences. Also, further research needs to be done to find out why library administrators rate certain activities so highly and give other activities a much lower rating.

In summary, the vast majority of both academic and public library administrators perceive continuing professional education, especially certain types of such education, to be very important in their professional development. Moreover, even those types rated low by a majority were rated high by a minority of respondents. Therefore, this writer agrees with the reasoning advanced by James Neal in his article discussed in this paper, that continuing education opportunities must be broad and that librarians should have the freedom to choose from a variety of different types of continuing education activities.[16]

NOTES

1. Elizabeth W. Stone, "Library Education: Continuing Professional Education" in *ALA World Encyclopedia of Library and Information Science.* 2nd ed. (Chicago: American Library Association, 1986), 476.

2. Elizabeth W. Stone, Ruth Patrick, and Barbara Conroy, *Continuing Library and Information Science Education: Final Report to the National Commission on Libraries and Information Science* (Washington, D.C.: American Society for Information Science, 1974), 23.

3. Elizabeth W. Stone, *Factors Related to Professional Development of Librarians* (Metuchen, N.J.: Scarecrow Press, 1969), 220–224.

4. Elizabeth W. Stone, Ruth Patrick, and Barbara Conroy, *Continuing Library and Information Science Education,* XVI–XVII.

5. *ALA Handbook of Organization, 1987/88* (Chicago: American Library Association, 1987), 160.

6. James G. Neal, "Continuing Education: Attitudes and Experiences of the Academic Librarian," *College and Research Libraries* 41 (March, 1980): 130.

7. Ibid., 132.

8. Ibid.

9. Karlene K. Edwards and Isabel Schon, "Professional Development Activities as Viewed by School Library Media Specialists," *School Library Media Quarterly* 14 (Spring, 1986): 138.

10. Ibid., 139.

11. Ibid.

12. Ibid., 140–41.

13. John A. McCrossan, Public Library Administrators' Opinions of Continuing Education Activities," *Public Libraries* 27 (Spring, 1988): 47–49.

14. *American Library Directory* (New York: Bowker, 1986); Laura James Hodges and E. Walter Terrie, eds., *Florida Library Directory with Statistics* (Tallahassee, Fla.: Florida Department of State, Division of Library Services, 1986); *Official Membership Directory of the Florida Library Association* (Winter Park, Fla.: Florida Library Association, 1987).

15. *American Library Directory* (New York: Bowker, 1987); Elizabeth A. Curry and E. Walter Terrie, eds., *Florida Library Directory with Statistics* (Tallahassee, Fla.: Florida Department of State, Division of Library and Information Services, 1987); *Official Membership Directory of the Florida Library Association* (Winter Park, Fla., Florida Library Association, 1987).

16. James Neal, pg. 5.

A CORE REFERENCE THEATRE ARTS COLLECTION FOR RESEARCH

Sharon Lynn Schofield, Helen K. Bolton,

Rashelle S. Karp and Bernard S. Schlessinger

INTRODUCTION

The reference tools in an academic research collection comprise bibliographies, dictionaries, guides, indexes, annuals, and source documents, including a core periodical collection, which provides the most current information available in print.

One area of growing academic research is the theatre arts. This fact is evident, if in no other way, in the number of groups which have formed to promote theatre research. Among these groups are the American Society for Theatre Research, the International Federation for Theatre Research, and the Theatre Library Association. As Lee Nemcheck has pointed out, "The recognition of

Advances in Library Administration and Organization,
Volume 8, pages 215-240.
Copyright © 1989 by JAI Press Inc.
All rights of reproduction in any form reserved.
ISBN: 0-89232-967-X

theatre as a valid field of study in universities [has] precipitated an increase in significant research in the field, which ultimately [has] led to the need for organized library collections of theatre materials'' (1981, p. 374). The writers' search of the literature, however, has revealed that there is no research based information available to identify reference or periodical core collections in the theatre arts that would support research.

The materials identified and annotated in this article have been selected as a basic core collection of English language reference materials and periodicals concerned with traditional stage drama. The bibliography may be used as an evaluative tool to examine an existing collection, as a guide for research, or, as a selection tool to develop a new or young collection.

Methodology

Three steps were utilized to identify the materials which comprise this suggested core collection.

1. The writers compiled a list of reference sources and periodicals for the theatre arts which appeared in five standard selection tools:

> Katz, Bill and Gargel, Berry. *Magazines for Libraries*. New York: R.R. Bowker, 1986.

> Rogers, A. Robert. *The Humanities: A Selective Guide to Information Sources* 2nd ed. Littleton, Co: Libraries Unlimited, 1979.

> Sheehy, Eugene Paul. *Guide to Reference Books*. Chicago, IL: ALA, 1986.

> *Ulrich's International Periodical Directory*. New York: R.R. Bowker Company, 1987–88.

> Whalon, Marion K. Ed. *Performing Arts Research: A Guide to Information Sources*. Detroit, MI: Gale Research Company, 1976.

These selection tools listed nearly 500 reference sources and periodicals published in the field of theatre arts.

2. The list of tools developed above was then compared to the tools in the theatre arts research collections at the Dallas, Texas, Public Library (known for its Fine Arts Department and drama collection); the Denton, Texas, Public Library (which supplements the collections of two universities, and supports an active community theatre program); and the North Texas State University and Texas Woman's University libraries (both of which support graduate and undergraduate study in drama).

Fifty-nine items (9 periodicals and 50 reference tools) which were listed in at least four of the standard selection tools, and were held in each of the four selected libraries, were identified as potential items for the core collection.

3. In order to test the identified core collection, a group of five subject specialists representing the areas of humanities, drama, art, fine arts, general reference, social sciences, and theatre research, were queried. Using a questionnaire designed by the writers, the subject specialists were asked to designate whether they considered each source "Indispensable," "Necessary," or "Questionable" in a core reference and periodical collection for the theatre arts. Additionally, they were instructed to add any sources they felt had been overlooked.

Upon receipt of the responses, a comparison was made between the core which was identified by the writers, and the core indicated by the subject specialists.

Results

Fifty-four of the sources identified by the writers received "Necessary" and/ or "Indispensable" ratings from the specialists, and were included in the final core collection.

Of the five which were not included, one (*The Jew in English Drama*), received a "Questionable" vote from four subject specialists, and four (*Black American Playwrites, 1800 to the Present: a Bibliography, A Dictionary of the English Costume: 900–1900, List of Masques, Pageants, etc., Supplementary to a List of English Plays*, and *American Theatrical Arts: A Guide to Manuscripts in the United States and Canada*) received "Questionable" ratings from three subject specialists. Each of these people noted that although the questioned items were valuable, they should only be a part of the core if the collection was quite large.

Of the 54 remaining reference tools on the list, 14 received one "Questionable" rating. Oddly enough, each of these also received at least one "Indispensable" rating. Reference sources and journals that received three "Indispensable" ratings are indicated with an asterisk (*) in the final bibliography, and those which received four "Indispensable" ratings are flagged by a double asterisk (**). Subject specialists added six sources (three periodicals and three reference tools) to the original list, bringing the total number of items to 60. These sources are identified with a plus symbol (+), in the final bibliography. No source received a perfect score of five "Indispensable" ratings.

ANNOTATED BIBLIOGRAPHY OF CORE RESOURCES

Prices listed for this final collection of reference tools were obtained from the 1987–1988 *Books in Print*, or directly from the publishers. Prices listed for the periodicals were obtained from the 1987–1988 edition of *Ulrich's International*

Periodical Dictionary. It should also be noted that some of the recommended sources are now out of print (identified as such in the bibliographic citation). However, since this recommended core collection may be used as an evaluative tool for existing collections, they have been included.

THE CORE COLLECTION

Bibliographies

Bergquist, G. William, Ed. *Three Centuries of English and American Plays: A Checklist—English 1500–1800 and United States 1714–1830.* London: Hafner, 1963. $37.50.

Purpose. To list English and American plays, published from 1500 to 1830.

Scope and content. Originally conceived as a guide to the contents of a microprint collection of the full text of plays published between 1500 and 1830 (*Three Centuries of English and American Plays, 1515–1830 in Microprint*) this comprehensive index lists important and less important plays published during the periods covered. Plays are listed by author and title, and entries give the author's full name (if known), birth and death dates (if known), main titles or alternative title, place of publication, publisher and date of the play. When applicable, numbers are given to access the Greg/Woodward and McManaway bibliographies.

Format. Arrangement is alphabetical by author and title, with cross references for alternate titles, spellings and translations, and added entries for joint authors and editors.

Brockett, Oscar G., Samuel Becker and Donald Bryant. *A Bibliographical Guide to Research in Speech and Dramatic Art.* Chicago, IL: Scott Foresman, 1963. Out of Print.

Purpose. To list, in a single volume, the important bibliographical aids and reference works in the fields of Speech and Dramatic Art, and to place these guides in the context of related materials.

Scope and content. More than 650 works printed through 1962 are listed and briefly annotated in three parts: (1) general reference works, (2) works in the field of speech and dramatic art, and (3) works in five related fields. Includes important bibliographical aids, dictionaries, encyclopedias, handbooks, and summary treatments of related fields. Excluded are standard histories, textbooks and summary treatments unless unusual.

Format. Access only through general subject headings in the table of contents. No index.

* Greg, Sir Walter Wilson. *A Bibliography of the English Printed Drama to the Restoration.* London: Bibliographic Society, 1970. (reprint of first edition published in 1939) 4 volumes. Out of print.

Purpose. To provide an annotated bibliography of "all [English] dramatic compositions which were either written before the end of 1642 or printed before the beginning of 1660.

Scope and content. Begun in 1939 and completed in 1958, Volumes I and II include descriptions of individual plays, Latin plays that are considered to belong within English literature, and collected editions of plays. Volume III comprises (1) lists of collections; (2) appendixes which include advertisements, prefaces, author and actor lists, publications lists, lists of private collections, and early play catalogs; and (3) various "reference lists" including, among others, theatre companies, court performances, play producers, artists, mottoes, and notabilia. Volume IV, written by the Bibliographical Society, contains a description of the first three volumes, additions, corrections, and an index to all four volumes. Entries comprise full bibliographic citations, and a detailed description of the printed edition, as well as plot synopses. At the end of the first three volumes can be found reproductions of advertising posters for many of the listed plays.

Format. Except for collected editions of plays, arrangement is chronological; collected editions are arranged alphabetically by author.

Harbage, Alfred. *Annals of English Drama. 975–1700: An Analytical Record of All Plays, Extant or Lost Chronologically Arranged and Indexed by Authors, Titles, Dramatic Companies, etc.* (revised by S. Schoenbaum). Philadelphia, PA: University of Pennsylvania Press, 1964. Out of print.

Purpose. To list, in chronological order, the authors, titles, years of performance, classification, auspices, and dates of first and latest editions of the printed form of plays. The author's stated purpose is to "aid the student in determining immediately the approximate environment of a given play," and to serve as a finding tool for librarians, historians, and teachers.

Scope and content. A list of plays, masks and other dramatic or quasi-dramatic English drama from the Middle Ages to the Restoration period. Included are plays in Latin, French and English, lost and extant, unacted and acted, translated, adapted, and original, and descriptions of royal receptions and entertainments.

Format. Items are arranged chronologically, at first by centuries, later by years (1495 on). Set up in unannotated and undocumented chart form, indexing is by playwright (with dates of birth and death, if known), plays titles, and dramatic companies. Also included are lists of editions, theatres, and dissertations, as well as an appendix of extant play manuscripts.

Hatch, James Vernon. *Black Image on the American Stage: A Bibliography of Plays and Musicals, 1770–1970.* NY: Drama Book Publications, 1972. Out of Print.

Purpose. To encourage teachers and students to explore and examine the development of black images and racial history in terms of the theatre.

Scope and content. Includes over 2,000 American, European, African and

Asian full length and one act plays, musicals, operas, revues and dance dramas, performed in the United States. All works have met at least two of four criteria: They must (1) contain at least one black character, (2) be written by a black playwright, (3) have a black theme, or (4) have been written or produced in America between 1767 and 1970. Excluded are radio, film, and television scripts (unless adapted for the stage), as well as minstrel shows, "darkie comedies," and plays or musicals in which black actors play neutral roles.

Format.   Arranged chronologically by decade, then alphabetically by author, entries include the following information: author, title of play, date, publisher, library where a script may be found, and sometimes productions groups for the play. Title and author indexes provide access to the main text and a bibliography of the theses and dissertations on which the book was based is also included.

Hill, Frank Pierce. *American Plays Printed 1714–1830: A Bibliographical Record.* NY: B. Franklin, 1968 (reprint of a 1934 edition). $19.00.

Purpose.   To provide a list of works by American-born authors or foreigners who lived in this country and published between 1714 and 1830.

Scope and content.   Four hundred and five plays (151 authors and 66 anonymous entries) known to have been written and published between 1714 and 1830 by American authors, foreign authors living in America, and American authors living abroad are listed and located in one or more of ten large libraries in the United States. Excluded are plays by foreign authors published in America, plays in manuscript, and "dialogues" (unless they have three or more characters). Entries include: author and author's dates, title, a synopsis of the play, number of acts, when and where the play was performed, publisher, date, pages, how long the performance runs and where the play can be obtained.

Format.   The main body is arranged alphabetically by authors and anonymous titles numbered serially for cross reference from two indexes: (1) an alphabetical list of titles, and (2) a title list in chronological order (both refer the user to the serially numbered main entry).

Salem, James M. *Drury's Guide to Best Plays.* 4th ed. Metuchen, NJ: Scarecrow Press, 1987. $35.00

Purpose.   To provide information on where plays can be obtained and royalties, as well as productions and their reception by the public.

Scope and content.   More than 1,500 "significant" plays written since 1953, and through the 1984–85 theatrical season are listed with the following information: source, title, translator or adaptor, a brief synopsis, first production date or copyright date, name of publisher handling amateur rights or citations to drama collections and anthologies, royalty information, sets, cast number and royalties. Includes all plays which have won Pulitzer or New York Drama Critic Circle awards, plays selected for inclusion in the *Best Plays of the Year* series, commercial successes, and those plays which are popular with amateur and high school groups. Excluded are one act plays (unless lengthy), and twentieth century American plays not currently offered by play publishers or especially recommended.

Format. Entries are alphabetized by author, and are made accessible through several separate indexes: selected subjects, title, plays requiring no scenery, award winning plays, most popular plays for amateur groups, plays recommended for all groups, popular plays for high school production, and frequently produced plays (high school theatre). Separate appendixes list the addresses of play publishers represented and index co-authors, original authors and adapters.

* Shipley, Joseph T. *The Crown Guide to the World's Great Plays: From Ancient Greece to Modern Times.* NY: Crown Publishers, 1984. $24.95. (revised edition of *Guide to Great Plays.* Washington: Public Affairs Press, 1956).

Purpose. To provide a select guide to the classics, defined as those which the "master critics have considered truly great" or those which "while not intrinsically great, [have] been at least a great success and may call for inclusion on the grounds of history."

Scope and content. Seven hundred and fifty plays by leading writers from every country, and covering the time period from the birth of drama to contemporary theater are detailed. Each play entry includes: author and a brief biography, a brief plot synopsis, the play's importance in history, leading actors, the play's stage history, and opinions by critics and reviewers.

Format. The alphabetical arrangement by author is supplemented by an extensive title index and cross references within the text (a glossary of terms was included in the earlier, 1956, edition).

Dictionaries and Encyclopedias

* Bowman, Walter Parker and Robert H. Ball. *Theatre Language: A Dictionary of Terms in English of the Drama and Stage from Medieval to Modern Times.* NY: Routledge/Theatre Arts Books, 1976. paperback $4.95. (reprint of a 1961 edition).

Purpose. To select and define words and phrases used for the past 500 years on the "legitimate" stage in the United States and Great Britain.

Scope and contents. Close to 4,000 technical terms, standard nontechnical terms, slang, jargon or cant are defined. Excluded are foreign terms (unless absorbed into the English language), expressions which have passed into nontheatrical use, copyrighted or trademarked names (unless commonly used), and proper names of persons, organizations, and places (unless they have become part of the theatre language).

Format. Arranged in strictly alphabetical order.

* Gassner, John and Edward Quinn. *The Reader's Encyclopedia of World Drama.* NY: Crowell, 1969. Out of Print.

Purpose. To provide a one volume, ready-reference resource which reflects John Gassner's vision of drama as literature.

Scope and content. Playwrights, plays (and their literary characteristics), theatrical terms, periods of drama history, and surveys by countries are described from as early as 525 BCE to near the present. Additionally, the author discusses radio and television drama in Europe. Excluded are actors, theatrical troupes, costumes, scenery and playhouses.

Format. Arranged alphabetically, and written narratively, the source includes one appendix which lists (and sometimes annotates or reproduces) "documents of dramatic theory."

+ Granville, Wilfred. *The Theatre Dictionary: British and American Terms in the Drama, Opera, and Ballet.* Westport, CT: Greenwood Press, 1970. (This reprint of a 1952 edition is currently out of stock, but is being considered for another printing as of 1/88). $55.00.

Purpose. To provide a permanent record of the technical, colloquial and slang speech of the twentieth century stage.

Scope and content. Definitions of approximately 3,000 terms (gathered throughout the author's active theatrical career as actor, producer, stage director and acting manager), include a few common rhyming terms, *Parlyaree* (mostly phrases or words originating from the circus, fairgrounds, and booth theatres), "critic's" words, and technical terms used in elocution and phonetics. Excluded is Cockney rhyming slang. Entries include the term's definition and origin (if known). No pronunciation guides.

Format. Arranged alphabetically.

Lewine, Richard and Alfred Simon. *Songs of the American Theatre: A Definitive Index to the Songs of the Musical Stage.* NY: H.W. Wilson, 1984. $70.00. (expands, updates, and supercedes his earlier edition entitled *Songs of the American Theatre: A Comprehensive Listing of More than 12,000 Songs, Including Selected Titles from Film and Television Productions.* NY: Dodd, Mead, 1973).

Purpose. To provide the answer for "every frustrated musical-comedy fan who's ever asked "what is that from?"

Scope and content. Includes over 17,000 songs from 1200 American musicals produced in Broadway and Off-Broadway theater, on television and on film from 1891–1983.

In the first section, entries for songs include composer names, lyricists, and year of original New York production. In the second section, entries for shows (alphabetically by title) include New York opening dates, number of New York performances, composers, lyricists, titles of songs, and reference to recorded and print editions.

Format. The alphabetical arrangement in the first two sections is supplemented by a composer, lyricists, and author index, as well as a chronological list of all shows, and a list of film and television productions.

* Matlaw, Myron. *Modern World Drama: An Encyclopedia*. NY: Dutton, 1972. Out of Print.

Purpose. To "provide a comprehensive reference to modern world drama in one extensively indexed volume containing a single alphabetical listing of plays, playwrights, countries, technical terms and national surveys."

Scope and content. Reflecting the author's "own tastes and attitudes," entries comprise 1,058 plays and drama terms, 688 major nineteenth and twentieth century playwrights, and 80 countries. The text includes plot synopses, factual data, historical and critical notes, geographical and ethnic surveys, trends and movements.

Format. A character index and general index provide specific access. Also helpful are a selective general bibliography, detail of content arrangement, and a list of illustrations.

** *McGraw-Hill Encyclopedia of World Drama: An International Reference Work*. NY: McGraw-Hill, 2nd ed, 1984. $310.00.

Purpose. To provide international and comprehensive coverage of world drama, and to focus on the achievements of playwrights who have influenced its evolution.

Scope and content. The achievements of approximately 1300 playwrights are detailed in entries which include (to varying degrees, depending upon the playwright's assessed importance) (1) biographical information, (2) information about the playwright's place in history, (3) synopses of major plays (including their importance and place in history), (4) a play list of titles in their original language and in published or literal translations, (5) a comprehensive bibliography of collected editions of a playwright's plays, and (6) a selective bibliography of works about the playwright. Major emphasis is on biographical material and western drama, but consideration is also given to the drama and theatre of Asia and Latin America, as well as lengthy survey articles ranging from African theatre to Yugoslav drama, and nonbiographical articles dealing with anonymous plays, theatre companies, genres, in-depth studies of the history of musical comedy, and Shakespeare on film. All articles were either revised (from the earlier 1972 edition) or newly written by experts who were allowed freedom to express critical evaluations.

Format. An extensive index, an alphabetical play title list, and extensive cross-referencing within the text are supplemented by a glossary covering dramatic terms, forms, movements and styles, and more than 2500 illustrations.

+ Rigdon, Walter. *The Biographical Encyclopedia and Who's Who of the American Theatre*. NY: J.H. Heineman, 1966. Out of Print. (Updated by

Notable Names in the American Theatre. Clifton, NJ: J.T. White, 1976. Also out of Print).

Purpose.   To provide a biographical reference for the theatre.

Scope and content.   Detailed biographical sketches of more than 3,000 people who have been active in the American theatre include actors, playwrights, directors, designers and others. Also included is a necrology of 9,000 "theatre greats," an alphabetical listing of more than 10,000 plays produced in New York from 1900–1965, reproductions of complete playbills from Broadway, off Broadway, and American experimental and repertory theatres (1959–1965), an awards section, a bibliography of over 600 titles, and a history of the American theatre.

Format.   Each section is arranged alphabetically. No index.

Histories

Bentley, Gerald E. *The Jacobean and Caroline Stage*. 7 volumes. NY: AMS Press, 1982. (reprint of a 1968 edition). $42.50 per volume.

Purpose.   To continue a survey begun by Sir Edmund Chambers on the Elizabethan Stage from 1616 to the closing of the theatres in 1642.

Scope and content.   The seven volumes survey the Jacobean and Caroline Stage from 1616 to 1642, citing literature about this time period written through 1950. Volumes I and II (published in 1941) chronicle the history of the London dramatic companies and the lives of the actors. Considered first, in rough order of importance, are the dramatic companies which performed in London before the death of Shakespeare. Later, companies are treated in the order of the appearance. A comprehensive index to both volumes is found in Volume II. Volumes III, IV and V (published in 1956) provide synopses of plays, masques, shows, and dramatic entertainments, as well as biographies of the playwrights. Entries for volumes I–V total 1200 plays and 220+ playwrights. Volume VI (published in 1968) describes 30 theatre buildings of the time, and lists performances which were put on in them. Volume VII (also published in 1968) were comprises appendixes on Lenten and Sunday performances, and a chronology of dramatic and semidramatic events.

Format.   Volume VII includes an analytical index and bibliography for the entire work.

Blum, Daniel. *A Pictorial History of the American Theatre: 1860–1985*. 6th ed, updated and enlarged by John Willis, ed. NY: Crown Publishers, 1986. $25.95.

Purpose.   To provide a pictorial record of the growth and development of acting and the American stage.

Scope and Content.   Over 5,000 photographs of famous actors and actresses in scenes from popular plays illustrate the history of the American theatre. The main text is preceded by a brief account of plays produced before 1860, and textual material which puts the pictures in context describes the popularity of the theatre, and events that affected the stage, actors, actresses and their roles. The most popular plays are described with interesting circumstances involved with their production and run. Broadway, Off-Broadway, and touring attractions include both musical and dramatic presentations, and Pulitzer Prize winners are mentioned.

Format. The quarto volume is comprehensively indexed by approximately 9,000 entries of personality and play names.

Brockett, Oscar G. *History of the Theatre.* 5th ed. NJ: Allyn and Bacon, 1987. (estimated price of $28.00).

Purpose. To provide a chronological narrative of the development of the theatre from its beginning up to the present, with special emphasis on Europe and America.

Scope and content. Playwriting, directing, acting, costumes, make-up, scenery, lighting, properties, theatre architecture, machinery, special effects, management, audiences and criticism are described in varying depths. Over 540 illustrations and photographs supplement the text.

Format. The chronological/geographical arrangement is complemented by a lengthy bibliography, a detailed index, and an appendix of theatre history for advanced research.

Brockett, Oscar G. and Findlay, Robert. *A Century of Innovation. A History of European and American Theatre and Drama. 1870–1970.* NJ: Prentice Hall, 1973. $49.33.

Purpose. To trace those changes in outlook and practice upon which the present dramatic era is based.

Scope and content. Concentrating on Western theatrical traditions from around 1870 until the early 1970s (as seen in several European countries and the United States), coverage is restricted to those persons and events either most characteristic of an era or of greatest significance in later times, as well as societal and environmental influences on theatre and drama, dramatists, theoreticians, practitioners (directors, actors and designers), and audiences.

Format. Organized chronologically, the textbook format is illustrated in black and white, and includes a bibliography, divided according to chapters and restricted primarily to works in English. Access to the text is through an extensive subject, author, and title index.

Chambers, Edmund Kerchiver. *The Elizabethan Stage.* Oxford: Clarendon Press, 1923. Reprinted in 1951, 1974. 4 volumes. Out of Print.

Purpose. To provide an exhaustive history of the Elizabethan stage from the middle of the 16th century to 1616.

Scope and content. Volume I (Book I) is devoted to a description of the Elizabethan court from the middle of the sixteenth century to 1616. Book II in the same volume records the settlement of the players in London and their conflicts with Puritanism. Volume II contains Books III and IV, which describe and chronicle the 38 individual playing companies and 18 theatres of the time. Volume III (Book V) discusses surviving plays which illuminate the history of the institution that produced them. Alphabetical entries of over 180 playwrights include lengthy annotations of their plays. Volume IV describes approximately 100 anonymous plays, masks, receptions and entertainments. Also, 13 separate appendixes include, among other topics, a court calendar, court payments, documents of criticism and control plague records, and lists of academic printed, lost, and manuscript plays.

Format. A table of contents in Volume I provides access to the contents and illustrations in all four volumes, and Volume IV includes separate indexes for plays, persons, places, and subjects.

Chambers, Edmund Kerchiver. *The Medieval Stage.* Oxford: Clarendon Press, 1903. Reissued in 1967. Reprinted by London: Lowe and Brydone Printers, Ltd, 1978. 2 volumes. Out of Print.

Purpose. To state and explain the pre-existing conditions which, by the latter half of the sixteenth century, made the Shakespearean stage possible.

Scope and content. Arranged in four books, Book I (Minstrelsy) shows how the organization of the Graeco-Roman theatre broke down before the onslaught of Christianity, and how the actors became wandering minstrels entertaining all society with *spectacula.* Book II (Folk Drama) describes the *ludi* of the village feasts, their origin in heathen ritual and primitive, deep-rooted mimetic instinct. Book III (Religious Drama) studies the process by which the church appealed to the mimetic instinct through miracle-plays as well as morality and dramatic pageants. The Book IV (The Interlude) summarily describes the transformation of the mediaeval stage; on the literary side under the influence of humanism, and on the social/economic side by the emergence from minstrelsy to a new class of professional players.

Format. A comprehensive subject index is supplemented by a detailed table of contents, a 30 page bibliography and 24 appendixes which include the texts of mediaeval plays, interludes, and poems; extracts from various documents; and lists of important people and events.

Cheney, Sheldon. *The Theatre: Three Thousand Years of Drama, Acting, and Stagecraft.* NY: Longmans, Green, and Co., 1952 (reprinted by McKay, in 1972). Out of Print.

Purpose. To present a history of the theatre, dramatic art, and artists, as they emerged from specific social backgrounds.

Scope and content. This "story" of drama interweaves fact, description, and commentary in a chronological narrative text. It begins with the origin of dance in primitive rituals, details the social influences and plays performed in Egypt as early as 2,000 B.C., and covers theatre development through 1950, century by century, and for various countries throughout the world.

Format. Chronologically organized by chapter with subject heading divisions, the text is complemented by numerous photographs and a comprehensive index of approximately 900 terms.

Davenport, Millia. *The Book of Costumes.* NY: Crown, 1964. $39.95.

Purpose. To provide a "chronological survey of dress through the ages."

Scope and content. For each civilization or century, an historical summary and outline of changes in its dress are followed by a picture section in which photographs of original artistic interpretations illustrate the preceding explanatory text.

Format. The chronological arrangement is supplemented by an index of names and subjects, as well as an appendix of bibliographical and documentary material, acknowledgements, and primary sources.

Genest, John. *Some Account of the English Stage, from the Restoration in 1660 to 1830.* 10 volumes. Reprint of 1832 edition. NY: B. Franklin, 1965. $375.00.

Purpose. To provide a richly detailed account of English theatre from 1660 to 1830.

Scope and content. This 10 volume set was originally published by England in 1832. It begins with a brief description of the theatre before 1660, then chronologically describes playhouses and their expenses, rigging, procedures, problems, and performances. Significant actors, playwrights, and historical figures that influenced the theatre are also discussed.

Format. The subject of the essay or illustrative article is identified at the top of each page. Often these headings are the name of a theatre or theatrical company and a date. Volume 10 has a short separate index. All other volumes are accessed through a comprehensive, alphabetical list of names, plays and theatres.

Halliday, Frank Ernest. *A Shakespeare Companion, 1564–1964.* NY: Schocken Books, 1964. Out of Print.

Purpose. To provide a handbook covering all aspects of Shakespeare's work and the people most intimately associated with it.

Scope and content. Includes a biography of Shakespeare, as well as descriptions of Shakespeare's works, friends and acquaintances, poems, plays and their characters, and, for his most important plays, the companies that performed them. Also detailed are Shakespeare's printers, publishers, editors, adapters, and critics, as well as the Elizabethan-Jacobean theatre and the other dramatists who wrote for it.

Format. The alphabetical arrangement by personal names, subjects, terms, and titles is complemented by a lengthy bibliography, and several appendixes.

One appendix describes the printed format of Shakespeare's plays, and others include Shakespeare genealogical trees.

Hogan, Charles Beecher. *Shakespeare in the Theatre, 1701–1800.* Oxford: University Press, 1953–1957. 2 volumes. Out of Print.

Purpose. To emphasize the meaning of Shakespeare's works as conveyed through actors to an audience.

Scope and content. Volume I covers the time period from 1701 to 1750, and is divided into two parts. The first part contains a list of performances grouped by theatre and arranged chronologically. Entries include nightly receipts and, where possible, details of the benefits allowed to actors and others involved with the performance. The second part is an alphabetical grouping of plays in which the complete casts are given (as available) for every performance. Volume II completes the account of performances from 1751– 1800.

Format. Both volumes are arranged chronologically, and each have the following appendixes: popularity of Shakespeare's plays by year, the comparative popularity of Shakespeare's plays, and the history of the London theatres. Both volumes have separate indexes for actors and for the characters in the plays.

Odell, George Clinton Dinsmore. *Annals of the New York Stage.* (reprint of edition by Columbia University Press, 1927–49). 15 volumes. NY: AMS Press, on demand. $1,425.00 per set; $95.00 per volume.

Purpose. To provide a thorough account of the history of the new York stage.

Scope and content. Developed in detail through information gathered from autobiographies, diaries, letters, newspaper notices, magazine articles, advertisements, programs, handbills, show receipts, and publishing records, this historical account spans close to 250 years. Beginning with amusements in the colonies through 1752, focus is soon directed solely to the activities of the theatres, influential theatrical families, companies, and actors in the New York City area. Earliest plays are limited only to those presented by white men.

Format. Each volume has a table of contents, a list of illustrations, and is indexed individually by authors, persons, plays, clubs and general subjects (interfiled). The number of photographs and illustrations increases with the development of the modern era. Separate areas of New York City are discussed in special chapters. Individual theatres are frequently used as subheadings with dates. The entire work is comprehensively indexed in Volume XV, with over 16,300 entries of persons, plays, playwrights, theatres and subjects.

Indexes

* Breed, Paul F. and Sniderman, Florence M. *Dramatic Criticism Index: A Bibliography of Commentaries on Playwrights from Ibsen to the Avant-Garde.* Detroit, MI: Gale, 1972. $66.00

Purpose. To index commentaries on modern playwrights and their plays.

Scope and content. This bibliography comprises nearly 12,000 entries in English on 300+ American and foreign playwrights, and was compiled from approximately 630 books and over 200 periodicals. The emphasis is on the 20th century, but a few 19th century playwrights are included.

Format. The playwrights are listed alphabetically. Indexed criticisms appear under the playwright's name, first general criticisms, and then alphabetically by play. Play title and critics indexes are supplemented by a list of the books that were indexed to create the work.

Chicorel Theater Index to Plays in Anthologies, Periodicals, Discs, and Tapes. NY: American Library Publishing Company. Chicorel Index Series. 1970–1976. $125/volume. Volumes 1, 2, 3, 8, 9, 21, 22/A, and 25 cover plays and drama.

Purpose. To provide a standard reference tool which analytically indexes play anthologies.

Scope and content. Access is provided to full plays, significant abridgements and selections, one act plays, radio and film plays, and children's plays. Entries include the full bibliographic citation for each indexed play.

Format. Authors, anthology titles and play titles are interfiled alphabetically, and (depending on the volume) are either interfiled with or complemented by separate lists of publishers (with addresses), anthologies and collections, playtitles, authors, editors, adaptors, translators, and subject indicators.

Cumulated Dramatic Index, 1909–1949. 2 volumes. (A Cumulation of the F.W. Faxon Company's Dramatic Index) Boston: G.K. Hall, 1965. $615.00

Purpose. To provide a cumulation of the 41 annual volumes of the now out of print *Dramatic Index*, the "only existing guide for articles and illustrations concerning the stage and its players that have appeared in American and British periodicals."

Scope and content. More than 150 quarterly, monthly, and weekly periodicals are indexed. Periodicals indexed in the *Annual Magazine Subject Index*, as well as others were scanned and indexed for articles and portraits of dramatic interest. The critical, historical and biographical articles cited cover information about dramatists, librettists, performers, notices of production, scenes, synopses and reviews of plays, and stage portraits that include costumes from Shakespearean productions, grand operas and famous characters.

Format. More than 300,000 entries comprise the body of the index. Entries are arranged alphabetically by subject with additional headings for titles, playwrights, and famous characters. There are three appendixes which are entitled "Author List of Books about the Drama," (6,500 entries), "Title List of Published Play Texts," (24,000 entries), and "Author List of Published Play Texts" (20,000 entries). A complete system of cross references identifies authors and plays; and the inclusion of birth and death dates with the author headings makes the index a valuable guide to biographical material.

Firkins, Ina Ten Eyke. *Index to Plays, 1800–1926.* NY: Wilson, 1927. *Supplement* published in 1935. Out of Print.

Purpose. To provide a guide to available editions of plays by nineteenth and twentieth century authors who are either well-known, or whose works have been popular enough to bring them to recognition.

Scope and content. The 1927 edition indexes 7,872 plays by 2,203 authors, selected on the basis of "general demand." The *Supplement* indexes 3284 titles by 1335 authors. In all, 113 periodicals are referenced. Entries include a full bibliographic citation to separate publications of plays, collected works of authors, composite collections, and periodicals.

Format. The main text is arranged alphabetically by author, and is complemented by a title/subject index.

Guernsey, Otis L. *Directory of the American Theatre. 1894–1971: Index to the Complete Series of Best Plays Theatre Yearbook.* NY: Dodd, Mead, 1971. Out of Print.

Purpose. To provide a comprehensive, cumulative index to the *Best Plays* Theater Yearbooks, 1894–1971.

Scope and content. 22,000 names of plays, playwrights, librettists, composers, lyricists, and sources are referenced to the appropriate *Best Plays* volume(s) and page(s).

Format. The alphabetical index is in two sections: (1) playwrights, composers, lyricists, and other authors of shows and sources; and (2) titles of shows and sources.

Guide to the Performing Arts. Metuchen, NJ: Scarecrow Press, published annually from 1960–1972 with a 1957–1967 compilation. Out of Print.

Purpose. To index the material in a "select" group of performing arts periodicals.

Scope and content. Persons, theatres, plays, operas, quartets, and musical groups in domestic and foreign periodicals are indexed.

Format. Entries are arranged by author, subject and title (when necessary). Book reviews are listed under the name of the reviewer, and cross references are provided.

Keller, Dean H. *Index to Plays in Periodicals.* Metuchen, NJ: Scarecrow Press, 1979. $52.50.

Purpose. To identify and provide access to plays published in periodicals.

Scope and content. This edition includes 9,562 play citations from 267 periodicals. Indexing begins with the first publication of individual periodicals and covers the entire run through 1976. Entries for plays include the full name, dates, title, number of acts, a brief one or two word description when known, full bibliographic citation to the periodical in which the play is published, and the language in which the play is published if other than English.

Format.   Arranged in two parts, the author index includes all entry information, while the title index refers the user to the entry in the author index.

Logasa, Hanna. *An Index to One-Act Plays*. Westwood, MA: Faxon, 1920–1964. 6 volumes. Out of Print.

Purpose.   To identify and provide access to a vast number of one-act plays published in books, periodicals and pamphlets from 1900 to 1966.

Scope and content.   The first volume contains over 5,000 titles of one-act plays written in English or translated into English, published from 1900–1924. The second volume (1924–1931) indexes over 7,000 plays from over 500 collections, as well as a large number of separate pamphlets. The third volume (1932–1940) includes 500 collections, and almost 8,000 titles. The fourth volume is an index to one-act plays for stage and radio (1941–1948), and includes 4,000 titles. The fifth volume (1948–1957) indexes one-act plays for stage, radio and television, and includes 2,000 titles, as well as a preponderance of plays for children on subjects such as holidays and great characters from history. The sixth volume (1956–1964) indexes 1,000 titles.

Format.   The title index contains the full entry for each title; author, subject and collection indexes refer the user to the title index.

*** Connor, John M. and Connor, Billie M.. *Ottemiller's Index to Plays in Collections: An Author and Title Index to Plays Appearing in Collections Published Between 1900 and Early 1975*. Metuchen, NJ: Scarecrow Press, 1976. This title is currently out of print, but as of this writing (11/87) a new edition is in preparation.

Purpose.   To provide an index to collections of plays published in England and the United States, from ancient to modern times.

Scope and content.   10,351 copies of 3686 different plays by 1937 different authors, in 1,237 collections are indexed. Entries include the full bibliographic citations for the play.

Format.   Arranged in three parts: (1) an author index comprises the main text, (2) a title index references the author entries, and (3) a list of collections analyzed and key to symbols index provide the full bibliographic citations to the referenced collections.

Manuals, Handbooks, Digests, Etc.

American Theatre Planning Board Staff. *Theatre Check List: A Guide to the Planning and Construction of Proscenium and Open Stage Theatres*. Middletown, CT: Wesleyan University Press, 1983. paperback $14.95.

Purpose.   To provide a list of important considerations for planning and designing open stage theatres.

Scope and content.   This technically detailed manual points out the possibilities and dangers inherent in each area of a theatre structure. Theatre designs representative of historical periods are described and illustrated, and some topics of modern day construction and arrangement include seats and seating patterns, lighting, dimmers and switchboards, overhead facilities, backstage space, orchestra floors, entrances and dressing rooms. A numbered list of practical considerations follows each subject heading. Pictures, drawings and diagrams appear on almost every page.

Format. A Table of Contents and a short index provide specific access to the text.

Anderson, Michael. *Crowell's Handbook of Contemporary Drama.* NY: Thomas Y. Crowell, 1971. Out of Print.

Purpose. To serve as a "guide to developments in drama in Europe and the Americas since the Second World War, or, in the case of Spain, since the Civil War."

Scope and content. Emphasis is entirely on written drama, and entries include general terms discussed in depth, biographical sketches of dramatists, playwrights (with bibliographies of their plays), actors, and theorists, as well as commentary on the social environment and response of the public and critics at the time that specific plays were published or produced.

Format. Alphabetical, no index.

Gassner, John. *Producing the Play, Together with the New Scene Technician's Handbook.* FL: Holt Rinehart, Winston, 1953. Out of Print.

Purpose. To provide a functional reference source of professional play production for the nonprofessional.

Scope and content. Section I provides an overview of the elements that enter into play production, with special emphasis on training the actor and the acting group. Section II deals with the actual production of the play; central emphasis is on direction, including the procedures in directing the script, the interpretation of the script and problem of style and form. Section III covers special aspects of production such as the use of music and dance, and directing social drama, comedy, Shakespearian plays, revivals, poetic drama, musical comedy and revue, and radio drama. Section IV comprises a technical handbook for the construction of scenery, making costumes, and the use of lighting and acoustical equipment.

Format. The text is complemented by a selective bibliography, extensive index and detailed Table of Contents.

Gassner, John and Dukor, Bernard F. *A Treasury of the Theatre.* 4th ed. NY: Simon and Schuster, 1970– . 3 volumes. (First three volumes are out of print, but new volumes are planned).

Purpose. To provide, in one set, a collection of plays that spans 2,500 years of world theatre from its beginnings in ancient Greece to the dawn of modern drama in nineteenth century Europe.

Scope and content. Volume I (World Drama from Aeschylus to Ostrovsky) contains the unabridged texts of 26 masterworks representing the major periods of theatre, and 41 plays from the range of western drama. Lengthy essays and biographical sketches of the playwrights are included, as a representative list of plays to 1875 (with very brief synopses). Volume II includes the text of 18 plays representing Scandinavian, German, French, Italian and Russian modern European drama from the earliest forms as exemplified in Ibsen and Strindberg, to the post-Second World War Existential movement, exemplified by Sartre. Again, the text of the plays is accompanied by an analysis of artistic significance, and a biography of the playwright. Volume III includes 27 English, Irish and American dramatic works from Wilde to Ionesco, with an additional selection of modern plays and drama from the 1890s to the middle of the present century.

Format. Each volume is divided by periods, localities, or type of world drama. Representative plays are arranged chronologically under each heading. All three volumes include two appendixes: a supplementary annotated list of as many as 68 to 200 plays, grouped by type and arranged alphabetically by author; and, a selected bibliography that lists from between 50 to 100 books groups by subject. There are no indexes.

* Hartnoll, Phyllis. *The Oxford Companion to the Theatre.* 4th ed. London: Oxford University Press, 1983. $49.95 (paperback).

Purpose. To provide a compilation of factual information on the history of legitimate theatre as it developed in English and throughout the world.

Scope and content. This encyclopedic work provides articles of varying length on famous historical and contemporary theatre personalities, companies, theatres, theatrical terms and theatre issues. Discussions of the development of drama in individual countries are listed under country names. Ethnic theatre is represented as well as such popular genres as music hall, vaudeville and musical comedy. British and American theatre is especially emphasized. Entries cover a time range from 400 B.C.E. to 1980. Theatrical technology, scenery, costume, lighting, architecture, and play production are mentioned in brief general histories. Ballet, other forms of dance, and opera, are not included.

Format. Entries are in an alphabetical arrangement. No index.

Heffner, Hubert C. (and others). *Modern Theatre Practice: A Handbook of Play Production.* 5th ed. NY: Appleton, 1973. Out of Print.

Purpose. To provide a standard, authoritative text for directors and workers in nonprofessional theatre.

Scope and content. Separate sections present and discuss directing, designing and building scenery, designing lighting equipment and the selection and use of equipment in creating design. A "General Summary of Theatre Arts" includes analyses of plays, illustrations from scenes of plays, construction diagrams, duties of a director, and directing principles and practices. Lighting plans and sound and music equipment are also covered.

Format. The text is followed by an appendix on costume and make-up, a glossary of approximately 300 terms grouped by type, and a 33 page annotated bibliography grouped by technical subject. A comprehensive, alphabetical index allows specific access.

Kienzle, Siegfried. *Modern World Theatre: A Guide to Productions in Europe and the United States since 1945*. Translated by Alexander and Elizabeth Henderson. NY: Ungar, 1970. Out of Print.

Purpose. Originally a German work (*Modernes Welt-Theater*), this resource is designed to give a cross-section of the theater from 1945–1970 by examining each work from the "viewpoint of its own aims" and evaluating its "success in achieving them."

Scope and content. 578 play entries include the following information: author and title, number of acts, type of writing, date of first edition, first performance, where performed, translator, time and place of play, and a lengthy annotation.

Format. Arranged alphabetically by author, and under each author, in alphabetical order by title. Index of play titles is included.

Lounsbury, Warren C. *Theatre Backstage from A to Z*. Seattle, WA: University of Washington Press, 1967 (reprinted in 1972). (paperback, spiral bound) $14.95.

Purpose. To provide an efficient reference source of theatre terms, methodologies, and materials.

Scope and content. Alphabetically arranged explanations of the terminology and methods peculiar to technical theatre, both professional and nonprofessional. Consideration is given to many economical methods and materials developed over the past 40 years as satisfactory substitutes for those of the professional theatre. Elementary material is included, as well as material for the experienced technician.

Format. In addition to a bibliography, an introduction traces the history of scenery and lighting practices in the United States.

Lovell, John. *Digests of Great American Plays: Complete Summaries of More than 100 plays from the Beginning to the Present*. NY: Crowell, 1961. Out of Print. [1972 updated edition is entitled *Great American Play Digest*, but is also Out of Print].

Purpose. (1) To provide synopses which capture "the story, flavor, mood, and dramatic essence of each play and its characters;" (2) to analyze the best components of each play, including "principle theme, plot and character, the probable goals of the author in writing it, the social and cultural characteristics of its period and milieu in which it was written;" and (3) "to provide a comprehensive sampling of a dramatic literature that has been unjustly neglected."

Scope and content. One hundred and two entries cover the time period 1766– 1959, and represent works by every major writer and many minor writers, significant theatrical trends, and every phase of American life treated in drama. Synopses include dates of writing or first performance, author's dates, identification of kind of play, theme and main characters, musical highlights, and notes on the play, its author, main performances, and prominent actors.

Format. The chronological arrangement is supplemented by a series of appendixes listing themes, periods, settings, actors, musical selections, and other aspects of the plays.

* *New York Times Theatre Reviews, 1920–1980.* NY: New York Times, 1981. 10 volumes. $975.00. OP, but can order some individual volumes from Random House.

Purpose. To provide, in one place, the text of play reviews from the *New York Times*.

Scope and content. Volume I, 1020–1926; Volume II, 1927–1929; Volume III, 1930–1934; Volume IV, 1935–1941; Volume V, 1942–1951; Volume VI, 1952–1959; Volume VII 1967–1970; Volume IX, Appendix of (1) theatre awards and prizes (with full text of the articles, as well as pictures of the award winners an dramatists); and (2) summaries of productions and runs by season.

Format. Volume X, Index by Personal names, titles and production companies.

Sobel, Bernard. *The New Theatre Handbook and Digest of Plays.* NY: Crown, 1959. Out of Print.

Purpose. To present both facts and "apocrypha" of the theatre for reference and pleasure reading.

Scope and content. In an alphabetical arrangement, essays, articles, and approximately 1000 play synopses are interwoven with the definitions of theatrical terms, descriptions of theatres and companies, and biographies of a host of personalities involved with the theatre. A special effort has been made to include entries on the Oriental Theatre. Television items are covered, but cinema and most radio plays are not. A special bibliography groups 403 outstanding theatre books (in English) by type, subject and country. The names and life dates of more than 1,000 famous theatre people are compiled in an alphabetical list.

Format. No index, but a table of contents provides general access to the text.

Vinson, James. *Contemporary Dramatists.* Chicago, IL: St. Martin's Press, 1982. $65.00. [The fourth edition, by Kirkpatrick, Daniel, and Vinson, James,

is in process. It is entitled *Contemporary Novelists*, and is to be published in
March, 1988, by St. James Press. Projected price is $75.00].

Purpose. To provide comprehensive bibliographic information on living
playwrights and their works.

Scope and content. More than 300 important living playwrights in the
English language are included in this biographical source. Entries include a
biography, a full bibliography, details of other published bibliographies, and the
locations of manuscript collections. Also included are listings of critical studies
the playwrights themselves consider important as well as comments by many of
the playwrights on their own work; followed by a signed essay by one of the 100
English, American or Commonwealth critics. First production in both the United
States and Great Britain, as well as subsequent productions in London and New
York (if different), are included. Excluded are reprints and revivals.

Format. The alphabetical format is supplemented by a title index, and three
appendixes which document forms of drama on the media, and which discuss
live theatre, and groups and happenings.

Periodicals

All prices are for institutions.

+ *American Theatre.* Theatre Communications Group. 1984– . Monthly.
$27.00.

Distinguished contributors provide comprehensive coverage of American theatre as well as significant theatrical events and trends in other parts of the world.
All aspects of theatre are examined, including acting, directing, design, playwriting, and management. *American Theatre* also deals with developments in
related arts fields and legislative and economic issues affecting theatre. Five
times a year, full-length plays are printed in a removable center section.

Regular features include: "Letters to the Editor," "Editorial," "Stages"
(short reports with photographs on productions of interest), "Trends,"
"Events," "People," "Awards," and "Plays and Playwrights." A monthly
directory, arranged geographically, lists performance schedules for approximately 200 theatres.

Drama: The Quarterly Theatre Review. British Theatre Association. 1919– .
Quarterly. $21.00.

Each quarterly issue features 5–10 articles on aspects of British and European
theater, interviews with actors, actresses, and producers, and drama awards.
Each issue also contains a "Plays in Performance" section which reviews
currently running plays in England, Scotland, New York, Los Angeles, and
Berlin, as well as reviews of opera, and plays on TV and radio. "Books"

contains 4–7 book reviews, and "An Actor's Diary" chronicles memorable incidents in the life of one actor per issue.

Drama Review. New York University Tisch School of the Arts. 1955– . Quarterly. $47.00.

Each issue of this quarterly explores a selected (usually avant-garde) theme through scholarly, detailed articles contributed by performance artists. Such varied topics as the West German Theatre, Women and Performance, the Jewish Theatre, and dance have been developed through personal interviews with actors/actresses, dancers, choreographers and playwrights. Descriptions of their works, ideas and specific performances, plus act by act presentations of plays are given. Sets, movement, illustrative musical scores and photographs are frequently included. An "Historical Section" offers essays and analysis on early theatre and drama personalities and their works, as well as theatres and dramatic theory.

The above mentioned articles often number from 9 to 13 per issue. In addition, a critically annotated "New Books" section (number varies) and a "Books Received" list are standard with each publication. Both are arranged alphabetically by title. The December issue has an index for the preceding year.

The Journal of Arts Management and Law. Helen Dwight Reid Educational Foundation. 1969– . Quarterly. $55.00.

With an emphasis on the business aspects of theater management, each issue includes articles by lawyers, accountants, law professors and educators in other fields, arts managers, theatre theoreticians and other professionals involved in the business of theater.

Regular features include "Commentary" (editorial comments on the content of the issue) and "Book Reviews" (in most issues). Articles vary in length, but writer's guidelines call for legal analyses up to 25 pages, with commentaries generally not to exceed 1,500 words. An annual index is published in the winter issue.

Modern Drama. University of Toronto, 1958– . Quarterly. $37.50.

The lengthy essays in this scholarly journal describe and analyze aspects of modern drama, with special attention given to drama as literature. Single topics, such as the interaction of a play with its audience and the theatre within the theatre, may be explored from differing perspectives by several articles in the same issue; and discussions of playwrights and plays, interviews with noted dramatists and performers, and state of the art reviews, are often included. Extensive reviews of plays and books are included in every issue, and an annual bibliography in the June issue includes materials (excluding reviews, reprints, and unpublished thesis) on dramatic literature and theatre history. Additionally, each year, one special issue is devoted to a single topic.

+ *New York Theatre Critic's Reviews*. Critic's Theatre Reviews. 1940– . Weekly. $90.00

This source provides weekly reproductions of theatre reviews from the *New York Times, New York Daily News, Wall Street Journal, Christian Science Monitor, Women's Wear Daily, New York Post, Time, Newsweek*, and ABC, NBC, and CBS television. An annual index includes access by cast, authors, producers, directors, set designers, lighting crew, composers and lyricists, choreographers, costume designers, and premier performances.

+ *Shakespeare Quarterly*. Folger Shakespeare Library. 1950– . 5/year. $40.00.

This publication is devoted solely to the study of William Shakespeare. Lengthy bibliographic essays explore the legendary author and playwright, his plays, casting patterns, the issues surrounding his plays and the historical background they reflect. In addition to the three or more well developed essays, each issue is divided into sections comprising "Shakespeare on Stage," which offers critical reviews of recently performed Shakespearean plays; "Book Review," which includes 8 to 15 critical, several page reviews of current books written on Shakespeare and his works; and "Notes," which describes present collections of Shakespeare documents. Annually, the International Committee of Correspondents provides an annotated bibliography of important books, articles, reviews of books, dissertations, dissertation abstracts, theatrical productions, reviews of productions and significant reprints of works related to Shakespeare. This compilation is organized into two divisions: (1) the "General Shakespearean" section groups publications that treat broad aspects of Shakespeare study into 10 categories, and (2) a section which includes criticism and productions. Four indexes allow specific entry to this extensive bibliography.

Theatre Crafts. Rodak Press, Inc. 1967– . 10/year. $24.00.

Well illustrated, with numerous color photographs, charts and drawings (approximately 8 per issue), the articles in this journal describe the present works of successful contemporaries. Such topics as the costumes and sets of recent productions, the roles of backstage workers, and computer-assisted lighting and sound are explored, as are staging for film and videos, and traditional theatre.

Theme designs characterize a year's publications. Throughout 1987, for example, each issue examined aspects of the theatre buildings of the 1960s and what users have done to adapt them to present needs. Resource sections provide buyers' guides, directories to product literature and listings of equipment rental houses. Changes of address, obituaries and the promotions of significant professionals are posted in "Industry News." A "Calendar" outlines the dates of conventions and meetings, trade shows and job openings. "Updates" announces new companies, what they sell, addresses and phone numbers. And "Call Board" advertises available jobs and items for sale.

Theatre Journal. University and College Theatre Association. 1949– . Quarterly. $37.00.

Scholarly essays, most often written by distinguished professors of English, develop the theme of each issue of this professional quarterly journal. Topics covered in the past have ranged widely to include explorations of dramatic terror, madness and narcissism, as well as racial, ethnic and feminist theatre. Analyses are given of how textual history and narrative concerns and desires influence the composition, performance, and study of drama. Individual entries may describe single plays in depth, or several related plays. Often they present histories, biographies or discuss theories and practices. The articles are frequently illustrated. A Theatre Review section offers numerous (15 to 20) lengthy and critical reviews of recent international productions. Each entry includes a producer and cast list, synopsis, critique, the name of the theatre in which it was performed and the date of the first performance. A Book Review section is similarly comprehensive, beginning with a major essay that may review several related books in depth, followed by 15 or more lengthy critiques which are sometimes illustrated. Preference is given to recent publications on history, criticism and new books or performance, theory and practice but all aspects of theatre and related arts are covered. A list of new titles is published twice a year. The Books Received section lists new books organized by general subject and then alphabetically arranged by author. Categories include acting, directing, autobiography, criticism, history, anthology, music, plays and dance. A "Comment" section by the editor provides an introduction to each journal theme, and hardbound volumes contain a comprehensive index to each year's issues.

Theatre Notebook: A Journal of the History and Technique of the British Theatre. Society for Theatre Research, 1945– . 3/year. $18.75.

Each issue of this publication presents six to eight scholarly essays that discuss aspects of the British Theatre from the 17th to the early 20th Century. Events, festivals, letters, early plays, theatres and theatre guilds are described and frequently illustrated. Actors' roles are annotated in detail and early cast lists are given. Articles conclude with bibliographies. In each issue, a "Notes and Queries" section provides subscribers with selected current communications from the society, and "Book Reviews" offers a few lengthy and critical evaluations of recent books of historical interest.

Theatre Research International. The Oxford University Press and the International Federation for Theatre Research. 1975– . 3/year. $50.00

Each issue features several (generally 4) comprehensive, scholarly, and excellently illustrated essays that focus on historically important plays, spectacles, playwrights, troupes, and staging. Different types and periods of dramatic presentations are also covered. Past articles have varied in length from 12 to 18 pages, and have covered such international topics as Greek shadow puppet theatre, India's Bhavai religious drama, early promptbooks, Shakespeare in America and a travelogue of a British actor's experiences touring the United States, Canada and Australia in 1856. Lengthy bibliographies follow each article. Annually, one issue focuses on Third World theatre, and three sections are regularly included in each publication: "Reviews" offers 18 to 22 in-depth synopses and critiques of recently published books on critical histories of countries, plays, theatres, actor training and audience response; French summaries of each issue's feature articles are contained in the "Resumes des Articles"; and bibliographic data for books received but not reviewed are listed in "Books Received."

Theatre Survey: The American Journal of Theatre History. The American Society for Theatre Research, 1960– . Semi-annual. $10.00.

The majority of essays presented in this journal focus on significant aspects of American theatre history (occasionally international topics are included). Excluded are dramatic criticism and literary history in relation to the theater. Past articles have explored such subjects as the "American Indians in European Pageants (1493–1700)," the "Social Life of the Performer on the Yorkshire Circuit (1766–1785)," "British Military Theatre in New York (1780–1781)," and "Louisville Burlesque (1908–1909)." Articles include bibliographies. A "Notes and Documents" section in each issue lists reader responses to past reviews and notes dates determined for previously undated plays, and a "Book Reviews" section offers synopses and critical essays on a small number of selected books.

REFERENCES

Nemchek, R. L. (1981). Problems of cataloging and classification in theatre librarianship. *Library Resources and Technical Services*, 25, 374–385.

THE LIBRARY BUILDINGS AWARD PROGRAM OF THE AMERICAN INSTITUTE OF ARCHITECTS AND THE AMERICAN LIBRARY ASSOCIATION

Roscoe Rouse, Jr.

Initially given various titles by various entities, the Library Buildings Award Program in the United States originated under the cosponsorship of three organizations: The National Book Committee, the American Institute of Architects and the American Library Association. Today its stated purpose is advertised as follows: "To encourage excellence in the architectural design and planning of libraries." This is virtually the same statement of purpose that was issued at the beginning of the program.

Advances in Library Administration and Organization,
Volume 8, pages 241-252.
Copyright © 1989 by JAI Press Inc.
All rights of reproduction in any form reserved.
ISBN: 0-89232-967-X

THE BIRTH OF AN IDEA

The first recorded discussion expressing interest in such a program was made in 1962. It was initiated by Emerson Greenaway, Director of the Free Library of Philadelphia, and at the time Chairman of the National Book Committee. He was a past president of the American Library Association. The minutes of the Board of Directors of the American Institute of Architects for January, 1962,[1] indicate that Mr. Greenaway, speaking as Chairman of the National Book Committee, and supported by Dr. Ralph Blasingame, Director of the State Library of Pennsylvania, had made an inquiry of AIA regarding the establishment of a library buildings award similar to the other awards given by AIA. The response made by the Board to Mr. Greenaway's inquiry was a favorable one.

The Executive Board and the Council of the ALA met in June of 1962 at Miami Beach at the annual Association conference and heard Alphonse L. Trezza, Executive Secretary of the Library Administration Division of ALA, recommend the cooperation of the Association in the program with the National Book Committee, the body which proposed the action, and the American Institute of Architects.[2] Mr. Trezza told the librarians that the LAD Executive Board had acted favorably on the matter and said the program "was almost certain to be instituted" in any case. He recommended that approval be given for participation and that the Awards Committee be asked to support the program. That support was subsequently provided.

The program was described to ALA Council members at their meeting in June, 1962 as including requisites such as the following: "Entries shall be buildings designed by registered architects practicing professionally in the United States; the buildings, erected anywhere in the United States, or abroad, must have been completed after January 1, 1958 and shall be school libraries, college and university and public libraries. Awards are to be made in the three categories on a regional basis with judging to be on the basis of a solution of the problem presented the architect and its worthiness for an award for excellence in library planning and architecture."[3] Though not specifically stated in official records, the program was obviously planned to be an annual affair.

The highest award would be titled First Honor Award for Distinguished Accomplishment in Architecture which might be made to one or more buildings with certificates presented to the architects and to the building owner. A stainless steel plaque suitable for placement on a wall in the building would also be prepared. In addition, as many Awards of Merit in Architecture as deemed deserving were to be issued, each consisting of certificates for the architects and the owners.

Members of the ALA Council were told that the jurors would be selected by the Board of Directors of the American Institute of Architects and the jury would name its own chairman. Representatives from each of the three sponsors would make up the jury with the number from each organization to be worked out by AIA and ALA at a later time.

There had been no consideration given at early ALA Executive Board meetings to the funding of the program but this matter was put on the agenda for the November, 1962 meeting.[4] A plan was described whereby it was expected the costs of the program would be covered by the payment of a stated fee paid by each architect submitting a plan for consideration. Members were told that both the AIA and the National Book Committee were prepared to support the award program, if necessary, by each assuming responsibility for one-third of any deficit that might be incurred. The ALA would, therefore, be expected to be responsible for one-third of any deficit occurring. Members were told that the experience of the AIA in their other award programs as regards the coverage of costs, had in the past been quite acceptable; when there had been deficits they were small ones. A motion was made and passed which stated that the Board recognized and accepted "the possibility that there might be an ALA expense" involved in the organization's participation in the buildings award program.

The Library Administration Division of ALA, the unit which had come to the ALA Executive Board with the request initially through Mr. Trezza, asked for the right to establish a contingency fund for the coming year so that any costs to which the program might obligate the Association would be covered in the budget. This was preferred, the proponents said, to the creation of an earmarked fund in the first year of experience.

Discussion was held in the same meeting as to the means of selecting jurors and it was learned that the AIA was asking that there by three representatives from that organization and one each from ALA and NBC.

1962: THE REAL BEGINNING

The first library buildings award competition was announced in November, 1962 by the American Institute of Architects. Applications were to be received in the AIA headquarters in Washington by December 17, 1962 along with a registration fee of $15. The brochure announcing the program detailed the terms of the competition in a brief summation which explained the basis for judging the new structures: "Entries will not be judged in competition with other entries, but on the basis of the solution of the problem presented to the architect and its worthiness for an award for excellence in library architecture and planning."

The first competition set out to select "one or more First Honor Awards for Distinguished Accomplishments in Architecture, and Awards of Merit in Architecture for as many exhibits as the jury deems deserving." The winners would be announced during National Library Week, April 21–27, 1963, the flyer continued. There was no statement in the rules one way or the other regarding renovations, additions or remodeled buildings.

The announcement described the jury as a body of architects and librarians distributed as follows: three architects plus one representative each of ALA and the NBC. "To insure adequate library representation, three librarians shall be named to represent each class of libraries, each one of whom shall serve only when his classification or category is being judged."

The jury of three architects and four librarians met at the AIA headquarters, the Octagon in Washington, in mid-February and selected four library buildings for First Honor Awards and thirteen buildings for Awards of Merit from a list of 207 entries. All winners were in the public library and academic library categories.

1964: THE SECOND ANNUAL EFFORT

The second award program took place the following year, 1964. The jury again consisted of seven people, three of whom represented the American Institute of Architects (although one of them was not named a professional architect but apparently was associated with the organization) and four librarians.

Sixteen exhibits were given awards, all three categories of public, academic and school libraries receiving a share of the prizes. Three First Honor Awards were given and eleven Awards of Merit given. While the rules had not specifically disallowed additions to older buildings, it did not include them, either. The 1964 program honored four library additions, all Awards of Merit.

CHANGES, QUESTIONS, PROGRESS

The frequency of the program most likely worked a hardship on the headquarters staff of both the AIA and the ALA. After the first two annual programs in 1963 and 1964, the third one was held in 1966. Thereafter it was designated a biennial program. It evenutally evolved, as well, that ALA became responsible for all deficit costs of the program.

The competition continued into the mid-seventies with the AIA and the ALA carrying the bulk of the workload, insofar as personnel, publicity and other activities were concerned. After 1974 there is no further mention of the National Book Committee as a cosponsor of the project.

A major change in the program took place in 1976, one which brought for all concerned a new look at the rules and regulations governing the award program. The Buildings and Equipment Section of the Library Administration Division within ALA established a Library Building Award's Committee, obviously a response to the overloading of staff with award duties or, perhaps, a reaction to membership's recognition for the need of membership involvement in the operation of the program.

The ALA Awards Committee, which had some responsibility for the issuing of the awards but not for running the program itself, is not by nature made up of specialists who are equipped to manage such a program. This being recognized, the new committee came into being and named to it were practicing library building consultants from the ranks of the Buildings and Equipment Section of the Association. From that time forward for a period of years, such questions and concerns were raised about the then-current rules and the practices prevalent that there seemed a need for some serious talk between representatives of the two remaining sponsoring organizations.

The first chairman of the committee asked the members these questions: "Should there be separate categories for different types of libraries? Sizes of libraries? Should building additions and remodeling projects be separated from new structures in the judging? Should the jury be restructured in any way, at least so far as representation from the library profession is concerned? How can we determine what impact, if any, the Building Awards Program is having on the design of contemporary library facilities?"[5] Other concerns expressed when the meeting convened included the need to evaluate building plans on both function and form. One proposal called for a Form A for judging on form or design and Form B for judging on function. At this point in time, the architects had stipulated that the majority of the jurors be practicing professional architects. The librarians responded to that requirement with the request that the ALA should insist on a minimum requirement of one ALA representative from the type of library being judged, e.g., a public librarian must vote on a public library in order for that library to receive an award.

FUNDING—AND OTHER DIFFERENCES

One point of contention between librarians and architects in the mid-seventies was the payment of costs. The fee had gone from the original $15 to $25 and the architects were proposing a $40 fee for the 1978 program.

The Executive Vice President of the AIA wrote to the Executive Secretary of the Library Administration Division in September, 1976 and closed with the following paragraph: "I must emphasize that for future programs, we must have your guarantee that ALA will be responsible for all costs of the program, including the 20 percent administrative fee. If you take issue with the above, it will be necessary for our Board of Directors to re-evaluate the program. I indeed hope that you will not take issue with this proposal because we would like to continue the program which is mutually beneficial to both organizations."[6]

At its first meeting, the ALA Library Building Awards Committee developed a paper of 12 issues that had a need for resolution between AIA and ALA as regards the program as it was then described. One point was a statement to the effect that "Neither ALA, nor any division therein, should be required to underwrite any portion of the cost of the Library Buildings Award Program." Another was the desire for separate evaluation scales for design and function. (A comment from the LAD president on this issue at a later time read as follows: "The program was originally designed to recognize exemplary library buildings which function well—not just for excellence in architectural design. This goal seems to have been lost and awards are now based almost solely on architectural design.")[7]

In the document prepared by the ALA Awards Committee the ALA was called upon to do a great deal more than was currently undertaken in promoting and advertising the program.

The thought was expressed that time was of the essence and unless action was taken immediately to sit down with AIA representatives to iron out the differences between the two groups, the AIA program would move forward on its usual time schedule and brochures would be in press very soon. The recommendation was made by the librarians that, unless a resolution to differences was made soon, the 1978 program should be postponed. The thought was expressed that the ALA LAD Buildings and Equipment Section could, if necessary, establish its own library buildings award program, but that would not be preferred over the joint endeavor.

Because matters were growing worse instead of better between representatives of the two organizations, a conference was set up for the two contingents in a meeting room at an airport hotel in Kansas City in October of 1978. Among the points discussed on which there was agreement were the following: (1) Both organizations would have the opportunity to present new or revised guidelines for the program; (2) A single classification of awards be utilized rather than the two classifications then in use; (3) The chair of the jury be rotated between the two organizations; (4) The categories no longer be for type of library but rather become a. new, b. additions, c. renovations, d. adaptive reuse.[8] It is worthy of note that, despite the expressions of concern from the librarians about the majority of favorable votes going to non-functional buildings, there was no point of agreement in this area.

A second meeting of the two groups was held at the AIA headquarters in January, 1979. The atmosphere was again cordial but business-like. Both entities held to specific needs which they insisted be a part of the program, or be removed from program requirements, or subjected to changed. Again, proposals were made from both sides, there was considerable give and take, and eventually a semblance of agreement took shape.

The meetings were, apparently, the exorcism needed to clear the air and bring two unharmonious segments back into euphony. While there was no question that neither side was fully satisfied with the results and the revisions agreed upon, a new set of rules came into being and the program did not falter because of the controversy.

It seems, however, that all was not well for all time. Although the 1980 award program came off without extreme disagreement between librarians and architects, that year's effort brought near disaster to the future of the ongoing program. The 1980 program resulted in a sizeable budget deficit for ALA which troubled the Executive Board of the Library Administration and Management Association to such a degree that an August, 1981 letter was sent to the architects' headquarters calling for an immediate halt to all activity on plans for the 1982 judging.[9] The explanation given was the unwillingness of the LAMA Board to give approval for the program without "guaranteed assurance" that it would not incur a deficit.

DECISIONS MADE, DISTINCTION EARNED

The president of LAMA looked for a solution to the problem with assistance from members of the Library Building Awards Committee. The result was a vastly reduced budget which included the removal of the judging from AIA headquarters in Washington and conjoining that event with the ALA midwinter meetings scheduled in January. The plan was instituted and although there was no judging held in 1982 as planned, there was a contest held in 1983 in conjunction with the ALA meeting in San Antonio, Texas.

Another major turn-about in future plans was the agreement that ALA would in the future handle all phases of the awards program as AIA had done in the past. A broader publicity campaign for the prize contest was announced and programs instituted at each annual conference of ALA at which slide shows of the winning buildings are presented and the awards made to the architects and the building owners. Following the program a wine and cheese reception is held, usually at a distinctive address in the city of the conference. Funding for this event has been successfully sought from interested furniture and/or equipment vendors.

To reach the level of improved relationships that was attained by the early 1980s, it had been necessary to hold some very forthright conversations which, fortunately, resulted in the resolving of some extremely variant differences between architects and librarians working in the programs. There were successful biennial award programs in both 1985 and 1987 and the future of the venture took on a brighter prospect.

POINTS OF VIEW

With all that, one still could not pronounce the program free of contraventions. Despite the fact that all seems to be on a even keel, there are those who would like to see drastic changes made in the operation of the program and in the rules by which it functions. At least one well known library building planner would not serve on the awards jury because he did not think the method of judging the plans was adequate. In his letter responding to the invitation sent to him, he said, "It is impossible to judge the quality of a building either esthetically or functionally on the basis of photographs and floorplans (which are not called for from applicants). For instance, you cannot tell a thing about the lighting or the interior feeling of the building proper, two critical factors in a building's success. For this reason these awards have passed over two of the finest libraries in the country, and have given awards to some real duds. I regret that I cannot accept your invitation for these reasons."[10]

In an attempt to determine whether librarians and architects who have been much involved in the awards program over the years think its original purpose has been served, the writer made telephone calls to some of them as part of the research for this paper. Permission was given by two of them to quote from their remarks.

1.   Frazer G. Poole, retired from the Library of Congress where he served as Preservations Officer and Director of Library Building Planning, is a library space and planning consultant, having experience with many planning assignments in the United States and abroad. He served on the AIA/ALA jury five times and was a member of the ALA Library Building Awards Committee for a number of years. When asked if he felt that the awards program was serving the purpose set down as its goal, i.e., "to encourage excellence in the architectural design and planning of libraries," Mr. Poole responded that he regretted having to be negative in his reply but he had no alternative, if he were to be honest. He spoke of the effort as "a nice program" but he had serious doubts that it had led to any improvement in the design and planning of library buildings. There has been little change in the approach to jurying the entries and he observed a great need for change. "There has always been much disagreement between librarians who call for a workable floor plan, a functional design, and the architects who stress only the form, the design of the building." He said architects are not interested in function but rather insist on the creative, the innovative, a building which will "make headlines." Mr. Poole claims that "something has to happen to make architects more aware of the need for a practical building plan designed to make the building function properly as a library." He spoke of experiences wherein units of the library which operate closely and need to be placed in a contigious relationship were so widely separated that it interfered very much with daily routines all libraries follow; this even after his insistence prior to the finalizing of the plan that such a relationship was necessary. He spoke of such instances in his experiences on many occasions in far flung places around the world. One architect with whom Mr. Poole works on occasion in the United States has designed a dozen library buildings. Mr. Poole said he still "has to force him to consider the important relationship between the circulation services

and the technical processes routines as he plans building after building without a thought for that need."[11]

2.   Lee Harris Pomeroy, FAIA, of Pomeroy, Lebduska Associates, New York City, winner of a building award in the contest in 1980 and chairman of the jury in 1983, told the writer in a telephone conversation in July that he considers the AIA/ALA Library Buildings Award Program "very valuable." He says it provides an opportunity for dialogue between two professionals, the ˙˙˙ʰitect and the user of the building. There is a chance for two separate points o. .iew to be expressed and for a better solution to result. In Mr. Pomeroy's opinion, an architect cannot successfully plan a library building without this kind of dialogue. It is unusual, he said, for a buildings jury to be comprised of two such differing backgrounds and it can work only for a better building plan. He pointed out the fact that awards in the program are not given to plans which compete against one another but to plans which best solve a problem.

When asked whether he thought librarians might on occasion be overbearing in their insistence upon a practical and logical floor plan with little or no concern with aesthetics, he said there is a need for both points of view to play a part in the planning of a library. It would be his wish that the librarian express the needs of the plans in his terms, not in architectural terms, so there would be little misunderstandng between the two. Mr. Pomeroy described the awards program as meeting the goals established for it and said it is, in his opinion, "highly successful." He claims to have seen improvement in the planning of library buildings during the time the program has been functioning.[12]

THE FUTURE OF THE PROGRAM

A quarter of a century provides a track record of sorts by which both librarians and architects should be able to make a judgment as to the success or the failure of the only known national library buildings award program in the world. We have heard from one very knowledgeable librarian/library building planner who does not think it has met its intended purpose, another who disagrees with the procedures used by the jury, and an architect who has worked in the program for a number of years maintaining that it is, indeed, serving to work toward the improvement of library planning. It may be that each of us has his/her own opinion of the program and that there might never be a consensus among us all. the fact remains, however, that the program continues and is, without question, a viable one that attracts attention from every quarter. It is utilized by large numbers of librarians and library board members who are writing building programs, by architects who are drawing plans for libraries, and by vendors who

Colby-Sawyer College Library—Cut-Away View.

Exterior View, Colby-Sawyer College Library New London, N. H.

Interior View

supply furniture, equipment and materials for them. The program continues to attract many entries to the competition each year.

At the very least, one can surmise that the program has raised the awareness of those who write programs for and plan new library buildings, as well as renovations and additions, to the importance of careful preliminary planning, program writing, and the observation of the experience of others. It has thrust to the fore a multitude of at least reasonably good examples of library architecture (even assuming that a few ''real duds,'' in the opinion of some, may slip through to win awards) and a large number of excellent buildings.

Competition in any kind of endeavor likely results in a greater consciousness of the need to surpass; collectively, members of the two professions most interested in achieving true success in the creation of a library building have unquestionably learned much from the awards program. In the opinion of the writer, both the American Library Association and the American Institute of Architects should expect more and better success stories to derive from future award programs.

ACKNOWLEDGMENT

This paper is reprinted by permission of the editor of the eighth International Federation of Library Association Proceedings, published by K. G. Saur.

Thanks also to Robert Burley, FAIA, The Burley Partnership of Waitsfield, Vermont for supplying the photographs and drawing of the Colby-Sawyer College Library in New London, New Hampshire.

NOTES

1.   American Institute of Architects. Board of Director's Minutes, January, 1962. (From the files of the Archives of the American Institute of Architects).

2.   American Library Association, Council Minutes, June 18–22, 1962, p. 9. and ALA, Executive Board Minutes, June 17–21, 1962, p. 12.

3.   American Library Association, Council Minutes, June 18–22, 1962, p. 9.

4.   American Library Association, Executive Board Minutes, November 9–11, 1962, p. 2.

5.   Letter, Raymond M. Holt to David R. Smith, May 18, 1976.

6.   Letter, William L. Slayton to Donald P. Hammer, September 9, 1976.

7.   Letter, Richard L. Waters to Robert M. Lawrence, June 20, 1978.

8.   ''Summary, Joint Meeting of the American Institute of Architects and The American Library Association/Library Administration and Mangement Association, October 20, 1978, Kansas City, Missouri.''

9.   Letter, Gloria Novak to the American Institute of Architects, attn. Maris F. Murray, August 2, 1981.

10.   Letter, Ellsworth Mason to Donald P. Hammer, November 11, 1977.

11.   Telephone conversation, the author to Frazer G. Poole, July 24, 1987.

12.   Telephone conversation, the author to Lee Harris Pomeroy, July 24, 1987.

BIBLIOGRAPHY OF SUB-SAHARA AFRICAN LIBRARIANSHIP, 1986–1987

Compiled by Glenn L. Sitzman

PREFACE

The present bibliography supplements the one in the compiler's *African Libraries* (Scarecrow Press, 1988). This supplement has been compiled, in the main, from *Library and Information Science Abstracts* (*LISA*) and *Library Literature* for the years 1986 and 1987, following the procedure used in the base bibliography. The dates 1986–1987 in the title are a bit misleading in that many of the titles were published earlier. For one thing, some journals, or some issues, do not come to the attention of indexing and abstracting services until several years after publication. Some journals, or issues, are never indexed. It is the latter category that should be of major concern to bibliographers and scholars.

Advances in Library Administration and Organization,
Volume 8, pages 253-292.
Copyright © 1989 by JAI Press Inc.
All rights of reproduction in any form reserved.
ISBN: 0-89232-967-X

With this supplement coverage has been extended to *Information Science Abstracts*, the service having been searched from its beginning in 1966 as *Documentation Abstracts* through 1987. Moreover, retrospective compilation continues, as older works that have been overlooked or were unavailable earlier come to the attention of the compiler. The importance of this practice is demonstrated by a chapter in a work which was published in 1981 but which the compiler was able to examine only recently. The chapter has a bibliography of 98 titles appended. Sixty-two of those titles had not been in the indexes and thus were unavailable to researchers generally. The inclusion of such unindexed material in the supplements provides accessibility. Absolute completeness of the bibliography is probably impossible, but widespread cooperation from scholars will increase accessibility of more obscure publications.

The base bibliography published in *African Libraries* contains approximately 2,700 titles. Roughly, one-third of those titles have a broader than national focus, one-third focus on Nigeria, and one-third focus individually on the remaining sovereign countries and some territories of the Sub-Sahara. The same proportions held for the years 1984–1985. The present supplement adds about 600 titles to the bibliography: 35 percent have a non-national focus, 23 percent focus on Nigeria, and 42 percent focus on particular countries or territory. Whereas in the base bibliography at least one title was retrieved for each of 43 sovereign countries, plus Namibia, Reunion (island), and the former Western Sahara, coverage in this supplement includes 40 sovereign countries, plus Namibia.

Numbers of titles related to a country are not necessarily conclusive; but, taken with other known factors, publications seem to indicate that library activity for the period covered, aside from Nigeria, was greatest in Botswana (17 titles), Kenya (21), Tanzania (27), Zambia (30), and Zimbabwe (31). Normally, library and library science publications in Ghana and Uganda have been among the highest. Titles retrieved for this period were down to ten for Ghana and seven for Uganda, perhaps a result of the dire economic conditions in both countries. Of the 139 titles for Nigeria, 14 deal with documentation and information services, 12 with library education, 26 with academic libraries, 9 with public libraries, 9 with school libraries, and 23 with special libraries.

The compiler acknowledges with sincere thanks the assistance of Busisiwe I. Dlamini, a graduate student from Southern Africa at Clarion University of Pennsylvania, who has checked uncertain titles in sources not readily available to the compiler. He is also deeply appreciative of permission to use the library facilities of the University of Puerto Rico (both at Mayagüez and Río Piedras) and of the Inter-American University at San Germán, PR.

Some incomplete citations, taken from bibliographies or footnotes in various publications, are included in the supplement as found, the compiler being unable to complete them. It is to be hoped that they can be given in complete form in a future supplement or cumulation. Completions, additions, or corrections to the bibliography will be appreciated by the compiler. They may be sent to The Sitzman Bibliographical Project, c/o Carlson Library, Clarion University of Pennsylvania, Clarion, PA 16214.

GUIDE TO ORGANIZATION OF BIBLIOGRAPHY

Africa in General

—— General and Peripheral
—— French-speaking Africa
—— Academic Libraries
—— Bibliographies and Bibliography
—— Biographies of Librarians
—— Book Trade, Printing and Publishing
—— Cataloging and Classification
—— Documentation and Information Science
—— Library Education and Training
—— Public Libraries
—— Special Libraries

Africana

—— General
—— Africana Collections outside the Sub-Sahara
—— Africana for Children

Inter-Regional and Regional

—— Inter-regional
—— Central Africa
—— Eastern Africa
   —— General
   —— Documentation and Information Science
   —— Library Education
—— Southern Africa
—— West Africa
   —— General
   —— Academic Libraries
   —— Library Education

International Meetings

1976, Brazzaville, Congo, Meeting of Experts on Planning Documentation and
       Library Networks in Africa
       Tangier, Morocco, Preparatory Workshop on African Government Docu-
       ments

1979, Helsinki, Finland, Afro-Scandinavian Library Conference

1980, Arusha, Tanzania, Unesco Regional Meeting of Computer Centre Direc-
       tors

1983, Dar es Salaam, Tanzania, African Standing Conference on Bibliographic
       Control (ASCOBIC)
       Nairobi, Kenya, International Conference on Education and Training for
       Agricultural Library and Information Work

1984, Arusha, Tanzania, DSE/ESAMI Workshop on Management of Informa-
       tion Services Harare, Zimbabwe, Standing Conference of Eastern,
       Central and Southern African Librarians (SCECSAL)
       Nairobi, Kenya, General Conference of the International Federation of
       Library Associations and Institutions (IFLA)

1985, Harare, Zimbabwe, Meeting of Information Experts

1986, Gabarone, Botswana, Standing Conference of Eastern, Central and
       Southern African Librarians (SCECSAL)
       Nairobi, Kenya, African Standing Conference on Bibliographic Control

Individual Countries

Angola
Benin
Botswana
Burkina Faso
Cameroon
Cape Verde
Central African Republic
Chad
Congo (People's Republic)
Djibouti
Equatorial Guinea

Ethiopia
Gabon
Gambia
Ghana
—— General
—— Library Education
—— Special Libraries
Guinea
Guinea-Bissau
Ivory Coast
Kenya
—— General
—— Academic Libraries
—— School and Children's Library Services
—— Special Libraries
Lesotho
Liberia
Madagascar
Malawi
Mali
Mauritania
Mauritius
Mozambique
Namibia
Niger
Nigeria
—— General
—— Acquisitions
—— Bibliographies and Bibliography
—— Book Trade, Printing and Publishing
—— Cataloging and Classification
—— Cooperation
—— Documentation and Information Services
—— Librarians and Librarianship
—— Libraries and Education
—— Library Education
—— Ahmadu Bello University
—— Imo State University
—— University of Maiduguri
—— Professional Associations
—— Academic Libraries
—— Ahmadu Bello University

―― University of Calabar
―― University of Ibadan
―― University of Ilorin
―― University of Lagos
―― University of Maiduguri
―― University of Port Harcourt
―― Children's Library Service
―― National Library of Nigeria
―― Public Libraries
  ―― Former Eastern Region
  ―― Anambra State
  ―― Bendel State
  ―― Kaduna State
―― School Libraries
―― Secondary School and College Libraries
―― Special Libraries, Materials, and Services
  ―― Agriculture
  ―― Handicapped
  ―― Medicine and Health Services
  ―― Social Sciences
Rwanda
Senegal
  ―― Library Education
Seychelles
Sierra Leone
  ―― Public Libraries
Somalia
Sudan
Swaziland
Tanzania
  ―― Public Libraries
  ―― School and Children's Library Services
  ―― Special Libraries
Togo
Uganda
  ―― Academic Libraries
Zaire
Zambia
  ―― Academic Libraries
  ―― Public Libraries
  ―― School Libraries
  ―― Special Libraries

Zimbabwe
—— Bibliographies and Bibliography
—— Library Education
—— Public Libraries
—— Special Libraries

Africa—General and Peripheral

Africa South of the Sahara, 1980-81. London, Europa Publications, 1980.

Bennett, Richard J., and John Ndegwa. "Interlending in Africa: a General View." *Interlending & Document Supply* 14(1986): 22-25.

Bouazza, Abdelmajid. "Resource Sharing among Libraries in Developing Countries. The Gulf between Hope and Reality." *International Library Review* 18(1986): 373-388.

Chandler, George. "Africa South of the Sahara." In *International and National Library and Information Services; a Review of some Recent Developments, 1970-80*. Pergamon, 1982.

Havard-Williams, Peter, and J. E. Jengo. "Library Design and Planning in Developing Countries." *Libri* 37(1987): 160-176.

International Federation of Library Associations, The Hague. *IFLA General Conference, 1984*. Round Table for the Management of Library Associations, Regional Activities Division, Section on Africa. 1984. ERIC. ED 259 730.

Jackson, Miles, ed. *International Handbook of Contemporary Developments in Librarianship*. Greenwood, 1981.

Kaungamno, Ezekiel E. *Libraries as a Means to Economic Transformation in Africa*. 1978. ERIC. ED 220 080.

——"Patterns of Library and Information Services in Some Anglophone Countries South of the Sahara." In *Aspects of African Librarianship: a Collection of Writings*, compiled and edited by Michael Wise, 264-313. London, Mansell, 1985.

——*Possibilities of an Integrated National Library Policy for African Countries*. 1978. ERIC. ED 220 078.

Kibirige, Harry. "Africa." In *World Librarianship; a Comparative Study*, by Richard Krzys and Gaston Litton, with the assistance of Ann Hewitt, 116-118. New York and Basel, Marcel Dekker, 1983.

Kirk-Greene, A. H. M. "A Crowded Conference Calendar." *African Research & Documentation* 38(1985): 26-30.

Kuroda, T., and J. R. M. Wolfe. "Role of the Registry of Scientific and Technical Services for the Asian and Pacific Region." *International Development Review - Focus: Technical Cooperation* 16(1974): 16-17.

Legum, Collin, ed. *Africa: a Handbook to the Continent*. Rev. and enl. ed. New York, Praeger, 1966.

Lough, T., et al. "LOGO on the Six Continents: Issues and Uses—Part I." In *Computers in Education: Proceedings of the IFIP TC 3 4th World Conference, Norfolk, VA, July 29-August 2, 1985, 631*. Amsterdam, Elsevier Science Publishers, 1985.

Loveday, T. "African Experience of Libraries." *Focus on International and Comparative Librarianship* 14(1983): 4.

McLellan, I. *Television for Development: the African Experience*. 1986. ERIC. ED 276 410.

Msimuko, A., and J. Z. Mtukwa. "Non-verbal Forms of Communication in Africa and their Use in Training." *Programmed Learning and Educational Technology*. 22(1985): 267-272.

Ndiaye, A. Raphaël. "Développement de la bibliothéconomie dans le Tier Monde (ALP)" (Development of Librarianship in the Third World). *IFLA Journal* 12(1986): 279-280.

——*What IFLA Brings to Africa*. 1984. ERIC. ED 259 759.

Obbema, P. F. J. "De bibliotheken door het boek bedreigd: de weerslag van de opkomst van de typografie in de bibliotheekwereld" (Libraries Threatened by Books: the Effect of the Rise of Typography on the Library World). *Open* 16(1984): 375-380.

Ogunsheye, F. Adetowun. *Provision of Library Service to Non-literates. Paper Presented at the Annual Meeting of the International Federation of Library Associations (Manila, Philippines, August 18-23, 1980).* 1980. ERIC. ED 211 038.

Onadiran, G. Tunde. "Library Users as Security Problems in Africa." *International Library Movement* 8(1986): 37-43.

Perraton, H. "Radio Broadcasting and Public Education in Africa." *Educational Media International* 4(1981): 4-10.

Simsova, S., and M. MacKee. "Africa South of the Sahara." Chapter 11 of their *A Handbook of Comparative Librarianship.* Hamden, CT, Archon Books & Clive Bingley, 1970.

Sine, Babacar. *Education and Mass Media in Black Africa. The Development of Educational Methods and Techniques Suited to the Specific Conditions of the Developing Countries. Problems Presented by the Adaptation of Educational Technologies.* Paris, Division of Methods, Materials, and Techniques, Unesco, 1975.

Sub-Saharan Africa Report: Table of Contents, JPRS-SSA-84-076, 13 July 1984-JPRS-SSA-134, 21 December 1984. Arlington, VA, Joint Publications Research Service, 1985.

Unesco. *Conference of Ministers of African Member States Responsible for the Application of Science and Technology to Development, Dakar, Senegal 21 to 30 January 1974. Final Report.* Paris, 1974.

———*National Science Policies in Africa/Politiques scientifiques nationales en Afrique. Situation and Future Outlook/Situation et perspectives.* Paris, 1974.

Union of International Organizations, Brussels, Belgium. *African International Organization Directory, 1984/85.* New York, K. G. Saur, 1985.

Varley, Douglas Harold. *Adventures in Africa.* Cape Town, University of Cape Town; Trustees of the South African Library, n.d.

Vol'pe, M. "Preodolenie: Afrika: tiazhkie posledstviia kolonializma" (Conquest: Africa: Burdensome Remnants of Colonialism [and the Contemporary African Writer]). *Bibliotekar* (USSR) 1(1983): 38-42.

Wise, Michael, comp. *Aspects of African Librarianship; a Collection of Writings.* London, Mansell, 1985.

Africa—French-speaking Africa

Amon, Benjamin, and Marcel Lajeunesse. "Les bibliothèques universitaires en Afrique de l'Ouest francophone: problèmes et perspectives" (University Libraries in French-speaking West Africa: Problems and Perspectives). *Libri* 37(1987): 109-125.

Gladden, Earle M. "French African Books." *Booklist* 83(1986): 35-36.

Jacquey, Marie-Clotilde. "Le Club des lectures d'expression française" (The Club for Readers of French-language Material). *Bulletin d'Informations de l'Association de Bibliothécaires Français* 132(1986): 37.

Maack, Mary Niles. "Library Research and Publishing in Francophone Africa." +IFLA Journal 13(1987): 45-53.

Ndiaye, N. "The Author and his Problems. The Case of Publishing in French-speaking Africa." In *International Publishing Today: Problems and Prospects,* 204-207. Delhi, Bookman's Club, 1984.

Africa—Academic Libraries

Aguolu, Christian C. "Centralization and Decentralization in African University Libraries: a Theoretical Critical Re-examination." *International Library Movement* 7(1985): 157-172.

Avafia, Kwami E. "University Libraries: the African Scene." In *Aspects of African Librarianship: a Collection of Writings*, comp. and ed. by Michael Wise, 1-30. London, Mansell, 1985.

Dipeolu, J. O. "Sharing Resources among African University Libraries—Some Problems and Solutions." *African Journal of Academic Librarianship* 2(1984): 44-47.

Mahood, Molly M., ed. *Overseas Universities; Special Issue on Libraries. no. 21, Sept. 1974.* London, Inter-University council for Higher Education Overseas, 1974.

Ndiaye, Théodore. "La normalisation dans les bibliothèques universitaires d'Afrique" (Standardization in African University Libraries). *African Journal of Academic Librarianship* 2(1984): 41-43.

Ojiambo, Joseph B. "Participatory Management and its Relevance to Academic Libraries in Africa: with Specific Reference to English-speaking Africa." *Bookmark* 45(1986): 56-63.

Schlie, Theodore W., and Albert H. Rubenstein. *The Role of African Universities and Research Institutes in the Technology Transfer Process.* Evanston, IL, Dept. of Industrial Engineering and Management Sciences, Northwestern University, 1974.

Africa—Bibliographies and Bibliography

Delancey, Mark W. *African International Relations. An Annotated Bibliography.* Boulder, CO, Westview, 1981.

Freer, Percy, and Douglas Harold Varley. *A Bibliography of African Bibliographies.* 1955.

Kotei, S. I. A. "Some Comments on National Bibliography in Africa." *Botswana Library Association Journal* 6(1984): 16-24.

Lagace, Robert O. "Trends and Prospects in Bibliographic Control Systems." *Behavior Science Notes* 4(1969): 267-270.

McGowan, Patrick J., et al. *Search Codes for a Bibliography for the Study of African International Relations. Technical Report. 1 July to 31 December 1974.* Los Angeles, Department of International Relations, University of Southern California, 1975.

Mbaye, Saliou. "La Conférence Africaine sur le Contrôle Bibliographique—ASCOBIC" (African Standing Conference on Bibliographic Control—ASCOBIC). *IFLA Journal* 12(1986): 343-347.

Miller, L. L. *Africa: a Military Bibliography of Periodical Articles.* Fort Sill, OK, Army Field Artillery School, 1985.

"Natsional'naya bibliografiya v razvivayuschikhsya stramakh tropicheskoĭ Afriki" (National Bibliography in the Developing Countries of Tropical Africa). *Sovetskaya Bibliografiya* 3(1985): 81-93.

Olderogge, D. A., ed. *Yazyki Afriki. Annotirovannaya bibliografiya* (The Languages of Africa. An Annotated Bibliography). Moskva, Nauka, 1974.

Page, J. A., and J. M. Roh, eds. *Selected Black American, African, and Caribbean Authors: a Bio-bibliography.* Littleton, CO, Libraries Unlimited, 1985.

Rochman, Hazel. "The African Experience." *Booklist* 83(1986): 53-56.

Seeley, Janet. "Famine in Africa: a Bibliographical Survey." *African Research & Documentation* 39(1985): 1-8.

Africa—Biographies of Librarians

Aje, Simeon B. "Ogunsheye, Felicia Adetowun." In *ALA World Encyclopedia of Library and Information Services*, 416. Chicago, American Library Association, 1980.

———— ————In *ALA World Encyclopedia of Library and Information Services*, 2d ed., 610. Chicago, American Library Association, 1986.

DeHeer, Andrew N. "Evans, Evelyn." In *ALA World Encyclopedia of Library and Information Services*, 195. Chicago, American Library Association, 1980.

"Hans Panofsky Receives first Distinguished Service to African Studies Award." *Leads* 28(1986): 1.

Keswani, D. G. "Akita, Jeremias Mama." In *ALA World Encyclopedia of Library and Information Services,* 30-31. Chicago, American Library Association, 1980.

———"Akita, J. M." In *ALA World Encyclopedia of Library and Information Services,* 2d ed., 37-38. Chicago, American Library Association, 1986.

Lalande Isnard, F. "Bousso, Amadou Alassane." In *ALA World Encyclopedia of Library and Information Services,* 95. Chicago, American Library Association, 1980.

———"Bousso, Amadou A." In *ALA World Encyclopedia of Library and Information Services,* 2d ed., 133-134. Chicago, American Library Association, 1986.

Ogunsheye, A. Adetowun. "Aje, Simeon B." In *ALA World Encyclopedia of Library and Information Services,* 30. Chicago, American Library Association, 1980.

———"Aje, Simeon Babasanya." In *ALA World Encyclopedia of Library and Information Services,* 2d ed., 36-37. Chicago, American Library Association, 1986.

Africa—Book Trade, Printing and Publishing

African Book World and Press. 3d ed. Detroit, MI, Gale Research, 198 .

"African Books in Print." *Unesco Bulletin for Libraries* 27(1973): 122-123.

African Books in Print: Master Roster of Publishers; Preliminary List. Ibadan, Nigeria, University of Ife Press, 1972.

Book Development in Africa: Problems and Perspectives. Paris, Unesco, 1969.

Collings, Rex. "Publishing in Africa; an Industry Emerges." *Africa Report* 15(Nov 1970): 31-33.

Crowder, Michael. "The Book Crisis: Africa's Other Famine." *African Research & Documentation* 41(1986): 1-4.

Currey, James. "The State of African Studies Publishing." *African Studies* 85(1986): 609-612.

DeBenko, Eugene. *Books and Publishing in Selected African Countries: a Report to the Midwest Universities Consortium for International Activities, Inc. on a Library Acquisitions and Publishing Survey Tour in Africa, November 1970-May 1971.* East Lansing, MI, Michigan State University Library, 1971.

Grover, Mark L. "Acquisition of Latin American Library Materials Published in Africa." In *Latin American Economic Issues: Information Needs and Sources. Papers of the Twenty-sixth Annual Meeting of the Seminar on the Acquisition of Latin American Library Materials . . . 1981,* 293-301. Los Angeles, University of California, Latin American Center, 1984.

Joint Publications Research Service. *Abbreviations in African Press. Reference Aid.* Arlington, VA, Joint Publications Research Service, 1975.

———*Reference Aid. Abbreviations in the African Press.* Washington, DC, Joint Publications Research Service, 1971.

Kotei, S. I. A. *The Book today in Africa. Books about Books.* Paris, Unesco, 1981.

Market Survey of Books and Publications in Kenya, Nigeria, and Tanzania. New Delhi, Indian Institute of Foreign Trade, 1980.

Mzee, S., and R. Rauter. *Printed and Published in Africa. An Exhibition of Books in Print by 200 African Publishing Houses at the 32nd Frankfurt Book Fair.* Frankfurt am Main, German Booksellers' and Publishers' Association, Exhibition Dept., 1980.

Nottingham, John. "Establishing an African Publishing Industry; a Study in Decolonization." *African Affairs* 68(1969): 139-144.

Stein, Ruth. "Franklin Book Programs; Activities in Africa." *African Studies Bulletin* 9(1966): 92-94.

Witherell, Julian W. *A Publishing Survey Trip to West Africa, Ethiopia, France, and Portugal.* Washington, DC, Library of Congress, African Section, 1968.

Zell, Hans M. "African Scholarly Publishing in the Eighties." *Scholarly Publishing* 18(1987): 97-107.

———"The Other Famine" [book famine in Africa]. *Libri* 37(1987): 294-307.

Africa—Cataloging and Classification

Igbinosa, Isaac Osa. "The Classification of African Literature with the Library of Congress Classification Scheme: Problems and Prospects." *Bendel Library Journal* 7(1984): 26-32.

Mlaki, Theophilus E. "Serials of the Poor Nations: their Nature, Importance, Problems and Suggested Solutions." *International Cataloguing* 14(1985): 39-41.

Africa—Documentation and Information Science

Abass, Olayide. "Guidelines for Informatics Laws in Africa." *Transnational Data Report* 7(1984): 325-326.

———"Problems of Education and Training in Informatics in some African Countries." In *Computers in Education. Proceedings of the IFIP TC-3 3rd World Conference on Computers in Education . . . 1981*, 575-581. Amsterdam, North-Holland, 1981.

Apeji, E. Adeche. "National Information Policies and Systems in Developing African Nations." *Bendel Library Journal* 7(1984): 48-58.

Chateh, Peter. *Documentation Centre of the Association of African Universities*. 1980. ERIC. ED 214 545.

Cunha, I. M. R. F. "African Documentation: Language and Ideology." *Ciencia da Informacao* 16(1987): 37-40.

Dramé, Cheick Oumar. "La société moderne africaine au sud du Sahara: quelques problèmes et perspectives de développement de la communication documentaire dans les services de bibliothèque" (Modern African Society South of the Sahara: Some Problems and Perspectives of Developing Documentary Communications within Library Services). *Libri* 33(1985): 348-362.

"Dreams and Data Banks." *Botswana Library Association Journal* 5(1983): 50-52.

Fajemirokun, F. A. "Establishing an African Data Bank." In *Proceedings of the International Symposium on Management of Geodetic Data, Copenhagen, Denmark, 24-26 August 1981*, 50-57. Copenhagen, Geodetic Institute, 1981.

Farid, M. *The Development of Information Manpower Resource*. 1982. ERIC. ED 235 833.

Faye, Makane. "ARSO-DISNET: an réseau africain de centres d'information sur la normalisation" (ARSO-DISNET: an African Network of Information Centers on Normalization). *Documentaliste* 23(1986): 29-32.

Gehrke, Ulrich. "Information for Development: Some Problems of National Co-ordination, Regional Co-operation and International Assistance." *INSPEL* 19(1985): 166-198.

Olden, Anthony. "Opinion Paper: Sub-Saharan Africa and the Paperless Society." *Journal of the American Society for Information Science* 38(1987): 298-304.

Onuigbo, Wilson I. B. "Reprint Requests—a Tool for Documentation." *International Forum on Information and Documentation* 10(1985): 7-9. Discussion: 11(1986): 40-41.

Rubama, Ibrahim, et al. *Spoken Language Vocabulary and Structural Frequency Count: Swahili Data Analyses. Special Report, 1 July 1972-30 June 1973*. New York, Syracuse University Research Corporation, 1973.

Sall, Djiby, and Maurice B. Catherinet. *Projet de réseau d'information et de documentation scientifiques et techniques pour le Sahel: étude d'une stratégie documentaire et vue de la création d'un tel réseau pour le CILSS à l'Institut du Sahel* (Project for an Information Network of Scientific and Technical Documentation for the Sahel: a Study of a Documentary Strategy in View of the Creation of such a Network for the CILSS at the Institute of the Sahel). Ottawa, Canada, Centre de Recherches pour le Développement International, 1978.

Stanley, Janet L. "African Art and AAT." *Art Documentation* 4(1985): 103-105.

Thiam, P. A. "Patent Documentation as an Aid to Technological Development in the Developing Member Countries of O. A. O. I." *World Patent Information* 6(1984): 184-186.

Africa—Library Education and Training

International Federation of Library Associations, The Hague. *Education for Librarianship on the Grassroots Level. Part I. Papers [on Library Science in Africa].* 1984. ERIC. ED 259 728.

Karani, F., ed. *Training Curriculum.* 1984. ERIC. ED 247 913.

Kotei, S. I. A. "The Social Order, Library Service and Library Education in Africa." *Botswana Library Association Journal* 5(1983): 26-37.

Nzotta, Briggs C. "The Staffing of African Library Schools." *Education for Information* 4(1986): 291-303.

Obi, Dorothy S. *Education for Library, Archive, and Information Science in Sub-Saharan Africa: a Blueprint for Regional Planning.* 1974. EDRS: ED 104 446.

Ogunsheye, F. Adetowun. "Library Education and Manpower planning in Africa." In *National and International Library Planning,* ed. by R. Vosper and L. I. Newkirk, 99-115. Munich, Verlag Dokumentation, 1976. First published in 1974 as EDRS: ED 105 826.

Africa—Public Libraries

Kaungamno. Ezekiel E. *The Public Library in a Changing Society Viewed in the Light of the UNESCO Manifest. The African Experience.* 1979. ERIC. ED 220 081.

Africa—School and Children's Library Services and Literature

Craver, K. W. "A Survey of Library Services to Children and Young Adults in Selected Developing Countries in Africa and Asia." *Top of the News* 42(1985): 33-43.

Africa—Special Libraries, Services and Subjects

Ajayi-Dopemu, Y. "Visual Aids and the Enhancement of Communication in Africa." *Journal of Educational Television* 8(1982): 203-209.

Aleybeleye, B. "Oral Archives in Africa: their Nature, Value and Accessibility." *International Library Review* 17(1985): 419-424.

Awosika, Diekolola. "Administrative Libraries and Universal Availability of Information: Comments from a Developing Country." *INSPEL* 20(1986): 98-107.

Bitoumbou, Jean-Pierre. "Le Lancement d'un programme d'archives dans les pays en développement" (Starting an Archival Program in Developing Countries). In *Proceedings of the 10th International Congress on Archives,* 82-87. np, Saur, 1986.

Cason, Maidel K. "African Government Documents in Microform." *Microform Review* 14(1985): 223-228.

Central Intelligence Agency, Washington, DC. *Maps: Algeria, Benin, Cape Verde, Congo, Djibouti, Guinea, Namibia and Walvis Bay, Rwanda and Burundi, Swaziland, Tanzania.* 1979. (NTIS:PB 82-928020)

Directory of Engineering Education Institutions. Africa - Arab States - Asia - Latin America and the Caribbean. Paris, Unesco, 1986.

Gilliver, B. "Information Sciences/Genetic Resources Program (IS/GR)." In *Crop Genetic Resources in Africa. Proceedings . . . 1978,* 23-24. Amsterdam, Elsevier, 1980.

"Inventaire des principaux répertoires d'institutions de sciences sociales et humaines en Afrique au Sud du Sahara" (Inventory of the Principal Repertories of Institutions in the Social and Human Sciences in Africa South of the Sahara). *Social Sciences Information sur les Sciences Sociales* 5(1966): 114-129.

Jongbloed, Harry J. L. *The Audio-visual Services in Fifteen African Countries. Comparative Study on the Administration of Audio-visual Services in Advanced and Developing Countries. Par four. First ed.* The Hague, International Council for Educational Media, 1974.

Long, Nina P. "Twinning of Hospital Libraries—International Resource Sharing." *Bulletin of the Medical Library Association* 74(1986): 374-375.

Mwiyeriwa, Steve S. "The Development of Archives in Africa: Problems and Prospects." In *Aspects of African Librarianship: a Collection of Writings,* comp. and ed. by Michael Wise, 222-263. London, Mansell, 1985.

Orleans, Jacques d'. *The Status of Archivists in Relation to Other Professionals in the Public Service in Africa.* Paris, Unesco, 1985.

Schüller, Dietrich. "Handling, Storage and Preservation of Sound Recordings under Tropical and Subtropical Climatic Conditions." *Fontes Artis Musicae* 33(1986): 100-104.

Van, L. E. *The Status of Archives and Records Management Systems and Services in African Member States.* 1985. ERIC. ED 260 722.

Africana

Blake, David. "Periodicals from Africa: the Next Step." *African Research & Documentation* 38(1985): 11-19.

Boylan, Ray. "The Cooperative Africana Microform Project." *Microform Review* 15(1986): 167-171.

Conference on the Acquisition of Material from Africa, University of Birmingham, 1969. *Reports and Papers,* compiled by Valerie Bloomfield. Zug, Switzerland, Inter Documentation Co. for the Standing Conference on Library Material on Africa, 1969.

Easterbrook, David L. " 'The Africans' and Academic Libraries: a New PBS series on a Timely Topic." *College & Research Libraries News* 8(1986): 486-490.

Freshwater, Peter B. "Scolma's Response to *Speaking for the Future." African Research & Documentation* 42(1986): 1-7.

Gosebrink, Jean E. Meeh. *African Studies Information Resources Directory.* Published for the African Studies Association. np, Zell, 1986.

Larby, Patricia M. "African Studies and Research: Parker's Piece." *African Research & Documentation* 41(1986): 40-43.

———"Resources for African Studies: the Role of Libraries." *African Affairs* 85(1986): 605-608.

Lass, Hans D. "Acquisition of African Government Publications." In *Proceedings of the Standing Conference of African University Librarians, Eastern Area Conference, Addis Ababa, 1971,* ed. by Rita Pankhurst and Joan Proudman, Addis Ababa, Haile Selassie University Library, 1971.

Library of Congress. *U. S. Imprints on Sub-Saharan Africa. v. 1, 1985: A Guide to Publications Cataloged at the Library of Congress.* Washington, DC, The African Section, African and Middle Eastern Division, Research Services, Library of Congress, 1986.

"Library of Congress African Section Launches Series of Guides to Monographs on Sub-Saharan Africa." *Library of Congress Information Bulletin* 45(1986): 384-385.

Lordereau, Paulette. "La coopération interbibliothèques sur la documentation africaine en France" (Interlibrary Cooperation on African Documentation in France). *Bulletin d'Information de l'Association des Bibliothécaires Français* 128(1985): 5-6.

Maack, Mary Niles. "The A. O. F. Archives and the Study of African History." *Bulletin de l'Institut Fondamental d'Afrique Noire,* Série B. (1980).

McMee, Malcolm. "Cooperation in African Acquisitions: SCOLMA Looks to the Future." *African Research & Documentation* 38(1985): 20-25.

Near East and Africa Serials. [Translations] Arlington, VA, Joint Publications Research Service, 1985. (NTIS.PB85-941500)

———[Translations of articles] Arlington, VA, Joint Publications Research Service, 1986. (PB86-941500)

Periviita, Pirkko. *Ns. Mustan Afrikan kielten ja kirjallisuuden tiedonlahteita* (Information Sources in the Languages and Linguistics of the Black African Countries). Helsinki, Finnish Association for Documentation, 1974.

Rahard, Maryse, and Jean Francois Bourdin. "FRANCIS Can Inform You on Africa." *African Research & Documentation* 42(1986): 8-10.

Rayfield, J. R. "The Use of Films in Teaching about Africa." *Film Library Quarterly* 17(1984): 34-52.

" 'Riders on the Earth Together' Exhibit Features Expressions of Faith." *Library of Congress Information Bulletin* 45(1986): 241-242.

Rønning, Helge. "Litteratur og utvikling—noen problemer i moderne afrikansk litteratur" (Literature and Development—Some Problems in Modern African Literature). *Bog og Bibliotek* 53(1986): 274-277.

Schmidt, Nancy J. "African Studies in the United States." *African Research & Documentation* 38(1985): 1-10.

Seeley, Janet. "The Use of Bibliographic Databases in African Studies." *African Research & Documentation* 41(1986): 7-12.

Witherell, Julian W. "Resources for the Study of Africa and the Middle East: an Overview." *Reference Librarian* 17(1987): 131-142.

Africana—Africana Collections outside the Sub-Sahara

Auer, L. "Africa, Asia and Oceania in the Austrian State Archives." *Information Development* 3(1987): 17-19.

Dorsey, Learthen. "Government Documents on Microfiche in the Sahel Documentation Center at Michigan State University." *Microform Review* 14(1985): 229-231.

The SCOLMA Directory of Libraries and Special Collections on Africa in the United Kingdom and Western Europe. Ed. by Harry Hannam. 4th rev. & expanded ed. np, Zell, 1983.

Africana—Africana for Children

Black Impressions: a Book List for Children and Parents to Share. Conceived and comp. by Sammie Allen and Others of the Enoch Pratt Free Library. Baltimore, Enoch Pratt Free Library Publications, 1986.

Inter-Regional and Regional

Musisi, Jafred S. "Development, Organization and the Working Process in Parliamentary Libraries in Eastern, Central and Southern Africa." In *Parlament und Bibliothek*, 238-249. np, Saur, 1986.

Namponya, Clemence R. "Agricultural Libraries in East and Central Africa." In *Aspects of African Librarianship: a Collection of Writings*, comp. and ed. by Michael Wise, 154-165. London, Mansell, 1985.

Unesco. *Conference on Resource Sharing in Southern and Central Africa*. 1986. ERIC. ED 270 109.

Inter-Regional and Regional—Central Africa

Allen, R. J., and S. W. Allen. "Computer-assisted Videodisc. An African Perspective." *Perspectives in Computing* 22(1983): 28-31.

Brock, Jean. "Les bibliothèques en Afrique centrale" (Libraries in Central Africa). *Archives et Bibliothèques de Belgique* (1972).

Made, Stanley M. "National Libraries in English-speaking Central Africa: Zimbabwe, Zambia and Malawi." In *Aspects of African Librarianship: a Collection of Writings,* comp. and ed. by Michael Wise, 50-68. London, Mansell, 1985.

Mazikana, Peter C. "A Joint Microfilming Project: Records of the Federation of Rhodesia and Nyasaland." In *Proceedings of the 10th International Congress on Archives,* 273-277. np, Saur, 1986.

Msiska, Augustine W. C. "Early Efforts at Creating African Literature: its Distribution, Local Authorship and Library Service in Northern Rhodesia (Zambia) and Nyasaland (Malawi)." *Libri* 36(1986): 240-246.

Varley, Douglas Harold. *Library Services in the Rhodesias and Nyasaland.* np, 1951.

Inter-Regional and Regional—Eastern Africa

Burt. E. C. *An Annotated Bibliography of the Visual Arts of East Africa.* Bloomington, IN, Indiana University Press, 1980.

Deboeck, G., and B. Kinsey. *Managing Information for Rural Development. Lessons from Eastern Africa.* 1980. NTIS.PG83-247122.

Kaungamno, E. E. *Centralized Services for Libraries. The African Experience.* 1979. ERIC. ED 220 077.

Matson, A. T. "A Unique African Journalistic Achievement: Four Decades of 'Coast Causeries'." *African Research & Documentation* 38(1985): 31-34.

Inter-Regional and Regional—Eastern Africa—Documentation and Information Science

"Conference on Information Networks in East Africa, 1973." *Unesco Bulletin for Libraries* 28(1974): 52-53.

Shayo, L. K. *Role of Computers in Developing Countries with Reference to East Africa.* Trieste, Italy, International Centre for Theoretical Physics, 1984.

Inter-Regional and Regional—Eastern Africa—Library Education

Abidi, S. A. H., et al. *The Introduction of Information Science Elements into Library Training Schemes in Eastern Africa: a Study.* Nairobi, Coordinating Centre for Regional Information Training, 1978.

———"Library Education in East Africa." In *Aspects of African Librarianship: a Collection of Writings,* comp. and ed. by Michael Wise, 182-199. London, Mansell, 1985.

Dean, John. *A Regional Library Science Program for Eastern Africa. A Report. 1974. EDRS: Ed 156 113.*

Inter-Regional and Regional—Southern Africa

Henley, Janet. "A Proposed Southern African Studies Information Database." *African Research & Documentation* 41(1986): 13-20.

Kotei, S. "IFLA Funds Southern Africa Study." *Focus on International and Comparative Librarianship* 14(1983): 6.

Lungu, Charles B. M. "Resource-sharing and Self-reliance in Southern Africa." *Information Development* 3(1987): 82-86.

Inter-Regional and Regional—West Africa

Akwule, R. U. "Telecommunications in West Africa. An Analysis of Selected Diplomatic Elite Perceptions of Regional Cooperation in the Field of Telecommunications within the Economic Community of West African States (ECOWAS)." *Dissertation Abstracts International* 46(1986): 2845-A.
Horrocks, Norman. "English-language Publishing in Librarianship outside the United States." *Drexel Library Quarterly* 15(1979): 95-115.
Knox-Hooke, S. A. "The Law Relating to Public Libraries in West Africa. A Comparative Study with the United Kingdom Public Library Laws." Thesis, Library Association, 1966.
Maack, Mary Niles. "The Role of External Aid in West African Library Development." *Library Quarterly* 56(1986): 1-16.
Stutzman, Mary. "The Role and Problems of Libraries in Developing Countries: the West African Experience." Master's thesis, UCLA, 1978. Published as ERIC. ED 176 744.
University of Ibadan. Institute of Librarianship. *Proceedings of a Seminar on Library Standards for West Africa.* April 1967. (unpublished)
"West African Book: a Vicious Circle." *West Africa* 2391(1963): 355.

Inter-Regional and Regional—West Africa—Academic Libraries

Ifidon, Sam E. "Establishment of Standards for Bookstock in West African University Libraries." *African Journal of Academic Librarianship* 2(1984): 54-60. First published in *Libri* 33(1983): 92-106.
Tamuno, Olufunmilayo G. "Local Publishing and Development of Academic Libraries." *African Journal of Academic Librarianship* 2(1984): 1-5.

Inter-Regional and Regional—West Africa—Library Education

Edoka, B. Eziukwu. "Library and Information Studies in English-speaking West Africa." *Information Development* 3(1987): 30-35.

International Meetings

1976, Brazzaville, Congo, Meeting of Experts on Planning Documentation and Library Networks in Africa.
Unesco. *Meeting of Experts on Planning Documentation and Library Networks in Africa (NATIS). Working Document.* Paris, 1976. Also published as EDRS:ED 156 220.
———Tangier, Morocco, Preparatory Workshop on African Government Documents
African Government Documents. Proceedings of the Preparatory Workshop on African Government Documents. Ed. by Mohamed M. El Hadi. Tangier, Morocco, African Training and Research Centre in Administration for Development (CAFRAD), 1977.
1979, Helsinki, Finland, Afro-Scandinavian Library Conference.
Afro-Scandinavian Library Conference, Espoo, Finland, 1979. *Libraries and National Development. Final Report* ... 1979. ERIC. ED 221 176.
1980, Arusha, Tanzania, Unesco Regional Meeting of Computer Centre Directors.

Unesco. *Unesco Regional Meeting of Computer Centre Directors in Africa (Arusha, Tanzania, Apr 14-18, 1980). Final Report.* Nairobi, Unesco, 1980.

1983, Dar es Salaam, Tanzania, African Standing Conference on Bibliographic Control (ASCOBIC).

Garebakwene, Basiamang. "Report on the African Standing Conference on Bibliographic Control (ASCOBIC), Dar es Salaam, 1st-8th August 1983." *Botswana Library Association Journal* 5(1983): 37-44.

————Nairobi, Kenya, International Conference on Education and Training for Agricultural Library and Information Work

Mann, E. J. "International Conference on Education and Training for Agricultural Library and Information Work, Nairobi, March 1983. Opening Speech." *Quarterly Bulletin of the International Association of Agricultural Librarians and Documentalists* 28(1983): 31-33.

International Conference on Education and Training for Agricultural Library and Information Work. Nairobi, Kenya, 1983. *Education and Training for Agricultural Library and Information Work. Proceedings ... 7-12 March 1983.* Edited by H. A. Liyai, B. N. Ayaka, R. Thomas; organized by International Association of Agricultural Librarians and Documentalists, Kenya Library Association, Kenya National Academy for the Advancement of Arts and Sciences, with the participation of the International Federation for Documentation Education and Training. Nairobi, Kenya Library Association, 1984.

1984, Arusha, Tanzania, DSE/ESAMI Workshop on Management of Information Services.

Mg'andu, Bathsheba. "The 1984 DSE/ESAMI Workshop on Management of Information Services: an Appraisal." *Zambia Library Association Journal* 16(1984): 13-29.

————Harare, Zimbabwe, Standing Conference of Eastern, Central and Southern African Librarians.

Liyai, H. A., and P. S. Weche. " 'We Are Our Own Liberators': Report on the Sixth Standing Conference of Eastern, Central and Southern African Librarians (SCECSAL) Held in Harare, Zimbabwe 17-21 September 1984." *COMLA Newsletter* 49(1985): 11-12.

————Nairobi, Kenya, General Conference of the International Federation of Library Associations (IFLA)

Berndtson, Maija. "IFLA:n 50. yleiskokous Nairobissa" (IFLA's 50th Conference in Nairobi). *Kirjastolehti* 77(1984): 556-557.

Bossuat, Marie-Louise. "Fédération Internationale des Associations de Bibliothécaires et des Bibliothèques: 50ème conférence, Nairobi, Kenya, 19-25 août 1984" (International Federation of Associations of Librarians and Libraries: 50th Conference, Nairobi, Kenya, 19-25 August 1984). *Bulletin d'Informations de l'Association des Bibliothécaires Français* 125(1984): 29-31.

Geh, Hans-Peter, et al. "Die 50. Generalkonferenz der IFLA in Nairobi (Kenia)" (The 50th IFLA General Conference in Nairobi, Kenya). *Zeitschrift für Bibliothekswesen und Bibliographie* 32(1985): 87-105.

IFLA Annual, 1984: Proceedings of the 50th Council and General Conference, Nairobi, 1984; Annual Reports; edited by Willem R. H. Koops and Carol Henry. Np, Saur, 1984.

"IFLA-motet 1984, sentralt tema: bibliotekets rolle i voksenundervisningen" (IFLA Meeting 1984, Central Theme: Role of the Library in Adult Education). *Bok og Bibliothek* 51(1984): 377-379.

Pereslegina, E. V. "Itogi 50-i sessi IFLA" (Summary of the 50th IFLA Session). *Sovetskaya Bibliografiya* 2(1985): 91-95.

Rückl, Gotthard, and Dieter Schmidmaier. "IFLA in Afrika" (IFLA in Africa). *Zentralblatt für Bibliothekswesen* 98(1984): 540-545.

1985, Harare, Zimbabwe, Meeting of Information Experts

Hüttemann, Lutz, ed. *Manpower Training Needs.* Bonn, Deutsche Stiftung Internationale Entwicklung, 1985.

1986, Gaberone, Botswana, Standing Conference of Eastern, Central and Southern African Librarians.

Motsi, Goodwell. "SCECSAL 7: Report of the Seventh Standing Conference of Eastern, Central and Southern African Librarians, Gabarone, Botswana, August 1986." *Zimbabwe Librarian* 18(1986): 37, 39, 41, 43.
Giggey, Shirley H. "Standing Conference of Eastern, Central and Southern African Librarians(SCECSAL) 7: Pre-conference, Conference, and Post-conference, 31 July-12 August 1986, Gaberone, Botswana—a Report." *African Research & Documentation* 42(1986): 35-42.
———Nairobi, Kenya, African Standing Conference on Bibliographic Control (ASCOBIC)
Armstrong, James C. "Sixth ASCOBIC Conference is Held in Nairobi, Kenya." *Library of Congress Information Bulletin* 46(1987): 35.
Mbaye, Saliou. "La Conférence Africaine Permanente sur le Contrôle Bibliographique— ASCOBIC" (The African Standing Conference on bibliographic Control—ASCOBIC). *IFLA Journal* 12(1986): 343-347.

Individual Countries

Angola

Van-Dúnem, Domingos. "Angola." In *ALA World Encyclopedia of Library and Information services*, 34. Chicago, American Library Association, 1980.
——— ———*Ibid.*, 2d ed., 49-50. Chicago, American Library Association, 1986.

Benin

Dufil, Marie-Hélene. "Där boken är lyxvara och läxorna läases under gatlyktan" (Where the Book is a Luxury and Homework is Done under the Street Lamp) *Biblioteksbladet* 70(1985): 114-116.
Etudes dahoméennes. Porto Novo, Institut de Recherches Appliquées du Benin, 1963-70.
McHugh, Neill. "Benin." In *ALA World Encyclopedia of Library and Information Services*, 78-79. Chicago, American Library Association, 1980.
——— ———*Ibid.*, 2d ed., 107-108. Chicago, American Library Association, 1986.

Botswana

Gibbons, Frank. "Forging Ahead: Library Education in Botswana." *COMLA Newsletter* 53(1986): 2-3.
Jones, Karla Lee. "Botswana Bibliography: a Review of the State-of-the-Art." *Botswana Library Association Journal* 7(1985): 8-21.
Kåri, Peter Wulff. "Vores bibliotek burde vaere dobbelt så stort" (Our Library Should be Twice as Large). *Bogens Verden* 67(1985): 320-321.
Kotei, S. I. A. "Prerequisites to Production of Teaching Materials: the Case of the Department of Library Studies, University of Botswana and Swaziland." In *Aspects of African Librarianship: a Collection of Writings,* comp. and ed. by Michael Wise, 216-221. London, Mansell, 1985.
Lekaukau, T. M. "Holdings of Botswana National Archives." *Botswana Library Association Journal* 6(1984): 12-15.
Mbaakanye, D. M. "Cultural Documentation in Botswana." *Botswana Library Association Journal* 5(1983): 13-20.
———"Educational Library Provision for the Blind in Botswana." *Information Development* 3(1987): 220-225.
Moore, Nick. *Library and Information Power Needs: a Study of the Situation in Botswana.* Np, British Council, 1984.

Neill, J. R. "Botswana: a Regional Approach to Library Education." *Information Development* 3(1987): 40-43.

———"Some Factors Influencing Curriculum Development in Library Education." *Botswana Library Association Journal* 6(1984): 34-46.

Phikani, Chris. "Publishing for Botswana: a Symposium on Problems and Issues." *Botswana Library Association Journal* 5(1983): 23-25.

Post, Mogens. "Bibliotekar i en flygtningelejr" (Librarian in a Refugee Camp). *Bibliotek* 70(1986): 596-598.

Qobose, Edwin Nkareng. "Library Promotion: Programmes in a Public Library." *Botswana Library Association Journal* 6(1984): 25-33.

Raseroka, Kay. "Botswana." In *ALA World Encyclopedia of Library and Information Services,* 94-95. Chicago, American Library Association, 1980.

——— ———*Ibid.*, 2d ed., 132-133. Chicago, American Library Association, 1986.

"Report of the Botswana Delegation to Algeria on New University Library Funding." *Botswana Library Association Journal* 5(1983): 59-62.

Simonsen, Grethe. "Bibliotekarer må snakke et språk folk forstår: møte med Thandiwe Kgosidintsi, bibliotekar fra Botswana" (Librarians Must Speak a Language People Understand: a Meeting with Thandiwe Kgosidintsi, Librarian from Botswana). *Bok og Bibliotek* 53(1986): 281-282.

Sturges, Paul. "International Transfer of Information and National Self-sufficiency: the Case of Botswana." In *ASIS '86; Proceedings of the 49th ASIS Annual Meeting . . .* ed. by Julie M. Hurd, 320-325. Np, Learned Information, 1986.

Burkina Faso

"[Bibliographical Services in] Upper Volta." In *Bibliographical Services Throughout the World 1970-74,* ed. by Marcelle Beaudiquez, 405-406. Paris, Unesco, 1977.

———"Burkina Faso." *Ibid.*, 2d ed., 146. Chicago, American Library Association, 1986.

Krissiamba, Larba Ali. "Upper Volta." In *ALA World Encyclopedia of Library and Information Services,* 582. Chicago, American Library Association, 1980.

Notes et documents voltaïques. 1967- . Ouagadougou, Centre National de la Recherche Scientifique et Technologique.

Recherches voltaïques. 1950- . Ouagadougou, Centre National de la Recherche Scientifique et Technologique.

Burundi

Kinigi, Firmin. "Burundi." In *ALA World Encyclopedia of Library and Information Services,* 105. Chicago, American Library Association, 1980.

——— ———*Ibid.*, 2d ed., 147-148. Chicago, American Library Association, 1986.

Cameroon

Chateh, Peter Nkangafack. "Cameroon." In *ALA World Encyclopedia of Library and Information Services,* 108-109. Chicago, American Library Association, 1980.

——— ———*Ibid.*, 2d ed., 153-155. Chicago, American Library Association, 1986.

Cape Verde

Cruzeiro, Maria Manuela. "Cape Verde." In *ALA World Encyclopedia of Library and Information Services,* 165. 2d ed. Chicago, American Library Association, 1986.

Central African Republic

Poutou, Alain-Michel. "Central African Republic." In *ALA World Encyclopedia of Library and Information Services*, 127-128. Chicago, American Library Association, 1980.
——— ———*Ibid.*, 2d ed., 177-178. Chicago, American Library Association, 1986.

Chad

Central Intelligence Agency, Washington, DC. *Chad.* (Map no. 505126/505125) 1982. (NTIS: PB82-928032)
McHugh, Neil. "Chad." In *ALA World Encyclopedia of Library and Information Services*, 130. Chicago, American Library Association, 1980.
——— ———*Ibid.*, 2d ed., 181. Chicago, American Library Association, 1986.

Congo (Peoples Republic)

Lalande Isnard, Fanny. "Congo, People's Republic of the." In *ALA World Encyclopedia of Library and Information Services*, 158-159. Chicago, American Library Association, 1980.
Wambi, Bruno. "Congo." In *ALA World Encyclopedia of Library and Information Services*, 216-218. 2d ed. Chicago, American Library Association, 1986.

Djibouti

"Djibouti." In *ALA World Encyclopedia of Library and Information services*, 180. Chicago, American Library Association, 1980.
———*Ibid.*, 2d ed., 252. Chicago, American Library Association, 1986.

Equatorial Guinea

Berman, Sanford. "Spanish Guinea: an Annotated Bibliography." Thesis, Catholic University of America, 1961.
Eléments pour le dossier de l'afrofascisme. De la Guinée Equatoriale (Elements for the dossier of afrofascism in Equatorial Guinea). 1983.
Guinea Ecuatorial. Bibliografía General. 1974-85. 5 vols.
Liniger-Goumaz, Max. *Historical Dictionary of Equatorial Guinea.* Metuchen, NJ, Scarecrow Press, 1979.
"Equatorial Guinea." In *ALA World Encyclopedia of Library and Information services*, 267-269. 2d ed. Chicago, American Library Association, 1986.

Ethiopia

Adhana Mengste-Ab. "Ethiopia." In *ALA World Encyclopedia of Library and Information Services*, 270-272. 2d ed. Chicago, American Library Association, 1986.
Cullen, Tim. "Have UDC, Will Travel." *State Librarian* 33(1985): 30-31; 34(1986): 11-13.
Ethiopian Publications. 1965- . Addis Ababa, University of Addis Ababa.
Pankhurst, Rita. "Ethiopia." In *ALA World Encyclopedia of Library and Information Services*, 193. Chicago, American Library Association, *1980*.

Gabon

Bouscarle, Marie Elizabeth. *Les bibliothèques au Gabon* (Libraries in Gabon). 1982.
———"Gabon." In *ALA World Encyclopedia of Library and Information Services,* 212-213. Chicago, American Library Association, 1980.
——— ———*Ibid.,* 2d ed., 296. Chicago, American Library Association, 1986.
Deschamps, Hubert. *Traditions orales et archives du Gabon* (Oral Traditions and Archives of Gabon). Paris, Berger-Levrault, 1962.
Haeringer, Danielle. *Documentation et planification au Gabon* (Documentation and Planning in Gabon). Libreville, Gabon, Ministère de la Planification du Développement et des Participations, Commissariat Général au Plan, Direction des Projets, 1981.

Gambia

N'Jie, Sally P. C. "Bibliotheksarbeit für Kinder und Jugendliche in Gambia" (Library Work for Children and Young People in Gambia). *Bibliothekar* 36(1982): 60-65.
———"Gambia, The." In *ALA World Encyclopedia of Library and Information Services,* 213-214. Chicago, American Library Association, 1980.
——— ———. *Ibid.,* 296-297. 2d ed. Chicago, American Library Association, 1986.

Ghana

Agyei-Gyane, L. "The Ghana Library Association: History and Development." *Libri* 36(1986): 113-118.
Council for Scientific and Industrial Research, Accra, Ghana, et al. *The Scientific and Technical Information (STI) in Ghana: Role of the CSIR in Developing a National STI Network.* Grant NSF-DSI-74-12167. Washington, DC, Committee on International Scientific and Technical Information Programs, National Academy of Sciences, 1976.
Dua-Agyemang, Henry. "Ghana." In *ALA World Encyclopedia of Library and Information Services,* 219-221. Chicago, American Library Association, 1980.
——— ———. *Ibid.,* 2d ed., 310-312. Chicago, American Library Association, 1986.
Franklin Book Programs, Inc. *Books for Ghana and Nigeria.* New York, Franklin Book Programs, Inc., 1962.
Husain, S., and A. A. Alemna. "Cataloguing of Ghanaian Names: Problems and Possible Solutions." *Annals of Library Science and Documentation* 31(1984): 13-17.
Maafo, E. Victor. "Ghana." *Reference Services Review* 15(1987): 88-91.
Ofori, A. G. T. "Ghana." In *International Handbook of Contemporary Developments in Librarianship;* ed. by Miles M. Jackson, 3-26. Westport, CT, Greenwood Press, 1981.
Wright, D. J., et al. "Forecasting Transport Requirements for District Primary Health Care in Ghana: a Simulation Study. *European Journal of Operational Research* 15(1984): 302-309.

Ghana—Library Education

Kotei, S. I. A. "Preparing Teaching Materials for Library Education in Ghana: a Historical Account of Developments, 1961-78." In *Aspects of African Librarianship: a Collection of Writings,* comp. and ed. by Michael Wise, 200-215. London, Mansell, 1985.

Ghana—Special Libraries

Agyei-Gyane, L. comp. *Directory of Special and Research Libraries in Ghana.* Accra, CSIR, 1977.

Guinea

Lalande-Isnard, Fanny. "Guinea." In *ALA World Encyclopedia of Library and Information Services*, 226. Chicago, American Library Association, 1980.
——— ———. *Ibid.*, 2d ed., 319. Chicago, American Library Association, 1986.

Guinea-Bissau

Cruzeiro, Maria Manuela. "Guinea-Bissau." In *ALA World Encyclopedia of Library and Information Services*, 226. Chicago, American Library Association, 1980.
——— ———. *Ibid.*, 2d ed., 319. Chicago, American Library Association, 1986.

Ivory Coast

Central Intelligence Agency, Washington, DC. *Maps: Ivory Coast, Africa.* 1981. (NTIS:PB82-928025)
Handloff, Robert E. "Ivory Coast." In *ALA World Encyclopedia of Library and Information Services*, 276-277. Chicago, American Library Association, 1980.
Handloff, Robert E., and Seydou Gueye. "Ivory Coast." In *ALA World Encyclopedia of Library and Information Services*, 400-401. 2d ed. Chicago, American Library Association, 1986.
Valerien, J. "Education by Television in the Ivory Coast." *Educational Media International* 4(1981): 11-15.

Kenya

Durrani, N. "Library [of Congress] Is Active in Collecting Rural Newspapers of Kenya." *Library of Congress Information Bulletin* 45(1986): 31.
Durrani, Shiraz. "Rural Information in Kenya." *Information Development* 1(1985): 149-157.
Holmberg, B. "Applications of Distance Education in Kenya." *Distance Education* 6(1985): 242-247.
Imhof, M., et al. *English by Radio. Implications for Non-formal Language Education.* 1984. ERIC. ED 243 470.
Kabeberi, Monicah. "Voice of Kenya's Role in Collection, Preservation and Dissemination Kenya's Cultural Heritage." *Fontes Artis Musicae* 33(1986): 105-108.
"Milwaukee-Kenya Partnership Agreement." *Leads* 28(1986): 3.
Musisi, J. S. "Kenya." In *International Handbook of Contemporary Developments in Librarianship;* ed. by Miles M. Jackson, 27-39. Westport, CT, Greenwood Press, 1981.
Ndegwa, John. "Kenya." In *ALA World Encyclopedia of Library and Information Services*, 288-289. Chicago, American Library Association, 1980.
——— ———. *Ibid.*, 2d ed., 416-417. Chicago, American Library Association, 1986.
Ng'ang'a, Damaris G. "Availability of Publications in Science and Technology in Kenya: Problems." *INSPEL* 19(1985): 199-209.
Ocholla, Dennis N. "Kenyan Libraries Today: their Academic and Research Potentiality." *The Bookmark* 44(1985): 60-63.
Otike, J. N. "The Problems of Library Co-operation in Kenya." *Interlending & Document Supply* 15(1987): 80-83.
Schwartz, S. *A National Documentation and Information Centre of the Kenya National Council for Science and Technology.* 1980. ERIC. ED 214 546.

Kenya—Academic Libraries

Anand, A. K. "Academic Libraries in Kenya." *International Library Movement* 8(1986): 69-81.

Kenya—School and Children's Library Services

Nguchu, R. R. *The Extent to which Radio is Used in Teaching of Home Science in Urban Primary Schools in Kenya.* 1981. ERIC. ED 222 193.

Onganga, O. O. *An Evaluation of the Effectiveness of Radio Programs in Teaching English Language to Class Six Pupils in Primary Schools in South Nyanza-Kenya.* 1982. ERIC. ED 235 788.

Kenya—Special Libraries

Durrani, Shiraz. "Agricultural Information Services in Kenya and Third World Needs." *Journal of Librarianship* 19(1987): 108-120.

Herbert, Shirley. "Into Africa: Visit to Kenya, February 1986." *State Librarian* 34(1986): 39.

Musembi, Musila. "Archives Development in Kenya." *Information Development* 2(1986): 218-222.

Omondi, Washington A. "Problems in Collection and Preservation of Music Data in Kenya and Suggested Solutions to the Problems." *Fontes Artis Musicae* 33(1986): 108-117.

Otike, J. N. "A Proposal for the Establishment of a Formalized Co-operative Programme for Special Libraries in Kenya." *INSPEL* 21(1987): 103-112.

Lesotho

Forshaw, Vincent. "Lesotho." In *ALA World Encyclopedia of Library and Information Services,* 313. Chicago, American Library Association, 1980.

————— —————. *Ibid.,* 2d ed., 451-452. Chicago, American Library Association, 1986.

Wilken, G. C., et al. *Catalog of Holdings and Other References in the Lesotho MOA/LASA Library.* 1980.

Liberia

Armstrong, Charles Wesley. "Liberia." In *ALA World Encyclopedia of Library and Information Services,* 313-314. Chicago, American Library Association, 1980.

————— —————. *Ibid.,* 2d ed., 452-453. Chicago, American Library Association, 1986.

—————"Liberia." In *International Handbook of Contemporary Developments in Librarianship;* ed. by Miles M. Jackson, 41-50. Westport, CT, Greenwood Press, 1981.

Newman, D. L. "Oral Interviewing in Liberia: Problems in Cross-cultural Communication." *International Journal of Oral History* 7(1986): 116-125.

Roper, M. *Liberia: National Archives Centre.* Paris, Unesco, 1983.

Madagascar

Rakoto, Rabakonirina. "Madagascar: développement de bibliothèques" (Madagascar: Library Development). *Information Development* 2(1986): 165-166.

Ratsimandrava, Juliette. "Madagascar." In *ALA World Encyclopedia of Library and Information Services,* 338-339. Chicago, American Library Association, 1980.

————— —————. *Ibid.,* 2d ed., 508-509. Chicago, American Library Association, 1986.

Malawi

Beinart, William. "Films in the National Archives of Malawi: a Preliminary Report." *MALA Bulletin* 4(1984): 13-17.

Chilambe, P. "The Malawi Foreign Trade Statistics Information System." *Information Technology Research and Development* 2(1987): 193-202.

Mamomba, Rodrick S. "Malawi." In *ALA World Encyclopedia of Library and Information Services*, 339. Chicago, American Library Association, 1980.

Malawi National Bibliography. 1967- . Zomba, National Archives of Malawi.

Malawi National Library Service Board. *Annual Report*. 1969- . Lilongwe.

Msiska, Augustine W. C. "Early Efforts at Creating African Literature: its Distribution, Local Authorship and Library Service in Northern Rhodesia (Zambia) and Nysaland (Malawi)." *Libri* 36(1986): 240-246.

Mwiyeriwa, Steve S. "Malawi." In *ALA World Encyclopedia of Library and Information Services*, 509-510. 2d ed. Chicago, American Library Association, 1986.

Namponya, Clemence R. "Agricultural Development and Library Services." *International Library Review* 18(1986): 267-274.

Ngaunje, Michael A. "Library Services in the North—in Brief." *MALA Bulletin* 4(1984): 31-33.

Mali

Koita, Al Hady. "Mali." (Trans. Mary Niles Maack) In *ALA World Encyclopedia of Library and Information Services*, 513-514. 2d ed. Chicago, American Library Association, 1986.

Konare, Alpha Oumar. "Mali." In *ALA World Encyclopedia of Library and Information Services*, 341-342. Chicago, American Library Association, 1980.

Mauritania

Diouwara, Oumar. "Mauritania, Islamic Republic of." In *ALA World Encyclopedia of Library and Information Services*, 347. Chicago, American Library Association, 1980.

————— —————. *Ibid.*, 2d ed., 520. Chicago, American Library Association, 1986.

Mauritius

Benoit, Marie. "Mauritius—et lite land med mange språk og kulturer: Bibliotekjenesten må vaere et produkt av lokalmiljøet" (Mauritius—a Small Country with Many Languages and Cultures: the Library Service Must be a Product of the Local Environment). *Bok og Bibliotek* 52(1985): 65-67.

Jean-François, Louis Sydney. "Mauritius." In *ALA World Encyclopedia of Library and Information Services*, 347-348. Chicago, American Library Association, 1980.

————— —————. *Ibid.*, 2d ed., 521-522. Chicago, American Library Association, 1986.

Wong Ko Nang, N. "The Sales Tax System in Mauritius." *Information Technology Research and Development* 2(1987): 203.

Mozambique

"Mozambique." In *ALA World Encyclopedia of Library and Information Services*, 566-567. 2d ed. Chicago, American Library Association, 1986.

Shechkov, Boris N. "The Computerized Documentary Information Retrieval System of the Mozambique Meteorological Services." *International Forum on Information and Documentation* 10(1985): 10-12.

Namibia

Armstrong, James C. "Report from a Seminar on Namibian Bibliography and Documentation." *Library of Congress Information Bulletin* 45(1986): 126-127.
Cimbebasia. 1962- . Windhoek, State Museum Library.
Pieterse, Patricia Barbara, and Maria Margaritha Viljoen. "Namibia." In *ALA World Encyclopedia of Library and Information Services,* 573-575. 2d ed. Chicago, American Library Association, 1986.
Pieterse, Patricia Barbara, and S. H. van den Berg. "Namibia." In *ALA World Encyclopedia of Library and Information Services,* 386-387. Chicago, American Library Association, 1980.
South West Africa Scientific Society Library. *Botanic Newsletter.* Windhoek.
————*Newsletter.* Windhoek.
————*Ornithological Newsletter.* Windhoek

Niger

Central Intelligence Agency, Washington, DC *Niger.* (Map no. 59203) 1969. (NTIS: PB82-928033)
Etudes nigériennes. 1953- . Niamey, Institut de Recherches en Sciences Humaines.
"Niger." In *ALA World Encyclopedia of Library and Information Services,* 604-605. 2d ed. Chicago, American Library Association, 1986.

Nigeria

Agumanu, Joan N. "Serials in Third World Academic and Research Libraries." *The Serials Librarian* 11(1986): 55–61.
Aguolu, Christian C. "The Future of Library and Information Services in Nigeria." *International Library Movement* 8(1986): 54–68.
Aina, L. O. "Availability of Periodical Titles Cited in the Literature of Nigeria's Scientific Research in Nigerian Libraries." *Bendel Library Journal* 7(1984): 18–25.
Ajayi-Dopemu, Y. "Educating through Television in Nigeria." *Journal of Educational Television* 11(1985): 115–122.
Aje, Simeon B. "Nigeria." In *ALA World Encyclopedia of Library and Information Services,* 411–413. Chicago, American Library Association, 1980.
Alali, A. O. "Nigerian Participation in INTELSAT. An Analysis of Communications Development." *Dissertation Abstracts International* 46(1986): 2845-A.
Dosunmu, J. A. "Nigeria." In *ALA World Encyclopedia of Library and Information Services,* 605–606. 2d ed. Chicago, American Library Association, 1986.
Egbon, M. "TV Development and Unity in Nigeria." *Media in Education and Development* 15(1982): 81–85.
Franklin Book Programs, Inc. *Books for Ghana and Nigeria.* New York, Franklin Book Programs, Inc., 1962.
Gana, F. Z. *Distance Education. A Nigerian Perspective.* 1984. ERIC. Ed 253 196.
Ifidon, Sam E. "The Evaluation of Performance." *Libri* 36(1986): 224–239.
Igwe, Ukoha O. "Planning Library Extension Services in Nigeria." *Library Scientist* 13(1986): 19–34.

Nwafor, B. U. "Staff Development in Nigerian Libraries." In *Aspects of African Librarianship: a Collection of Writings*, comp. and ed. by Michael Wise, 166–181. London, Mansell, 1985.
Nwagha, Georgiana Ngeri. "Nigerian Users and Document Delivery." *Canadian Library Journal* 44(1987): 46–47.
Nwoye, S. C. "Nigeria." In *International Handbook of Contemporary Developments in Librarianship*, ed by Miles M. Jackson, 51–69. Westport, CT, Greenwood Press, 1981.
Nzotta, Briggs C. "Serials Librarianship in Nigeria, 1975–1985." *Serials Librarian* 10(1985): 269–279.
Ogundipe, O. O. *Conservation of Library Material in Tropical Conditions. The Example of Nigeria.* 1980. ERIC. ED 211 037.
Olanlokun, S. Olajire, ed. "Reference Services in Nigerian Libraries Today." *Lagos Librarian* 10(1983): 1–184.
Olden, Edward Anthony. "Expatriates." In *Information consultants in Action*, ed. by J. Stephen Parker, 98–108. London, Mansell, 1986.
Talabi, J. K. "Maintenance Needs of Educational Equipment in Nigeria." *Journal of Educational Television* 12(1986): 49–53.

Nigeria—Acquisitions

Ayeni, Emmanuel Olu. "The Benefits, Politics and Attendant Problems Associated with Gifts, Donations, and Exchanges." *Library Scientist* 13(1986): 79–86.

Nigeria—Bibliographies and Bibliography

Baldwin, C. *Nigerian Literature. A Bibliography of Criticism, 1952–1976.* Boston, G. K. Hall, 1980.
Bankoke, Beatrice S. *Use of the International Standard Bibliographic Description (ISBD) in Nigeria.* 1980. ERIC. ED 208 800.
Ita, Nduntuei O. "Problems of Bibliographic Control in Nigeria." *Libri* 36(1986): 320–335.

Nigeria—Book Trade, Printing and Publishing

Franklin Book Programs, Inc. *A Book Development Project in Nigeria, 1964–1968.* Final Report Submitted to the Ford Foundation [and] the United States Agency for International Development. New York, Franklin Book Programs, Inc. 1968.
—— *Books for Ghana and Nigeria.* New York, Franklin Book Programs, Inc., 1962.
Mohammed, Zakari. "Arguments for and against Nigerians Publishing at Home or Overseas." *Library Scientist* 11(1984): 104–114.
Olanlokun, S. Olajire. "Publishing of Learned Journals in Nigeria." *Libri* 35(1985): 333–340.

Nigeria—Cataloging and Classification

Adegbule-Adesida, E. K. "The Use of Cataloguing in Publication (CIP) Data in Cataloguing Practice: a Survey." *Bendel Library Journal* 7(1984): 20–33.

Nigeria—Cooperation

Malumfashi, Mansur Usman. "Library Resource Sharing: a Challenge to Nigerian Libraries in the Period of Economic Emergency." *Library Scientist* 13(1986): 99–115.

Nigeria—Documentation and Information services

Agajelu, S. I. "On the Establishment of a Geodetic Data Base in Nigeria." In *Proceedings of the International Symposium on Management of Geodetic Data, Copenhagen, Denmark, 24–26 August 1981*, 283–303. Copenhagen, Geodetic Institute, 1981.

Agha, Stella J. "Constraints on Library Automation in Nigeria." *Information Development* 2(1986): 159–162.

—— "Library Automation in Nigeria: Achievements and Constraints on Progress." *Program* 20(1986): 409–414.

Akinyemi, A. "The WAI Game. A Case Study of a Low Cost Social Reform Approach in Nigeria." *Simulation/Games for Learning* 17(1987): 19–28.

Alabi, G. A. "Constraints on Library Automation in Nigeria." *Information Development* 2(1986): 163–164.

—— "Some Technical Factors for the Design of a Computer-based Circulation System for Nigerian University Librarians." *Journal of Library and Information Science* (India) 8(1983): 146–156.

Banjo, A. Olugboyega. "Efforts at Computerization in Nigerian Libraries: a State of Online Development Review." *INSPEL* 20(1986): 221–223.

Igwe, Paul O. E. "The Electronic Age and Libraries: Present Problems and Future Prospects." *International Library Review* 18(1986): 75–84.

Jimba, Samule Wodi. "A Thesaurus for Indexing Nigerian Newspapers—a Research Report." *Library Scientist* 12(1985): 60–68.

Oguntunde, A. Omatayo. "Problems of Scientific Terminology in Nigeria." In *Networking in Terminology*, 253–258. Saur, 1986.

Olorunsola, R. A Case for the Application of Computers in Nigerian Libraries." *Library Scientist* 13(1986): 46–54.

Tague, Jean, and Isola Ajiferuke. "The Markov and the Mixed Poisson Models of Library Circulation Compared." *Journal of Documentation* 43(1987): 212–231.

Vega-Catalan, F. "A Nonlinear Curve Fitting Program for Functions with Separable Parameters." *Computers and Chemistry* 11(1987): 185–194.

Nigeria—Librarians and Librarianship

Aina, Lenrie O. "Factors Affecting Development of Librarianship in Nigeria." *International Library Review* 11 (1979): 57–67.

Nzotta, Briggs Chinkata. "A Comparative Study of the Job Satisfaction of Academic and Public Librarians in Nigeria." *African Journal of Academic Librarianship* 2(1984): 6–11.

—— "Job Mobility of Librarians in a Developing Country." *Pakistan Library Bulletin* 16(1985): 1–10.

Nigeria—Libraries and Education

Bello, Nassir. "Libraries and the New National Policy on Education in Nigeria." *Library Scientist* 11(1984): 54–64.

Mohammed, Zakari. "An Autopsy of the Role of Libraries as Agents of Education in Nigeria." *Library Scientist* 12(1985): 98–123.

Nigeria—Library Education

Aboyade, B. Olabimpe. "Education and Training of the Information Professionals in Nigeria—Establishing an Identity." *Journal of Library and Information Science* (India) 9(1984): 65–84.

Ashby, R. "Report to Nigerian Library Association on Library Training." 1960. (unpublished)

Igwe, Benedict Onyechinyere. "The Values of the Librarian: a Cross-cultural Study of the Students of Library and Information Science in the United States and Nigeria." Ph. D. diss., University of Maryland, 1981.

Nzotta, Briggs Chinkata. "Education and Training of Library Personnel in Nigeria: Some Challenges for the Next Decade." *Education for Information* 3(1985): 39–49.

Ochai, Adakole. "In Search of Relevance in Library Education in Nigeria." *International Library Review* 19(1987): 261–269.

Onadiran, G. Tunde. "Library Experience as a Requirement for Admission into Library Schools in Nigeria." *International Library Movement* 7(1985): 16–22.

Nigeria—Library Education—Ahmadu Bello University

Afolabi, Michael. "Subject and Geographical Analyses of Final Year Undergraduate Library Science Projects." *Library Scientist* 11(1984): 32–44.

Ekoja, Innocent Isa. "The Proposed Four-year A. B. U. Bachelor of Library Science Programme and the Place of its Graduates in Academic Libraries." *Library Scientist* 11(1984): 24–31.

Onadiran, G. Tunde. "Bachelor of Library Science Programme of Ahmadu Bello University, Nigeria." *Library Scientist* 11(1984): 14–23.

Osaniyi, Olanrewaju. "The Popularity of the Courses on Organization of Knowledge among Library Science Students of the Ahmadu Bello University." *Library Scientist* 12(1985): 26–40.

Nigeria—Library Education—Imo State University

Nwakoby, M. A. "Field Work: a Component of the Library Education Program at Imo State University, Nigeria." *Journal of Education for Library and Information Science* 27(1987): 302–304.

Nigeria—Library Education—University of Maiduguri

Alemna, Anaba A., and Dittakavi N. Rao. "Library Education in Nigeria: a Review of the Bachelor of Library Science Programme at the University of Maiduguri, Nigeria." *Library Scientist* 11(1984): 45–53.

Nigeria—Professional Associations

Obi, Dorothy S. *The Role of Library Associations in the Continuing Education of School Librarians.* 1985. ERIC. ED 274 342.

Ogunyemi, Olatunji. "Keynote Address." *Nigerian School Library Journal* 1(1978): 3–9.

Ogunsheye, F. Adetowun. "Welcome Address to the Launching of the Nigerian School Library Association." *Nigerian School Library Journal* 1(1978): 1–2.

Nigeria—Academic Libraries

Adelabu, Adedeji. "Wanted: Research Oriented Professionals in Nigeria's Academic Libraries to Meet the Changing Demands and New Challenges in Academia." *African Journal of Academic Librarianship* 2(1984): 61–64.

Alabi, G. A. "Library Automation in Nigerian Universities." *Information Development* 2(1986): 163–164.

Elemide, I. B., and P. Havard-Williams. "University Libraries in Nigeria's National Library Provision." *International Library Review* 18(1986): 179–186.

Ibrahim, J. L. "Serials Librarianship in Nigerian University Libraries: the Experience of a Serials Librarian." *Library Scientist* 11(1984): 80–85.

Ifidon, Sam E. "Collection Development in Nigerian University Libraries." In *Aspects of African Librarianship: a Collection of Writings*, comp. and ed. by Michael Wise, 31–49. London, Mansell, 1985.

—— "Scientific Approach to Library Management." *African Journal of Academic Librarianship* 2(1984): 12–20.

Igbinosa, Isaac Osa. "AVM [audio-visual materials] in Nigerian Academic Libraries." *Audiovisual Librarian* 12(1986): 23›5.

Kadiri, J. A. "Problems with Non-book Materials in Nigerian Academic Libraries." *Audiovisual Librarian* 13(1987): 23–25.

Ochai, Adakole. "Management Development Needs of Library Managers in University Libraries in Nigeria." *Library and Information Science Research* 7(1985): 357–368.

—— "Management Development Needs of Lower and Middle Managers in University Libraries in Nigeria." *Dissertation Abstracts International* 46(1985): 827-A.

Sanusi, K. A. "Processing in Acquisition Department of a University Library (Collection Development)." *Library Scientist* 13(1986): 87–98.

Unomah, J. I. "Student Utilization of Academic Libraries in Nigeria: an Assessment." *Journal of Library and Information Science* (India) 10(1985): 170–182.

Womboh, Simmons H. "A Plan for the Development of Selected Technological University Libraries in Nigeria." *Collection Management* 8(1986): 79–99.

Nigeria—Academic Libraries—Ahmadu Bello University

Akhidime, J. A. Fab. "The Status of Reference Books in the Social Sciences in Kashim Ibrahim Library Ahmadu Bello University, Zaria." *Library Scientist* 12(1985): 79–89.

Alafiatayo, Benjamin O., and Joash T. Aleraiye. "Samaru Public Library: an Example of a University Public Library Service in Nigeria." *Information Development* 3(1987): 36–39.

Sanusi, K. A. "Participative Management in Nigerian University Libraries: a Practical Application in the Case of Kashim Ibrahim Library." *Library Scientist* 11(1984): 121–127.

Stephen, Peter. "The Stripdex Catalogue." *Library Review* 21(1967): 137–139.

Nigeria—Academic Libraries—University of Calabar

Kwasitsu, Lishi. "The University of Calabar Definitive Library Building: History and Future Development." *International Library Review* 19(1987): 73–80.

Nigeria—Academic Libraries—University of Ibadan

Alabi, G. A. "A Cost Comparison of Manual and Automated Circulation Systems in University Libraries: the Case of Ibadan University Library." *Information Processing & Management* 21(1985): 525–533.

Odularu, S. S. A. "The Manuscript Collection of Ibadan University Library." *Libri* 37(1987): 321–333.

Nigeria—Academic Libraries—University of Ilorin

Ajileye, E. O. "User Frustration in Libraries: a Case Study of University of Ilorin Library." *Bendel Library Journal* 7(1984): 33–45.

Nigeria—Academic Libraries—University of Lagos

Agboola, A. T. "Shelvers and their Attitudes to Shelving in a University Library." *Bendel Library Journal* 7(1984): 3–17.
Olanlokun, S. Olajire, and H. S. Issah. "Collection Development in an African Academic Library during Economic Depression: the University of Lagos Library Experience." *Library Acquisitions* 11(1987): 103–111.
Osundina, Oyeniya. "Improved Accessibility and Undergraduate Use of the Academic Library." *International Library Review* 7(1975): 77–81.

Nigeria—Academic Libraries—University of Maiduguri

Akhidime, J. A. Fab. "Focus on the University of Maiduguri Library Services." *African Journal of Academic Librarianship* 2(1984): 65–68.

Nigeria—Academic Libraries—University of Port Harcourt

Obiagwu, M. C. "Foreign Exchange and Library Collections in Nigeria." *Information Development* 3(1987): 154–160.

Nigeria—Children's Library Services

Ibeabuchi, Aloysius. "Many Things to Exploit—the Work of the Nigerian Illustrator Charles Ohu." *Bookbird* [24], no. 2(1986): 63–64.
Obokoh, N. P. "Toy Library: a Missing Link in the Life of the Under School Age Child in Nigeria." *Bendel Library Journal* 7(1984): 43–47.
Segun, Mabel D. "Children's Literature at the 10th Ife Book Fair." *Bookbird* [24], no. 2(1986): 32–34.

Nigeria—National Library of Nigeria

Adeniji, Adegoke, and H. S. Issah. "National Library of Nigeria: Objectives, Functions, Achievements." *Libri* 36(1986): 136–145.
"Nigerian National Library." *Federal Nigeria* 7(1964): 10–13.

Nigeria—Public Libraries

Alegbeley, G. D. "The Non-use of Nigerian Public Libraries by the Silent Majority: a Historical Survey and Discursus." *Libri* 36(1986): 187–201.
Harrison, Kalu U., and Peter Havard-Williams. "Motivation in a Third World Library System." *International Library Review* 19(1987): 249–260.
Igbinosa, Isaac Osa. "The Public Library Services in Nigeria: Need for Information and Referral (IR) Service." *Public Library Quarterly* 7(1986): 63–71.
Nzotta, Briggs C. "Acquisitions Policy in a Developing Economy: a Case Study of Nigerian State (Public) Libraries." *Collection Building* 7, no. 4(1985): 3–8.

Nigeria—Public Libraries—Former Eastern Region

Eastern Nigeria Library Board. *Consolidation and the Future. 7th Annual Report.* Enugu, 1965.

Nigeria—Public Libraries—Anambra State

Muogilim, Emma S., ed. *Three Decades of Librarianship in Anambra State of Nigeria.* Np, Nigeria Library Association, Anambra State Division, nd.

Nigeria—Public Libraries—Bendel State

Egor, F. O. "A Preliminary Study of the Clientele Structure of Public Libraries: Bendel State Library, Benin City." *Bendel Library Journal* 7(1984): 46–57.

Nigeria—Public Libraries—Kaduna State

Boman, Daniel D. "Job Satisfaction among the Junior Staff of Kaduna State Library Board." *Library Scientist* 12(1985): 132–138.

Gwabin, John Nuhu. "User Satisfaction Survey of Kaduna State Library Services." *Library Scientist* 13(1986): 71–78.

Nigeria—School Libraries

Akinyemi, K. "A Study of Technophobia among Primary School Teachers in Nigeria." *Programmed Learning and Educational Technology* 23(1986): 263–269.

"Guidelines for Nigeria Legislation for School Libraries/Media Resource Centres." *Nigerian School Library Journal* 1(1978): 39–43.

Ihebuzor, N. A. "Appropriate Instructional Media Selection (AIMS): an Issue in Educational Technology in the Nigerian School System." *British Journal of Educational Technology* 17(1986): 94–102.

Igwe, Paul O. E. "The Trainee-Teacher and Instructional Media." *Herald of Library Science* 24(1985): 189–194.

Nigerian School Library Journal. Oct. 1978– . Nigerian School Library Association.

Ogunsheye, F. Adetowun. "Abadina Media Resource Centre (AMRC): a Case Study in Library Service to Primary Schools." *Nigerian School Library Journal* 1(1978): 11–25.

——— *A Perspective from Developing Countries.* 1982. ERIC. ED 239 615.

Utor, J. K. "School Librarian as Educational Facilitator." *Library Scientist* 11(1984): 70–79.

Wali, Mu'Azu H. "The Role of School Libraries." *Nigerian School Library Journal* 1(1978): 35–38.

Nigeria—Secondary School and College Libraries

Gwang, James Mato. "Collections of Three College Libraries in Plateau State, Nigeria." *Library Scientist* 12(1985): 69–78.

Rao, Dittakavi N. "College Libraries within Library Networks." *Library Scientist* 11(1984): 65–69.

Sekharan, K. Raja. "On Visiting College Libraries." *International Library Movement* 7(1985): 23–26.

Nigeria—Special Libraries, Materials and Services

Adedigba, Yakub A. "Forestry Researchers as Information Users in Nigeria." *Information Development* 1(1985): 229–233.

Igwe, Paul O. E. "Audiovisual Network for Nigeria: a Proposal." *Herald of Library Science* 25(1986): 27–36.

Nzotta, Briggs Chinkata. "Providing Information for Research: Federal Research Institute Libraries in Nigeria." *Information Development* 1(1985): 223–228.

Okorafor, E. E. "Maintaining Local Newspaper Collections in Nigerian Libraries." *Information Development* 3(1987): 161–166.

Ononogbo, R. U. "Audio-visual Resources in Some Major Nigerian Libraries." *Library Scientist* 13(1986): 35–45.

Samuel, Sarah. "The Relationship between the Organizational Placement and Budgeting in Some Selected Special Libraries in Zaria." *Library Scientist* 12(1985): 124–131.

Utor, J. K. The Use of Research Libraries in Zaria: two Case Studies." *Library Scientist* 13(1986): 56–70.

Woakes, Harriet. "Recent Developments in the Use of Audiovisual Materials in Nigeria: Implications for Librarians." *Audiovisual Librarian* 12(1986): 26–31.

Nigeria—Special Libraries, Materials and Services—Agriculture

Aina, Lenrie O. "Agricultural Information Provision in Nigeria." *Information Development* 2(1986): 242–244.

———— "Grey Literature and Agricultural Research in Nigeria." *Quarterly Bulletin of the International Association of Agricultural Librarians and Documentalists* 32(1987): 47–50.

———— "Information Needs and Information-seeking Involvement of Farmers in Six Rural Communities in Nigeria." *Quarterly Bulletin of the International Association of Agricultural Librarians and Documentalists* 30(1985): 35–40.

Ezeji, J., and F. C. Ekere. "Readers' Requirements of Catalogue, Descriptive Items in a Special Library." *Library Scientist* 11(1984): 86–91.

"Library Automation at IITA [International Institute of Tropical Agriculture]." *Quarterly Bulletin of the International Association of Agricultural Librarians and Documentalists* 31(1986): 174–175.

Odiba, N. K. "An Evaluation Survey of the Information Services in the National Crop Research Institute Library, Umudike, Umuahia." *Library Scientist* 12(1985): 90–97.

Oladele, Benedict Adekunle. "Toward an Integrated Agricultural Information Consolidation Scheme for Farmers in the Nigerian Rural Areas." *Quarterly Bulletin of the International Association of Agricultural Librarians and Documentalists* 32(1987): 97–101.

Oruma, Oviss. "The Problem of Information Management in Agriculture." *Quarterly Bulletin of the International Association of Agricultural Librarians and Documentalists* 29(1984): 91–94.

Nigeria—Special Libraries, Materials and Services—Handicapped

Gupta, Sushma. "Library Resources and Services for the Deaf Children in the Secondary Schools of Ibadan—a Survey." *International Library Movement* 7(1985): 129–140.

Nigeria—Special Libraries, Materials and Services— Medicine and Health Sciences

Agbalajobi, F. "The Unstructured Approach to Medical Computing in Nigeria." In *MEDINFO 80. Proceedings of the Third World Conference on Medical Informatics, Tokyo, Japan, 29 Sept.-4 Oct. 1980*, 656–659. Amsterdam, Netherlands, North-Holland, 1980.

Fowowe, Samuel O. "An Appraisal of Library Facilities and Services at the Medical Library of the University of Ilorin, Nigeria." *Bulletin of the Medical Library Association* 75(1987): 39–41.

Hunponu-Wusu, O. O. "Information Systems and Computer Science Modules in the Training of Community Physicians in Developing Countries. The Experience of Lagos, Nigeria." In

Medical Informatics Europe 82. Proceedings, Dublin, March 1982, 662. Berlin, Springer Verlag, 1982.

Igwe, Paul O. E. "Overcoming Communication Barriers in a Multi-campus Teaching Hospital through the Use of Two-way Radio: a Nigerian Example." *Bendel Library Journal* 7(1984): 8–19.

Osiobe, Stephen A. "A Study of the Use of Information Sources by Medical Faculty Staff in Nigerian Universities." *Journal of Information Science* 12(1986): 177–183.

Nigeria—Special Libraries, Materials and Services—Social Sciences

Banjo, A. Olugboyega. "Problems in the Storage and Dissemination of Newspaper Information: a Nigerian Example [Nigerian Institute of International Affairs]." *INSPEL* 19(1985): 65–80.

Rwanda

Borchardt, Peter. "Bibliotheken in Rwanda. Kleines Land-grosse Problems" (Libraries in Rwanda. A Small Country-Big Problems). *Bibliotheksdienst* 20(1986): 1111–1118.

Hategekimana, Grégoire. "L'information scientifique et technique, la politique de développement et la circulation de l'information nécessaire à l'application de la science et la technique au Rwanda" (Scientific and Technical Information, the Policy of Development and the Circulation of Information Necessary to the Application of Science and Technology in Rwanda). *Education et Culture* (Apr-June 1980)

Serugendo, Emmanuel. "Rwanda." In *ALA World Encyclopedia of Library and Information Services*, 489. Chicago, American Library Association, 1980.

————————. *Ibid.*, 2d ed., 717–719. Chicago, American Library Association, 1986.

Senegal

BLIBAD: Bulletin de Liaison à l'Intention des Bibliothécaires, Archivistes, et Documentalistes Africains. Jan. 1976– . Dakar, Senegal, Ecole des Bibliothécaires, Archivistes et Documentalistes, Université de Dakar.

Ndiaye, Théodore. "Seminaire national sur l'acces universel aux publications (UAP), Dakar, 6–9 janvier 1986" (National Seminar on Universal Availability of Publications (UAP), Dakar, January 6–9, 1986). *IFLA Journal* 12(1986): 336–338.

Ndiaye, Waly. "Senegal." (Tr. Mary Niles Maack). In *ALA World Encyclopedia of Library and Information Services*, 755–756. 2d ed. Chicago, American Library Association, 1986.

Séne, Henri. "Le commerce du livre de langue arabe au Sénégal jusqu'au début de 20e siecle" (The Arab Language Book Industry of Senegal to the Beginning of the 20th Century). *Libri* 36(1986): 146–159.

Veaux, Marie Gabrielle. "Senegal." In *ALA World Encyclopedia of Library and Information Services*, 520–521. Chicago, American Library Association, 1980.

Senegal—Library Education

Abid, Abelaziz, and Mohamed Benjelloun. "La formation des spécialistes de l'information au Mahgreb et au Sénégal" (The Training of Information Specialists in the Maghreb and in Senegal). *Bulletin des Bibliothèques de France* 30(1985): 62–67.

Seychelles

Roda, Jean-Claude. "Seychelles." In *ALA World Encyclopedia of Library and Information Services*, 521. Chicago, American Library Association, 1980.
——— ———. *Ibid.*, 2d ed., 757. Chicago, American Library Association, 1986.

Sierra Leone

Fourah Bay College. *Library Catalog of the Sierra Leone Collection, Fourah Bay College Library, University of Sierra Leone.* Boston, G. K. Hall, 1979.
Jusu-Sheriff, Gladys M. "Sierra Leone." In *ALA World Encyclopedia of Library and Information Services*, 526–527. Chicago, American Library Association, 1980.
——— ———. *Ibid.*, 2d ed., 764–765. Chicago, American Library Association, 1986.
Kamara, Kade. "Library Services to Children and Young People in Sierra Leone." *Bookbird* [24], no. 1(1986): 15–17.

Sierra Leone—Public Libraries

Havard-Williams, Peter. *Sierra Leone. Development of Public Library Services.* Paris, Unesco, 1984.

Somalia

Gowda, G. Thimme. "Somalia." In *ALA WORLD Encyclopedia of Library and Information Services*. 767,,68. 2d ed. Chicago, American Library Association, 1986.
Hutchinson, P. "The Installation of a Microcomputer System in Somalia." *Information Technology Research and Development* 2(1987): 223–230.
Rajagopalan, T. S. "Somalia." In *ALA World Encyclopedia of Library and Information Services*, 529. Chicago, American Library Association, 1980.
——— *Somalia: Development of Services in the National Library.* Paris, Unesco, 1983.

Sudan

Aman, Mohammed M., and Sha'Ban A. Khalifa. "Sudan." In *ALA World Encyclopedia of Library and Information Services*, 786–787. 2d ed. Chicago, American Library Association, 1986.
El Sammani, A. Y. "Information Required by Scientists, Research Managers and Science Policy-makers for Conditions in the Sudan." In *UNISIST International Symposium on Information Systems and Services in Ongoing Research in Science. Proceedings*, 103–111. Hungarian Central Technical Library and Documentation Centre, 1976.
International Federation for Documentation. *Sudan: Librarianship, Documentation.* Budapest, FID/DC "Developing Countries" Secretariat, Hungarian Central Technical Library and Documentation Centre, 1974.
Nur, Qasim Osman. "Sudan." In *ALA World Encyclopedia of Library and Information Services*, 548–549. Chicago, American Library Association, 1980.
O'Connor, Brigid. "The Role of Training in Development: Some Reflections from Sudan." *Focus on International & Comparative Librarianship* 17(1986): 4–5.
Sewell, Philip Hooper, and Cecile Wesley. "The Development of Library and Information Services in the Republic of Sudan in Relation to International Developments." In *Information Consultants in Action*, ed. by J. Stephen Parker, 224–251. London, Mansell, 1986.

Wesley, Cecile. "Information on Current Research in the Sudan." *Information Development* 1(1985): 217–222.

Swaziland

Kuzwayo, A. W. Z. *Information Systems and National Information Services in Swaziland.* Kwaluseni, University College of Swaziland Library, 1978.
——— "Swaziland." In *ALA World Encyclopedia of Library and Information Services*, 549–550. Chicago, American Library Association, 1980.
——— ———. *Ibid., 2d ed., 788–789.* Chicago, American Library Association, 1986.
Swaziland. Development of Library Services. Paris, Unesco, 1981.
Swaziland National Bibliography. 1976– . Kwaluseni, University of Swaziland Library.

Tanzania

Bourne, Charles P. *United Republic of Tanzania. Planning for a National Research Information Centre.* Paris, Unesco, 1974.
Grenholm, Lennart H. *Radio Study Group Campaigns in the United Republic of Tanzania.* Paris, Unesco, 1975.
Gulbraar, Kari, and Jorum Moen. "Bibliotek i Tanzania: Informasjon = utvikling" (The Library in Tanzania: Information = Development). *Bok og Bibliotek* 53(1986): 286–287.
Hall, B. L. *Mtu Ni Afya (Man in Health): Tanzania's Health Campaign.* 1978. ERIC: ED 216 682.
Kagan, Alfred. "Literacy, Libraries, and Underdevelopment—with Special Attention to Tanzania." *Africana Journal* 13(1982): 1–23.
Kaungamno, Ezekiel E. *The Book Industry in Tanzania.* 1980. ERIC: ED 220 083.
——— "Tanzania." In *ALA World Encyclopedia of Library and Information Services*, 554–555. Chicago, American Library Association, 1980.
——— ———. *Ibid., 2d ed.*, 796–797. Chicago, American Library Association, 1986.
——— ———. In *International Handbook of Contemporary Developments in Librarianship*, ed. by Miles M. Jackson, 105–116. Westport, CT, Greenwood Press, 1981.
Lahti, Marjatta. "ANC kiittää suomalaista kirjastoväkeä avusta" (ANC[African National Congress] Thanks Finland's Library Community for its Help). *Kirjastolehti* 78(1985): 330–331.
Massamba, D. P. B. "Terminology as a Prerequisite for Language Development—the Case of Kiswahili." In *Networking in Terminology: International Co-operation in Terminology Work*, 572–580. Munich, West Germany, K. G. Saur, 1986.
Mdee, James S. "Terminology and Knowledge Transfer in Tanzania." In *Networking in Terminology*, 259–268. Munich, West Germany, K. G. Saur, 1986.
Petersen, Jette. "Bibliotheker i Tanzania: Kommunikation og fremskridt" (Libraries in Tanzania: Communication and Progress). *Bibliotek* 70(1985): 700–702.
Rulagora, D. K. *Proposal for a Technical Information System for Transfer of Technology to Small Industries in Tanzania.* (Information Technology and Development Series. vol. 2. Informatics and Industrial Development). 1982. NTIS. AD-P001 498/5.
Schwarz, S., and A. Winkel. *Support for a National Research Information Service in Tanzania.* 1984. ERIC. ED 260 726.

Tanzania—Public Libraries

Ilomo, Charles S. "The History and Work of Tanzania Library Service 1963–80." In *Aspects of African Librarianship: a Collection of Writings*, comp. and ed. by Michael Wise, 98–153. London, Mansell, 1985.

—— *Is the NCL [National Central Library, Dar es Salaam] a National Library?* 1979. ERIC. ED 220 086.

Mung'ong'o, C. G. *An Investigation into the Nature, Trend, and Implications of the 1973–1976 TLS [Tanzania Library Service] Issue Decline.* 1978. ERIC. ED 220 075.

Mwasha, A. Z. *Some Considerations for the Planning of Village Libraries in Tanzania.* 1979. ERIC. ED 220 084.

Ngozi, I. S. "Public Libraries and Local Government: Challenges ahead in Tanzania." *Libri* 37(1987): 72–83.

Tanzania—School and Children's Library Services

Ilomo, Charles S. *Towards More Effective School Library Programmes in Tanzania.* 1978. ERIC.ED 220 088.

Nyalusi, G. P. J. *The Role of Tanzania Library Service in Informal Education to Pre-school and Primary Schools in Tanzania.* 1979. ERIC. ED 220 085.

Slang, Live. "Bibliotektilbud til barn og unge i Tanzania" (Library Services for Children and Youth in Tanzania). *Bok og Bibliotek* 53(1986): 283–285.

Tanzania—Special Libraries

Gessesse, Kebede. "The Role of the Sokvine University of Agriculture Library as Provider of Agricultural Information." *Quarterly Bulletin of the International Association of Agricultural Librarians and Documentalists* 32(1987): 113–114.

Kaungamno, E. E. *Information for Agricultural Development.* 1979. ERIC. ED 220 076.

Masdalen, Kjell-Olav. "Arkivsamarbeid Tanzania-Norge" (Archival Cooperation between Tanzania and Norway). *Nordisk Arkivnyt* 30(1985): 76–76 [sic]

Mlaki, Theophilus E. "The National Bibliographic Agency of Tanzania" *IFLA Journal* 12(1986): 352–355.

Thurston, Anne. "The Zanzibar Archives Project." *Information Development* 2(1986): 223–226.

Togo

Etudes togolaises. 1965– . Lomé, Institut National de la Recherche Scientifique.

Giradot, Nicole. Relations entre les bibliothèques de la ville de Grenoble et la bibliothèque de Dapaong au Togo" (Relations between the Libraries of the City of Grenoble and the Library of Dapaong in Togo). *Bulletin d'Information de l'Association des Bibliothècaires Français* 132(1986): 11–12.

"Togo." In *ALA World Encyclopedia of Library and Information Services,* 559. Chicago, American Library Association, 1980.

—— *Ibid.,* 2d. ed., 802–803. Chicago, American Library Association, 1986.

Uganda

Harris, Gordon. "Political Instability and the Information World in Uganda." *African Research & Documentation* 37(1985): 42–46.

Kawesa, Boniface M. "Uganda." In *ALA World Encyclopedia of Library and Information Services,* 811–813. 2d ed. Chicago, American Library Association, 1986.

Kibirige, Harry M. "Libraries and Illiteracy in Developing Countries: a Critical Assessment." *Libri* 27(1977): 54–67.

—— "Uganda." In *ALA World Encyclopedia of Library and Information Services*, 563–564. Chicago, American Library Association, 1980.

Unesco. *Regional Meetings of Experts on the National Planning of Documentaton and Library Services: Arab Republic of Egypt, 1974; Uganda, 1970; Sri Lanka, 1967; Ecuador, 1966. Summary of Main Recommendations.* Paris, 1974.

Uganda—Academic Libraries

Macpherson, Margaret. *They Built for the Future: a Chronicle of Makerere University College, 1922–1962.* Cambridge [Eng.], University Press, 1964.

Wood, Kate. "We Knelt Down and Prayed and God Spared Us." *Library Association Record* 89(1987): 29–30.

Zaire

Komba, Mafwala. "Formation des bibliothécaires—documentalistes au Zaire" (Training of Librarians—Documentalists in Zaire). *Documenatliste* 23(1986): 189–191.

Zaire. Bibliotheque Nationale. *Bibliographie nationale.* 1955– . Kinshasa-Gombe.

Zaire. Ministry of Fine Arts and Cultural Affairs. *Liste des bibliothèques publiques.* Kinshasa, 1971.

"Zaire." In *ALA World Encyclopedia of Library and Information Services*, 598–599. Chicago, American Library Association, 1980.

—— ——. 2d. ed., 865–866. Chicago, American Library Association, 1986.

Zambia

Hansen, Jens L. "Biblioteket i bushen" (The Library in the Bush). *Bibliotek* 70(1985): 629–631.

Kari, Peter Wulff. "Biblioteksarbejde i Zambia" (Library Work in Zambia). *Bogens Verden* 68(1986): 386.

—— "Et kulturhus i Zambia—med 5 bøger, produktion af tagplader og knaninavl—en historie fra det virkelige liv" (A Cultural Center in Zambia—with 5 Books, Production of Roofing Boards and Breeding of Rabbits—a Story of Real Life). *Bogens Verden* 67(1985): 207–208.

Mbewe, Godfrey L. "The Library and the Zambian Society." *Zambia Library Association Journal* 17(1985): 39–48.

Mohemedali, O. N. "Types of Educational Programmes in Zambia: Role and Relevance." In *Librarianship and Documentation Studies: a Handbook of Teaching and Learning Materials*, II, 82–90. Bonn, German Foundation for International Development, 1986.

—— "Zambia." In *ALA World Encyclopedia of Library and Information Services*, 867–869. 2d ed. Chicago, American Library Association, 1986.

Msiska, Augustine W. C. "Early Efforts at Creating African Literature: its Distribution, Local Authorship and Library Service in Northern Rhodesia (Zambia) and Nysaland (Malawi)." *Libri* 36(1986): 240–246.

National Bibliography of Zambia. 1970/71– . Lusaka, National Archives.

Nyirenda, J. E., and A. Kakanda. "Distance Education at the University of Zambia." *Media in Education and Development* 15(1982): 22–25.

Phiri, Zilole M. K. "Book Budgets, Foreign Exchange Restrictions and their Impact on Collection Development in University, College, Technical and Research Libraries in Zambia: a Survey." *Zambia Library Association Journal* 15(1984): 30–50.

—— "Introducing AACR2 Zambian Libraries." *Zambia Library Association Journal* 17(1985): 1–6.

────── "Performance of the Library Profession in Zambia." *International Library Review* 18(1986): 259–266.

Siaciwena, R. M. C. "Continuing Education in Zambia." *Media in Education and Development* 16(1983): 165–169.

Wamulwange, Margaret S. "Informal Communication—a Feasible Alternative in Zambia?" *Zambia Library Association Journal* 17(1985): 19–30.

Wina, Danson K. "Librarianship in the Zambia Civil Service: a Case Study of Institutions of Higher Learning." *Zambia Library Association Journal* 15(1983): 13–24.

"Zambia." In *ALA World Encyclopedia of Library and Information Services*, 599–600. Chicago, American Library Association, 1980.

Zambia—Academic Libraries

Lundu, Maurice Chimfwembe. "Information Processing, Evaluation, and Utilization: the Role of Academic Libraries in Research and Development (R&D) in Zambia." *Information Processing & Management* 21(1985): 443–457.

Msiska, Augustine W. C. "An Attempt to Establish an Oral History Project in the University of Zambia Library, Lusaka Campus." *American Archivist* 50(1987): 142–146.

Phiri, Zilole M. K. "Groundwork for Implenting AACR2 in the University of Zambia (UNZA) Library." *Zambia Library Association Journal* 17(1985): 31–38, 64–71.

Rooke, Andrew, and A. Msiska. *Problems with the Acquisition and Bibliographic Control of Official Documents and their Accessibility to Citizens and Researchers. The Univeristy of Zambia Library Experience.* 1980. ERIC. ED 208 803.

Wina, Danson K. "Academic Status for Academic Libraries: the Zambian Experience." *Zambia Library Association Journal* 17(1985): 49–63.

Zambia—Public Libraries

Ocaya, Helen. "Outreach Library Services in Zambia: Possibilities." *Zambia Library Association Journal* 17(1985): 7–18.

Zambia—School Libraries

Kasheki, Mubanga E. "Keynote and Opening Address by the Principal of the University of Zambia at Ndola to the Copperbelt Branch of the Zambia Library Association Seminar." *Zambia Library Association Journal* 16(1984): 1–12.

Lundu, Maurice C. "Closing Address." *Zambia Library Association Journal* 16(1984): 65–69.

Lungu, Charles. "Secondary School Libraries on the Copperbelt: Report on Survey Conducted by the Copperbelt Branch of the Zambia Library Association in 1982." *Zambia Library Association Journal* 16(1984): 13–26.

Mwacalimba, Hudwell. "Manpower Training and Provision for School Libraries." *Zambia Library Association Journal* 16(1984): 27–34.

Tembo, Ethel M. "The Importance of Libraries in Zambia Secondary Schools." *Zambia Library Association Journal* 16(1984): 35–41.

Zambia—Special Libraries

Dall, Frank. "VILLAGE—a Minimum Structure Simulation Game Developed for Agricultural Extension Training in Central Africa (Zambia)." *Simulation/Games for Learning* 14(1984): 14–29.

Egaas, Marit. "Reisebrev frå Zambia" (Travel Letter from Zambia). *Bok og Bibliotek* 53(1986): 288–289.
Goldberg, Beverly. "Making Waves." *American Libraries* 18(1987): 624.
Sewell, Philip. "The Library of the Theological College of Central Africa (TCCA)." *Bulletin of the Association of British Theological and Phiosophical Libraries* 34/35(1986): 17–18.

Zimbabwe

Alison, William A. G. *A National Library Service for Zimbabwe: a Report to the British Council.* 1981.
Bright, S. "Video for Extension Workers in Zimbabwe." *Media in Education and Development* 18(1985): 171–174.
Dickinson, R. J. "A Structured Approach to the Production of Teacher Education Materials. The ZeSTT [Zimbabwe Science Teacher Training Project] Experience." *Journal of Educational Television* 10(1984): 79–83.
Dube, Sam R. "Zimbabwe: a National Library and Documentary Service Is Launched." *Information Development* 2(1986): 45–48.
Greenfield, Sir Cornelius, Chairman. *Report of the Rhodesia Library Commission, 1970.* 1971.
Hartikainen, Riitta. "Kehittyvän kirjaston maa: Zimbabwe" (Library Development in Zimbabwe). *Kirjastolehti* 78(1985): 14–15.
Johnson, Norman. "Zimbabwe Rhodesia." In *ALA World Encyclopedia of Library and Information Services*, 600–601. Chicago, American Library Association, 1980.
——— ———. *Ibid.*, 2d ed., 869–870. Chicago, American Library Association, 1986.
Kidd, R. *From People's Theatre for Revolution to Popular Theatre for Reconstruction. Diary of a Zimbabwean Workshop.* 1984. ERIC. ED 259 694.
Lahti, Marjatta. "Yhteistyöllä eteenpäin: pamberi ne kubutana!" (Cooperation is the Watchword: pamberi ne kubutana) *Kirjastolehti* 78(1985): 12–13.
Lalloo, Chagan, Kerstin Jonsson, and Nina Bergstrom. *Zimbabwe; National Library and Documentation Service: Report of the Swedish Library Mission.* 1982.
Made, Stan M., and Goodwell C. Motsi. "Alternative Ways of Providing Rural Information. Culture Houses: the Zimbabwean Experience." *Zimbabwe Librarian* 18(1986): 45–50.
Mupawaenda, Odysseus T. "Information Technology Transfer for Rural Development in Zimbabwe. *Zimbabwe Librarian* 18(1986): 11, 13–15, 18.
——— "A Zimbabwean Librarian Visits North Korea." *Information Development* 3(1987): 44–45.
Pakkiri, Devi. "Literacy in Zimbabwe: a Challenge to Libraries." *Zimbabwe Librarian* 18(1986): 4–5, 7–9.
——— "Time to Reflect." *Zimbabwe Librarian* 17(1985): 47, 50.
Robson, M. "Developing Teacher Education Resource Materials in Zimbabwe." *Media in Education and Development* 15(1982): 85–91.
Samuelson, Jeff. "The British Council and the Education and Training of Librarians in Zimbabwe." *Zimbabwe Librarian* 17(1985): 21, 23, 25, 27.
Stang, Kirsten Winsnes. "Zimbabwe Publishing House" [text in Norwegian] *Bok og Bibliotek* 53(1986): 290+.
Waungana, Ellen. "Oral Tradition, Reading and Issues Associated with the Transmission of Culture and History in Non-book-based Cultures." *Zimbabwe Librarian* 16(1984): 59, 61, 63–64.

Zimbabwe—Bibliographies and Bibliography

Kamba, Angeline S. "Bibliographic Control: Zimbabwe's Present Practices and Hopes for the Future." *Zimbabwe Librarian* 16(1984): 48–51.

Zimbabwe—Library Education

Kotei, S. I. A. *Zimbabwe: Library and Information Service Training School.* Paris, Unesco, 1984.
Podmore, Ann. "Library Education Begins in Zimbabwe." *Zimbabwe Librarian* 16(1984): 65, 67.

Zimbabwe—Public Libraries

Chinyemba, A. "Harare Municipal Library Services." *Zimbabwe Librarian* 18(1986): 59–61.
Doust, Robin. "Service to Samathonga: Bookmobile in the Bush." *Zimbabwe Librarian* 16(1984): 41–46.
Nkiwane, L. "Bulawayo Municipal Library Services." *Zimbabwe Librarian* 18(1986): 57–58.
Phillips, E. M. "Role of Municipal Libraries in the Development of Urban Communities." *Zimbabwe Librarian* 17(1985): 36–37, 39–40.

Zimbabwe—Special Libraries

Kamba, Angeline S. "Archives and National Development in the Third World." *Information Development* 3(1987): 108–113.
Lodge, J. I. "Air Zimbabwe Technical Library." *Zimbabwe Librarian* 18(1986): 51, 55–56.
Mazikana, Peter C. "Archives and Oral History. Overcoming a Lack of Resources." *Information Development* 3(1987): 13–16.
Patrikios, Helga. "Zimbabwe's National Medical Library: its new Role." *Zimbabwe Librarian* 18(1986): 19–20, 23.
——— "Zimbabwe's National Medical Library: its Origins." *Zimbabwe Librarian* 17(1985): 43, 45–46.

BIOGRAPHICAL SKETCHES
OF THE CONTRIBUTORS

HELEN K. BOLTON was a graduate student in the College of Library Science, Clarion University of Pennsylvania. Formerly she was a teacher for the visually impaired.

ELAINE LOIS DAY is cataloger, Fishburn Library, Hollins College, Roanoke, Virginia. In 1987–88 she was an intern in the library of the National Institute of Environmental Health Sciences at Research Triangle Park, North Carolina.

PETER V. DEEKLE is University Librarian at Susquehanna University. He is the author of "Literature and Non-print Media Resources" which appeared in *English and American Literature: Sources and Strategies for Collection Development*. American Library Association, 1987.

EUGENE R. HANSON teaches Library Science at Shippensburg University of Pennsylvania. He writes on professional topics for professional journals in the field of Library Science.

Advances in Library Administration and Organization,
Volume 8, pages 293-295.
Copyright © 1989 by JAI Press Inc.
All rights of reproduction in any form reserved.
ISBN: 0-89232-967-X

BARBARA J. HENN, a librarian at Indiana University, Bloomington, Indiana, is head of the Acquisition Section, and assistant head of Monographic Processing Services. She is chair of the LAMA Middle Management Discussion Group of the American Library Association. She is the author of "Securing Asian and African Materials for Library Collections: Practical Advice and Considerations" which appeared in *Technical Services Quarterly*, volume 5, no. 4, 1988.

SHELIA S. INTNER is editor of *Library Resources and Technical Services*. An associate professor in Simmons College Graduate School of Library and Information Science, she teaches courses in cataloging and classification, collection development and bibliographic instruction. An author and speaker, her most recent publication is *The Library Microcomputer Environment: Management Issues* published by Oryx Press, 1988. Currently, she is chair of the Cataloging and Classification Section, Resources and Technical Services Division, American Library Association.

RASHELLE S. KARP is an assistant professor of Library Science in the College of Library Science, Clarion University of Pennsylvania. She has contributed papers to ALAO in the past.

JOHN A. McCROSSAN is a professor in the School of Library and Information Science, University of South Florida. He is author of "Public Library Administrators' Opinions of Continuing Education Activities," *Public Libraries*, 27, Spring, 1988.

EUGENE S. MITCHELL is Associate Director for Collection Management at the Sarah Byrd Askew Library, William Paterson College, Wayne, NJ 07470. He received his B.A. from Canisius College and his M.L.S. and Ph.D. from Rutgers University.

LARRY J. OSTLER is Assistant University Librarian for Personnel and General Services, Brigham Young University. A contributor to professional literature, he writes on such topics as planning, preventing theft, and library history.

ROSCOE ROUSE, JR. was born in Valdosta, GA, earned degrees at the University of Oklahoma and the University of Michigan, receiving the Ph.D. from the latter institution. He was library director at Baylor University, at SUNY-Stony Brook, and at Oklahoma State University. He is currently University Library Historian at OSU.

BERNARD S. SCHLESSINGER is a professor and Associate Dean of the School of Library and Information Studies, Texas Woman's University. He is a speaker, consultant and author on library topics.

SHARON LYNN SCHOFIELD is the Head Librarian of the Audio-Visual Department at the Ector County Library in Odessa, Texas.

GLENN L. SITZMAN, retired from Clarion University of Pennsylvania libraries, has served as a librarian in Africa, notably at the National Library of Nigeria and at Makerere University in Uganda. He has traveled extensively in Africa and Europe and has spoken to library science students at Clarion on many occasions about African libraries.

INDEX

Access [databases], 137
Adams, Charles Kendall, 183
Adams, Judith A., 72, 85, 105
African Libraries, 253
ALA Handbook of Organization, 203
Allegheny College, 185
Ambrose, Lodilla, 188, 193
American Catalogues, 178
American: History and Life, 138, 139
American Library Directory, 205, 206
Anderson, Rosemary, 101
Atkinson, Hugh, 100
Automation funding, 104
Automation funding for, 73
Automation
  of library processes, 71
  enhancing access, 71, 82
  expanding services, 71
Automation planning, research questions, 80–1
Automation system, selection, 94
Auram, Henriette D., 80, 87, 89
Axford, H. William, 70, 74

Baatz, Wilmer H., 116
Baker, Betsy, 102
Baldridge, Victor J., 44
Bare, A. C., 30
Bellassai, Marcia C., 43
Benson, S. H., 164
Bibliotheca Americana, 178
Bishoff, Lizabeth J., 101
Biskup, Peter, 114, 122
Blanchard, K., 27
Bland, Robert, 89
Blasingame, Ralph, 242
Book costs, 179
Boulding, Kenneth E., 42
Bradsher, Earl L., 179
Braude, Robert M., 43, 45, 48, 55, 62, 63, 64
Bridge, Frank R., 96, 98
Brockett, O. G., 131
Broderick, Dorothy, 121
Brough, Kenneth, 182
Brown, Irving, 135
Bryant, Bonita, 116
Burgin, Robert, 101
Burns, James McGregor, 25
Byrd, Cecil K., 115

Cameron, Kim, 41, 42, 43
Camp, John A., 96
Carlton, W. N. Chattin, 182
Carpenter, Michael, 82
Cashman, J. F., 27
Cataloging, by Library of Congress
    highest standard of quality, 2
    quality control, 3
Chan, Lois Mai, 84
Cheney, S., 131, 132
Choice, 140
Cline, Hugh F., 117, 125
Cochrane, Pauline A., 85
Coles, Elizabeth, 91
Colonial College Library, book
    collection, 180
Computer hardware, upgrade, 92
Coney, Donald, 122
Conroy, Barbara, 202, 203
Consultants, automation, 74
Continuing Library Education
    Network and Exchange, 203
Continuing education [definition],
    202
Cooperative Institutional Research
    Program, 145–6
Corey, James F., 97, 98–9
Cost effectiveness, as affordability,
    70–1
Crawford, C. C., 176
Crawford, D., 142
Crawford, Walt, 75, 85, 90, 93
Curley, Arthur, 121
Cutter, Charles A., 186
*Cutter's Rules for a Dictionary
    Catalog*, 82

Danton, J. Periam, 114
Davis, Betty Bartlett, 88
Day, Elaine Lois, 86
Declerck, Luc, 87
Deekle, Peter V., 146, 149

De Gennaro, Richard, 42, 43
DeHart, Florence E., 85
Derlega, V. J., 26
Dewath, Nancy V., 43
Dickinson, Dennis W., 117, 125
Dissertation Abstracts Online, 138
Dobler, Richard P., 175
Dolan, Elizabeth, 87
Donelly, Robert M., 45
Dougherty, Richard M., 40
Dragon, A. C., 25
Drucker, Peter F., 43
Duino, Russell, 115

East, Mona, 115, 126
Edelman, Hendrik, 120, 195
Edinger, Joyce A., 45
Edwards, C., 134, 135, 136
Edwards, Karlene K., 204
"Enhance Libraries", 3
Etchingham, J. B. Jr., 142
Evans, Charles, 177
Evans, G. Edward, 123
Everett, Edward, 176, 184

Falk, Joyce Duncan, 134, 137, 138,
    139, 140, 141
Farber, Evan, 165
Fayollat, James, 91
Fenly, Judith G., 89
Ferguson, Douglas K., 84, 101
Fiedler, F. E., 27
Flecker, Dale P., 89, 92, 98
Fleishman, E. A., 27
Ford, Stephen, 121, 122
Freedman, Maurice J., 99, 100
Frost, Carolyn O., 87
Fussler, Herman H., 71, 85

Gallanger, George W., 45
Germany, 114

Good, Harry G., 171, 173
Gorman, Michael, 3, 76
Graen, G., 27
Great Man Theory, 26
Greenaway, Emerson, 242
Greene, Evarts B., 173
Grieder, Theodore, 118, 119, 123
Growell, Adolph, 177
Guide for Writing a Bibliographer's Manual, 121, 123

Hafter, Ruth, 4, 22, 79, 100
Harding, Thomas, 194
Hardy, C. DeWitt, 173, 175, 176, 183
Haro, Robert P., 115, 126
Harper, William Rainey, 196
Harrington, Sue Anne, 99
Haskell, John D., Jr., 115, 116, 121
Haynes, L. L., 26
Henn, Barbara, 102, 103
Herbert, I., 134, 135, 136, 137
Hernon, Peter, 79–80
Hersey, P., 27
Hickey, Doralynn J., 118, 119, 120
High, Walter M., 119, 121
Higher Education Act of 1965, 115
Highsmith, Anne L., 88
Hildreth, Charles R., 80, 84, 86, 90, 91
Hill, W., 25
Hirshon, Arnold, 74, 97
Historical Abstracts, 138, 139, 172
Historical Statistics, 172
Hofstadter, Richard, 173, 175, 176, 183
Horny, Karen L., 103, 106
House, R. J., 27
Hudson, Judith, 88
Huesman, Heinrich, 134
Humphreys, K. W., 124, 125
Hunt, J. G., 26

Indiana University Library, 103
Instructors, Library oriented, 150
International Bibliography of Theatre, 136

Jamieson, Alexis J., 87
Jewett, Charles C., 180, 181, 182, 185, 186, 188, 189, 190, 191, 192, 194
Johns Hopkins University, 114, 176
Jordan, Robert T., 163

Kandel, I. L., 173
Kelly, James, 178
Kennedy, Gail A., 121, 126
Knowles, Malcolm, 146
Koch, Theodore, 175, 190, 192, 196
Koos, Leonard V., 176
Kotler, Philip, 41
Kraus, Joe W., 184
Krausse, S. C., 142
Kullman, Colby H., 136

Lawrence, Gary S., 84
Leach, Ronald G., 39
Lehman-Haupt, Hellmut, 177, 179
Library as Heart of Institution, 187
Library automation
  benefits of, 80
  motives for, 75
  purposes and effects, 72
  uses, 95
Library Leadership Project, 26
Likert, R., 27
Linked systems project, 80, 89
Literacy rate, 172
London Stage Information Bank, 133, 136
Lowell, Mildred H., 186, 187
Lubans, J., 163

McCallum, Sally H., 80
McCarthy, C., 163
McClure, Charles R., 79–80
McCrossan, John A., 205
MacGregor, J., 164
McInnis, R. G., 164
McKenna, David L., 174
McKinley, Margaret, 102
Magazine Index, 80, 91
Magrill, Rose Mary, 115, 118, 119, 120, 126
Marc
  coding, 5
  formats, 78–9
Markey, Karen, 84, 89
Martin, Susan K., 75
Matthews, Joseph R., 84, 94
Matthews, Karen, 85
Maxwell, Margaret F., 87
Melvyl, 80, 90, 91, 97
Metzger, Deborah A., 79
Michalak, Thomas J., 124
Mirabel-Acte [database], 137
Moran, Barbara B., 75
Morita, Ichiko, 88
Morse, J. J., 30
Mott, Frank Luther, 179, 180
Murphy, Patrick E., 41

Naisbitt, John, 56, 146
National Coordinated Cataloging Program, 80
National Council on Quality Continuing Education for Information, Library, and Media Personnel, 202
National Endowment for the Humanities, 133, 136
Neal, James G., 204
Nemcheck, Lee, 216
New York Times Index, 141
North American Online Directory, 141

North American Review, 187
Northwestern University Library, Technical Services reorganization, 103
NOTIS, 96, 98

Okimi, Patricia H., 44
Oldman, Christine, 45
Online Computer Library Center, 2
Online Public Access Catalog, patron attitude toward, 90–1
Orion, 91, 102
Osburn, Charles B., 124, 125, 126

Palmour, Vernon, 43
Paterson, Judy, 87
Patrick, Ruth, 202, 203
Pearson, L., 163
Plum, S. H., 140
Pomeroy, Lee Harris, 249
Poole, Frazer G., 248
Poole, William Frederick, 191
Popa, Opritsa D., 79
Port Folio, 177
Post, William, 103
Potter, William Gray, 87, 92, 96, 97, 98
Publisher's Weekly, 178

Quadrivium [education], 174
Quality control, of cataloging, 3

Reavis, C. A., 26
Redundancy of catalog records, 77
Reid, Marion T., 119, 121
Research Libraries Information Network, 2
Response time, 76
Rhees, William J., 181, 185
Rhine, Leonard, 102
Rice, James, 91
Rider, Fremont, 184

Riggs, Donald E., 41, 42, 48, 55, 56, 64
Robinson, T. E., 163
Rocke, Hans J., 90
Roorbach, Orville A., 178
Ross, Johanna C., 90
Rubin, I., 42
Rudolf, Frederick, 173

Saffady, William, 71, 73, 92, 94
Sandler, Mark, 40
Sandore, Beth, 102
Schmidt, Karen A., 120
Schneider, B. R., Jr., 133, 134
Schon, Isabel, 204
Scrivener, J. E., 114, 117
Sellberg, Roxanne, 102, 103
Sessions, Judith, 103
Sewell, Robert G., 120
Shared cataloging, 100
Shaw, Debora, 95
Shores, Louis, 180
Shrum, John W., 174
Simpson, Charles W., 22
Singleton, James A., 79
Sinnott, Loraine T., 117
Sitts, Maxine K., 95
Sloan, Elaine F., 116
Smith, Eldred R., 116, 117
Sohn, Jeanne, 117
Sowell, Steven L., 124
Speller, Benjamin F., Jr., 101
StatPac, 9
Steiner, George A., 45, 52
Stevenson, Gordon, 100
Stogdill, R. M., 27
Stone, Elizabeth W., 202, 203
Stories, Catherine, 191, 194
Stress, 42
Stueart, R. D., 115, 120, 121
Svenonius, Elaine, 82
Subject specialist/bibliographer, Germany, Great Britain, 114

Tandem, 134–5, 136
Tappan, Henry, 185
Tarratus, Edward A., 174
Tatum, G. M., 195
Taylor, Arlene G., 22, 87
Tebbel, John, 177, 178, 179
Terwilliger, G. H. P., 164
Tewksbury, Donald G., 181
Theatre arts bibliographies, 218
  dictionaries and encyclopedias, 221
  digests, 231
  handbooks, 231
  histories, 224
  indexes, 228
  manuals, 231
  periodicals, 236
Theatre arts
  as research subject, 215
  reference sources, 216
  research collections, 216
Theatre link-up [database], 137
Theatre Research Data Center, 135
Thurber, Evangeline, 187, 191, 193
Thwing, Charles F., 173
Ticknor, George, 176, 184
Trezza, Alphonse L., 242
Triuium [education], 174
Trudeau, Pierre, satired in play, 141
Tuttle, Helen Welch, 118

U.S. Bureau of Education, 182, 183, 184, 190, 191, 192
Utah College Library Council, 44

VanGundy, A. B., 26

Wagner, F. R., 30
Walonick, David S., 9
Walton, Robert A., 96, 98
Wang, R., 136
Watson, Peter, 103
Weber, David C., 42, 189

Wiggins, Beacher, 80, 89
Williams, James W., 100
Wilson, Patrick, 79
Winkler, Paul W., 3
Winner, Langdon, 72
Wood, Elizabeth J., 55, 56

Wots-up Analysis, 52
Wulfekoetter, Gertrude, 119, 121, 122

Zemke, R., 146
Zemke, S., 146

Advances in
Library Administration
and Organization

Edited by
Gerard B. McCabe
Director of Libraries
Clarion University of Pennsylvania

and

Bernard Kreissman
University Librarian Emeritus
University of California, Davis

REVIEWS: "Special librarians and library managers in academic institutions should be aware of this volume and the series it initiates. Library schools and University libraries should purchase it."
—Special Libraries

"... library schools and large academic libraries should include this volume in their collection because the articles draw upon practical situations to illustrate administrative principles."
—Journal of Academic Librarianship

Volume 1, 1982, 148 pp. $58.50
ISBN 0-89232-213-6

CONTENTS: Introduction, *W. Carl Jackson.* **Continuity or Discontinuity-A Persistant Personnel Issue in Academic Librarianship,** *Allan B. Veaner, University of California, Santa Barbara.* **Archibald Cary Collidge and "Civilization's Dairy: Building the Harvard University Library",** *Robert T. Byrnes, Indiana University.* **Library Automation: Building and Equipment Considerations in Implementing Computer Technology,** *Edwin B. Brownrigg, Division of Library Automation, University of California.* **Microforms Facility at the Golda Meir Library of the University of Wisconsin, Milwaukee,** *William C. Roselle, University of Wisconsin, Milwaukee.* **RLIN and OCLC - Side by Side: Two Comparison Studies,** *Kazuko M. Dailey, Jaroff*

JAI PRESS

Grazia and Diana Gray, *University of California, Davis.*
**Faculty Status and Participative Governance in Academic
Libraries,** *Donald D. Hendricks, University of New
Orleans.*

Volume 2, 1983, 373 pp. $58.50
ISBN 0-89232-214-4

CONTENTS: Introduction, *Bernard Kreissman.* **Manage-
ment Training for Research Librarianship,** *Deanna B.
Marcum, Program Associate, Council on Library
Resources.* **Subject Divisionalism: A Diagnostic Analysis,**
J.P. Wilkinson, University of Toronto. **Videotext
Development for the United States,** *Michael B. Binder,
Fairleigh Dickinson University.* **The Organizational and
Budgetary Effects of Automation on Libraries,** *Murray S.
Martin, Tufts University.* **The Librarian as Change Agent,**
Tom G. Watson, University of the South. **Satellite Cable
Library Survey,** *Mary Diebler, PSSC.* **Deterioration of
Book Paper,** *Richard G. King, Jr., University of California.*
**Evaluation and the Process of Change in Academic
Libraries,** *Delmus E. Williams, Western Illinois University.*
**Towards a Reconceptualization of Collection Develop-
ment,** *Charles B. Osburn, University of Cincinnati.*
**Strategies and Long Range Planning in Libraries and
Information Centers,** *Michael E.D. Koenig and Leonard
Kerson, Columbia University.* **Project Management: An
Effective Problem Solving Approach,** *Robert L. White,
University of California, Santa Cruz.* **A Preliminary and
Selective Survey of Two Collections of Juvenilia,** *Michele
M. Reid, New Jersey Institute of Technology.* Biographical
Sketch of the Contributors.

Volume 3, 1984, 320 pp. $58.50
ISBN 0-89232-386-8

CONTENTS: Introduction, *Gerard B. McCabe.* **Interna-
tional Exchange and Chinese Library Development,**
Priscilla C. Yu, University of Illinois Library. **Measuring
Professional Performance: A Critical Examination,**
*Andrea C. Dragon, School of Communication, Informa-
tion and Library Studies, Rutgers University.* **The
Turnover Process and the Academic Library,** *James G.
Neal, Pennsylvania State University Library.* **Subject**

Bibliographers in Academic Libraries: An Historical and Descriptive Review, *John D. Haskell, Jr., College of William and Mary.* University of California Users Look at Melvyl: Results of a Survey of Users of the University at California Prototye Online Union Catalog, *Gary S. Lawrence, Vicki Graham and Heather Presley, University of California Library System.* Job Analysis: Process and Benefits, *Virginia R. Hill, University of Southern Mississippi, and Tom G. Watson, University of the South.* College Library and Nonusers, *Nurieh Musavi and John F. Harvey, International Library and Information Science, Consultant, Western Michigan University.* David Milford Hume, M. D., 1917-1973, *Mary Ellen Thomas, Virginia Commonwealth University.* The Association of Research Libraries 1932-1982 50th Anniversary. The Impact of Changes in Scholarship in the Humanities Upon Research Libraries, *Ralph Cohen, University of Virginia.* The ARL at Fifty, *Stephen A. McCarthy, Consultant to the Council of Library Resources.* ARL/LC: 1932-1982, *William J. Welsh, Deputy Librarian of Congress.* The Influence of ARL on Academic Librarianship, Legislation, and Library Education, *Edward G. Holley, University of North Carolina, Chapel Hill.* Biographical Sketch of the Contributors.

Volume 4, 1985, 233 pp. $58.50
ISBN 0-89232-566-6

CONTENTS: Introduction, *Bernard Kreissman.* The Third Culture: Managerial Socialization in the Library Setting, *Ruth J. Person, The Catholic University of America.* Public Library Unions: Bane or Boon?, *Rashelle Schlessinger, Clarion University of Pennsylvania.* Satisfaction with Library Systems, *Larry N. Osborne, University of Hawaii.* Budgeting and Financial Planning for Libraries, *Michael E.D. Koening and Deidre C. Stam, Columbia University.* Library Support of Faculty Research: An Investigation at a Multi-Campus University, *Barbara J. Smith, Pennsylvania State University.* Staff Development on a Shoestring, *Helen Carol Jones and Ralph E. Russell, Georgia State University.* The Impact of Technology on Library Buildings, *Rolf Funlrott, Karisruhe University.* Whither the Book? Considerations for Library Planning in the Age of Electronics, *Roscoe Rouse, Jr., Oklahoma State University.* Attempting to Automate: Lessons Learned Over Five Years, Pittsburgh Regional

Library Center, *Scott Bruntjen and Sylvia D. Hall,
Pittsburgh Regional Library Center.* **Annotated Bibliographer of Materials on Academic Library Service to
Disabled Students,** *Rashelle Schlessinger, Clarion
University of Pennsylvania.* Biographical Sketch of the
Contributors.

Volume 5, 1986, 307 pp. $58.50
ISBN 0-89232-674-3$29.25

CONTENTS: Introduction, *Gerard B. McCabe.* **A
Longitudinal Study of the Outcomes of a Management
Development Program for Women in Librarianship,** *Ruth
J. Person and Eleanore R. Ficke, The Catholic University
of America.* **Volunteers in Libraries,** *Rashelle Schlessinger
Karp, Clarion University of Pennsylvania.* **The History of
Publishing as a Field of Research for Librarians and
Others,** *Joe W. Kraus, Director of Libraries Emeritus,
Illinois State University.* **The Respone of the Cataloger and
the Catalog to Automation in the Academic Library
Setting,** *Joan M. Repp, Bowling Green State University.*
**Accredited Master's Degree Programs in Librarianship in
the 1980s,** *John A. McCrossan, University of South
Florida.* **Collection Evaluation - Practices and Methods in
Libraries of ALA Accredited Graduate Library Education
Programs,** *Renee Tjoumas, Queens College, and Esther E.
Horne, The Catholic University of America.* **Integarted
Library System and Public Services,** *Marcia L. Sprules,
University of South Dakota.* **Bibliographic Instruction
(BI): Examination of Change,** *Fred Batt, University of
Oklahoma Libraries.* **The University Library Director in
Budgetary Decision Making,** *Susan E. McCargar, El Paso
Herald Post.* **Getting From Here to There: Keeping an
Academic Library in Operation During Construction/
Rennovation,** *T. John Metz, Carleton College.* **Three
Studies of the Economics of Academic Libraries,** *Paul B.
Kantor, Tantalus, Inc.* Bibliographical Sketches of the
Contributors. Author Index. Subject Index.

Volume 6, 1987, 323pp. $58.50
ISBN 0-89232-724-3

CONTENTS: Introduction, *Bernard Kreissman.* **Proactive
Management in Public Libraries - In California and in the**

Nation, *Brian A. Reynolds, Siskiyou County, Librarian.*
**Library Resource Sharing in Massachusetts, Traditional
and Technological Efforts,** *Robert Dugan, Massachusetts
Board of Library Commissioners and MaryAnn Tricarico,
Lynn Public Library, Massachusetts.* **On the Nature of
Information Systems,** *Charles B. Osborn, University of
Alabama.* **Fiscal Planning in Academic Libraries: The Role
of the Automated Acquisitions System,** *Carol E.
Chamberlain, Pennsylvania State University.* **Taking the
Library to Freshmen Students via The Freshmen Seminar
Concept,** *John N. Gardner, University of South Carolina,
Debra Decker and Francine G. McNairy, Clarion
University of Pennsylvania.* **Conceptualizing Library Office
Functions as Preparation for Automated Environment,**
Edward D. Garten, University of Dayton. **A Survey of the
Sixth-Year Program in Library Schools Offering the ALA
Accredited Master's Degree,** *Alice Gulen Smith, University
of South Florida.* **The Evolution of an Endangered Species:
Centralized Processing Centers and the Case of the
University of South Carolina, University of South
Carolina. Libraries and the Disabled Persons: A Review
of Selected Research,** *Marilyn H. Karrenbrock, University
of Tennessee and Linda Lucas, University of South
Carolina.* Biographical Sketches of the Contributors.
Author Index. Subject Index.

Volume 7, 1988, 287 pp. $58.50
ISBN 0-89232-817-7

CONTENTS: Introduction, *Gerard B. McCabe.* **A
Comparative Study of the Management Styles and Career
Progression Patterns of Recently Appointed Male and
Female Public Library Administrators (1983-1987),** *Joy M.
Greiner, University of Southern Mississippi.* **Library
Services for Adult Higher Education in the United
Kingdom,** *Raymond K. Fisher, University of Birmingham,
England.* **Chinese Theories on Collection Development,**
Priscilla C. Yu, University of Illinois Library. **An Overview
of the State of Research in the School Library Media Field,
with a Selected Annotated Bibliography,** *P. Diane Snyder,
Clarion University of Pennsylvania's College of Library
Science.* **A Comparison of Content, Promptness, and
Coverage of New Fiction Titles in Library Journal and
Booklist, 1964-1984,** *Judith L. Palmer, North Texas State
University and Irving Texas Public Library.* **Librarians as
Teachers: A Study of Compensation and Status Issues,**

**J
A
I

P
R
E
S
S**

Barbara I. Dewey and J. Louise Malcomb, Indiana University. **Academic Library Buildings: Their Evolution and Prospects,** David Kaser, Indiana University. **Accreditation and the Process of Change in Academic Libraries,** Delmus E. Williams, University of Alabama, Huntsville. **College and University Libraries: Traditions, Trends, and Technology,** Eugene R. Hanson, Shippensburg University of Pennsylvania. **A Reference Core Collection for a Petroleum Library,** Nancy Mitchell-Tapping, Texas Woman's University, Valerie Lepus, Rashelle S. Karp, Clarion University of Pennsylvania, and Bernard S. Schlessinger, Texas Women's University. **Private Institutions and Computer Utilization in Community Service and Education: The Case of the Abdul-Hamid Shoman Foundation,** As'ad Abdul Rahman, Abdul-Hamid Shoman Foundation. Abdul-Hameed Shoman Public Library, Nahla Natour, Ministry of Planning, Amman, Jordan. Bibliographical Sketches of the Contributors. Index.

Volume 8, 1989, 302 pp. $58.50
ISBN 0-89232-967-X

CONTENTS: Introduction, *Bernard Kreissman.* **Quality in Bibliographic Databases: An Analysis of Member-Contributed Cataloging in OCLC and RLIN,** *Sheila S. Intner, Simmons College.* **The Library Leadership Project: A Test of Leadership Effectiveness in Academic Libraries,** *Eugene S. Mitchell, William Paterson College.* **Applying Strategic Planning to the Library: A Model for Public Services,** *Larry J. Ostler, Brigham Young University.* **Management Issues in Selection, Development, and Implementation of Integrated or Linked Systems for Academic Libraries,** *Elaine Lois Day, Hollins College.* **Acquisitions Management: The Infringing Roles of Acquisitions Librarians and Subject Specialists-An Historical Perspective,** *Barbara J. Henn, Indiana University.* **Development and Use of Theatre Databases,** *Helen K. Bolton, Clarion University of Pennsylvania.* **The Academic Library and the Liberal Arts Education of Young Adults: Reviewing the Relevance of the Library-College in the 1980s,** *Peter V. Deekle, Susquehanna University.* **College Libraries: The Colonial Period to the Twentieth Century,** *Eugene R. Hanson, Shippensburg University of Pennsylvania.* **Library Administrators' Attitudes Toward Continuing Professional Education Activities,** *John A.*

McCrossan, *University of South Florida*. **A Core Reference Theatre Arts Collection for Research,** *Sharon Lynn Schofield, Ector Community Library, Odessa, Texas, Helen K. Bolton, Rashelle S. Karp, Clarion University of Pennsylvania, and Bernard S. Schlessinger, Texas Woman's University*. **The Library Buildings Award Program of the American Institute of Architects and the American Library Association,** *Roscoe Rouse, Jr., Oklahoma State University*. **Bibliography of Sub-Sahara African Librarianship, 1986-1987,** *Glenn L. Sitzman, Clairon University of Pennsylvania Libraries*. **Bibliographical Sketches of the Contributors. Index.**

JAI PRESS INC.
55 Old Post Road - No. 2
P.O. Box 1678
Greenwich, Connecticut 06836-1678
Tel: 203-661-7602